Introductory Economics

G. F. Stanlake M.A. B.Sc.(Econ)

Head of the Economics Department
Wyggeston Boys' School, Leicester

Longman

LONGMAN GROUP LIMITED
London
*Associated companies, branches and representatives
throughout the world*

© G. F. Stanlake, 1967

This edition © Longman Group Ltd 1971

First published 1967
Second edition 1971
Second impression 1972
Third impression with revisions 1973
Fourth impression 1973
Fifth impression 1974
ISBN 0 582 35048 4

Printed in Great Britain by
Lowe & Brydone (Printers) Ltd., Thetford, Norfolk

Preface to second edition

The knowledge that the first edition of this book appears to have met the needs of so many students embarking on their first course in Economics has been most gratifying. In view of this, and in the light of my own teaching experience, I have decided not to make any substantial changes in the general layout of the book.

There has been, however, a fairly extensive revision of the text. To a large extent this has taken the form of bringing up to date the factual material relating to the British and international economies, but I have amended various parts of the theoretical treatment where an improvement seemed to be called for.

Among these latter changes, the student familiar with the book will find a more extended treatment of the functions of the price mechanism; some amendments to the chapter on supply and demand and to the section on the laws of production; some changes and additions to the material on marginal productivity; a more extended treatment of monopoly, and additional material on demand-pull and cost-push inflation.

In the sections on applied economics, the balance of payments now includes the new official presentation, and the material on Britain's foreign trade and the European Communities has been brought up to date. The section on industrial structure has been largely rewritten and there is now a short account of the changing policies on industrial relations. An improved account of regional policy is now included in the text. On money and banking, there is a new account of the money supply and a short section on the Giro.

In short, the student will find numerous changes in the original text, but no major changes in the structure of the book.

G. F. STANLAKE 1971

Note to 1973 *impression*
For this printing chapters 21 and 23 have been completely rewritten to take account of recent changes in banking and current experience of inflation.

G.F.S. 1973

Acknowledgements

We are indebted to the following for permission to reproduce copyright material:
George Allen & Unwin Ltd for material from *Full Employment in a Free Society*
by Lord Beveridge and *The Principles of Economic Planning* by Professor Arthur
Lewis; the Controller of Her Majesty's Stationery Office for material from
Economic Trends, May 1965, *Economic Trends*, November 1965 and *National
Plan Command Paper 2764, Ministry of Labour Gazette*, January 1966, *Board of
Trade Journal*, 7 December 1962, *The Annual Abstract of Statistics*, 1965, *Economic Report*, 1964, *Preliminary Estimates of National Income and Balance of
Payments* 1959 to 1964, *Command Paper 2629*, and *Monthly Digest of Statistics*
September 1965; Hill Samuel & Co. Ltd, Bankers, for material from *U.N.
Commodity Trade Statistical Papers*, 1965, *U.N. Monthly Bulletin of Statistics*,
June 1965, *O.E.C.D. Overall Trade by Countries Series A*, October 1966, and
I.M.F. International Financial Statistics; Lloyds Bank Ltd for material from
'Does Money Always Depreciate' by Professor R. G. Lipsey printed in *Lloyds
Bank Review*, October 1960; Longmans, Green & Co. Ltd for material from
The Structure of Industry in Britain by G. C. Allen; The National Institute of
Economic and Social Research for material from *National Institute Economic
Review*, No. 34, November 1965, and No. 35, February 1966; Prentice-Hall, Inc.
for material from *Economic Development: Past and Present* by Richard T. Gill,
© 1963, and The Council of London Stock Exchange for material from *Notes on
Share Ownership: Stock Exchange*, October 1964.

Contents

Part Three: The Business Unit

Part Four: Prices

Part Five: The National Income and its Distribution

Part Six: Money and Banking

The London Money Market
The Commercial Banks
Reserve Assets
The Control of the Money Supply
Monetary Policy
The Giro

Part Seven: Public Finance

Part Eight: Employment and Unemployment

Part Nine: International Trade and Finance

Part Ten: Economic Policies and Problems

Part One: Introduction

Chapter 1

The Subject Matter of Economics

What is economics about? Most people would be able to attempt an answer to this question. In recent years, the word 'economics' has become part of our everyday vocabulary, and the daily news invariably contains some reference to the economic situation of the country. But what sort of answers would they be? We would probably be told that economics is about the cost of living, takeover bids, nationalisation, exports and imports, wages and profits and so on. In fact economics is not about these things any more than chemistry is about sulphuric acid. Sulphuric acid is merely an application of chemistry, just as stainless steel is an application of metallurgy.

Economics is a social science. This means that it is concerned with the study of an aspect of human behaviour. It is concerned with that part of human activity which is commonly described as 'getting a living' or with 'the earning and spending of money' or, again, with 'the production and consumption of wealth'. It is of interest to note the definitions of the subject which some famous economists have given to us.

Adam Smith, one of the earliest writers on economics as we know the subject, said that his work was 'an inquiry into the nature and causes of the wealth of nations'. John Stuart Mill described the subject as 'the practical science of the production and distribution of wealth'. Alfred Marshall, a famous Cambridge professor, defined economics as 'the study of mankind in the ordinary business of life' and then went on to say that it is concerned with the study of those human activities which are connected with the attainment of the means for wellbeing. It is difficult to devise a satisfactory and concise definition of economics, but the subject matter is easy to recognise. We are all aware of those matters which may be described as 'economic' – prices and productivity, unemployment, the location of industry, the size of firms, monopolies, wages, profits, taxation, exports, and so on.

Production, Consumption, Exchange

There are three types of human activity which may be classified as economic. They are Production, Consumption and Exchange.

Production is the process whereby man transforms the resources available to him (land, labour and capital) into the products which people want, making them available where they are wanted. It includes, therefore, all the operations which are required to provide the suit in the tailor's shop; operations which began no doubt on an Australian sheep farm.

Consumption is the process of using up the products of man's labour; the burning of coal, the wearing of clothes, the eating of food, the use of the television set and so on.

The acts of *Exchange* make up by far the greater part of the subject matter of economics. In general, goods and services are exchanged for money and this money is subsequently exchanged for other goods and services. We all recognise the purchase and sale of an article as an act of exchange.

Perhaps not so easily recognisable as acts of exchange are the renting of houses, the hiring of labour, and the lending of money. When a house is rented, the use of the house is exchanged for a money payment. When money is borrowed, the use of 'present' money is exchanged for 'future' money. The amount repaid in the future is greater than the amount borrowed by a sum of money known as interest. The interest is the payment made for the use of the money during the period of the loan.

When labour is hired, the worker exchanges hours of labour for a money payment known as wages.

Economics, then, is concerned with the production, consumption and exchange of goods and services. But it is not sufficient merely to note that these activities are carried on. We must note also the *quantities* which are involved. The economist is interested in the factors which determine the *output* of coal, the *numbers* unemployed, the *wages* of engineers, the *tariff* on motor cars, and the *price* of meat. All these are economic quantities.

A further part of the study of economics is devoted to the organisations which control and direct a large part of the economic activity of our country. The acts of production, consumption and exchange are performed by individuals, but the individual usually carries out his economic activities as part of some organisation. In the case of the one-man business, the individual is acting on his own behalf, but most people work for a limited company, a local council, a public corporation or a government department. It is within and through such institutions that the greater part of economic activity takes place.

Scarcity and Choice

Modern economics is said to be based upon a theory of scarcity and choice. We should look at some of the reasons for this particular view of the subject.

SCARCITY

We are aware, or should be, of the extremely low standard of living of a very large proportion of the world's peoples. We would not dispute the use of the word 'scarcity' to describe the supply of goods and services which are available in the underdeveloped countries. But, to an economist, all economic goods (i.e. goods which command a price) are scarce goods. In our own country, where shops are well stocked with a very wide variety of goods, there would appear to be ample supplies of almost every type of article. Yet it is still true that these goods are scarce. We are using the word 'scarce' in a relative sense; economic goods are scarce in relation to the desire for them. Most people would like to have more or better things than they possess at the moment. If they already possess a car then a bigger or a newer car may be the object of their desire. They would like better houses, more domestic appliances, better furniture, and more opportunity to travel abroad. It seems that people's wants do not diminish as their living standards rise. The average standard of living in this country is very much higher than it was only fifty years ago, yet the desire for more and better things to consume seems to be just as strong as ever. The pressures for higher living standards appear to be just as insistent in the wealthier countries such as the U.S.A. and Great Britain as they are in the very poor countries.

People's wants are many, but the economic resources required to satisfy them are limited. It is impossible to satisfy all wants. If an infinite amount of every good could be produced, then everyone could have all they desired and human wants would be fully satisfied. There would be no economic problem, no economic goods, and no need for 'economising'. But the fact remains that people's wants are not limited; as soon as one level of satisfaction is achieved a new and higher level becomes the objective. Hence we have an economic problem – goods and services are scarce relative to the demand for them.

CHOICE

Since wants are many but the resources available for their satisfaction are limited in supply, we are faced with a problem of choice. We cannot have more of everything. At any given moment of time the economic resources (raw materials, machines, factories, land, and labour) are limited and so, therefore, is the quantity of goods and services which these resources can produce. It is true that, over time, man's technical knowledge continues to grow and enables him to increase his *total* output, but this is a relatively slow process. The economic problem is how best to use the resources available at any given time to satisfy human wants; how to achieve the highest level of economic welfare with the means available.

3

The individual is constantly confronted with this problem of choice. He has a limited income and must therefore choose between alternatives when he spends his income. He must decide whether to buy a car *or* take a holiday abroad; to spend more on clothes *or* more on entertainment; to buy cigarettes *or* spend the money on books. Just as a person and a family have to make these choices in disposing of their incomes, so a society has to choose between alternative uses for the resources it has available.

OPPORTUNITY COST

The true cost of using economic resources in any given project is the loss of the alternative output which they might have produced. If we use land, labour, and capital to build a school, the economic cost of the school might be the houses which these resources could have produced. This view of cost is known as *opportunity cost*, because it represents the loss of the next most desired alternative. The purchase of this textbook could be viewed in terms of the alternatives foregone – the opportunity cost might well have been a new fountain pen or an evening at the theatre.

The Fundamental Economic Problems

Any society, whether it is an advanced capitalist society, a communist state, a dictatorship, or a primitive tribe, must face three basic economic problems:

1. *What variety of goods should be produced and in what quantities.*
2. *How these goods should be produced.* Society has to decide who should produce the goods, the resources to be used and the methods of production to be adopted.
3. *How the goods produced should be distributed.* Some decision must be made on the manner in which the national output is to be distributed among the citizens.

In primitive societies these decisions are not made consciously by the members of the community. There are traditional and customary ways of growing crops, raising livestock and sharing out the produce. The people follow methods of production and distribution which have been unchanged for centuries.

In a communist or socialist society these three basic choices would be made by planning committees which may or may not be elected by the people. These committees would draw up production programmes for the different industries and allocate resources to them. The distribution of the goods and services produced would also be decided by central planning of incomes.

In a dictatorship the problems might well be solved by the decisions of one man, but more likely by committees appointed by him without any reference to the people.

The Price Mechanism

In a free enterprise or capitalist state, the pattern of economic activity is largely determined by the free choices of the citizens operating through the price mechanism. In such a system the goods and services produced have prices, and so do the factors of production (land, labour and capital) which produced them. Wages are the price of labour, rent is the price of land, and interest is the price of capital. Everyone receives money in exchange for whatever he has to sell and then uses this money to satisfy his material wants by buying whatever goods and services he requires. People are free to spend their incomes as they wish, and, in doing so, they provide indicators for producers. If consumers show an increasing preference for some particular commodity by increasing their purchases, the increase in demand will cause the price of the goods to rise. This makes production of this commodity more profitable and producers will respond by increasing output.

The sequence of events, higher demand $\longrightarrow$ higher prices $\longrightarrow$ greater profits $\longrightarrow$ greater output, represents the linkages between consumer preferences and the manner in which economic resources are utilised. The free choices of consumers exercised in the market-place determine the manner in which economic resources are used in a free enterprise society. It is sometimes said that in such a society the consumer is sovereign.

The second problem, '*How* shall things be produced?', is decided by competition between different producers. Those producers who adopt more efficient methods of production will be able to operate at a lower cost per unit and hence sell at lower prices than their less efficient competitors. Price competition will decide the methods of production used in a capitalist society. Those producers who are best able to meet the demands of consumers will make profits and expand their firms; the inefficient will be driven out of business. If the larger firm can operate at lower costs, it will tend to replace the smaller firm. Electricity will be generated with oil-fired furnaces rather than coal-fired ones if this means cheaper electricity. Motor-cars will be manufactured by large scale mass production methods if consumers demand cheap standardised models rather than expensive specially designed cars. If consumers demand greater variety, the small firm will survive.

How will the fruits of economic activity be distributed? The share of the national output which any individual obtains depends upon the level of his income. Incomes are paid in the form of money, and this money represents a claim to goods and services. The greater a person's income, the greater his purchasing power and the greater is his claim to the goods and services available. The manner in which the national output is distributed, therefore, depends upon the pattern of income distribution. If incomes are very unevenly distributed then the available goods and services will be distributed unevenly.

Incomes are derived in two ways, either as a reward for the provision of labour services, or as a return on the ownership of property. Interest, rent and profits are incomes which are derived from property while wages and salaries are the rewards for the provision of labour services. These incomes are also prices and, like other prices in a free enterprise economy, they are determined by the forces of supply and demand. The demands for land, labour, and capital are derived from the demands for the goods and services they create. If the public is increasingly demanding, say, motor-cars, the demands for the factors of production required to produce motor-cars will be increasing and so will the prices of these factors. If the demand for houses is increasing, the price of houses will tend to rise. This will encourage building firms to expand their activities and they will increase their demands for land, building materials, and workers. The incomes of landowners, cement and brick manufacturers, and building workers will all tend to rise. On the other hand when the consumers' demand for a product is declining, the incomes of those who produce the product will tend to fall.

In a free enterprise economy, therefore, the goods which are produced, the methods of production adopted, and the distribution of incomes are all determined by the price mechanism operating in free markets. It is a system where prices, profits and losses provide the indicators and stimuli to which consumers and producers respond. Scarce resources are allocated according to consumer choice – they move to profitable activities and away from unprofitable activities.

Now this is a very simplified picture of a system which is not found anywhere in the real world, because in all societies, to a greater or lesser extent, governments intervene to influence economic activity. But even if they did not do so, it is very doubtful if the economy would work as smoothly and efficiently as our brief account seems to imply. If the efficient are to prevail, by their superiority in the competitive process, this could well lead to the most efficient firms achieving monopoly powers. The continuous movement of resources from industries experiencing a falling demand to those which are growing, is a difficult and often painful process. In modern economies specialisation is widespread and labour and capital have been trained and designed for highly specific tasks.

The system may be criticised on grounds of equity. A free enterprise economy will produce those goods which are in demand – purchasing power will decide what is produced. It may well be that luxuries will be produced for the rich while the poor lack necessities. The system responds to *demand* (i.e. the willingness and ability to pay) rather than to *wants*.

Only those activities which offer the prospect of profit will be undertaken. It is very doubtful whether such a system would provide such things as public parks, a universal system of education, or a national health service which makes medical attention available to all irrespective of the ability to pay.

A Mixed System

The system we have described is commonly known as a system of private enterprise. This particular type of society allows private individuals to own the means of production. Individuals are allowed to buy and control land, buildings and machines, to hire labour and to undertake production with a view to profit. An alternative system is known as public enterprise where the means of production are owned and controlled by the State. In our own country, and in most other western countries, there are mixed economic systems which contain elements of both public and private enterprise. In the U.K. a large part of the economy is under the direct control of public authorities. The coal, electricity, and gas industries, the railways, the post office and civil aviation are examples of nationally owned enterprises. In addition local authorities own and operate local bus companies, build and own houses, schools, public baths and many other forms of social capital.

Quite apart from these forms of direct ownership, the State also plays a large part in dictating the conditions under which the private sector is allowed to operate. Factory Acts and Office Acts govern the conditions under which people are allowed to work in these places. Conditions in shops are also subject to official regulation. The Companies Acts lay down the methods by which companies are allowed to conduct their financial affairs. The Monopolies Commission and the Restrictive Practices Court exist to investigate and to control the procedures of businessmen in fixing their prices and in supplying their goods and services. A variety of statutes control the decisions of businessmen in matters of industrial location; and buildings of all kinds are subject to planning regulations. A complete list of all the official regulations which influence and control economic activity in the private sector would be a very long one indeed.

Chapter 2

The Population Basis

World Population

The most striking feature about world population has been the explosion in its growth since the Industrial Revolution, but more especially during the last twenty-five years. It is now increasing faster than ever before.

The present rate of growth is estimated to be about 1·8 per cent per annum – a rate of growth which, if maintained, would cause total population to double in less than forty years. In the present century, the total increase in world population to date amounts to 1,900 million and more than half this increase (about 1,100 million) took place during the last twenty years. About four-fifths of this more recent increase occurred in the less developed parts of the world.

Whereas it took thousands of years for the world to attain its first billion (1,000 million) people, the second billion was added in about 100 years. The third billion was added in about thirty years and the fourth billion is expected to be achieved in only sixteen years after the third billion.

Table 1 and Figure 1 illustrate some of these developments.

Table 1. *World Population (millions)*

		Average annual % *increase from preceding* *date*
1750	791	
1800	978	0·4
1850	1,262	0·5
1900	2,516	0·9
1969	3,551	1·8

The population explosion started in Europe, because the Industrial Revolution started there. Rapid technical progress made possible the great increases in productivity, the higher living standards, and the improvements in medicine, sanitation, and transport which enabled man to reduce the incidence of disease and famine. The principal cause of the rapid increase in the population was a drastic fall in the death rate. The

8

Source: Compiled from *UN World Population Situation 1969*.

WORLD POPULATION

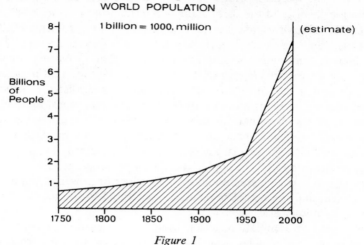

Figure 1

population of Europe trebled in the period 1750–1914 and, together with the European technological and military superiority, it was a major factor in the great European expansion overseas. During the eighteenth and nineteenth centuries Europeans settled all over the world.

The first round of the world demographic explosion is over. Europe, North America and Russia have reached a population equilibrium of the 'industrial' type—with low birth rates and low death rates. We are now facing the second round which gives every indication of being even more remarkable than the first. Asia, South America and Africa are undergoing population growth of unprecedented magnitude.

The explanation for the present great upsurge in population is to be found chiefly in the applications of medical science developed in the advanced countries. This has had tremendous consequences. In Europe medical knowledge advanced relatively slowly and the growth of population, due to the control of disease, was fairly gradual. In the under-developed countries the accumulated knowledge of two centuries is immediately available and death rates have fallen very much faster than they ever did in Europe. In Ceylon, the conquest of the malaria mosquito by D.D.T., cut the death rate from twenty per thousand to fourteen per thousand in a single year (1946–7), a fall which took seventy years in Europe.

The basic problem in the underdeveloped countries is that they are still agricultural societies. In Europe the growth of population *accompanied* the industrial revolution, and the growth in production more than kept pace with population growth. In the developing countries, rapid population growth has *preceded* economic development.

9

The current trends in world population have revived interest in the population theories of the Rev. Thomas Malthus whose *Essay on Population* (1798) led to the first serious discussions of the problem. Malthus .wrote at a time when the British population was increasing rapidly and his observations seemed to confirm his views that increasing numbers could only increase the misery of the masses. He declared that population had a persistent tendency to outstrip the means of subsistence. Any rise in the standard of living would only lead to early marriages, more births and more babies surviving. The increased numbers of people would lower the standards of living back to subsistence level. His purpose was to demonstrate 'That the increase in population is necessarily limited by the means of subsistence. That population does invariably increase when the means of subsistence increase and that the superior power of population is repressed, and the actual population kept equal to the means of subsistence, by misery and vice'.

The checks on population, which Malthus summarised as misery and vice, were famines, plagues, wars and infanticide. He was concerned with the British problem, and believed that agricultural output could not possibly increase at the rate at which population had a tendency to grow. He was proved wrong in the case of Britain, for the population quadrupled during the nineteenth century. He did not foresee the great improvements in transport which enabled the British population to feed itself from the vast lands of the new continents. Nor did Malthus foresee that rising standards of living may bring falling birth rates as they did in most western nations after 1870.

Nevertheless, the germs of truth in his doctrines are still important for an understanding of the population problems of China, India and other areas where the balance between the numbers of people and the means of subsistence is often very precarious. Where inexpensive science greatly reduces the death rate without increasing productivity, Malthus still has some relevance.

Changes in Population

Changes in population come about in two ways, (1) by natural increase or decrease due to changes in birth rates and death rates and (2) by migration.

The natural increase in population which is a feature of the modern world is due to an excess of births over deaths. The birth rate is the number of births per thousand of the population per annum, and the death rate is the number of deaths per thousand, per annum. The natural growth rate will be the difference between the two, i.e. Natural growth rate = Birth rate – Death rate.

The more or less stable populations up to about 1750 were due to a combination of high birth rates and high death rates. In Britain death rates began to fall about 1750, while birth rates remained high and population began to increase. Birth rates began to fall about 1880 and fell sharply from thirty-five per thousand, to fifteen per thousand in a matter of fifty years, but population continued to rise because birth rates remained higher than death rates. Birth rates in Britain and Europe remained low between the wars, but since the Second World War they have tended to increase. Death rates in the developed countries are at a very low level. In these countries the general pattern seems to have been as follows: a process of industrialisation leading to greater output per head, better living conditions, better food, improved sanitation and a marked advance in medical science. This led to a sharp fall in death rates and a rapid increase in population, but output increased even faster. After a fairly long interval (about 100 years), there followed a sharp fall in birth rates and a slowing down in the rates of population growth. The age of affluence, however, has brought a tendency for birth rates to move upwards again.

Migration represents the net balance between the numbers leaving the country (emigration), and the numbers entering the country (immigration). Between 1846 and 1930 over 50 million Europeans sought new homes overseas, the bulk of them going to North America. Between 1891 and 1920 they were leaving at an average rate of nearly one million a year. The population of the U.S.A. has been greatly increased by immigration particularly during the latter part of the nineteenth century. The decline in the population of Ireland after 1840 was partly due to large-scale emigration. In the U.K. one-third of the increase of 520,000 in the total population between 1961 and 1962 was due to immigration.

Age Distribution

Changes in birth and death rates change the age distribution of the population (i.e. the proportions in the different age groups). A country which has a high birth rate and a high death rate will have a large percentage of young people in its population. The typical age distribution of such a population is represented graphically in Chart A. It resembles a pyramid, and is typical of the populations of most developing nations.

In South Asia, Africa, and Latin America more than forty per cent of the population is under fifteen years of age. In Europe this proportion is about twenty-six per cent.

A static population, with low birth rates and low death rates balancing each other, and no migration, would have an age distribution like the one represented in Chart B. It resembles a beehive and is fairly typical of the populations of western Europe, although recent increases in the birth rates will have 'pushed out' the lower tiers. Notice that the greater expectancy of life in the European-type population is shown by the

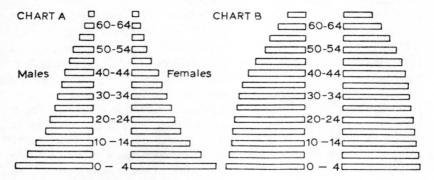

CHART A   CHART B

Males — 40-44 — Females

greater proportion of the population in the higher age groups.

In Europe, life expectancy is about seventy years whereas in much of the less developed world it is less than forty years.

Economics of Population

UNDERPOPULATION AND OVERPOPULATION

Countries may be overpopulated (too large a population for maximum efficiency) or underpopulated (too small a population). These concepts of overpopulation and underpopulation do not refer to population densities (number of people per square mile), but to the relationship between the size of the population and the economic resources available to it. A country with more than adequate amounts of fertile land and capital may be underpopulated with a density of 200 people per square mile, while a poor country may be overpopulated with twenty persons per square mile. That population, which, with existing resources and a given state of technical knowledge, gives the maximum output per head, is known as *the optimum population*.

In overpopulated countries there is generally too little land per head, and the average size of farm is much too small. Most of the people are engaged in agriculture and productivity is very low. The solution lies in moving many peasants from the land, redistributing the land into much larger holdings and making use of machinery, fertilisers and high-yielding varieties of crops. This would mean finding work for the displaced persons in industrial occupations. But these changes would require a massive increase in the amount of capital available. Overpopulation can be clearly seen in terms of deficiencies of capital and land in many eastern countries.

Underpopulation exists when there is a deficiency of labour relative to the supply of land (and capital). Such a country cannot take full advantage of large-scale production. The high efficiency of modern industry comes about as the result of specialisation, and very little of this

12

specialisation would be possible in an underpopulated country. Modern agriculture with its use of machinery is itself dependent upon large-scale industry and large markets. Comprehensive road and rail networks, power supplies and other public utilities are only economic if they are fully utilised. In an underpopulated country they would be costly to operate.

INCREASING AND DECREASING POPULATIONS

When a population is increasing due to an excess of births over deaths, the proportion of young people will be increasing. This will affect the pattern of demand for goods and services; more of those goods preferred by the young will be demanded. A declining population will have an increasing proportion of older people and a consequent increase in demand for such things as medical services, old people's homes and pensions.

An expanding population will provide a more flexible labour force. With increasing numbers entering the working population, it becomes possible to change the occupational distribution by means of a greater number of young workers entering the expanding industries. Industries in decline will reduce their labour forces more gradually by means of natural wastage; retirement will exceed recruitment. With a static or declining population industrial change is rather more difficult since growing industries must attract labour away from other industries. An expanding population will have a larger proportion of younger people who are usually more amenable to economic and industrial changes.

A growing population makes possible a more rapid rate of technical progress because new industries, new factories, and new machines can come into operation alongside (i.e. additional to) the old. With a stationary or declining population, technical progress means replacing the older equipment, which often means waiting until it wears out.

An expansion of the population will create an increased demand for goods and services and this will stimulate investment and employment. But a growing population also raises the demands for houses, schools, hospitals and other forms of social capital. The resources which have to be devoted to meeting these demands might have been used to raise the standards of living of the existing population.

In the case of Britain, and other countries heavily dependent upon foreign trade, a growing population might cause serious balance of payments difficulties. A larger population would necessitate larger imports of food, raw materials and manufactured goods. To pay for these extra imports there would have to be a substantial increase in exports.

The Population of the United Kingdom

TOTAL POPULATION

A full census of the population of the United Kingdom is taken every ten years. The first official census was carried out in 1801.

During the nineteenth century, Britain's population grew quite rapidly at a rate of nearly 1½ per cent per annum, but during the first half of the twentieth century there was a marked fall in the rate of growth to about ½ per cent per annum.

Table 2. *U.K. population* (millions)

1700	6·5 (estimate)
1801	10·5
1851	22·25
1901	38·25
1951	50·2
1971	55·7

Britain's population density is one of the highest in the world and in mid-1968 was approximately 587 persons per square mile. In England Wales there were about 833 persons per square mile.

On the basis of the present trends in birth rates, death rates, and migration, the total population is expected to rise to over 60 millions by the end of the century. The estimates are:

	(millions)
1981	57·7
1991	60·3
2001	63·1
2011	66·3

BIRTH AND DEATH RATES

For most of the nineteenth century the birth rate was about thirty-five per thousand and the death rate just over twenty per thousand. Both birth and death rates fell during the last thirty years of the century. These high rates produced a population of low average age, but the rapid fall in the death rate after 1880 more than offset the effects of the fall in the birth rate and population continued to increase. By the 1930s the birth rate had fallen to less than half the nineteenth-century rate. The population continued to increase slowly but the average age increased considerably. The fall in the birth rate ceased in 1933. It rose during the Second World War and reached a post-war peak in 1947. The birth rate then declined slighty until 1955 when it rose again until 1964, since when there has been a slight fall. The birth rate in 1968 was seventeen per thousand. The death rate has remained fairly steady for some time now at around twelve per thousand.

THE SEX RATIO

The ratio of male births to female births varies little from 106 : 100.

Although there are more male births than female births, the number of females in the total population exceeds that of males. In 1968 there were 105 females to every 100 males. This situation is due to the fact that still-birth rates, and mortality rates at almost all ages are higher for males. But the pattern is changing. Until fairly recently women outnumbered men in every age group from adolescence onwards, but the reduction in infant mortality and in the number of stillbirths has changed the sex ratio so that males exceed females in every age group up to forty-seven years. On the other hand the lengthening expectation of life has been rather more marked for women than for men so that there are now some twenty-eight women over seventy-years old to every fifteen men.

AGE DISTRIBUTION

In looking at the age distribution of the population, the most useful division for economic purposes is the three groups: young persons, persons in the working age groups, and older persons. By 'young persons' is meant persons aged 0 to 15 years (i.e. below the official school leaving age). The working age groups are assumed to be 15 to 64 years[1] in the case of men and 15 to 59 years in the case of women. This group is not to be to be confused with the working population which is discussed later. The expression 'older persons', therefore, comprises men aged 65 and over and women aged 60 and over. The 'dependent age groups' include all those persons outside the working age groups.

Since 1945 the average rise in the birth rate has been somewhat greater than the average fall in the death rate so that the increase in the average age of the population which was taking place during the inter-war period has not continued. The rather higher birth rates since the Second World War together with the continuing rise in the numbers over 65 (who were born in an era of high fertility) have tended to increase the proportion of the population in the dependent age groups. This high proportion of young and old is expected to increase still further.

Table 3. *Age Distribution – U.K. Population*

Age group	1961		1971		1981	
	000s	%	000s	%	000s	%
0–14	12,346	23·3	13,498	24·2	13,400	23·1
15–59 (F) 15–64 (M)	32,869	62·1	33,270	59·8	34,628	59·9
60+ (F) 65+ (M)	7,741	14·6	8,898	16·0	9,711	17·0

[1] The school-leaving age has now been raised to 16.

15

Age group	1991		2001		2011	
	000s	%	000s	%	000s	%
0–14	14,219	23·6	14,840	23·5	15,151	23·3
15–59 (F) ⎱ 15–64 (M) ⎰	36,212	60·1	38,796	61·5	40,096	61·3
60+ (F) ⎱ 65+ (M) ⎰	9,832	16·3	9,452	15·0	10,089	15·4

Source: *Annual Abstract of Statistics.*

REGIONAL DISTRIBUTION OF THE U.K. POPULATION

The south-east and the Midlands occupy 28 per cent of the area of the United Kingdom, but contain 49·9 per cent of its population. The most densely populated area, however, is the north-west with a density of 3·4 persons per acre. This density is due to the large conurbations centred on Manchester and Merseyside. The next most densely populated area is the south-east with 1·9 persons per acre, followed by the East and West Ridings with 1·67 persons per acre. The most sparsely populated regions are Scotland, Wales and Northern Ireland.

There is considerable internal migration in the United Kingdom, a major part of which takes the form of a movement from the north to the south-east, and, to a lesser extent, to the Midlands. The economic causes and consequences of this movement are briefly discussed in Chapter 11. During the decade 1951–61, the gross interregional movements of *employees* averaged over 450,000 a year.

Table 4. *Regional distribution U.K. population*

Region	Population density (persons per acre) 1964[1]	% U.K. population 1964[2]	Annual net migration (000s) 1959–64[3]	Estimated % increase 1964–81[4]
North England	·69	6·1	−7	9·7
E. and W. Ridings	1·67	7·8	−6	8·6
N.W. England	3·38	12·3	−7	11·9
N. Midlands	·93	7·0	+13	18·7
W. Midlands	1·53	9·1	+19	21·2
S.E. England	1·86	33·8	+89	16·7
S.W. England	·61	6·6	+28	14·3
Wales	·52	5·0	−2	9·2
Scotland	·26	9·6	−33	8·5
N. Ireland	·42	2·7	−9	14·6

Sources: [1] [2] [4] *Economic Trends*, November 1965.
[3] *The National Plan*, Cmnd 2764.

Note that in all the regions the population is increasing. The migration figures indicate net movements into and out of the regions and do not refer to changes in the total population.

THE WORKING POPULATION OF THE UNITED KINGDOM

Size

In mid-1972 the total working population of the United Kingdom was about 25 million. This represents about 45 per cent of the total population and about 73 per cent of those persons in the working age groups. About 92 per cent of the men and 53 per cent of the women in the working age groups are in, or are seeking, gainful employment. Besides those of normal working age, there are more than one million older men and women still at work.

The size of the working population increased slowly between 1959 and 1966 but has since fallen. The reasons for this change include the growing tendency for young people to stay longer in full-time education, a reduction in immigration, and the fact that a higher proportion of women are marrying and interrupting their working life. No net growth in the size of working population is expected between 1967 and 1973 when the raising of the school leaving age to 16 years will cause the numbers in the working population to fall below the 1967 level. After 1976, the working population is expected to increase again giving a total increase of about 3 per cent between 1967 and 1981.

Occupational distribution

Of all employees, about 40 per cent are employed in the mining and manufacturing industries and only about 2 per cent in agriculture and fisheries.

Most industries employ women as well as men, but the industrial groups in which women are chiefly employed are: the metal-using trades, textiles and clothing; food, drink and tobacco; the distributive trades; and professional and miscellaneous services. It should be noted that the numbers given in Table 5 as working in any industry include those engaged on administrative, technical, and clerical work, so that the totals given for production industries are greater than the numbers engaged on productive processes. In manufacturing industries it is estimated that 26·2 per cent are administrative, technical and clerical workers.

Changes in occupational distribution

Very significant changes have taken place in the occupational pattern during the present century. The primary (or extractive industries) have experienced a steep decline in the numbers employed. This has been due to the large decreases in the numbers employed in agriculture (due to increased mechanisation) and in coalmining (due to shrinking markets and mechanisation). Employment in agriculture has fallen from 9 per cent of the labour force in 1900 to less than 2 per cent in 1969.

The proportion engaged in the service industries has not changed very much during the past sixty years, but the nature of the employment within this category has undergone a very marked change. At the beginning of the century most of the employment in services was made up of people in domestic service (about 10 per cent of the working population). At the present time this proportion is about 1½ per cent. The number of women employed in domestic service fell by more than 1 million between 1901 and 1951. But there has been a great expansion of employment in other service trades. This expansion has been most noticeable in professional (especially health and education), administrative, technical and clerical work, and in the personal services. There has also been a growth in the numbers employed in the distributive trades.

The secondary industries (manufacturing) now occupy a much more important place in the economy than they did before the First World War. Within this group there have been changes in the relative importance of different industries as employers of labour. The large old-established industries such as shipbuilding and textiles have declined, while the metal trades, chemicals, engineering and vehicles have greatly expanded. The growth is most marked in those sections of the industries concerned with relatively new, or technically advanced products such as motor-cars, electrical engineering, electronic equipment and chemical products.

The future trends in occupational distribution are expected to show a continuing decline in the numbers employed in the primary industries and in public transport. Some decline in employment is also expected in industries such as textiles, clothing. and aircraft. Industries where there should be major increases in the numbers employed are engineering and the service sectors such as health, education, and public administration. It is also estimated that the demand for skilled man power, at all levels, is likely to increase.

Table 5. *Recent changes in the occupational distribution of the U.K. Working Population*

| | 1950 | | 1971 | | Percentage change |
	000s	%	000s	%	1950–71
Agriculture, forestry, fishing	1,262	5·6	353	1·5	− 72
Mining, quarrying	856	3·8	404	1·8	− 53

Manufacturing:

Food, drink, tobacco	841	3·7	867	3·6	0·3
Chemicals and allied industries	473	2·1	527	2·2	11·4
Metal manufacture	542	2·4	555	2·3	2.4
Engineering and allied industries	3,522	15·6	3,849	15·8	9·3
Textiles, Leather and Clothing	1,902	8·4	1,211	4·9	− 36·3
Other manufacturing	1,436	6·3	1,604	6·6	11·7
Total manufacturing	8,716	38·7	8,613	35·4	− 1·2
Construction	1,468	6·5	1,291	5·4	− 12·0
Gas, electricity, water	360	1·6	377	1·6	4·7
Transport and communications	1,812	8·0	1,587	6·5	− 12·4
Distributive trades	2,360	10·5	2,634	10·8	11·6
Services	4,040	17·9	5,811	23·9	43·8
Total in civil employment	22,539		24,329		

Note: Certain groups have been omitted from this table and the totals do not represent summations of separate categories shown.
Source: *Annual Abstract of Statistics.*

Chapter 3

Production and the Division of Labour

Definition of Production

The purpose of production is the satisfaction of wants, and any activity which helps to satisfy wants must be considered as productive. This is a wider meaning of the word 'production' than it carries in everyday speech, where it implies the 'making of something'. It is still common practice to talk of 'productive' and 'non-productive workers'. Productive workers are generally understood to be those who work directly on the goods which are being made. Turners and grinders in an engineering factory, coal-miners, bricklayers, joiners, etc., would be classified as productive workers. On the other hand, teachers, clerical workers, supervisors, entertainers, doctors, and clergymen, would be classified as non-productive workers, because they do not 'produce', or help *directly* in the production of any physical commodity.

But the economist does not restrict the meaning of production in this manner. All those efforts which are directed towards satisfying people's wants must be considered as productive. If the public are prepared to pay for the services of the teacher, the accountant, the surveyor, the estate agent and the entertainer, then the services of these people must be satisfying some want. The narrowness of the popular usage may be a little clearer if we visualise the effect of the withdrawal of the services of some of the so-called non-productive workers, for example telephone operators, bank clerks, shop assistants, doctors and teachers. What would be the effect upon the total output of goods and services? The total production of the country would undoubtedly fall to an alarming extent. These people are productive in the economic sense: they do not produce commodities, they produce *services*.

Production must be understood as comprising all those activities which provide the goods and services which people demand, and for which they are prepared to pay a price. Another important point must be made— production is not complete until the commodity is in the hands of the consumer. The man driving the lorry which carries the goods from the factory to the shop, the wholesalers and retailers who help to move the goods towards the customer, and the insurance companies which insure the goods, are all part of the productive process.

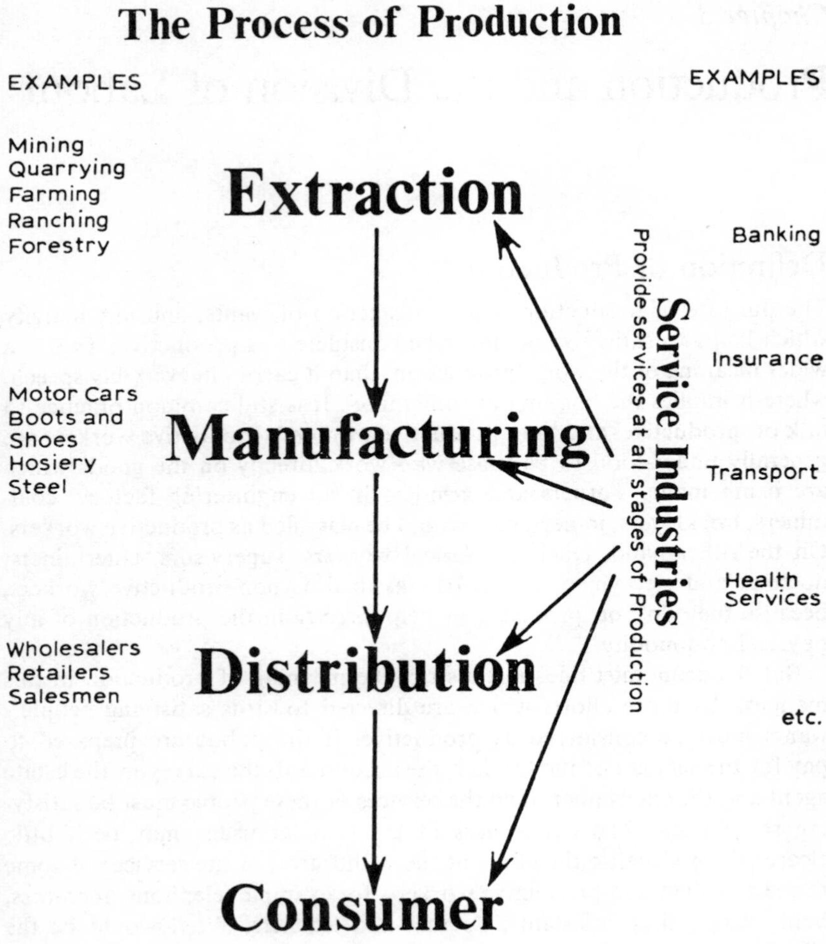

The Process of Production

EXAMPLES   EXAMPLES

Mining
Quarrying
Farming
Ranching
Forestry

Extraction

Banking

Insurance

Motor Cars
Boots and
Shoes
Hosiery
Steel

Manufacturing

Transport

Wholesalers
Retailers
Salesmen

Distribution

Health
Services

etc.

Service Industries
Provide services at all stages of Production

Consumer

Figure 2

The Division of Labour

By far the most striking feature of production in an advanced economy is that a person's daily work does not consist of providing his own wants directly. We consume hundreds of different goods and services during the course of our daily lives, few, if any, of which we make or provide ourselves. The food we eat, the clothes we wear, the furniture we use, the electricity we consume, the house in which we live, were all made by hands other than our own.

Most workers *specialise*; they contribute a very small part to the production of some article or the provision of some service. The most outstanding aspect of presentday production methods is the extent to which the principle of the division of labour is applied. The productive process is broken down into a number of separate operations, each operation being the single task of one man.

At a very early stage in his development, man realised the gains to be achieved from the application of this most important principle. Earliest man must have attempted to provide all his daily wants by his own efforts. He would be obliged to provide food, clothes, shelter and protection for himself and his family. In so doing, he would have been able to provide little more than the barest essentials for survival.

By living in communities and specialising in one, or very few activities, he learned that the total production of the group could be greatly increased. One man would specialise in hunting, another in making clothes, another in making weapons and so on. Each would exchange his surplus product for the goods produced by other specialists.

In modern economies this principle of specialisation has been carried to a high degree, and it is being extended every day. We have progressed far beyond the elementary specialisation of primitive man. The making of the simplest articles today is divided into hundreds of separate operations, and a man may perform no more than one of these individual operations.

Adam Smith, writing in the second half of the eighteenth century, saw great possibilities in a system which made use of the division of labour. On a visit to a small factory engaged in the making of pins, he observed: 'One man draws out the wire, another straightens it; a third cuts it; a fourth points its; a fifth grinds it at the top for receiving the head; to make the head requires two or three distinct operations; to put it on is a peculiar business; to whiten it is another; it is even a trade in itself to put them into paper. The important business of making a pin is, in this manner, divided into about 18 distinct operations.'

He estimated that production per day in this factory was about 5,000 pins per person employed. If the whole process had been carried out from start to finish by each employee it was estimated that he would not have been able to make even twenty per day.

ADVANTAGES OF THE DIVISION OF LABOUR

Why should the division of labour lead to such great increases in output? 1. A person who spends his time doing one job, or performing one simple operation, becomes extremely efficient at that particular task. His speed of operation is very much greater than the man who is attempting to carry out the whole of the production process. Constant repetition leads to great dexterity or, as most people would say, 'practice makes perfect'.

2. No time is wasted in moving from one task to another. The necessity of moving from one station to another, putting down one set of tools and picking up another, is eliminated.

3. There is also a great saving of time in the training of operatives. A man can be trained very quickly for the performance of a single operation.

4. There is a saving of skill. Specialisation means the creation of a very large number of different occupations, each one of which requires a particular skill. It is possible for each worker to specialise in that task for which he is best suited.

5. A great advantage of the division of labour is that it makes possible the greater use of machinery. Once a complex process has been broken down into a number of separate simple processes, it is possible to devise a machine to carry out each of the individual operations. It would be extremely difficult, for example, to devise a machine to carry out the entire process of making a chair, but once the manufacture of chairs has been reduced to a large number of separate tasks, then use can be made of planing machines, electric saws, and power-driven lathes.

With regard to the fourth point, it might be objected that one man might be more efficient at all tasks than another man. In such a case specialisation is still advantageous. A simple arithmetical example will make this point clear. Let us suppose there are two leather workers, Jones and Smith, producing shoes and handbags.

In 1 week Jones can make *either* 10 pairs of shoes *or* 10 handbags
In 1 week Smith can make either 8 pairs of shoes or 4 handbags
In the absence of any specialisation we will suppose that, each week,
Jones makes 5 pairs of shoes *and* 5 handbags
Smith makes 4 pairs of shoes and 2 handbags

It can be demonstrated that, although Jones is more efficient in producing both goods, specialisation would still increase their total output. Let us assume that Smith specialises completely in the production of shoes, and Jones spends more of his time producing handbags than producing shoes, but does not specialise completely.

Jones now produces 2 pairs of shoes and 8 handbags
Smith produces   8 pairs of shoes and 0 handbags

If we now contrast the situations before and after specialisation we have the following:

	Total production	
	Pairs of shoes	*Handbags*
Without specialisation	9	7
With specialisation	10	8

DISADVANTAGES OF THE DIVISION OF LABOUR

There are a number of reasons why the development of specialisation has not been an unmixed blessing. The drawbacks of the system are mainly concerned with the loss of 'job satisfaction' which results from the constant repetition of some relatively simple operation.

1. *Monotony*

A few simple movements which are repeated every few minutes are all that are required of a large number of workers in many factories. Observers often remark that such tasks must be very monotonous. While there is undoubtedly some truth in this charge, it has probably been exaggerated. There are many workers, especially, it is said, large numbers of women and girls, who prefer a daily task which makes limited calls upon the intelligence, demands little initiative, and carries very little responsibility. The almost completely automatic reactions which they develop leave them free to dwell on their domestic and social interests, and to indulge in pleasant conversations with their colleagues.

2. *Loss of Craftsmanship*

The gradual extension of the principle of specialisation has meant a steadily increasing use of machinery, which, in turn, has tended to become more and more automatic. We may say that the basic skills have been gradually transferred from the hands of the worker to the machine. This has led to a decline in the degree of craftsmanship required of the worker. The satisfaction to be derived from 'making something' – the pride in the creation of a product – is denied to the machine-minder. Again, much of this is true, but we must not forget that the development of machines has produced new types of craftsmen, the designers and creators of the machines themselves. The use of machines has also removed much of the heavy labour which hand methods of production require. Imagine the work involved in reducing the trunk of an oak tree to a dining table without the use of power-driven tools.

3. *Increased Risk of Unemployment*

Specialisation means that the worker is trained to perform a small narrow task, so that he is at the mercy of every industrial change. He does not have the kind of wide industrial training which would make him adaptable to changes in the techniques of production. A new invention may make him redundant, and his kind of specialised skill may be useless elsewhere. Such a worker, it is held, is peculiarly liable to spells of unemployment. In answer to this argument it has been pointed out that the division of labour, by simplifying tasks, makes the jobs in one industry very similar to those of another and so makes it very much easier for a worker to move from one industry to another. The training period for a very large number of jobs in most of our industries is very short, so that, technically,[1] a large proportion of our labour force is occupationally mobile.

4. *Interdependence*

The more specialised the pattern of production, the greater the degree to which different sectors of the economy are dependent upon one another. This may be a disadvantage in the sense that a strike, or a breakdown in production in any one part of a production process, will lead to serious disruptions elsewhere in the economy. This is perhaps best seen in the structure of the motor-car industry where extensive specialisation has led to the disintegration of production into a large number of highly specialised units. Delays in the supply of any one component may cause massive hold-ups throughout the industry.

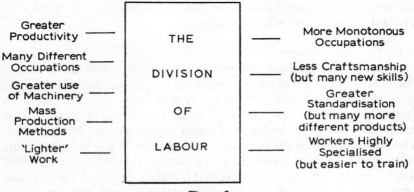

Figure 3

The advantages of the division of labour greatly outweigh the disadvantages. It has made possible enormous increases in output which have enabled men to enjoy much longer periods of leisure. The great increase in productivity has made it possible to bring about a gradual reduction in the working week, the extra hours of leisure bringing the opportunity for men to lead fuller and richer lives. The medieval craftsman may have obtained more satisfaction from the nature of his work, but the price he had to pay was a very much longer working day.

The widespread application of the division of labour, together with the extensive use of machinery which it makes possible, has meant that, in Great Britain, a working population of 25 million can produce, in a working week of 40–50 hours, sufficient output to maintain a population of 55 million at a very high standard of living. This could not have been achieved by an economic system which used hand methods of production.

[1] This qualification is necessary, because there are many other barriers to occupational mobility—see pages 44 and 282.

The Development of Specialisation

Division of labour began by dividing the work among the members of the family. The man would spend his day fishing or hunting, the woman would prepare food and make clothes, the children worked in the home and in the fields. The family was an economic unit.

The second stage of development came with the growth of communities such as the tribe and the village, and men began to specialise in one particular craft. Each community would have its potter, its shoemaker, and its blacksmith. This system reached its highest point of development with the growth of towns where the craftsmen organised themselves into guilds which regulated almost every aspect of their work.

The growth of the factory system meant the decline of the craft guilds and the manufacture of commodities by methods which made much greater use of the principle of specialisation. In the factory a man made but a small contribution to the creation of the completed product. Under the early factory system one firm would make the whole product, but as output increased, the firms themselves came to specialise.

At this stage we find each firm or factory carrying out only one stage in the total productive process. In the cotton industry we find firms which are specialists in spinning, weaving, bleaching, or dyeing. This is especially noticeable when the industry is concentrated in one region. This concentration of an industry in one part of the country is particularly apparent in the industrial development of this country. Lancashire is the centre of the cotton industry, North Staffordshire of the pottery industry, Birmingham of the engineering industry and South Wales is the centre of the tin-plate industry.

But we find not only specialisation by region; the world itself is specialised to a high degree. International trade is based upon the principle of the international division of labour. Countries tend to specialise in the production of certain commodities in which they have some cost advantages. They exchange their surpluses for the specialised products of other countries.

Division of labour has extended from the family to the town, from the town to the region, and from the region to the country itself.

Specialisation and Exchange

Robinson Crusoe had to provide his daily needs by his own efforts. If we all lived like Crusoe we could only provide ourselves with a very limited variety of goods. It is only because we have this complex system of specialisation that we can enjoy the luxuries of modern life. But once a system of specialised production has been developed we are dependent upon some system of exchange for the variety of goods and services which we need to satisfy our daily wants. Without some means of exchange, the farmer would have far too much corn for his personal needs, but he would have no coal, no oil, no electricity, and no machinery. As specialists we are absolutely dependent upon some efficient means of exchanging the products we make, or the services we provide, for the products and services provided by other specialists. Our highly developed economic system enables us to exchange hours of labour for a new suit, for a haircut, for a holiday abroad, for a gallon of petrol and for a thousand and one different commodities. Such exchanges and hundreds of thousands of similar transactions take place every day, smoothly and efficiently. We take all this for granted, rarely, if ever, stopping to think how very complex is this system of exchange on which we are so dependent.

It should be clear now that the division of labour necessitates exchange, which in turn depends upon the development of efficient markets and systems of transport. When we specialise we are no longer independent economic units, but are highly dependent upon the work of others.

Specialisation and the Market

There is one other important point which must be made regarding the extent to which the division may be applied. This is dependent upon the size of the market. Large-scale production and mass production methods can only be utilised if there is a large demand for the product. If the demand for some particular product amounts to no more than say six per week at the current price, then it would be absurd to establish a massive production line which will produce thousands per week. Mass production, making extensive use of the division of labour, is possible only where there exists a very large demand for a standardised article. This point is illustrated in the manufacture of cigarettes, electric light bulbs, ball-point pens, soap, and motor cars. In all these cases there is a large demand for a standardised product. Where the demand is for individual styles rather than standardised products, production can only take place on a small scale, and, hence, only very limited use can be made of the division of labour. Clothing (particularly ladies' clothes), ladies' footwear, jewellery, racing cars, and fur coats are examples of products which are not suited to mass production because there is no 'mass' demand.

Chapter 4

The Factors of Production

No production can take place unless the means of production are available. The economic resources required for the productive process are usually grouped into four categories, land, labour, capital and the entrepreneur. They are usually referred to as the factors of production. Early economists recognised only three factors, land, labour and capital. Even for the very simplest types of production these three factors are required. Some fruit grows wild, but labour is still required to gather it and some simple equipment (capital) will be required to store and transport it. The fourth factor, the entrepreneur, is the person who is responsible for taking the decision to produce, bearing the risks involved in this decision and organising the other factors into a production team.

Land

The term 'land' is used to include all kinds of natural resources – all the gifts of nature as distinct from man-made resources. It includes all the minerals available in the earth's crust, the forests, the farmlands, the fishing grounds, and the space on which productive activity takes place. Land is essential for all kinds of production. Traditionally, land has been regarded as being different in several respects from the other factors of production.

1. Land is strictly limited in supply. The area of land available to man cannot be increased, whereas it is possible to change the supply of the other factors.
2. Land is not geographically mobile.
3. It is particularly subject to the Law of Diminishing Returns.

These three characteristics of land have some important economic implications, but they cannot be left unqualified.

It is true that the total surface area of land cannot be significantly changed, although certain areas have been reclaimed from the sea, notably in Holland. But in economics we are concerned principally with land which can be used for the purpose of production and the supply of this land can be altered. Deserts can be irrigated, jungles can be cleared, barren land can be fertilised and marshlands may be drained. By such means the supply of land suitable for particular economic purposes may be extensively changed over the long period.

Land is not geographically mobile; the situation oi any given plot of land cannot be changed. But most land has some degree of occupational mobility; it is capable of more than one use. Some land may be used for many purposes: for the growing of crops, as building land for the erection of houses or factories, as a public park or as a storage space. Other land may be useful for only one purpose, e.g. moorland for the grazing of sheep.

The geographical immobility of land – that is, the inability to change the location of any given site – has important economic consequences. Some countries are very densely populated, while others have a very low density of population. This situation cannot be changed by moving land from, say, Australia to Holland. Countries which have very limited areas of land in relation to the size of their population, must, if they are to develop economically, concentrate on those industries which require a great deal of labour and small amounts of land. Countries such as Great Britain, Japan, and Belgium, which are in this position, must specialise in manufacturing. Australia, Canada, and the South American countries, which are sparsely populated, are able to develop great agricultural and pastoral industries which require large tracts of land but relatively little labour.

There is another economic aspect of the geographical immobility of land which is revealed in the great differences which are to be found in the valuation of similiar areas of land situated in different parts of our towns and cities. In any city the number of corner sites, and the number of sites on the main thoroughfares are strictly limited. A site of similar area in the suburbs is no substitute for a location in the High Street. No matter how much the demand for these central sites increases, their supply cannot be increased. All that can happen, and in fact does happen, is that their value continues to rise.

The third point, concerning the Law of Diminishing Returns, is dealt with later, in the chapter on the laws of production.

Labour

In economic theory, labour is no different from the other factors of production. It is merely one of the essential resources which are needed before production can take place. But labour is provided by human beings; it is not only a factor of production, but the reason why economic activity takes place. The persons who take part in productive activity are also consumers – the sum of whose individual demands provides the business man with the incentive to undertake production.

For this reason, when considering real-life economic problems, it is necessary to treat labour somewhat differently from the other factors of production. There are ethical and moral problems which have to be taken into account. For example – if a machine is capable of working a twenty-four hour day, the question whether it is right (i.e. desirable) to use it in this manner would be judged in terms of efficiency, output, costs, etc. The same question applied to labour would raise additional considerations of individual freedom and human rights.

The following section refers to the supply of labour, but it must be borne in mind that we are concerned with the 'services of labour' rather than 'labour'. The businessman does not purchase men and women, but the services of men and women. Only in a slave society can 'labour' be purchased in the strict sense of the term.

THE SUPPLY OF LABOUR

Of great economic significance to any society is the supply of labour which is available to produce the goods and services which the people require. The supply of labour is not the same thing as the number of people in that society. We are concerned with labour as a factor of production and it is the number of hours of labour available which comprises the supply of labour in this context. Keeping in mind this definition of the supply of labour – the hours of labour which are available for productive purposes – we can examine the factors which govern its size.

The Size of the Total Population

This is obviously a most important factor, for the size of a country's population, sets an upper limit to the supply of labour available.

The Age Composition of the Population

The age composition of the population is measured by the numbers of people in the different age groups. Two countries may have the same total population, but very different age compositions. One country may have large numbers of older people but relatively few in the younger age groups, whereas the other may have large numbers of young people, but comparatively few in the older groups. The supply of labour will be very different in these two communities.

The Working Population

In our own country and in many others the age at which a person may engage in full-time work is legally restricted. In Great Britain no one may work in a full-time capacity until he has reached the age of fifteen years (soon to be 16 years); the normal age of retirement is sixty-five years. This does not mean, however, that the total working population

31

comprises all those between the ages of fifteen and sixty-five. It is a much smaller number. There are many people in this age group who continue their full-time education beyond the age of fifteen. Another large group, which must be excluded, consists of the housewives who do not indulge in paid employment outside the home. A number of people retire before the age of sixty-five and hence do not form part of the working population although they are part of the fifteen to sixty-five group.

The working population may be defined as the number of people who are eligible and who offer themselves for employment. As a proportion of the total population it varies greatly from country to country, depending on such factors as –

(a) The official school leaving age.
(b) The normal age of retirement.
(c) The proportion of married women who take up paid employment.
(d) The numbers pursuing full-time education beyond the age of fifteen years.
(e) The number retiring before the accepted retirement age.

In this country the working population is a little less than half the total population. Of our total population of some 55 million (1972) about 25 million are defined as the working population. Countries which have no compulsory system of education, and no social services which provide old-age pensions, will have a very much greater percentage of their total population classified as the working population. The total supply of labour is very much affected by the factors which determine the size of the working population (see also Chapter 2).

The Working Week

The number of people who work (or are available for work) is an important determinant of the supply of labour, but so is the number of hours which these people work. The supply of labour provided by twenty people working for forty hours is the same as that provided by forty people working for twenty hours. The accepted working week in most advanced countries has been progressively reduced and many countries now have a recognised working week of forty hours. The shorter the working week the smaller will be the supply of labour.

Holidays

The gradual reduction of the working week has been accompanied by an extension of the annual holiday period. Again, this amounts to a reduction in the supply of labour.

It must not be assumed, however, that a reduction in the supply of labour implies a reduction in the amount of work done. In spite of the fall in the number of hours worked by each employee, output per worker has, in the past, continued to rise. In other words, the reduction in the hours worked has been more than offset by the increases in productivity.

THE EFFICIENCY OF LABOUR

In discussing the relationship between labour and output, another condition, in addition to the number of workers and the number of hours worked, is relevant, namely – the efficiency of labour.

Productivity is usually measured in terms of the number of units of output produced by a worker in a given period of time, usually one hour. The unit of measurement is output per man-hour. There is a very great difference between the productivity of workers in the modern industrial nations and those who work in the underdeveloped countries. Even between industrial nations great variations are to be found in the output per man-hour of workers in similar industries. Teams of productivity experts which visited America in the years following the Second World War found that in many industries the productivity of the American worker was two or three times as great as that of his counterpart in British industry. Efficiency of labour is the term we use to describe the ability of labour to produce goods and services. Its basis is the productivity of labour, which is measured by output per man-hour. The efficiency of labour may be increased in a number of different ways.

Education and Training

An educated labour force which has had the benefit of a sound technical training is much more efficient than a working population which is denied these benefits. Modern industrial techniques require highly skilled scientists and technicians, and, to maintain its position as a leading manufacturing country, Britain is very dependent upon the institutions which will provide the required technical training. This training is provided by the technical colleges, the universities and by industry itself. But these establishments can only provide the technicians and administrators if there is a well-established system of general education such as that provided by our schools.

Working Conditions

A dark, cold, and cheerless workshop will not encourage industrious and careful effort. The efficiency of labour is undoubtedly influenced by the conditions under which it is carried out. During the present century there has been a continuous improvement in working conditions in all our industries. Great attention is now paid to such matters as good ventilation and the removal of dust and smells; to satisfactory lighting, pleasing decoration, comfortable temperatures and better working positions. Many of our modern factories are very pleasant places, far removed from the damp, ill-lit, badly ventilated 'dark Satanic mills' in which so many nineteenth-century workers toiled for anything up to sixteen hours a day.

Welfare Services

The state now provides a National Health Service which makes medical attention available to all, irrespective of the ability to pay. A National Insurance Scheme provides unemployment pay, sickness benefit, and national assistance grants. These services are designed to assist the workman and his family when he is out of work and when he is unable to work due to sickness. In helping to maintain a healthy population and in greatly reducing the working time lost owing to sickness and injury, the health services make possible a much more efficient labour force. Unemployment and sickness benefits prevent the deterioration in health and morale of those workers who are suffering from loss of earnings due to sickness and unemployment.

Most of our larger firms also provide welfare services for their staffs. Playing fields, social and recreational facilities, staff canteens, trained nurses and factory medical services are all common features of the larger industrial and commercial undertakings. These provisions all contribute towards a happier, healthier, and more efficient labour force.

The Cooperating Factors

It is often argued that the greater efficiency of the American worker is due to the fact that he has 'more and better power at his elbow'. It cannot be denied that the worker using more efficient tools is likely to be the more efficient worker. This is an aspect of production which concerns the proportions in which the factors of production are combined and is discussed later in this chapter. Since we are using output per man-hour to measure the efficiency of labour, it is apparent that the more efficient the means with which labour has to work, the greater will be the output per worker. Perhaps the most important advance made recently in this connection has been the growing practice of adopting Work Study and Method Study.

These are techniques which are designed to increase output by a careful, systematic analysis of each particular process. The individual movements of the operator, the layout of the machines, the movement of materials and the positions of the tools are all carefully investigated, measured, and photographed. The result of this investigation is often a completely new layout for the production process and new methods of operation for the workers. Such changes have frequently resulted in great increases in productivity.

Capital

Capital is a means of production. It consists of all those goods which man produces, not because he wishes to obtain satisfaction from them directly, but because he wants them to help him to produce other goods. Capital is, in fact, a stock of goods. It includes factories, machines, raw materials, railways and docks. We must also include the stocks of finished goods which are held by manufacturers and traders, because the production process is not complete until the commodity is in the hands of the consumer.

Capital was created when man began to make simple tools and implements to assist him in the production of food; in the hunting of animals, and in the transportation of his possessions. In the most primitive methods of production some capital is used in conjunction with land and labour. The most backward peoples use simple ploughs, axes, bows and arrows, and water-bags.

One distinguishing feature of capital is that it is artificial. It is produced by man and is not a natural resource. Another feature of capital goods, already mentioned, is that man does not produce them because they give him immediate satisfaction, but because they help him to increase his output of consumer goods. Bread, clothing and footwear are examples of consumer goods; they are wanted for their own sake because they render immediate satisfaction. Lathes, steam-hammers, power stations, steel, and cement are examples of capital goods; they are desired because they help man to produce the commodities he needs for shelter, sustenance, and enjoyment.

The production process, as we noted earlier, is not complete until the commodity is in the hands of the ultimate consumer. All those tools, materials, and equipment which man uses directly or indirectly in the process of production are capital goods.

There are several categories or types of capital of which the following may be noted:

1. *Fixed Capital*

This term is used to describe all those assets which have a relatively long life and do not change their form in the process of production. Under this heading we would include instruments of production such as factories, machines, railway systems, roads, and docks, because they are not transformed into different economic goods and are 'used up' very slowly.

2. *Circulating Capital*

Some commodities, such as wheat, rubber, clay, and cotton, change their form completely as they pass through the process of production. Such materials are known as circulating capital. They are classified as capital because they assist in the production of final or consumer goods, but they differ from fixed capital because the businessman is constantly changing his stock of such commodities. He uses money to buy his raw materials; transforms them into manufactured products; sells these products for money, and uses the money to buy fresh stocks of materials. This is a 'circular' process, which gives rise to the term Circulating Capital.

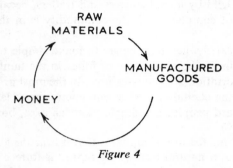

Figure 4

3. *Social Capital*

A large proportion of the nation's stock of capital consists of houses, hospitals, schools, parks, public baths, and other kinds of property which people use for purposes which are not directly concerned with the production of goods. The term 'social capital' is normally used to describe this type of property which is used for social rather than for industrial or commercial purposes. In a society which enjoys a high standard of living a large part of the total supply of capital will consist of social capital. Why should houses, hospitals and schools be described as capital? Because they do assist man in the production of his material wants, but in an indirect way. We can ask ourselves the question, 'Would the nation be more or less productive if it did not have its present stock of houses, schools and hospitals?'

CAPITAL ACCUMULATION

If man had to work without the assistance of capital equipment, productivity and living standards would be very low indeed. We have to visualise men working with bare hands on virgin soil in order to get a picture of production without the aid of capital. The simplest tools are capital, as are fertilisers, drainage, ditches and fences. Over the centuries our economic system has amassed a tremendous stock of aids to production and we now have industries such as the steel industry, which uses about £25,000 worth of capital equipment *per man employed*.

But man cannot use capital goods until he has first produced them, and while he is producing capital goods, he cannot also be producing consumer goods. If a man spends a week producing a simple plough, he is still consuming each day a variety of consumer goods, and unless he has a stock of such goods available to him, he cannot devote his time to making the plough. The production of capital goods demands *abstinence* from consumption. The man making the plough must sacrifice the consumer goods which he could have produced during the time which he devotes to the construction of the plough. The sacrifice might be made by other members of the community who give up part of their stock of consumer goods in order to sustain the workers who are producing capital goods. In essence, the creation of capital means the foregoing of present consumption for the prospect of a much greater level of consumption in the future. People are prepared to make this sacrifice because the capital goods will greatly increase their future productivity.

A castaway might survive by catching fish with his bare hands. He is able, perhaps, to catch six fish each day by using this simple method. A net would enable him to catch the same number in half an hour, leaving him valuable time to devote to other activities. But the net might take two days to construct. The castaway can only obtain his capital equipment by sacrificing consumption in the form of twelve fish.

This is the reality of capital accumulation, and it is as true of our complex society as it is of the primitive communities. The houses, machines, factories, and roads which we are building today, involve the use of resources which could be used to make more consumer goods and so give us a higher *present* standard of living. But we are prepared to sacrifice higher standards today for the even higher standards which these capital goods will make possible *in the future*. In our very complicated economic system it is difficult to see that the manufacture of capital goods necessitates any sacrifice. An abundance of consumer goods appears to be pouring forth from our factories simultaneously with the building of factories, the manufacture of machines and the construction of roads. But the present large output of consumer goods is the result of capital accumulation in the past.

The people of this country do not spend the whole of their incomes on consumer goods. That part of their income not spent is saved. Saving involves refraining from consumption, and it is these savings which enable the construction of capital goods to be financed. This will be dealt with more fully later in the book.

CAPITAL CONSUMPTION

Not all the capital goods being produced involve additions to our stock of capital. Capital goods are continually wearing out or becoming out of date. Repairs and replacement are required as capital depreciates. In any one year a large proportion of the total output of capital goods is required to replace worn out or obsolete equipment. The value of the output required to maintain our existing stock of capital is known as depreciation. The total output of capital goods in any one year is known as Gross Investment; the addition to our existing stock of capital is termed Net Investment. Hence:

Gross Investment – Depreciation = Net Investment.

It may happen that depreciation is taking place at a faster rate than the manufacture of capital equipment. In this case net investment would be a minus quantity. A nation in this position is said to be consuming capital; it is not making good the wear and tear of capital which is taking place continually. This is most likely to happen during a war when a country is obliged to devote a large part of its economic resources to the manufacture of military supplies. During the last war Britain allowed her railway network to depreciate, many houses were destroyed and damaged whilst practically none were built, and many industries were unable to obtain replacements for machines which were wearing out or becoming obsolete.

If a country is consuming capital, then its future production must fall. If the worn-out capital equipment is not replaced then more primitive methods of production will have to be adopted and productivity must decline.

CAPITALISTIC METHODS OF PRODUCTION

The greater the proportion of capital used in any system of production, the more capitalistic is the system. In advanced countries goods are produced by highly capitalistic methods. The greater the degree to which capital is employed the more 'roundabout' or 'time consuming' is the productive process. Although the use of capital greatly increases total output, the time interval between the first steps in production and the completion of the product is often greatly extended. Production processes which make use of machinery and other forms of capital are very efficient and very productive, but they are roundabout processes. Time which could be spent producing consumer goods must be devoted to the production of the machines, railways, ships, lorries, docks and so on. The ultimate flow of consumer goods will be increased enormously, but the total production process is greatly lengthened.

The Entrepreneur

We have now discussed Land, Labour and Capital and indicated their essential features as factors of production. No productive activity is possible without the cooperation of all three factors. Many economists identify a fourth factor – the entrepreneur. They point out that, left to themselves, land, labour and capital will not produce anything. There must be some person or persons to organise these three factors into a production unit. There must be someone who will take the decisions:

1. what to produce (i.e. the type of article and the quantity);
2. how to produce (i.e. the methods of production);
3. where to produce (i.e. the location of the factory),

and who will bear the risks which the taking of such decisions involves.

Whoever takes these decisions and bears the risks is known as the entrepreneur. (There is no really suitable English word to describe such a person, perhaps the word 'enterpriser' is as near as we can get.) The entrepreneur is the man who undertakes production with a view to earning a profit. He undertakes to produce a commodity for which, he believes, a satisfactory demand exists at a price which will yield him a profit. He decides upon the location of his factory, hires the factors of production, and combines them in the proportions which he considers to be the most efficient. He must also be prepared to risk his savings (or borrowed funds) in meeting all payments (for resources) which have to be made before his products reach the market. He must also decide the quantity and the quality of the product to be manufactured. In a capitalist or free enterprise economy, production would not take place unless someone was prepared to carry out these functions.

The entrepreneur is also the risk-bearer. Most production takes place *in anticipation of demand*. We said earlier that the entrepreneur will produce those commodities which he *believes* will yield him a profit – he does not *know* that they will do so, because the future is always unknown. Since it takes time to produce and market the goods, the entrepreneur must finance the production during the period which elapses from his decision to produce to the marketing of the final product. He must pay rent for his land and premises, wages to his workers, interest on the money he has borrowed, and, usually within three months, he must pay for his raw materials. These payments he must make without being certain of the amount of money he will obtain from the sale of his products. If his revenue from the sale of his goods exceeds his costs, he will make a profit; if his costs exceed his receipts then he will make a loss.

The risks borne by the entrepreneur arise from uncertainty – he cannot know for certain what the market conditions will be in the future. Economic conditions are constantly changing and there are many things which can affect the demand for his product. His success as a businessman depends to a large extent upon his ability to forecast future trends and to adjust his production plans to meet the changes in market conditions.

The enterpreneur then is the risk-bearer and the decision-taker. In a one-man business both functions are carried out by the same person – the sole proprietor. In the larger enterprise, the joint stock company, these functions, as we shall see later, may be carried out by different groups of people.

Chapter 5

The Mobility of the Factors of Production

The Need for Mobility

Economic conditions are constantly changing and the present century has been a period of particularly rapid economic change. All sorts of conditions give rise to changes in our economic environment; some of the more important of these are:

1. *Wars*

Modern wars have the effect of completely disrupting the economic life of the country. The two world wars which have taken place in the twentieth century brought significant economic changes in the pattern of life in Britain. They led to rapid technological progress in certain industries (e.g. aircraft, chemicals, radio and television, engineering and transport). Large numbers of people changed their jobs and acquired new skills, and large numbers of workers moved to different parts of the country to work in essential industries. The pattern of world trade was drastically altered as a result of the wars and Britain lost many of her former markets.

2. *Changes in Population*

Immigration, emigration and changes in birth rates and death rates can bring about significant changes in the size of the population and in the age composition of the population. Such population changes can have important economic effects. A rapidly rising population will mean an increasing demand for schools and schoolteachers and for those goods which are principally consumed by the young. A population which is growing rapidly because of large scale immigration will cause an increase in the demand for houses, but will also increase the supply of labour. Such changes will affect the price of houses and the price of labour (i.e. wages).

3. *Technological Changes*

New materials, new products and new techniques of production are constantly being devised. These innovations, as they are called, are responsible for important changes taking place in the conditions of supply of, and the demand for, existing products. They lead to the growth of new industries and the decline of some older industries.

4. Political Changes

The British economy is affected by political changes both at home and abroad. At home the government is the biggest 'business' in the country and is responsible for spending about one-third of our total annual income. Any changes in government policy must have important economic effects. Perhaps the most obvious examples of governmental influence on the economy lie in the field of taxation. Try to visualise what might be the economic effects of an increase in purchase tax, or a reduction in income tax.

This country is very dependent upon world trade. We depend upon a high level of exports for the means of buying a large proportion of our food supply and for many of the raw materials used by our industries. Political developments in other countries can have serious effects upon Britain's overseas trade. British-owned industries in other countries might be nationalised; a country which formerly bought British cotton goods might decide to establish its own cotton industry; a nation which imported British goods might decide to raise its tariffs in order to protect its own industries. Such changes, and others of a similar nature, could well have a serious effect upon Britain's overseas trade, and upon our ability to pay our way in the world.

5. Changes in Taste and Fashion

Changes in taste and fashion affect the demands for most consumer goods to some extent, but they are of especial importance to the manufacturers of such goods as footwear, clothing, furniture and domestic appliances. Most advertising in this country is a deliberate attempt to bring about changes in taste and fashion.

These things, and many others, lead to changes in the economic system which have far-reaching effects.

A fall in the demand for product A, and an increase in the demand for product B can only be matched by the necessary changes in supply if factors of production are able to move out of industry A, and more factors are able to move into industry B. New products, and new methods of production and distribution can only be developed if economic resources can be transferred into these fields. In other words, factors of production must have some degree of mobility.

Occupational and Geographical Mobility

There are two aspects of mobility (1) *Occupational mobility* – the movement of a factor from one industry or trade to another, and (2) *Geographical mobility* – the movement of a factor from one location to another.

LAND

Land, as we have already seen, is not mobile in the geographical sense, although much land has a high degree of occupational mobility. These aspects of land were discussed in the previous chapter.

CAPITAL

Capital is mobile in both senses, but some types of capital equipment are relatively immobile. Capital items such as buildings, railway systems, blast furnaces and dock installations are virtually immobile in the geographical sense. It may be physically possible to dismantle such equipment and to move it to another site, but the cost of doing so is likely to outweigh any advantages in the new location. Neither is such equipment mobile in the occupational sense. Blast furnaces and railways cannot be used effectively for any purposes other than those for which they were constructed. Many buildings, however, can be effectively adapted to other uses. Many of the former cotton mills in Lancashire are now housing a variety of industries. Some capital equipment is extremely mobile both geographically and between industries. Electric motors, machine tools, hand tools, and lorries can be effectively used in a wide variety of industries and are capable of being moved from one location to another.

LABOUR

Theoretically we should expect labour to be the most mobile of the factors of production both occupationally and geographically. Economic history does indeed provide abundant evidence of great movements of labour from one industry to another and from one region to another. During the nineteenth century and the early years of the twentieth, millions of people left Europe to settle in North America and in the British Dominions. In the second half of the nineteenth century there occurred the great movement westwards in the United States, when large numbers of people left the eastern states to settle the interior and the western seaboard. The last quarter of the eighteenth century saw the beginnings of the great movement of British workers from the country to the town, a movement which is still taking place. At the end of the eighteenth century some 80 per cent of the British population lived in the countryside; by the end of the nineteenth century, 80 per cent were living in towns.

In spite of all this, the fact remains that there is abundant evidence of an unwillingness of workers to move from one area to another. In the 1930s the rates of unemployment in different regions of Britain varied enormously. While some regions experienced unemployment rates as high as 60 per cent, others had rates well below 10 per cent. Although some movement of population, from areas of severe unemployment to areas more fortunate, did take place, it was nothing like so great as the differences in unemployment rates might have led one to expect.

Barriers to Mobility of Labour

There are a number of impediments to the mobility of labour. We shall examine first *the barriers to geographical mobility*.

1. The monetary cost of moving to a new district. Moving a family, together with all its possessions, can be an expensive operation. In addition to the costs of transport, it may well include the numerous expenses involved in the sale and purchase of a house. To overcome this particular barrier to mobility, many firms, anxious to attract more labour, are meeting the whole or part of the cost of removal.

2. The housing shortage, which has been a feature of the British economy since the war, has proved to be the most serious handicap to the geographical mobility of labour. Even where the worker has been willing to move, the inability to obtain a house in the new locality has often proved an insuperable obstacle. Here again a number of firms have undertaken to provide housing for their workers, especially key workers.

3. Social ties. Many people are very loath to 'tear up their roots'. They do not wish to leave behind their friends and relatives and face the prospect of establishing new relationships in a strange town. The question of interrupting a child's education is another factor which often weighs heavily against a decision to move.

The determinants of the ability of a worker to change his trade and to move from one industry to another are more complex. The major *barriers to occupational mobility* are:

1. The prevailing system of apprenticeship in many trades is designed to train people between the ages of sixteen and twenty-one. A man who has 'served his time' in a particular trade, and is earning the appropriate rate for a skilled man, is not usually prepared to accept a trainee's rate of pay for a number of years while he learns a new trade.

2. People differ in natural ability, and certain occupations require a high level of ability and intelligence, or a particular natural aptitude which is only possessed by a certain proportion of the population. For this reason occupations such as surgeons, physicists, mathematicians, designers, and entertainers, are closed to those who do not possess the requisite abilities.

3. An increasing number of occupations require a long period of training (e.g. doctors, dentists, lawyers, architects). In spite of the government aid in the form of grants which is now available to finance such training, considerable financial sacrifice is still required of the student and his family. Many people cannot afford the sacrifice or are unwilling to make it. The length of the period of training is, itself, sometimes a deterrent.

4. To enter some occupations a certain amount of capital is required. In order to establish oneself as an entrepreneur either by opening a retail shop or some other form of one-man business (e.g. garage proprietor, window-cleaner, hairdresser or jobbing builder), capital is required to purchase the necessary stock and equipment. The purchase price of a practice or a partnership is often required in order to become established as a solicitor, an accountant or an estate agent.

5. It is still held by many people that the existing class structure provides some restrictions on the occupational mobility of labour. A certain type of social background and an education at one of the more famous public schools provide, it is believed, definite advantages in certain fields of employment.

It is undeniable that a certain degree of mobility is essential if we are to use our economic resources in the most efficient manner. What can be done to assist the movement of labour from one job to another? We have already mentioned some of the measures which might help. The problem of housing is a difficult one, but both private firms and local authorities are doing a great deal to remedy the serious shortages in particular areas. Another problem is lack of knowledge; workers may be ignorant of opportunities and employers may be unaware of labour which is seeking alternative employment. The main function of our Employment Exchanges and Youth Employment Bureaux is to remove this ignorance; their role is to bring together men seeking jobs and employers seeking labour. The local and national press are being utilised to an increasing extent in giving publicity to employment opportunities. Our schools are developing career departments to assist the school-leaver in his choice of employment.

An important feature of government policy in this field has been the development of Government Re-training Centres where men who have lost their jobs in one industry are given a training which helps them to obtain work in another industry.

Industry itself plays an important part. Most of the larger firms offer training to new recruits. Increased mechanisation and the greater use of automatic and semi-automatic machinery has tended to reduce the problem of mobility. It has led to the creation of a very large number of jobs of an unskilled or semiskilled nature which call for no more than a few weeks' training. Unskilled and semiskilled workers in many of our manufacturing industries tend to be very mobile between industries.

Labour Turnover

While a measure of mobility in the labour force is essential, too much mobility is inefficient and very costly. It appears that a great deal of the movement from job to job which takes place nowadays, is not of a nature which leads to a more efficient distribution of the labour force. It has been found from studies of particular industrial regions that very large movements of workers into and out of certain industries are taking place continually, but the totals employed by these industries remain virtually unchanged. *Labour turnover*, as this movement is called, is unnecessarily high and represents an aimless wandering from job to job – a restless movement of workers seeking 'a change' rather than advancement to a better paid or more suitable situation. If more attention were paid to the selection of employees in order to ensure that those engaged had the aptitude for the work, and more care and thought were given to the training of operatives and to those conditions which lead to boredom and unrest, then much of this unnecessary labour turnover might be eliminated. Labour turnover is costly, because each time an operative leaves his employment and a replacement is required, the employer incurs costs in the form of (*a*) a fall in output, (*b*) the cost of training a new worker, and (*c*) the loss of a skilled man's output while he spends his time training the new worker.

Mobility of the Entrepreneur

The most mobile of the factors of production is probably the entrepreneur. While labour tends to be trained for some special task and acquires skills and knowledge appropriate to some trade or industry, the basic functions of the entrepreneur are common to all forms of production. Whatever the type of economic activity, there will be a need to raise capital, to organise the factors of production, and to take the fundamental decisions on where, what and how to produce. The welding of men and capital into an efficient productive unit is a task of human relations, the basic features of which are common to all industries. First-class entrepreneurial ability can perform this task in almost any industry.

Immobile factors of production are sometimes known as specific factors. Thus, a blast furnace would be described as a highly specific factor as would an eminent surgeon or a nuclear physicist. Such resources have been created, or trained, to perform one highly specialised function – they are specific to one particular job.

Chapter 6

The Laws of Production

The Law of Diminishing Returns

For most economic activities the proportions in which the different factors are combined can be varied. This is quite apparent if we consider the different ways in which men produce crops such as wheat, or maize, or rice in different parts of the world. In advanced countries the crops are grown by combining land with relatively large amounts of capital and relatively few units of labour. In less developed countries, the crops are grown by combining land with very little capital and large amounts of labour.

Since the proportions are variable, economists are interested in observing the effects of varying them. Such observations have resulted in the formulation of the law of variable proportions, more commonly known as the Law of Diminishing Returns.

Let us assume that wheat is to be grown on a fixed area of land, say 10 acres. We shall also assume that the amount of capital to be utilised is also fixed in supply. The number of workers put to work with these fixed factors (land and capital) can be varied and the resultant variations in output duly noted. Table 6 sets out some hypothetical results of such an experiment. The figures themselves are not important, what matters are the relationships between them.

Table 6. *Labour returns*

No. of men	Total product (cwt)	Average[1] product (cwt)	Marginal product (cwt)
1	10	10·0	10
2	25	12·5	15
3	45	15·0	20
4	65	16·3	20
5	80	16·0	15
6	92	15·3	12
7	102	14·6	10
8	110	13·8	8
9	116	13·0	6
10	120	12·0	4

Area of land: 10 acres

[1] Figures rounded to 3 significant figures.

Column 1 shows the variations in the numbers of men employed and column 2 indicates the total products resulting from the employment of these different numbers of men. Column 3 gives us the average product per man and is obtained from the formula,

$$\frac{\text{Total Product}}{\text{No. of men employed}} = \textit{Average Product (AP)}$$

Column 4 shows the changes in total product brought about by varying employment. The addition of the eighth man adds eight units to total product while the employment of the fourth man increases total product by twenty units. *The changes in total product* brought about by taking on one more man, or by reducing employment by one man, are known as *Marginal Products* (MP).

As the number of men is increased from one to ten, the total product continues to increase, but this is not true of average and marginal products. As more men are employed, both the AP and MP begin to rise, reach a maximum and start to fall. These movements are seen more clearly in Fig. 5 which shows the movements of AP and MP as the number of men employed is varied.

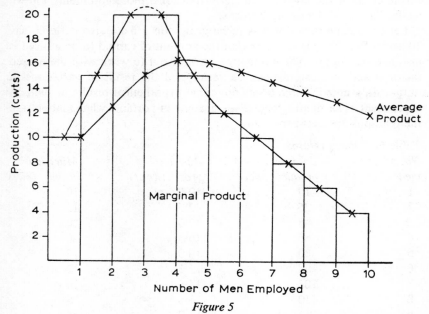

Figure 5

The fact that average and marginal products vary as the number of workers varies is not due to the fact that some men are more efficient than others. We are assuming that they are all equally efficient. The changes in

AP and MP are due entirely to the changing proportions between the fixed factors (land and capital) and the variable factor (labour). As the number of men increases from one to four, the average product of labour increases. Up to this point, the fixed factors are too large for the men to work them efficiently – they are 'too thin on the ground'. As the number of men is increased beyond four, the average product begins to fall – an indication that the proportions between the fixed and variable factors are less favourable – the land is becoming overcrowded. When four men are employed we get the *maximum output per man* – labour productivity is at its highest point.

This simple arithmetical example provides an illustration of one of the most famous and fundamental laws of economics – the Law of Diminishing Returns. The units of output are referred to as 'returns' and the law refers to the *returns to the variable factor* – in our case, labour. A more precise statement of this law might be:

As more and more units of a variable factor of production are used in combination with a fixed quantity of other factors, there is some point at which the returns to the variable factor will start to decline.

In our example we have made labour the variable factor, but the law is equally applicable when land or capital is the variable factor. The average and marginal productivity of capital will start to decline at some point when more and more capital is applied to a fixed supply of land and labour.

It should be apparent that a continuation of Figure 5 would bring us to a point where the total product itself begins to decline and the MP of labour becomes negative. This state of affairs indicates that, not only have the men become too numerous, they are positively hindering one another.

The law of diminishing returns only applies when 'other things remain unchanged'. The efficiency of the other factors and the techniques of production are assumed to be constant. Now we know that these things are always changing and improvements in technical knowledge have tended to offset the effects of the law of diminishing returns. Improved methods of production will raise the productivity of the factors of production and move the AP and MP curves upwards. But this does not mean that the law no longer applies. It is still true that in the short period (during which other things can change very little), if more and more men were set to work on a fixed area of land, there would come a point where the MP and AP of labour would begin to decline.

Increasing and Constant Returns

Referring back to Table 6 (p. 47) we can see that as employment increases from one to four men, production is taking place under conditions of *increasing returns* – the average product of labour is rising. It is possible, under certain conditions, for the average product of labour to remain constant over certain ranges of output. Where this is so, production is said to be taking place under conditions of *constant returns*.

But, if other things remain unchanged, increasing and constant returns must give way sooner or later to diminishing returns. This fact may be demonstrated by asking ourselves the questions, 'Why are crops grown on lands which differ so widely in fertility?', and 'Why not grow all the food we need on the most fertile land?' As we put more labour to work on the most fertile land, output will increase, so why should we bother with inferior land when the more fertile land yields so much more per acre?

The answers to these questions may be found in Table 6 and Figure 5. Output will certainly increase as we apply more variable factors to the fertile land, but the increases in output from each successive application of capital and labour will, at some point, start to fall. They will continue to fall until, eventually, the units of the variable factors will be yielding less on the more fertile land than they would yield if applied to the less fertile land.

The Least-Cost Combination

This demonstration of a fundamental economic law must not be taken to imply that the ratio labour to land and capital which gives the maximum output per worker is the ratio which should be adopted. All we have done is to show the tendency of output per unit of the variable factor when the proportions between the factors are varied. The most profitable ratio of land to capital and labour depends upon the prices of the factors as well as their productivity.

In this chapter we have been concerned with physical inputs and physical outputs. In other words we have been discussing *technical* efficiency, that is, the ratio of output to input in physical terms. If we are concerned mainly with the productivity of labour as the indicator of efficiency, then Table 6 demonstrates that a ratio of 4 units of labour to 10 acres of land is the most efficient combination since it is this combination which gives the greatest output (units of the product) per unit of input (labour).

But the entrepreneur is concerned with economic efficiency and he will measure output and input in monetary terms. His input he measures as costs and his output he measures as revenue. The physical productivity of the factors is important, but the businessman must also take account of their prices. He will not be so concerned with maximising labour productivity if labour is very cheap and land is very expensive.

For any given output there will be several possible ways of combining the factors of production. Let us suppose that a firm wishes to produce 100 units per week of some given commodity. This output, we will suppose, may be produced with any of the following combinations:

	Land	Labour	Capital
Method 1	10	2	10
Method 2	8	4	9
Method 3	6	10	8

Of these possibilities, the entrepreneur will choose that which minimises his costs. Let us assume that the prices of the factors are as follows:

£

Land: 5 per unit
Labour: 10 per unit
Capital: 8 per unit

£

Now, Method 1 will cost 150
Method 2 will cost 152
Method 3 will cost 194

The entrepreneur will choose Method 1.

The reader should now check the effects of varying factor prices. It will be observed that any change in the relative prices of the factors will lead to the substitution of the cheaper for the dearer factor.

The least-cost combination of the factors of production depends on:
(i) the productivity of the factors and
(ii) the prices of the factors.

Returns to Scale

The law of diminishing returns deals with what are, essentially, short-run situations. It assumes that some of the resources used in production are fixed in supply and examines the effects of changing the amounts of the variable factors which may be combined with these fixed factors. In the long run, however, it is possible to vary all the factors of production which a firm may be using; more land may be acquired, more buildings erected, and more machinery purchased. What we are saying is that *in the long run* it is possible for a firm to change *the scale* of its activities. Strictly speaking, a change of scale takes place when all the factors are increased by the same percentage so that the proportions in which the factors are combined is not changed.

It is of interest, therefore, to consider the effects on output of a change in the scale of production. In the example used earlier it was established that the maximum output per man was achieved when land and labour were combined in the ratio of $2\frac{1}{2}$ acres per man. Suppose, now, that the scale of production is increased whilst the ratio of land to labour remains unchanged. What will be the effect on output? It is more than likely that output, for a time, will increase more than proportionately. The reasons for this phenomenon are given in Chapter 8 where the various economies of scale are examined.

In Table 7 the figures are purely hypothetical but they serve to show the manner in which output might vary as the scale of production increases.

Table 7. *Returns to scale*

Units of labour	Units of land	Total output	Marginal product	Average product
			(cwt per man)	
4	10	65		16·25
8	20	135	17·5	16·88
12	30	215	20	17·92
16	40	305	22·5	19·06
20	50	385	20	19·25
24	60	455	17·5	18·96
28	70	520	16·25	18·57
32	80	570	12·5	17·81
36	90	615	11·25	17·08

Up to the point where twenty men are employed on ᴊᴜ acres of land, output per man increases as the size of the firm increases. The firm is experiencing *increasing returns to scale*. The growth in total output is more than proportionate – doubling the size of the firm is providing more than double the previous output. As the size of the firm increases from four men and 10 acres of land, to eight men and 20 acres of land, total output changes from 65 cwts to 135 cwts (an increase of about 108 per cent).

As the size of the establishment increases beyond twenty men and 50 acres of land, the returns to scale are diminishing. This is another feature of economic activity; the enterprise can become too large and, beyond a certain output, efficiency begins to decline. This subject is discussed in Chapter 8.

Changes of scale require all factors to be changed in the same proportion. There is a widespread view that, although increasing and constant returns to scale are possible, there will be reached, eventually, a scale of production where diminishing returns must apply because management (the entrepreneurial function) is limited in supply. This is a subject of disagreement among economists, many of whom hold that with modern management techniques it is possible to get proportionate increases in management skills to match the increases in the amounts of the other factors.

Chapter 7

The Costs of Production

Output and Costs

We have seen that production may be carried on under conditions of increasing returns, constant returns, or diminishing returns. These terms describe the relationship between changes in the quantity of resources used in production (i.e. the Input) and changes in the total product (i.e. the Output).

Increasing returns apply when the ratio $\dfrac{\text{Output}}{\text{Input}}$ increases as output increases.

Constant returns apply when the ratio $\dfrac{\text{Output}}{\text{Input}}$ remains constant as output increases.

Diminishing returns apply when the ratio $\dfrac{\text{Output}}{\text{Input}}$ falls as output increases.

These changing conditions of production affect costs. It is apparent that a greater output per unit of input implies falling costs, and a declining output per unit of input must lead to rising costs. This may be clearer if we refer back to Table 6 and see how many extra men would be required to raise output by twenty units. When three men are employed the 'cost' of the extra twenty units would be the labour of one extra man. But when six men are employed, an extra twenty units of output would 'cost' the labour of $2\frac{1}{3}$ men (i.e. two men working some overtime).

If a firm doubles the size of its labour force and as a result output is trebled then costs of production per unit must have fallen. The last sentence carries an assumption that the prices of the factors of production do not change as more, or less, of them are employed. This assumption also applies to what follows in respect of the individual firm.

In dealing with changes in output and costs, there are two situations to consider, (1) changes in output which result from *changes in the quantity of the variable factors*, one or more factors remaining fixed in supply, and (2) changes in output which are the result of *changes in the amounts of all the factors*.

The first situation applies to short-run changes. It would apply where a firm varies its output by changing its labour force and the quantity of raw materials it uses, with the same amounts of land, buildings and machinery. In this case, we speak of returns to the variable factors.

The second case is the long-run situation, because changes in the sizes of plant and buildings can only be carried out in the longer period. Changes of this nature bring increasing, constant or diminishing returns to scale, because the entire scale of operations is being altered.

But the entrepreneur is not interested solely in the productivity of his factors of production, he must take account of their prices. There will be a variety of ways of producing any given output. One method might use a lot of capital and very little labour, while another would require much labour and small amounts of capital. For any given output the firm will adopt that combination of factors which is the least costly (i.e. the least-cost combination). The output which will be produced will be that which gives the widest margin between total receipts and total costs, that is, the output which yields maximum profits.

Fixed and Variable Costs

It is useful, for the purposes of economic analysis, to classify costs into *fixed costs* and *variable costs*.

Fixed costs (sometimes called overhead or indirect costs) are those costs which do not vary as output varies. Some factors of production are 'indivisible' (e.g. a blast furnace or an oil tanker) and once committed to production they cannot be changed over the short period. If a firm increased (or reduced) its production by 20 per cent, it is most unlikely that such a change would affect the depreciation on its assembly line, or its power press; the interest it pays on its loans and its insurance charges would likewise remain unaffected.

Variable costs (sometimes called prime or direct costs) are those expenses of production which are directly related to output. The costs of most types of labour, the costs of raw materials, fuel and power charges are typical examples of expenses which bear a direct relationship to production.

These costs may be examined in more detail by subdividing them into four main categories, Technical Costs, Commercial Costs, Financial Costs and Administrative Costs.

TECHNICAL COSTS

All firms must use some capital equipment – buildings, machines, transport and so on. The amounts will vary enormously from one industry to another. A modern steel or chemical plant uses capital equipment worth many millions of pounds, while a hairdresser will require capital assets which may be purchased for a few hundred pounds. Capital costs are made up of (1) interest on the money borrowed (dealt with below), (2) maintenance costs and (3) depreciation.

Maintenance costs will contain an element of fixed costs, for some maintenance work will be required even when the machines are idle, but other maintenance costs will be variable (i.e. vary according to use).

Depreciation will be a major item, for machines and other equipment wear out and must be replaced. Depreciation charges are classified as a fixed cost. This may seem illogical because the life of any piece of capital equipment might be regarded as dependent upon the extent to which it is used. Nowadays, however, the life of capital assets (especially machinery) is measured in economic terms rather than technical terms. Machinery depreciates even when not in use, and more important in an age of rapid technical progress – it becomes obsolete. A machine which is rendered out of date by a newer and much improved model is as uneconomic as one which has worn out. It is normal practice, therefore, to fix an annual depreciation charge which will write off the cost of the equipment within some period of time which is less than the physical life of the asset. There are many ways of doing this; the simplest of these, is to charge, annually, a fixed proportion of the total value. If a machine costs £10,000 and has an expected life of five years, then £2,000 per annum will be added to costs and placed in a depreciation fund to cover the cost of replacement.

Other technical costs are the wages of direct labour, the costs of materials, and fuel and power charges. They are all variable costs since they are subject to adjustment as output changes. Fuel and power are probably the most flexible items because they can be linked directly with production. Some wages and salaries are not subject to rapid adjustment. The wage payments of foremen and the salaries of supervisors and executive staff will not vary much as output varies. A firm will not dismiss foremen, designers, inspectors, maintenance engineers or department heads as soon as any fall in output occurs, if the fall is expected to be only of a fairly temporary nature. The costs of some raw materials may not be very flexible, especially where the firm buys in bulk at intervals of three or four months.

COMMERCIAL COSTS

The expenses of maintaining a sales staff, a buying department, and advertising, are classified as commercial costs. They will contain some items of a variable nature, but in the main they are fixed costs.

FINANCIAL COSTS

The financial costs will be fixed costs and will depend upon the size of the sums of money borrowed. Interest charges will usually be fixed for

c

the duration of the loan and will in no way be affected by changes in output. The interest will have to be paid whether the capital assets on which the money has been spent are used or not. If the entrepreneur has used his own savings (or ploughed back profits) the interest charge (at market rates of interest) must be regarded as a cost. The loss of interest which has been incurred by committing the funds to the purchase of buildings or machinery is a measure of the cost involved in this decision. The firm must set aside, each year, sums of money in order to meet the annual interest burden and to create a fund for the purposes of repayment.

ADMINISTRATIVE COSTS

Most of these costs will be fixed, because they include the salaries of permanent staff. Some small items such as postage, stationery and telephone expenses will be variable.

Fixed costs are only 'fixed' in relation to some period of time. All costs in the very long run are variable, since all assets wear out and, when the time arrives, they need not be replaced or they may be replaced by very different types of equipment. When we use the expressions fixed and variable costs we are referring to some given period of time.

Total and Average Costs

We now turn to an examination of the manner in which costs change as output changes. When output is zero, total costs will be equal to fixed costs and variable costs will be nil, but when production commences total costs will increase as variable costs increase. But total costs are not likely to vary proportionately with output. In the early stages increasing returns will probably apply and as production continues to increase, a point will be reached where diminishing returns are experienced.

Of vital concern to the entrepreneur are the changes in average cost (the cost per unit). Average cost is equal to $\dfrac{\text{Total cost}}{\text{No. of units produced}}$. When output is small, average cost will be high, because the fixed costs will be spread over a small number of units. As output increases average cost will fall because the fixed costs are being distributed over a larger output and each unit is 'carrying' a smaller element of fixed costs. Average costs will fall, because, for a time, there will be increasing returns to the variable factors as more of them are added to the fixed factors. The falling average cost may also be due to the fact that increasing output makes possible better organisation and greater specialisation. When a firm is producing at minimum average cost we say that it has reached its *optimum output*; it has achieved its most efficient size.

At outputs beyond the optimum, diminishing returns and increasing costs will be experienced, although there may be an interval where production is carried on under conditions of constant returns and constant costs.

Beyond the optimum certain diseconomies arise. The fixed factors become overloaded as more variable factors are used – the proportions between the factors become progressively less efficient. Management problems increase; it is more difficult to coordinate the activities of the firm and flexibility and speed of decision deteriorate. These latter points are, in fact, another aspect of changing factor proportions. The entrepreneur is a fixed factor and as more and more variable factors are combined with a fixed supply of entrepreneurial ability there will come some point where diminishing returns are encountered.

These cost relationships are illustrated below. Table 8 indicates the changes in the different types of costs as output changes, and Figures 6a and 6b (page 58) show the same relationships in graphs.

Table 8. *Cost relationships*

Units of output	Fixed costs £s	Variable costs £s	Total costs £s	Average costs £s
10	100	20	120	12
20	100	120	220	11
30	100	200	300	10
40	100	260	360	9
50	100	300	400	8
60	100	320	420	7
70	100	390	490	7
80	100	460	560	7
90	100	620	720	8
100	100	800	900	9
110	100	1,000	1,100	10
120	100	1,220	1,320	11

As output expands, the average cost per unit falls. The firm is enjoying increasing returns – extra output is being obtained for proportionately smaller increases in input. Average cost continues to fall until sixty units of the product are being manufactured. At this point average costs level out and we have conditions of constant returns or constant costs over a range of output from sixty units to eighty units. As output is expanded beyond eighty units, average costs begin to rise and production is taking place under conditions of diminishing returns or increasing costs.

Figure 6a shows the movements of total costs, but details of variable and average costs, for any given output, can be obtained from the same diagram. For the output OC, fixed costs are given by the vertical distance

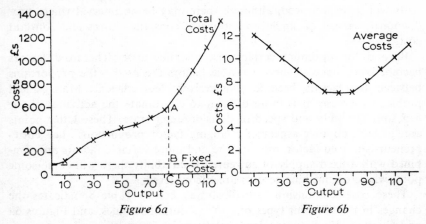

Figure 6a *Figure 6b*

BC, variable costs by the distance AB and the average cost per unit is obtained from the ratio $\dfrac{AC}{OC}$.

If we drop the assumption that factor prices will remain unchanged, there is another reason why average costs might increase as production is expanded. The firm may be obliged to offer higher wages in order to attract more labour and to pay higher prices for its materials as the demand increases.

The long run situation where changes can take place in the quantities of all the factors used by the firm is dealt with in Chapter 8. When the scale of production is changed entirely, new cost conditions apply, and new cost curves must be drawn. This aspect of changes in production is also considered in Chapter 12 (page 115).

Marginal Costs

Before leaving this subject it is necessary to introduce one further aspect of cost, namely, *marginal cost*. Marginal cost is the addition to total cost resulting from the production of one more unit (or the savings in costs resulting from the production of one less). Once in business, the entrepreneur is normally concerned with decisions which involve changes in output – should he produce more or less? Only the prospective new entrant, or the firm about to close down, is faced with decisions of the type 'Do we produce or not?' Existing businesses are thinking about the likely consequences of making changes in their output. This is the reason for the economist's interest in *the margin*. Marginal cost is the variation in total costs which results from changing output by one unit. Likewise, marginal revenue is the addition to, or subtraction from, total revenue which will result from the sale of one unit more, or one less. An understanding of average and marginal costs is very important in the later work on Supply and Demand.

Average cost = Total costs ÷ no. of units produced

Marginal cost = Total cost of x units − Total cost of $(x-1)$ units.

The relationships between average and marginal costs can be seen quite clearly in Table 9 and Figure 7. Both curves are U-shaped. When marginal

Table 9. *Average and marginal costs*

Output (units)	Total costs £s	Average costs £s	Marginal costs £s
0	18·0	Infinity	
1	33·2	33·2	15·2
2	46·4	23·2	13·2
3	58·0	19·3	11·6
4	68·4	17·1	10·4
5	78·0	15·6	9·6
6	88·0	14·7	10·0
7	99·2	14·2	11·2
8	112·8	14·1	13·6
9	130·4	14·5	17·6
10	152·4	15·2	22·0

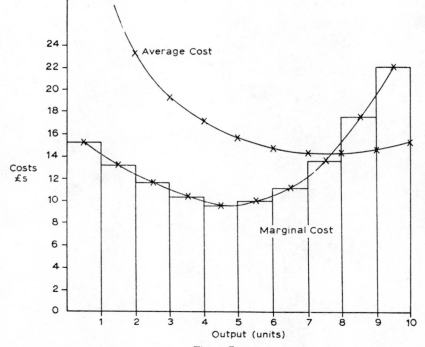

Figure 7

cost is below average cost, average cost is falling. When marginal cost is above average cost, average cost is rising. Marginal cost is equal to average cost, when average cost is at a minimum.

Consider a cricketer's batting average. If, in his next innings, his score (i.e. his marginal score) is less than his existing average score then his average will fall. If his score is more than his existing average, then his average score will rise. This relation between average and marginal quantities plays a great part in economic theory.

Chapter 8

Large-scale and Small-scale Production

Economies of Scale

One of the entrepreneur's major decisions concerns the size of his firm, and we must consider the facts which determine the size of the business unit. We shall see later that firms vary enormously in size, ranging from the giant enterprise such as I.C.I., which employs more than 100,000 workers, to very small organisations which have ten or fewer employees. The general tendency over the past hundred years has been for the size of the average firm to grow, but the number of small firms in this country is very large indeed. There are many motives which lead firms to increase their size, but in this section we are concerned principally with various economies of scale, i.e. *those aspects of increasing size which lead to falling average costs*. It is convenient to group these economies into different classes according to their nature.

1. TECHNICAL ECONOMIES

(a) Increased Specialisation

As the unit of production increases in size it becomes possible to employ the principle of the division of labour to an increasing extent. The larger the establishment, the greater are the opportunities for the specialisation of men and machines.

(b) Indivisibility of Plant

A large output of a standard product makes possible the continuous use of specialised machines. Some types of capital equipment can only be employed efficiently in units of a minimum size, and this minimum may well be too large for the small firm. There is a lower limit to the size of a blast furnace, a rolling mill, a car assembly line and a power press. This lower limit is often a technical limit; a smaller version of the equipment is impracticable. More generally the lower limit is an economic one, smaller versions of the equipment could be made but their usefulness would not justify their cost. Such indivisibility of plant means that small enterprises with small outputs cannot make use of large specialised plant and machinery. With a limited output it means that such plant would not be fully utilised, and would be standing idle for most of the time. The cost of using such equipment would be disproportionately high. Let us assume that such a piece of capital equipment operates with the following cost structure:

Overhead costs	£25 per day
Direct costs	5p per piece produced

1. With a daily output of 1,000 units, the cost per unit attributed to this particular machine would be:

Overhead costs	£25
Direct costs	£50
	———
	£75

Average cost per unit   £75 ÷ 1,000 = 7½p

2. With a daily output of 100 units the costs will be:

Overhead costs	£25
Direct costs	£5
	———
	£30

Average cost per unit   £30 ÷ 100 = 30p

To some extent the small firms can overcome their disadvantage in this respect by combining in order to own and operate a pool of large machines. An excellent example of this policy is to be found in agriculture. No one small farmer could afford to own and operate a combine harvester, but a number of such farmers might well find it profitable jointly to own such a machine.

(c) Economies of increased dimensions

Costs do not always increase proportionately with size. A double-decker bus does not cost twice as much as a single-decker, nor does it use twice as much petrol. It only requires the same staff to operate it as does a single-decker. If we double the dimensions of a ship we increase its capacity by eight times. A very large modern oil tanker of 80,000 tons is only twice the size of a 10,000 ton tanker in terms of its length, width and height. The larger ship will require very few, if any, more men to operate her, and she will certainly not need eight times the fuel and power to propel her through the water. In fact, the water resistance increases as the square of the increase in the dimensions.

This particular economy of scale accounts for the tendency of industries which use tanks, vats, and furnaces, to operate larger and larger units. The average size of blast furnaces, oil tankers, oil refineries, and chemical works, has greatly increased during the past twenty-five years. It is also apparent in the transport industry, where lorries, buses, and railway trucks have considerably increased in size in recent years.

(d) The Principle of Multiples

In most industries a variety of machines is used in the productive process, each machine carrying out a different operation. Each of these different machines is likely to have a different capacity. The machine which moulds the blocks of chocolate will produce at a very different rate from the machine which wraps the blocks. Assume that a particular process requires a team of four machines A, B, C and D, the productive capacities of which are 50, 60, 20, and 30 units per hour. If the team comprises only one machine of each type, the maximum output per hour will be 20 units and machines A, B and D will be working below capacity. This would be the kind of problem facing the small firm which tries to make use of such machines. For small outputs it is not possible to obtain a balanced team of machines such that each machine is being fully utilised.

The lowest common multiple of 50, 60, 20 and 30 is 300. This is the smallest output per hour which will enable machines of this type to operate at full capacity. Such a balanced team of machines would be:

Machine A	Machine B	Machine C	Machine D
6	5	15	10

This assembly of machines would give an output of 300 units per hour and all the machines would be fully utilised. These machines can only be operated at full capacity if output is increased by multiples of 300 units (i.e. 600, 900, 1,200, etc.). The reader can test this statement by trying to work out the most economical way of producing intermediate outputs, say 450 units or 700 units. The smallest size which will allow the fullest operation of the machines will be the lowest common multiple of the separate capacities of the machines.

(e) Research and Development

The large firm can afford to maintain its own research laboratories and development departments. It is able to carry out, within its organisation, a constant search for new products, for new and better methods of production, and for ways of improving its existing products. The small firm is unable to afford its own research facilities, but in many industries where small firms predominate, collective research organisations have been established (e.g. in the boot and shoe industry and in the pottery industry). In these industries a central research establishment is maintained by subscriptions from member firms, all of which benefit from the work of the establishment.

2. MARKETING ECONOMIES

A large firm is able to buy its requirements (e.g. raw materials) in large quantities. Bulk buying enables the large enterprise to obtain preferential terms; it will normally obtain its goods at lower prices than the small firm, and will be able to dictate its requirements with regard to quality and delivery much more effectively. Large firms will be able to employ expert buyers, whereas in the small firm buying will be a function of an employee who will have several other tasks to perform. An expert buyer has the knowledge and skill which enables him to buy 'the right materials at the right time at the right price'. Expert buying can be a great economy – unwise buying can be very costly.

The selling costs of the large firm will be very much greater than those of the small firm, but the selling cost *per unit* will generally be very much lower. Remember that we are discussing economies of scale, and the word 'economy', in this context, means the ability to produce at a lower average cost per unit. The selling costs of a large business might be £100,000 per annum while those of a small business might be as low as £5,000 per annum. But if the large firm is selling 1,000,000 units each year, while the small firm sells 20,000 units, the selling cost per unit in the large firm (10p), is very much less than in the small firm (25p). In selling, as in buying, the large enterprise can afford to employ experts whose specialised skill and knowledge can give it great economic advantages.

Packaging costs per unit should be lower. A package containing 100 articles is very much easier to pack than ten separate packages each containing ten articles. The clerical and administrative costs of dealing with an order for 1,000 articles is little, if any, greater than those involved in an order for 100. To type an invoice for 1,000 articles involves no more work than typing one for 100. The salesman booking an order for 100 tyres does no more work than the salesman booking an order for two.

Although many large firms spend huge sums on advertising, their advertising costs per unit sold may very well be less than those of the small firm.

3. FINANCIAL ECONOMIES

The large firm has several financial advantages. The fact that it is large and well known will enable it to borrow money more readily and more cheaply than the small firm. Its larger assets and greater selling potential provide the banks with greater security and make it possible for them to provide loans at lower rates of interest than would be charged to the smaller firm. The larger firm has access to the long-term capital market where it can raise substantial sums by a public issue of shares. This source of capital is only available to the large public company, and is only economic when large sums of money are required. The terms will be favourable because the lending of money in large quantities, like the bulk buying of materials, is less costly than lending in small quantities.

4. RISK-BEARING ECONOMIES

Large firms are much better equipped to meet the risks of trading than are small firms. The larger the firm, the greater is the share of the total market under its control. A firm which has a large share of the total market is able to judge much more accurately than the small firm the shifts which are taking place in the demand for the product and hence is able to adjust its production schedules accordingly. The small firm is not likely to have such a comprehensive picture of, or to be in such close contact with, total demand.

The law of averages operates to the advantage of the large firm. Accidents and mistakes will take place in all firms, but in the larger firm their incidence can be calculated and allowed for in total production costs. The delivery of wrong components, the spoiling of a batch of products, the under-costing of a particular order, are errors which can be disastrous for the small firm, but they will be only a small part of the total activity of the large firm, and while they may damage the reputation of such a firm, they are not likely to mean financial disaster.

Many large firms are able to reduce the risks of trading by means of a policy of diversification. They manufacture either a variety of models of a particular product, or, more likely nowadays, a variety of products. All their eggs are not in one basket. This variety of products or models means that a fall in the demand for any one of them does not mean serious trouble for the firm; it may well be offset by a rise in the demand for one of the other products. A small firm, on the other hand, is likely to be specialising in one product, any change in the demand for which may have serious consequences.

A large firm is likely to have a number of different markets for its products. In the national market, demand fluctuations between regions might offset one another. A fall in demand in the home market might be balanced by a rise in the demand overseas. A small firm with a restricted market for its goods is much more vulnerable to changes in market conditions.

There are other aspects of size which might be considered advantageous. The Americans have an expression – 'the economy of big brains' – which is, in fact, merely another example of the indivisibility of certain factors of production, in this case human beings. Highly talented specialists can be fully utilised in the large firm. The brilliant designer, scientist, mathematician, salesman or accountant can be employed full-time on the work for which he has been trained. The small firm employing such a man would not have the amount of specialist work to keep him fully employed and would have to use him, for part of the time, on other work where his special skills are not required. This is a diseconomy because a valuable economic resource is working below capacity.

The large firm is likely to enjoy an advantage in the composition of its labour force. The giant enterprises attract a large proportion of the talented young men. They are attracted to the larger firms by the excellent training facilities which are offered, the wide variety of work which is available in the large organisation, and the attractive prospects for promotion. It is very likely, therefore, that the large firm will have a labour force, particularly in the specialist field, of a higher level of ability than the small firm possesses.

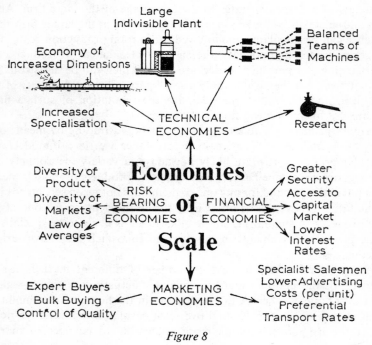

Figure 8

Market Limitations on Mass Production

The major limitation on the size of the firm in any industry is the extent of the market for the product. No firm can achieve a great size where the total market for the product is small. The total demand for the commodity may be restricted by a number of factors.

1. VARIETY OF PRODUCT

Some industries are faced with the problem that consumers demand a great variety of styles, patterns and designs. Obvious examples of this state of affairs exist in the clothing, millinery, furniture, shoe, and jewellery trades. Economies of scale can only be significant where some degree of standardisation of product can be achieved. Mass production methods depend upon a large demand for identical items. Where variety of product is required, the market for any one style or pattern will be very limited, and, in these industries, we will find that the average size of the firm is quite small.

2. GEOGRAPHICAL LIMITATIONS

If the commodity has great bulk in relation to value, transport costs will be high relative to production costs. In such cases the market for the product is likely to be a local one rather than a national one. The market may also be subject to geographical limitations due to the perishable nature of the product. Bread, bricks, and coal may be cited as examples of commodities where markets have been confined to fairly small regions, but recent improvements in transport have tended to weaken this particular restriction on the size of firms.

3. PERSONAL SERVICES

Industries which provide services rather than commodities are usually characterised by a large number of small firms. Where the element of personal attention required by the purchaser is an important part of the service, then it is not possible to introduce standardisation and mass production methods.

Hence we find small firms in hairdressing, all kinds of repair work, house-building, and, most especially, in retailing. It is interesting to note in respect of the last example, the recent technical revolution, which has enabled large firms to develop in retailing. Branding, new techniques in packaging, the introduction of frozen foods, and other developments, have led to the adoption of a high degree of standardisation of product, and the use of large scale methods is becoming increasingly common in the marketing of consumer goods. This has gone hand in hand with a great reduction in the element of personal service.

Diseconomies of Scale

Increasing size brings many advantages, but it can bring disadvantages too. It may well be that growth in the size of the business unit beyond some optimum size will cause average costs of production to start rising. The average cost curve in Figure 6b (page 58) is U-shaped and most economists believe this to be the normal shape of a firm's long run cost curve. Why should costs begin to rise? What causes are at work to offset the economies of scale which we have just discussed? There are a number of facts which might give rise to inefficiencies as the size of the firm increases, although practical experience in industries such as the motor industry, the chemical industry, and the oil industry, appears to contradict some of these suggested diseconomies. In some industries, such as those mentioned, firms have grown to enormous size without any apparent diminution of efficiency, but this might only prove that the optimum size of firm in such industries is very large indeed, or that the technical economies are so great that they outweigh administrative or other diseconomies. Some of the developments which might cause costs to rise as size increases, together with other factors which might limit the size of the firm, are discussed below.

As the firm continues to expand, the tasks of organisation and coordination become more and more difficult. Essentially, management consists of two basic activities, the taking of decisions and seeing that the decisions are carried out. In the small business, the entrepreneur can both decide and supervise – he is able to exercise all the management functions. In the large business it is impossible for one man to carry out all the activities of management. The only solution is to subdivide the duties and responsibilities of control. Hence it becomes necessary to create specialist departments such as production control, sales, purchasing, accounts, and personnel departments. As the departments multiply and grow in size, the task of welding them into a whole, and getting them to work as a team, becomes more and more difficult. A hierarchy of authority becomes established (managing director, director, head of department, manager of section, and foreman), and the taking of decisions becomes a very much more complex matter than it is in the small firm, where the proprietor is aware of all the facts and can take immediate decisions.

The complexity of organisation is illustrated by the fact that the proportion of clerical and administrative workers to direct labour is always much higher in the large firm than it is in the small firm. In other words, management may become top-heavy; it may become less flexible in that numerous meetings at different levels are required before any significant changes can take place, and it may suffer from a multiplicity of departments making coordination difficult and costly.

There are good reasons for the entrepreneur deciding not to expand his firm where the expansion would require the raising of additional finance. The acquisition of further capital often means the sacrifice of a measure of control. The sole proprietor may be obliged to offer a partnership in order to persuade the would-be lender to invest his money in the business. The limited company may be obliged to issue further shares in order to raise its capital. If these shares carry voting rights the existing pattern of control may be seriously affected. If an individual, a family or a particular group of persons previously held the majority of the voting shares, a further issue of voting shares to new shareholders might well mean that the individual, or family, or group, no longer holds the majority of votes.

Interest on loans must be paid whatever the results of the year's trading. If the business has already a fairly heavy burden of fixed interest payments, it may be unwise to increase this burden, especially in industries where demand fluctuates from year to year. Where the only feasible way of raising more capital is to obtain a loan at a fixed rate of interest, many firms, in the situation described above, will decide not to expand.

Lenders will normally require some kind of security for their loan, and the normal practice is for the firm seeking the loan to pledge some of its assets. The inability of the firm to offer adequate security may well be a restriction on its ability to expand.

Many businessmen are reluctant to increase the size of their firms even where trading results fully justify such an increase. One reason, already mentioned, is the desire to maintain a full measure of personal control over all the activities of the enterprise. Where an expansion of the firm would mean sharing the responsibilities for the operation of the firm, many businessmen would prefer not to expand.

Many proprietors are content with a modest income, and prefer leisure and freedom from anxiety to the extra monetary rewards which a larger enterprise might bring them.

The Size of the Firm in British Industry

There are some problems of definition. It is not at all easy to define 'an industry', for it is possible to group economic activities in a variety of ways. They may be classified according to the nature of the markets they serve, or the nature of the processes carried out, or the kind of technology used, or on the basis of the type of factors of production used. There is no single classification which is best for all purposes. The most common definition of an industry is that used in official statistics which groups firms into industries according to the physical and technical properties of their principal products. The classification is often self-evident as is the case with say, footwear, furniture, and pottery where the nature of the product clearly defines the industry. Sometimes it is the nature of the process which is relevant as is the case with the hosiery industry which includes all those firms where knitting is the principal activity. The statistics must be used with great care, however, because there are now so many multi-

INTRODUCTORY ECONOMICS

product firms and the whole of a firm's output is officially classified in the industry of its principal product.

It is also necessary to be clear on the meaning of two more very common terms – factory and firm. A *factory* is defined as the unit of production and official statistics generally refer to it as an *establishment*. A *firm* is the unit of ownership or control and is often referred to in official statistics as an *enterprise*. A firm, of course, may own several factories.

A further problem of definition concerns the methods used to measure the size of a firm or industry. Again there is no 'right' method. The size of the firm (or industry) may be assessed on the basis of the value of the capital employed, or on the value of its output, or on the number of its employees. The use of different measurements will give different answers to questions about size. Great care must be used in discussing the size, or changes in size, of an industry or firm. An industry which is being increasingly mechanised may be employing less labour whilst its output may be increasing. This is true of agriculture. Some indication of the differences resulting from the use of different measurements is provided by the gas, electricity and water industries. In 1966 these industries accounted for about 10 per cent of the total capital employed by industry. They employed about 1·7 per cent of the working population and provided about 3 per cent of gross output.

THE SIZE OF FIRMS AND FACTORIES

In the U.K. is is only possible to get detailed information on the size structure of factories and firms for manufacturing industry. The most recent details available (from the *Census of Production*) show a continuing pattern of a very large number of small scale production units with a fairly small number of very large plants. Some 75 per cent of all factories employ fewer than 100 workers. The Census only collects detailed information from factories employing ten or more workers, so that if *all* factories are included about 84 per cent would be classified as having fewer than 100 workers.

These figures usually come as something of a surprise to the general observer since the popular impression of British industry is of the rapidly increasing domination of the large scale producer. These figures indicate that the small-scale producer must be a viable economic unit in most of the industry groups.

Although small establishments are numerically predominant, it is the larger establishments which account for the greater share of output and employment. In 1963, the 16 per cent of all factories which employed more than 100 workers accounted for 73 per cent of total employment in manufacturing industry. The really large plants (those with 1,500 or more workers) which represented 1·0 per cent of all plants, employed 28 per

70

cent of all the workers in manufacturing industry. There is a very similar contrast when we compare the shares of small and large factories in total output – if anything, the predominance of the larger unit is even more marked. The larger units tend to be more capital intensive and one would expect their contribution to output to be more significant than their contribution to employment.

Data referring to the size distribution of *firms* reveals a similar pattern to that outlined above. The great majority of firms employ less than 100 workers, but they are responsible for a relatively small part of total employment. Recent studies have shown a marked trend towards the larger plants and larger firms, particularly those employing more than 10,000 workers.

Table 10. *U.K. Manufacturing Industry—size of establishment— employment*

Size	Percentage of Total Employment		
(*numbers employed*)	1935	1951	1963
11–49	13·9	11·5	9·0
50–99	11·7	10·4	8·3
100–299	26·2	22·2	20·3
300–499	12·8	11·6	11·4
500–999	13·9	13·6	14·6
1,000–1,499	6·3	7·2	8·2
1,500 and over	15·2	23·5	28·2

Table 11. *U.K. Manufacturing Industry—size of establishment, 1963*

Size (*numbers employed*)	No. of establishments	%	Net output £m	%
1–24	51,723	57·49	629	5·80
25–99	18,257	20·29	1,143	10·54
100–499	11,440	12·72	3,089	28·46
500–1,499	2,137	2·37	2,537	23·37
1,500–4,999	583	0·66	2,204	20·31
5,000–9,999	63	0·07	626	5·77
10,000 and over	23	0·03	480	4·42
Total[1]	89,949	100·00	10,851	100·00

Concentration

The size of the firm has some important implications for economic policy. Closing a very large factory will have a serious impact on the local em-

[1] Includes unsatisfactory census returns.
Source: *Census of Production.*

ployment situation. Where a firm becomes so large that it acquires a dominant share of the market, it may be tempted to use its market power in order to earn excessive profits. It may be powerful enough to eliminate smaller competitors and create formidable deterrents to any new firms wishing to enter the industry. It may use its great size in order to put strong pressures on much smaller suppliers to cut their prices to uneconomic levels.

Such considerations have led to an analysis of the size structure of firms which reveals the degree of concentration in an industry. Concentration is usually measured by taking the three largest firms in an industry and expressing the total labour force of these firms as a percentage of the labour force in the industry.

$$\text{Degree of concentration} = \frac{\text{Total employment in the three largest firms} \times 100}{\text{Total employment in the industry}}$$

Alternatively concentration ratios may be measured in terms of the share of the total output of an industry accounted for by the three largest firms.

The use of concentration ratios in economic analysis requires some care since they refer to the employment and output ratios and do not tell us anything about the nature of the market. It is possible for an industry to consist of very few, very large firms, but competition in such an industry may be extremely keen. A higher degree of concentration does not necessarily mean a lessening of the intensity of competition.

A study by Messrs. Evely and Little[1] of 219 Census of Production trades employing a total of $6\frac{1}{2}$ million people has been widely used in commentaries on the extent of concentration in British industry. The study, as might be expected, showed a wide spread. There were trades such as valves and cathode ray tubes, and sugar refining where the employment concentration ratio was more than 80 per cent. At the other extreme trades such as vehicle repair and the weaving of cotton cloth had ratios of about 5 per cent. If we classify the concentration ratios into three groups, high, medium and low, the following picture emerges.

Concentration ratio	No. of trades	% of total employment in the 219 trades
High (more than 66%)	50	11
Medium (34%–66%)	69	26
Low (33% and less)	100	63

As one would expect following the earlier discussion on economies of scale, large-scale production is very common in manufacturing, but the

---

[1] EVELY and LITTLE, *Concentration in British Industry*, C.U.P.

average size of firm varies widely from industry to industry. We find very large firms predominant in the following industries: vehicles, engineering, chemicals, oil, tobacco, and tyres. In other industries the size of the firm is much smaller, notably, in textiles, clothing, footwear and hosiery. We find some industries dominated by a few giants, some industries comprise a few giants with many pygmies, while other industries are made up of a large number of pygmies.

Increasing the Size of the Firm

There are two principal motives which lead to growth in the size of the business unit. The first of these is the *economies motive* – the desire to operate on a larger scale in order to achieve lower costs of production. The second is the *monopoly motive* – the desire to operate on a larger scale in order to exercise a dominating influence in the market for the product. There are also two methods by which growth may be achieved. The first and more obvious method, is by internal growth. The firm increases its size by making more of its existing product, or increases the range of its products, but grows within the framework of its existing management and control structure.

The second, and much the most common method, is growth by *amalgamation*, *merger*, or *takeover*. A firm may amalgamate with one or more existing firms to form an entirely new enterprise, or a firm may take over another firm, the firm taken over losing its identity completely. Another common method by which the large business unit may come into being is by the formation of a *holding company*. Such a company is formed for the sole purpose of acquiring controlling interests in a number of separate companies, the trading policies of which are then directed by the holding company. The Imperial Tobacco Company is a holding company controlling several major tobacco companies. Sears (Holdings) Ltd, controls footwear companies, engineering companies and shipbuilding companies.

Growth by amalgamation is usually referred to as integration, which may be either vertical or horizontal.

Vertical Integration

When a merger takes place between firms engaged in different stages of the productive process, it is an example of vertical integration. It occurs when a manufacturer takes over the source of his supplies. Dunlops may acquire rubber plantations, Brooke Bonds may develop tea plantations and Cadburys may decide to run their own cocoa plantations. A more recent example would be the acquisition of body-building firms by the leading motor car manufacturers. Another case of vertical integration would be where manufacturers have taken over the market outlets for their products. When the movement is towards the source of supplies we speak of vertical integration backwards, and a movement towards the market for the product is known as vertical integration forwards.

There are a number of motives for this kind of integration. Integration backwards is often carried out in order that a firm may exercise greater control over the quantity and quality of its supplies and to be in a position of greater security with regard to delivery. It may also wish to embrace the profit margin at the previous stage of production. Integration forwards may stem from a desire to secure an adequate number of market outlets, and a wish to raise the standards of marketing by bringing the outlets under its own control. Since manufacturers carry the main burden of advertising costs, it is only natural that they should be concerned that their products reach the purchaser in a form and in an environment that lives up to the image created by their advertisements. Firms are often driven to acquire market outlets when their major competitor has already made a move in this direction. In recent years oil companies have taken over most of the petrol stations, and breweries have acquired the majority of public houses.

There are a few examples of production being completely integrated. The oil companies now control the whole process from exploration to the petrol pump. The co-operative movement is fully integrated, in the production of some grocery items, from the plantation to the retail counter.

Horizontal Integration

When firms engaged in the same stage of the productive process are brought under unified control, the movement is described as horizontal integration. Examples of this development occur when two or more retail chains merge, or when two or more manufacturers amalgamate. Some of our largest firms have emerged as the result of a long process of horizontal integration. British Leyland, G.E.C., E.M.I., and Unilever are good examples.

There are several motives which lead firms to integrate horizontally. It may be the wish to reduce competition and to become more influential in the market. Amalgamation of firms is a direct way of reducing competition by cutting the number of competitors. It may be that manufacturers or distributors wish to carry out some rationalisation of the capacity in the industry. If we have three firms all making similar products and each firm is only working at two-thirds capacity, then a merger of these firms will enable the new business unit to close down one firm and work the two remaining firms at full capacity, with a consequent lowering of costs. Integration will facilitate the implementation of a policy of greater specialisation of resources. Suppose there are three firms each making a washing machine, a refrigerator and a vacuum cleaner. A merger would enable the group to concentrate the production of each product in one factory or firm. The desire to diversify the range of products is another incentive to amalgamate. By taking over, or merging with firms making or selling different commodities, the business unit is spreading the risks of private enterprise -- all its eggs are not in one basket.

Horizontal integration enables firms to reap considerable economies of scale. The materials required by the group of firms can be bought in bulk; the firms may operate a group transport service, and the capital reserves of one firm may be used to finance the expansion of another.

But integration may bring with it several problems which are difficult to solve. The management of a diversified group of firms, operating in different industries, is a very complex task. Vertical integration is often difficult when the optimum output of one stage is very different from that of another. Technical change may alter the basic materials used by an industry and the firm that has acquired its own source of supplies may then find itself with a wasting asset.

Figure 9

VERTICAL INTEGRATION

	British Petroleum Co	Bata Shoe Co	Unilever
EXTRACTION	Oil Wells		Palm Oil Plantations
MANUFACTURE	Oil Refining	Shoe Factories	Soap Manufacture
DISTRIBUTION	Petrol Stations	Shoe Shops	

MOTIVES

Backwards: Security of supplies; control of quality and certainty of delivery; absorb intermediate profit margins.

Forwards: Secure market outlets and raise standards of same; squeeze out competitors; absorb wholesale margins.

HORIZONTAL INTEGRATION

Amalgamated Roadstone Ltd

← EXTRACTION → Granite + Gravel + Sand Quarries

Unilever

← MANUFACTURE → Soap + Detergents + Toothpaste + Margarine + Frozen Foods

Great Universal Stores

← DISTRIBUTION → Clothing + Footwear + Furniture Shops

MOTIVES

Rationalisation. Economies of Scale. Reduced competition. Diversification of Activities.

Part Three: The Business Unit

Chapter 9

Types of Business Organisation

Production and distribution are carried on by a variety of business enterprises, which differ, not only in their size, but in the form of organisation. The different types of business organisation found in this country may be classified under five headings: the sole proprietor, the partnership, the limited company, co-operative societies, and public enterprise.

The Sole Proprietor

This is the simplest and oldest form of business enterprise and is often referred to as the one-man business. A single person provides the capital, takes the decisions, and assumes the risks. He is solely responsible for the success or failure of the business and has, therefore, the sole rights to such profits as may be made or, alternatively, bears the sole responsibility for such losses as may accrue. The one-man business is still far more numerous than any other type of business organisation, although it is declining in importance. If we measure importance by the number of people employed, or the value of the capital employed, then companies are far more important, if less numerous, than sole proprietors.

The strength of this type of firm lies in the direct personal interest of the proprietor in the efficiency of his enterprise. Ownership and control are vested in one person, who enjoys all the gains of success and, hence, has a great incentive to run the firm efficiently. Since the entrepreneur is the sole decision-taker and has no need to consult colleagues when any changes of policy are required, we should expect this type of firm to be extremely flexible, and capable of easy adjustment to customers' whims and changes of mind.

The great disadvantage of the one-man business lies in the fact that the entrepreneur is liable for the debts of his business and this liability is unlimited; all his personal possessions may be seized in the event of the business becoming insolvent.

Another disadvantage of this type of firm is the strict limitation on its ability to acquire capital for expansion. Finance is restricted to the amounts which the entrepreneur is able to provide from his own resources, and to whatever sums he can borrow on his own security.

We find the sole proprietor prevalent in farming, retailing, hairdressing, building, window cleaning, automobile repair and maintenance, and in most of the service industries where the element of personal attention is very important.

Partnership

The legal definition of a partnership is 'the relation which subsists between persons carrying on business with a view to profit'. A partnership may consist of any number of partners between two and twenty. It is the logical development from the sole proprietor, since the obvious method by which such a firm may acquire further capital is to form a partnership. The motive, however, may not be financial, and partnerships are often formed in order to bring new ability and enterprise into the business.

The partners usually share in the task of running the firm, each being responsible for a particular aspect of the business, but a partner need not play an active role. A person who joins a partnership, supplying capital and sharing in the profits, but taking no part in the management, is known as a dormant or sleeping partner. Partnerships are a common form of business organisation in such professions as law, accountancy, estate management, and medicine.

The advantages of this type of firm are similar to those of the one-man business. It is a flexible organisation which allows a greater degree of specialisation than the one-man business. It is possible for partners to specialise in some particular aspect of the business; one may be responsible for buying, one for selling, one for production and so on. Since it has greater access to capital, it can achieve greater size than the sole proprietor.

In view of the greater risks involved, it has tended to dwindle in importance in this country. Its survival depends on the continued harmonious relationships between a number of people in an environment which gives so much opportunity for disagreement. Partnerships are not legal entities and terminate with the death or resignation of any partner.

The great disadvantage of this type of organisation, like that of the one-man business, is the fact that the liability of the partners is unlimited. All the partners may be held legally responsible for the acts of any one of their number.

It is possible for a partner to avoid the unlimited liability referred to above. There are some limited partnerships which have to be registered with the Registrar of Companies, but at least one partner must have unlimited liability.

Joint Stock Companies

This is the most important form of business organisation in the United Kingdom. Basically, it consists of an association of people who contribute towards a joint stock of capital, for the purpose of carrying on business with a view to profit.

The distinguishing feature of this type of firm is *limited liability*. Each member's liability for the debts of the company is limited to the amount of capital which he has agreed to subscribe. This means that, when the shareholder has fully paid for the shares which he has taken up, he cannot be called upon to make any further contribution to meet any debts of the company. A company of this type must include the word 'Limited' (or 'Ltd') in its name, so that anyone dealing with the company is aware of the fact that the members' liability is limited.

The limitation of shareholders' liability makes the task of raising large sums of capital much easier, for the investor is far readier to provide capital on these conditions. He will not be so afraid of going into business with people whose names he may not even know. In many of the large companies there are many thousands of shareholders, the vast majority of whom have contributed only a small fraction of the total capital of the business. The total number of individual investors, in Stock Exchange securities, is estimated to be about $2\frac{1}{2}$ million. The number is growing at the rate of 100,000 per annum. About 22 million people are 'indirect' shareholders through the investments of life assurance companies and pension funds. These figures and the following details are taken from a recent Stock Exchange publication.

Table 12. *Numbers of ordinary shareholders in some large companies*

Imperial Chemical Industries	450,000
'Shell' Transport	290,000
Imperial Tobacco Company	187,500
Unilever (British part)	59,000

Another great attraction of this form of enterprise to the prospective investor is the ease with which he can transfer the ownership of his shares. A shareholder in a public company can sell his shares in the business to anyone else. This transfer of share ownership is the main function of the Stock Exchange.

PUBLIC AND PRIVATE COMPANIES

There are two kinds of joint stock company, the *private company* and the *public company*. At the present time there are about 500,000 private companies and 11,000 public companies. The public companies are much larger units and account for something like two-thirds of the capital of all companies. The average size of the public company, in terms of capital employed, is about fifty times that of the average private company.

The essential differences between the public and private company relate to (i) size, (ii) methods of raising capital, and (iii) the transferability of shares.

In general, private companies are small firms where there are few shareholders (often the members of one family) and the amount of capital involved is not very large. Private companies must have at least two members, public companies at least seven, but, whereas the number of shareholders in the public company is unlimited, a private company cannot have more than fifty members. Public companies may raise capital by issuing a prospectus and offering their shares to the general public. Private companies are not permitted to invite the public to subscribe to their share capital. A shareholder in a public company may freely transfer his shares to other members of the public, but the transferability of shares in the private company requires the approval of the directors.

Prior to the Companies Act 1967 the majority of private companies enjoyed certain privileges in respect of the disclosure of information since they were not obliged, as was a public company, to file (with the Registrar of Companies) annual details of turnover, profits, assets, etc. This situation no longer applies and both types of company must file annual returns.

Company formation

The State has introduced, through a succession of Companies Acts, many regulations concerning the formation and organisation of joint stock companies. We can only mention a few of the more important requirements.

The persons forming a company (the promoters) are required to prepare two important documents which must be submitted to the Registrar of Companies for his approval. They are:

1. *The Memorandum of Association.* This document must contain: the name of the company with the word 'limited' as the last word; the address of the registered office; the amount of the authorised capital, and details of the objects for which the company has been formed. Nowadays the objects of the company would be set out in very broad general terms so that the company would not be restricted in its future development. The memorandum must be signed by two persons if it is to be a private company and seven persons in the case of a public company.

2. *The Articles of Association.* This is a document which sets out the proposed internal constitution of the company. It will contain details of the manner in which shares are to be issued and transferred; the company's borrowing powers; the rights of the different classes of shareholder; the frequency and type of company meetings; the ways in which the company will elect its officers; the powers of the directors and so on.

In addition to these documents the promoters must submit to the Registrar a statement of the nominal capital; a list of the directors together with their written consents to act and their promises to take up shares in the company, and a declaration that the Companies Acts have been complied with.

If these documents are in order, the Registrar will issue a Certificate of Incorporation which bestows on the company a separate legal identity. The private company may now commence business, but the public company must file a further document known as the Prospectus (or a statement in lieu thereof). The prospectus is a detailed statement of the history of the company, its profit record, its assets, its future prospects and any information which is deemed necessary in providing the potential subscriber with adequate safeguards. The Registrar must try to ensure that the public are not being misled. When this document has been registered and approved the Registrar will issue a Certificate of Trading which authorises the company to start business operations.

All the documents referred to above, together with the annual statements of accounts, are available for public inspection at the office of the Registrar of Companies.

The joint stock company (particularly the public limited company) has played a vital role in the development of modern capitalism. Modern means of production require heavy investment in plant and machines. The economies of large-scale production invariably call for large and costly units of capital equipment and large sums of money for working capital. These developments could not have taken place had the forms of business organisation been restricted to those of the one-man business and partnership. Joint stock enterprise makes possible the bringing together, in large aggregates, the small savings of many thousands of people, with a greatly reduced risk of loss. The company has an enduring life of its own and can afford to take longer views of the future than the one-man business. It is not dependent upon the ability of the founder, or of a few partners, for it can afford to buy first-class managerial talents, highly skilled men, who cannot afford to set up in business on their own. But, as is pointed out in the discussion on economies of scale (Chapter 8), the company can grow too large.

TYPES OF SHARES

People invest in joint stock companies with a view to profit. If their expectations are realised they receive profit in the form of dividends according to the number and type of shares which they hold. Shares normally carry some right to participate in the control of the company, but these rights vary considerably according to the type of share.

Preference Shares

Preference shares, as their name implies, carry a prior right to a share in the profits of the company. The holders of these shares must receive payment of their dividends before the holders of other types of share are paid. Normally the rate of return on preference shares is a fixed percentage of the capital invested. A holder of a £100 5 per cent Preference Share is entitled to a return of £5 per annum from the profits of the company. If the company makes no profit then the holder will receive no dividend, but there is a class of Cumulative Preference Shares, and holders of this type will receive payment of any arrears of dividend when the company does have a profitable year. Even when the company has an exceptionally profitable year the preference shareholders will receive no more than the fixed rate of interest, unless they hold another class of preference share, the Participating Preference Share. This type of share entitles the holder to a fixed rate of interest on his capital plus an additional share in the profits after the ordinary shareholders have been paid.

Preference shareholders usually have little say in the management of the enterprise since their income is less dependent upon the amount of profits than that of other types of shares. Their voting rights will be set out in the Articles of Association and, normally, they qualify for a vote only if their dividends have not been paid.

Ordinary Shares

The dividend on ordinary shares is not fixed and depends entirely on the profitability of the company. The dividend may be very high or it may be zero. The ordinary shareholder is entitled to the residue of profits after all other claims have been met. Ordinary shares are, therefore, the riskiest type of investment and dividends on them may fluctuate from year to year. Since they bear the major risks, the ordinary shareholders have the greatest say in the management and control of the enterprise, and most ordinary shares carry voting rights.

Debentures

A debenture is not a share in the strict sense of the word. The investor who purchases debentures is making a rather special kind of loan to the company and the debenture is really a kind of I.O.U. The rate of interest on debentures is fixed and debenture holders are guaranteed payment of this interest. Debentures rank first, before all classes of shares, for payment out of profits, and the holders of these securities are normally given special rights which add to the security of their loans. The company will give a pledge that certain of its assets will be attached to the debentures so that, in the event of a default by the company, the holders of the company's debentures may sell these assets, and use the proceeds for repayment of their loan.

The following simple example is intended to show how profits will be distributed and to illustrate the variable nature of the return on ordinary shares.

The X. Y. Z. Company Limited

Loan capital	20,000 £1 6% Debentures	£20,000
Share capital	80,000 £1 Pref. Shares (5%)	£80,000
	100,000 £1 Ordinary Shares	£100,000
		£200,000

Year 1

Profits available for distribution	£7,700

This will be distributed as follows:

Debentures, 6% of £20,000	£1,200
Pref. shares, 5% of £80,000	£4,000
Ordinary shares, dividend $2\frac{1}{2}$%	£2,500
	£7,700

Year 2

Profits available for distribution	£15,200

This will be distributed as follows:

Debentures, 6% of £20,000	£1,200
Pref. shares, 5% of £80,000	£4,000
Ordinary shares, dividend 10%	£10,000
	£15,200

Yields

There is a difference between the dividend on a share and the yield on a share. The dividend is expressed as a percentage of the face value (or nominal value) of the share. But shares are rarely marketed at their face value and the prices of shares quoted on the Stock Exchange vary from day to day. Investors are primarily concerned with the yield on the shares they hold or are contemplating buying. The yield on a share is the money value of the dividend, expressed as a percentage of the market price. For example:

The X. Y. Z. Company Ltd. declare a dividend of 10 per cent on their £1 Ordinary Shares.

These shares stand at 200p on the Stock Exchange.

$$\text{The yield} = \frac{10\% \text{ of } £1}{£2} \times \frac{100}{1} = 5\%.$$

CONTROL OF JOINT STOCK COMPANIES

The management of joint stock companies is in the hands of the Board of Directors which is elected by the shareholders. In public companies directors are required to be shareholders. Directorships are often only part-time appointments and it is possible for a person to hold director-ships in a large number of companies, but it is increasingly the case, especially in the larger companies, for the directors to be full-time executives. They normally specialise and take responsibility for some particular aspect of the company's activities, hence we have the Sales Director, the Works Director, and so on. The directors elect one of their number to be the Managing Director, who has the overall responsibility for the running of the company.

The normal situation, in a company which is successful, is for only a very small percentage of the shareholders to attend the annual general meeting. Although, in fact, the shareholders are the owners of the company and have considerable powers, they are not able to exercise any significant influence on the company's affairs. There are three principal reasons why the control of the company is effectively in the hands of the directors.
1. The shareholders are often very numerous.
2. They are distributed throughout the country – in some cases many shares are held abroad.
3. They lack the necessary technical and commercial expertise to play any effective part in the running of the company.

Shareholder control does operate to some extent, since shareholders can exercise their voting rights at the annual (or extraordinary) general meeting in order to bring about changes in the Board of Directors.

Co-operative Societies

The basic principles of co-operative enterprise are those of worker ownership and worker control. The first experiments in this type of organisation were tried in the field of production when workers established their own productive units, raising the capital by their own efforts, electing the management from their own ranks, and sharing in the rewards accord-ing to some agreed formula. In this country most of the attempts at co-operative production have proved unsuccessful. There still remain some few examples of this kind of productive enterprise but the total employ-ment is very small. They are to be found chiefly in the footwear industry, the printing industry and the clothing industry. Although we have very few examples of co-operative production in the United Kingdom, this kind of organisation has been notably successful in Danish agriculture and is being widely adopted in the agricultural industries of many under-developed countries.

In marked contrast to the failure of cooperation in production is the great success of the co-operative movement in the field of distribution. Beginning with a small retail shop, opened by some poor weavers in Rochdale in 1844, co-operative retailing has greatly expanded, until, at the present time, retail co-operative societies claim some 13 million members in some thousand retail societies.

The distinguishing feature of a co-operative society lies in its ownership. The capital is contributed by the members, but their contribution to the share capital is limited to £500 per member. The nominal value of each share is normally £1. In contrast to the joint stock company where there is no limit on the shareholdings of any one member and where voting rights are proportionate to the number of shares held, each member of a co-operative society has one vote. The management of a co-operative society is in the hands of a management committee elected by the members at the annual general meeting. The members of this committee, who are all part-time members, appoint full-time staff to run the society according to a policy decided by the committee.

The profits are not distributed to members according to the size of their investment, but are paid out in the form of a dividend which is distributed to members in proportion to their purchases. The dividend is expressed as 'so many pence, in the £'. In most societies, during the post-war period, the 'divi' has been in the region of 5p in the pound, but the rate will vary according to the size of the profits. Traditionally, co-operative societies spend a proportion of their profits on social and educational programmes for the benefit of their members.

About 12 per cent of the retail trade is done through the co-operative movement which is particularly strong in the grocery trade (about 20 per cent) and in milk distribution (about 33 per cent of the total trade). The retail societies combined in 1873 to form the Co-operative Wholesale Society. The C.W.S. now manufactures and provides about one-third of all the retail societies requirements.

The following points are often raised when the advantages and disadvantages of this form of business organisation are discussed.

1. The dividend payment is undoubtedly popular, and is looked upon as a kind of short-term savings fund. It accounts for much of the success of the movement.

2. The movement began as a working-class movement, and there still remains a strong sense of loyalty to the societies by members of the working class, although it cannot be distinguished as a class movement today.

3. It is very doubtful whether the best managerial talent will be obtained by the process of popular election.

Public Enterprise

A considerable sector of the British economy is controlled by public, and not by privately owned, enterprise. Some of these public bodies are run by local authorities, but most of them are run by the State, either by government departments or public corporations.

PUBLIC CORPORATIONS

In recent years whenever the State has decided to transfer ownership of industry from private hands to the public sector, the public corporation has been the type of business organisation adopted for the purpose of running the industry. Some of these public corporations have been in existence for many years, including:

The Port of London Authority, set up in 1909 to run the London docks;
The British Broadcasting Corporation, set up in 1927 to control sound broadcasting;
The British Overseas Airways Corporation, established just before the war.

Most of the larger public corporations, however, date from the period of the Labour Government 1945–51, when several important industries were nationalised. We shall discuss the process of nationalisation later, here we are concerned only with the type of business organisation to which it has given rise. In the postwar period we have seen public corporations established to control gas, electricity, coal, transport, airways, independent television, and atomic energy.

The control of a public corporation lies ultimately with Parliament and a Minister of the Crown is responsible for the overall performance of the corporation. The Secretary of State for Trade and Industry has responsibilities for the public corporations in the gas, electricity, coal, atomic energy, steel and civil air transport industries. The Secretary of State for Environment has responsibilities for the road, rail and water transport corporations. The Minister can influence the major policy decisions of the corporations but he is not responsible for the day-to-day running of the enterprises. For this purpose he appoints a Board for each industry (e.g. the National Coal Board).

The main purpose of a public corporation is to provide an efficient public service at a reasonable price. Its main aim, unlike that of the joint stock company, is not to maximise its profits, but it is charged with the duty of paying its way. Any profits made by public corporations must be used for capital investment, the lowering of prices, or the raising of wages. Such losses as have been made by these bodies are financed by government loans.

The nationalisation Acts of the Labour government brought into being some of the largest business organisations in the world. The largest joint stock company in Britain is the Imperial Chemical Industries with a labour force of about 100,000, but at the time of its creation the National Coal Board had more than 700,000 employees. In contrasting the public corporation and the joint stock company, the following features should be noted:

1. *Control*. The joint stock company is controlled by a board of directors elected by the shareholders, whereas the public corporation is controlled by a board (with similar functions) appointed by a Minister of the Crown.

2. *Size*. Some of the public corporations are many times larger than the largest joint stock company.

3. *Ownership*. A joint stock company is owned by the shareholders, but there are no shareholders in the public corporation which is owned by the State.

4. *Finance*. The joint stock company raises its capital by the issue of shares, but, at the present time, the public corporations obtain their capital requirements direct from the Exchequer.

5. *Motives*. While the joint stock company exists primarily for the purpose of making profits, the purposes of the public corporation are to provide a public service, to operate in the public interest, and to cover its costs.

(See also section on Nationalisation in Chapter 31.)

Chapter 10

Financing the Enterprise

Businesses require finance to meet their capital requirements which may be of two kinds, short term and long term. Short term finance is required for working capital – the purchase of materials and the payment of wages. Long term capital is required for the purchase of plant, machinery, land and buildings. The sources of finance for industry are many, and vary according to the type of firm and the nature of the capital required.

Personal Loans and Self-Financing

The sole proprietor and partnerships are financed mainly by this oldest method of raising funds. The one-man business relies mainly on his personal savings and loans from relatives and friends as does the partnership, which has, however, more sources available. This type of loan is not important in other forms of business organisation.

Bank Loans

All types and all sizes of businesses borrow from the commercial banks, which provide, in the main, loans of the short term variety, but the loans are often renewed and this will give them a longer term nature. There are two forms of bank lending:

(a) The bank loan, where a sum of money is placed to the credit of the borrower, and interest is charged on this amount regardless of the use made of the loan facilities.

(b) The overdraft, where the borrower is granted the right to overdraw his account by some agreed sum, and interest is charged only on the amount overdrawn.

Share Issues

For the larger firms a main source of external funds is the share issue. Very large sums of money may be raised by selling shares to the general public, but the method is only available to the public company and is only economic for fairly large capital requirements. Since the costs do not increase proportionately with the size of the issue, a public issue of shares is expensive where requirements are less than £300,000. The raising of capital by offering shares to outsiders may be carried out in several different ways.

(a) THE PUBLIC ISSUE

This is the most straightforward method and takes the form of a direct offer of shares to the general public. The formalities of such an issue are normally carried out by a specialist firm, an issuing house, probably one of the merchant banks. When the issuing house has decided on the class of shares to be offered, the price at which they will be offered, and the rights they will carry, it will prepare an advertisement. This advertisement, known as the prospectus, must appear in at least two national newspapers and must contain information on the company's financial position, trading position, organisation and management, in very great detail. A copy of the prospectus must be filed with the Registrar of Companies. The advertisement will contain an invitation to the public to apply for the shares, and a closing date for applications will be announced. The next procedure is the allotment of the shares. If the issue has been oversub-scribed, the issuing house must allot each applicant some proportion of the shares for which he applied. If the issue has been undersubscribed then the issuing house will be left with unsold shares. This possibility is norm-ally avoided by having the issue underwritten. Underwriting is carried out by specialist firms and is, in effect, a kind of insurance against failure to sell the entire issue. The underwriter, for a commission, will guarantee to take up any unsold shares. The public issue, as mentioned earlier, is costly, for it involves fees to the issuing house, underwriter's commission, legal fees, advertising costs, and accounting charges. For smaller issues it is much too expensive and other methods are used.

(b) OFFER FOR SALE

This is an alternative method of issuing shares which is less expensive than the public issue. The company sells the shares directly to the issuing house which then disposes of them to the public. The issuing house sells the shares as a principal, not as an agent for the company.

(c) PLACINGS

The shares need not be offered to the public at all. The company, or most likely, the issuing house or firm of brokers, acting on its behalf, may attempt to place the shares. This means contacting investors directly, and getting them to buy blocks of the shares offered. Such placings may be made with insurance companies, firms of stockbrokers, or investment trusts.

(d) THE RIGHTS ISSUE

One method of raising finance by the issue of shares which is in general use, and is probably the cheapest method of all, is the rights issue. This procedure is only available to an existing company, since it involves an approach to existing shareholders. The company writes to its shareholders offering them the chance of buying new shares in proportion to their present shareholdings. As shareholders they have 'rights' to a certain number of the new shares. The rights are valuable since the new shares are offered at less than their current market price.

Institutional Sources of Finance

There are a number of institutions of various types which provide a channel for savings of all kinds. Many of these bodies invest some proportion of their funds in industrial enterprise.

(a) INSURANCE COMPANIES

Insurance companies provide protection from certain risks in return for regular payments which are known as premiums. The annual total of the premiums paid to insurance companies in this country is a very large sum indeed, part of which becomes available for investment in industry. Insurance companies are easily the largest institutional investors, having something like £400 million per annum available for investment.

(b) PENSION FUNDS

Public and private pension schemes have grown rapidly since the war, and funds from these sources are an increasing element in the provision of capital for the government and for industry. Much of the investment by these bodies goes into government securities, but an increasing proportion is finding its way into the various stocks and shares of private industry.

(c) BUILDING SOCIETIES

A rather specialised source of finance for industry is the building society. It provides funds almost exclusively for investment in buildings. Most of the funds of British building societies are used to facilitate house purchases.

(d) INVESTMENT TRUSTS

Investment trusts are limited companies, registered in the usual way, but their assets do not consist of land, buildings, and machines, as is the case with most companies. They exist solely for the purpose of holding shares in other companies. The managers of investment trusts are full-time experts in the field of investment. In purchasing a share in an investment trust, the investor is, indirectly, investing in a very large number of different companies. The income of an investment trust consists of the dividends it receives on its holdings in other trading companies.

(e) UNIT TRUSTS

The unit trust is an organisation very similar in function to the investment trust. It aims to attract the small saver who is invited to buy low-priced 'units' in the trust. The funds accumulated in this way are invested by experienced managers in the shares of many different companies. Investors in unit trusts do not receive shares, but certificates (units) which entitle them to a share of the returns from the invested funds. The managers of a unit trust will repurchase units on demand, whereas shares in an investment trust must be sold on the Stock Exchange (or privately), in order to recover the money invested.

(f) SAVINGS BANKS

Most familiar to the small saver are the facilities provided by the Post Office and Trustees Savings Banks, and the National Savings Movement, now called the National Savings Bank. The savings of any one individual in these institutions is limited in amount, but there are many millions of accounts, so that the total savings is very large. The funds collected by these institutions are channeled to the government and other public authorities.

Specialist Finance Corporations

A number of specialised institutions were set up during the 1930s which were mainly intended to help small and medium sized businesses. Some of these corporations had the support of the banks and they invest rather than lend money, by taking up securities in the business receiving assistance. Typical of these organisations is the Charterhouse Industrial Development Company founded in 1934 by an issuing house, with the support of an insurance company and two joint stock banks. Its purpose is to advance sums of up to £100,000 to small businesses which can show evidence of their ability to use the funds effectively. Money has generally been advanced in the form of payments for preference shares.

Two new financial institutions were established in 1945 on government initiative.

1. *The Finance Corporation for Industry* was created with an initial capital of £25 million, subscribed by a number of insurance and investment companies and the Bank of England. It has power to borrow up to

£100 million. It is intended to provide loans for larger companies in sums in excess of £200,000. Most of its lending takes the form of fixed interest loans secured by a mortgage on the assets of the business, but it may, if it wishes, purchase ordinary shares.

2. *The Industrial and Commercial Finance Corporation* is the smaller of the two institutions with a capital of £15 million provided by the commercial banks and the Bank of England. It can borrow up to £30 million, and provides loans of up to £300,000. Like the F.C.I. it can advance capital either on fixed interest terms, or by participation in the equity of the business. It has done a great deal to meet the long-term capital requirements of smaller businesses.

Hire Purchase

Hire purchase may not, at first sight, appear to qualify as a source of finance since it is not a direct loan of money. But if a firm buys a machine valued at, say, £5,000, on hire purchase terms over three years, it has, in fact, received a loan. The effect is exactly the same as if the firm had negotiated a loan of £5,000, repayable over three years, from a finance institution, and then bought the machine for cash. A number of firms – finance houses, or industrial bankers – exist for the purpose of providing funds to support hire purchase schemes. The bulk of the business done by hire purchase companies is in the field of consumer goods, but an increasing part of their work covers the sale of industrial equipment on hire purchase terms. This form of financial assistance is of considerable importance to the smaller firm.

Trade Credit

Trade credit is a very important source of finance to the smaller firm, and the total sums outstanding in the form of trade credit is very much greater than the total of bank loans to industry. A firm supplying goods on credit terms, which allow the purchaser three months or six months to pay, is providing a short term loan to the buyer. Trade credit represents, for many firms, a valuable saving of working capital.

Retained Profits

For the large firm the provision of funds from its own reserves is the most important source of capital for purposes of expansion. These reserves are accumulated by the retention of some proportion of profits, within the firm, as an alternative to distribution to the shareholders.

Public Money and Private Industry

One important source of finance for industry is the Government. The emphasis which has been placed on economic planning in recent years has led to a greater involvement by the public authorities in private industry. Total Government financial assistance to private industry increased from £358 million in 1960/61 to £1,150 million in 1969/70. The pattern has also changed considerably. In 1960 about 90 per cent of the assistance went to agriculture, but this proportion has diminished to about one quarter. Government financial aid is now concentrated more towards promoting employment in the development areas (see page 111) and to increasing the efficiency of manufacturing industry.

AGRICULTURE AND FISHING

Government aid to agriculture takes two forms: price guarantees and production grants. Price guarantees amount to a subsidy equal to the difference between the market price of the farm produce and the guaranteed price negotiated each year by the farmers and the government. The Government also provides the farmers with grants designed to improve farm buildings and farming techniques.

Financial assistance is also rendered to the fishing industry (about £10 million per year in 1970). It takes the form of a subsidy to reduce operating costs.

It is not proposed to change this system and protect agriculture by means of levies on imported foodstuffs.

DEVELOPMENT AREAS

Substantial aid in the form of investment grants, building grants, and subsidies on labour costs has been made available to firms in the development areas. This subject is dealt with in some detail in Chapter 11.

RESEARCH AND DEVELOPMENT

For a long time now the government has had a well-established programme of support for industrial research and development. This takes the form of grants to the National Research Development Corporation and to research associations established by private firms. There has also been major financial support in the form of loans for the development of advanced technical projects (e.g. the Concorde). Loans have also been provided to industries undertaking major restructuring (e.g. shipbuilding) and to infant industries struggling to get established (e.g. computers).

EXPORT ASSISTANCE

Aids to exporters take the form of marketing services, financial assistance to firms taking part in trade fairs and exhibitions abroad, and the provision of favourable insurance terms on export contracts.

THE INDUSTRIAL REORGANISATION CORPORATION

Established in 1966, the I.R.C. was a very controversial Government agency. It was granted £150 million of public money to invest in private industry with the aim of promoting industrial efficiency and improved productivity. The major objectives of the I.R.C. were to encourage programmes of rationalisation, mergers, and regroupings where these changes would lead to greater standardisation, substantial economies of scale and greater competitiveness in the export markets. It instigated and encouraged several important mergers. It contributed £35 to the British Leyland merger and £15 million to the mergers which established the G.E.C. combine. It could provide funds in a variety of ways (fixed interest loans or the purchase of shares), but its investment in any one project was intended to be relatively short term. Once the project was successfully launched, the I.R.C. sold its holdings and reinvested the money elsewhere. The purpose was to 'rotate a chunk of public money through private industry in a way which will leave the industrial structure stronger and more competitive'. It has been said that the I.R.C. tended to provide a conflict with the Government's policy measures on monopoly. This is discussed later in the book.

In 1970 the Government announced that the I.R.C. was to be disbanded.

Loan Capital and Risk Capital

Capital for industrial and commercial enterprises may be classified as either *loan capital* or *risk capital*. Loan capital consists of those funds advanced at fixed rates of interest and secured by some kind of mortgage on the assets of the company. The interest payments on loan capital are regarded as part of the fixed costs of the business, and, hence, may be deducted from profits before any assessment is made for tax purposes. Risk capital is that part of the capital stock which is raised by the sale of shares. The interest and dividends payable on these shares do not rank as a cost of production for taxation purposes and they must be paid out of profits after taxation demands have been met. On the other hand, the interest charges on loan capital must be paid each year, otherwise the lenders may take legal action to recover their loans. Dividends and interest on risk capital need not be paid in those years when the company has not prospered. Companies which operate in industries where the market for the product is subject to constant fluctuation would not take the risk of having a high proportion of loan capital. Loan capital is more appropriate to firms operating in stable markets and which have a large part of their assets in the form of land and buildings which are good subjects for mortgages (e.g. brewery companies).

The ratio of loan capital to risk capital is of some significance since it has considerable influence on the variability of the returns from investment. The ratio of a company's ordinary share capital to that provided by prior claimants (debenture and preference shareholders) is known as *the gearing* of the capital structure. The greater the proportion of ordinary to other capital, the lower the gearing of the capital structure. Thus, if profits are rising, the dividends on ordinary shares will rise very much faster in companies with high gearing than in those with low gearing. The examples on page 83 might be used to illustrate this point. If the proportions between ordinary shares and the fixed interest securities are varied, the returns to ordinary shares will be much more variable when the gearing is greater.

Table 13 gives an indication of the manner in which the larger companies (those quoted on the London Stock Exchange) have been raising their funds in recent years.

Table 13. *Quoted companies – sources of funds: 1969*

	% of Total	
Issues:		
Ordinary shares	17·3	
Preference shares	–·8	
Long-term loans	8·0	
	——	24·5
Short-term credit:		
Bank loans	3·4	
Trade credit	9·2	
	——	12·6
Internal sources:		
Profits	55·5	
Other	7·4	
	——	62·9
		——
		100·0

Source: *Board of Trade Journal*

Fig. 10 refers to all companies, hence the greater relative importance of bank loans.

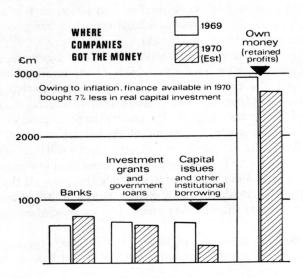

Figure 10

Source: *Sunday Times*, 7 March 1971.

The Problems of the Small Firm

The financing of small firms provides special and important problems. Small firms are denied access to the new issue market. Many of the smaller firms are often newly established and have been created to develop some new product, or new techniques of production. They are seeking to grow, and it is most important that new enterprise should not be stunted by lack of opportunities to raise the necessary capital.

Small and growing firms will not be making the big profits necessary to finance rapid expansion, so that 'ploughing back' is not likely to be a source of substantial funds. There is often a greater degree of risk involved, especially with newly established firms, which makes it more difficult for them to raise capital on such favourable terms as the older and larger firm. In the nineteenth century the traditional sources of capital for the small firm were the private fortunes of the local business man, professional man, landowner and the like. But high taxation has tended to diminish the importance of this personal source of finance. In any case, more and more private wealth is being channelled into the capital market through such institutions as insurance companies, superannuation funds, and investment trusts, which tend to invest in quoted securities.

The specialist finance corporations, mentioned earlier, do support the smaller firm, although they tend to look to the well managed business with a good profit record and a fairly certain future.

There is now a subsidiary of the I.C.F.C. known as the *Technical Development Capital Limited* (T.D.C.) which has been formed to provide finance for novel processes and developments which require capital, and involve greater risks than existing organisations are prepared to take. There is evidence that valuable British innovations have been exploited abroad owing to difficulties in obtaining financial backing, and an important aim of T.D.C. is to keep worth-while projects in British hands.

LEASING AND RENTING

Many firms now prefer to lease or rent their capital equipment. This alternative to purchasing plant, machinery, and commercial vehicles, reduces the need for medium and long term capital and is very advantageous to the small firm. These rental schemes may be operated by the manufacturers themselves, or by a finance company. The I.C.F.C. now operates a scheme for the finance of leased and rented equipment.

The Stock Exchange

A large part of the capital raised by industry and by public authorities takes the form of long-term or permanent loans. Most share certificates are acknowledgements of permanent loans; the company does not undertake to repay the shareholder at some definite future date. It would be extremely difficult for joint stock companies and the Government to raise the large sums they require for investment purposes unless the would-be lenders were provided with some means of selling their stocks and shares. No one can reasonably be expected to lock up money in a company (or the government) for ever. What is needed is some kind of market where shareholders and security-holders can sell their claims. The Stock Exchange is such a market, since it provides the means whereby buyers and sellers of *existing* securities can carry out the necessary exchanges.

Although dealings in shares have a much longer history, the development of an organised market for securities became vitally important when the privilege of limited liability became generally available. The limitation of shareholders' liability, together with a market where they might dispose of shares at any time, are essential requirements for the raising of large sums of money from the general public.

The Stock Exchange is not open to members of the general public; only members may transact business there. Membership is restricted, and there are about 3,500 members representing about 400 firms. The Stock Exchange is governed by a council of thirty-six members elected by ballot.

BROKERS AND JOBBERS

Members are of two kinds, *brokers* and *jobbers*. Brokers are agents for the persons wishing to buy or sell shares. The broker acts upon his clients' instructions and is paid a commission for his services. The person wishing to buy or sell shares on the Stock Exchange must use the services of a firm of brokers who are members of the Stock Exchange.

Jobbers do not deal with members of the public. They operate inside the Stock Exchange and are only allowed to deal with brokers or other jobbers. The jobber does not act as an agent, but as a principal. He buys and sells shares on his own account, and usually specialises in one group of shares (e.g. shipping or oil). The jobber's income is derived from the difference between the price at which he sells and the price at which he buys. Since there is usually keen competition between the jobbers, this margin is often very small. Of the 3,500 members about 520 are jobbers divided among 28 firms.

THE TRANSACTIONS

Let us imagine that a broker has received instructions from his client to purchase 100 shares in Company A. The broker will proceed to the Stock Exchange and make his way to that part of the floor where the jobbers who deal in this class of share are congregated. He will approach one jobber and say, 'What are Company A?' The jobber does not know whether the broker wishes to buy or sell, but he must be prepared to deal with him. He might reply, '126p to $127\frac{1}{2}$p'. The lower price represents the one that he will pay for these shares, and the higher price is the one at which he will sell. The broker will now move on to the other jobbers and note the prices quoted by each one. Since he is interested in buying shares, he will return, eventually, to the jobber quoting the lowest selling price.

Jobbers are wholesalers who adjust prices according to supply and demand. If, at the current price, there are more willing sellers than willing buyers, he will lower prices, hoping to attract buyers and reduce the number of sellers. If buyers are predominant, he will raise prices in order to attract more sellers. The successful jobber is able to adjust his prices to ever-changing conditions.

SHARE PRICES

Share prices are subject to daily, even hourly, changes in price. The Stock Exchange publishes its own Daily Official List showing the prices at which transactions have taken place. Over 9,000 different types of stocks and shares are quoted on the London Stock Exchange, and about one-third of the business is in British government securities and local authority stocks.

Share prices are determined by supply and demand which, in turn, are influenced by such things as:

1. The recent profit record of the company and the rates of dividend paid, together with the growth prospects of the market in which the company operates.

2. Rumours of, and announcements of, proposed takeovers and mergers.

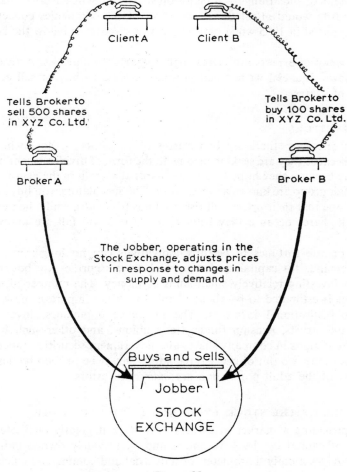

Client A Client B

Tells Broker to
sell 500 shares
in XYZ Co. Ltd.

Tells Broker to
buy 100 shares
in XYZ Co. Ltd.

Broker A Broker B

The Jobber, operating in the
Stock Exchange, adjusts prices
in response to changes in
supply and demand

Buys and Sells

Jobber

STOCK
EXCHANGE

Figure 11

3. Changes in government policy. When the government embarks upon measures to restrict consumer spending, the shares of companies making consumer durable goods will fall in price. A proposed increase in public spending on roads and houses will raise the value of the shares of construction companies.

4. Foreign political developments will have some effect on the shares of companies which have a large export trade.

5. Changes in the rate of interest on government securities will sometimes affect share prices. A rise in the market rate of interest might cause some 'switching' from shares to government securities.

6. The news of such things as a major oil strike or the discovery of natural gas deposits would affect the share prices of the companies concerned. This happened in 1965 when natural gas was discovered below the North Sea.

7. The views of experts are increasingly important influences. Articles by well-known financial writers can persuade people to buy or sell certain classes of shares.

THE INVESTORS

Broadly speaking, there are two classes of 'investors' – those who buy shares because they are seeking income in the form of dividends, and those who buy because they hope to sell the shares at a profit in the near future. This latter group are known as *speculators*. The speculators who buy shares in the hope that their prices will rise are known as *bulls*, while the persons who sell shares because they believe that prices will fall are known as *bears*.

The private fortunes of wealthy individuals can no longer meet the huge demands for capital, and more and more securities are bought by persons investing relatively small sums of money. The number of *direct* investors is estimated to be about $2\frac{1}{2}$ million. More important nowadays are the institutional investors. The insurance companies, investment trusts, unit trusts, pension funds, trade unions, and other such bodies invest huge sums in company shares and government securities. Since it is estimated that two out of every three adults subscribe to such bodies, the majority of the adult population are *indirect* investors.

THE ROLE OF THE STOCK EXCHANGE IN THE ECONOMY

1. By providing a market in existing securities, it greatly facilitates the raising of capital by the government and by privately owned industry.

2. It provides a daily 'barometer' of industrial and commercial efficiency, to the extent that movements in share prices reflect commercial success.

3. Stock Exchange prices provide a means of valuing wealth held in the form of securities. This is important for the assessment of death duties and capital gains' taxation. The prices of shares are also used as a basis for the assessment of compensation payments when a firm is nationalised. It is usual, in such cases, to take an average of shares prices over the five years immediately preceding nationalisation.

4. The Stock Exchange is a market where existing securities are bought and sold – it is not a market for new capital (although some new shares are privately 'placed'). Nevertheless, it does serve to direct the flow of new capital, since Stock Exchange valuations provide the prospective lenders with an indication of the potential growth prospects of different firms.

London is by far the largest, but not the only, stock exchange in Great Britain. There are stock exchanges in twenty-two of the larger provincial towns. In order to get its shares quoted on the London Stock Exchange a company must satisfy the Council by complying with requirements more stringent than those in the Companies Acts.

Chapter 11

Locating the Enterprise

One of the fundamental decisions to be taken by the entrepreneur concerns the geographical location of his enterprise. He has not only to decide 'How to produce' and 'What to produce' but '*Where* to produce'. We must now consider the various influences which bear upon this problem of industrial location. The great importance of this particular aspect of economic activity is evidenced by the increasing attention which the Government has given to this problem in recent years.

From the economic viewpoint the major determinant of location is that of cost, but political and social considerations loom very large in government policy regarding the location of industry. There are normally several locations where it is possible for the firm to operate, but the entrepreneur will tend to choose that situation which affords the lowest cost of production per unit. The variations in costs which are due to location arise because some areas have particular advantages over other areas for the performance of various economic activities. Even so, the firm, in deciding on its location, will generally be faced with a difficult problem for its needs as a producer might conflict with its needs as a seller. One location might provide an excellent site in relation to the source of raw materials, but another site would be more suitable in relation to the market for its products. The decision tends to rest upon some calculation of the maximum net advantages to be obtained in any one site.

Raw Materials and Power

In the early days of industrialisation the great localising factors were those of proximity to raw materials and power. The first factories depended upon water power and were sited on the banks of fast flowing streams. Arkwright built his mill on the banks of such a stream at Cromford in Derbyshire. The introduction of steam power brought about a concentration of industrial activity on the coalfields. Transport facilities at this time were extremely primitive and the cost of moving a bulky commodity like coal made any location other than coalfield sites hopelessly uneconomic. With coal replacing charcoal as the fuel for the iron industry, all the basic industries in Britain, cotton, wool, iron and steel, became established on or near the coalfields. It should be noted that these two factors, the proximity to raw materials and power, no longer exert such a great pull on industry. New sources of power, notably electricity and oil, are readily available in most parts of the country, and the remarkable developments in transport have both expedited and cheapened the movements of raw materials and finished products.

But proximity to raw materials, particularly where they are bulky, still exerts an influence on the location of some industries. Where the industrial process is *bulk-reducing* the tendency is for processing to take place near the source of the basic materials. The iron and steel industry has tended to move to the Lincolnshire and Northamptonshire ore deposits. This is because British ore has a very low iron content and technical progress has led to great economies in the use of coal. It is now cheaper to move the coal to the ore, than vice versa. The sugar-beet processing plants are located on or near the beet fields, since the yield of sugar is very low. Chemical plants are located on the salt beds of Cheshire and South Lancashire for similar reasons.

Proximity to Markets

Where the industrial processes are *bulk increasing* then the pull of the market is a more important factor. This is true of the furniture industry, and of the manufacture of domestic appliances such as refrigerators and washing machines. These activities tend to be concentrated in the southeast near to the mass London market. Transport developments have made it possible for industries originally concentrated near the source of raw materials to remain there long after the deposits have been exhausted. The pottery industry of North Staffordshire was sited on the basis of local clays, long since abandoned, and the industry now works clay transported from Cornwall. The woollen industry developed in Yorkshire on the bases of local coal and wool, but it now processes imported wools and uses electricity as its source of power. The desire to be near the source of raw materials helps to explain the siting of some industries on coastal sites. Some of our iron and steel plants are located on the coast due to a dependence on foreign ores.

In certain industries the locational pattern may be easily explained. The location of extractive industries such as coal mining, iron ore mining, forestry, etc., are fixed by the distribution of the natural resources. Many of the service industries cannot be concentrated in any one region, but must be situated according to the geographical distribution of the population. In providing services which must be supplied direct to the customer, industries such as hairdressing, window cleaning, retailing, and petrol distribution, must remain dispersed and local in character.

The market for the product has always exercised some influence on the siting of industrial activity, but its importance relative to that of other factors has tended to increase. One reason for this is the fact that as a nation grows richer the proportion of consumer goods in the total output tends to increase. The demand for a rapid and regular delivery of consumer goods, together with the need for after-sales service of such durable goods as electrical appliances, tends to increase the attractiveness of sites near to the major markets. The practice of charging a uniform price means that proximity to the market reduces the total selling costs and hence allows a lower uniform price.

Physical Features and Accessibility

For some industries, the physical features of the site are of prime importance in deciding location. Industries producing steel, rayon, paper and chemicals require very large quantities of water and tend to be found on rivers. The atomic power stations, built since the war, are all located on estuaries because of the vast quantities of water required for cooling purposes. Certain industries have a difficult problem of waste disposal, especially the chemical-based industries like bleaching and dyeing, and, usually, they are to be found on river-bank sites. The problem of dust control has made it necessary to site cement works in fairly remote situations.

The accessibility of the site is a vital factor. Before the development of road transport, proximity to the railway network was an essential requirement. The rapid development of road transport has greatly widened the scope and choice of location and many new factories are not sited so as to make use of the railway facilities.

Economies of Concentration

A general survey of the causes which have influenced location in the past gives the impression that their operation was frequently unknown or little understood by the initiators. Usually there was some major factor such as proximity to raw materials or local craftsmanship which led to the establishment of the industry. Once the industry becomes localised *the acquired advantages* of the situation become cumulative. It is the acquired advantages of existing centres of industry which now exert the greatest influence on location. These advantages, sometimes referred to as *economies of concentration*,[1] take many forms:

1. *A local supply of labour*, skilled in the various techniques of the industry, becomes available. For the establishment of a new firm, in many industries,

---

[1] Or, *external economies of scale* in order to distinguish them from the economies which arise from the growth of the firm.

this is still an essential requirement. The alternative to setting up an enterprise in the existing centre of the industry would be the costly procedures of establishing a scheme for the training of labour, or of attracting key workers to the new site. But the existence of a local supply of skilled labour is not such an important factor nowadays as it was in former times. Technical progress has taken the form of eliminating the human element, and skills have been transferred from men to machines. Industry now demands large numbers of semi-skilled workers who can be trained very quickly by modern methods.

2. In areas which have a high degree of industrial concentration, sub-. sidiary industries, catering for the special needs of the major industry, gradually develop. *Ancillary services* are provided by specialist firms. Taking as an example a highly localised industry like the boot and shoe industry, we see that the major manufacturers of boot and shoe machinery are located in the City of Leicester. Here too, are to be found firms which provide specialist services in the marketing of all forms of leather, in the wholesaling of footwear, and in processing the waste products of the footwear industry. The banks in the city have a special knowledge of the needs of the industry.

3. The division of labour within a firm increases productivity and lowers the average cost of production. Where an industry is highly concentrated, this principle can be extended to the whole industry. When firms are situated close together, it becomes possible for *individual firms* to *specialise* in a single process – the industry tends to 'disintegrate'. The classic example of this development is to be found in the structure of the Lancashire cotton industry, where the preparation of cotton cloth is broken down into a large number of separate operations, each carried out by a specialist firm (spinning, weaving, dyeing, finishing, etc.). A glance through the Trades' Telephone Directories for centres like Stoke-on-Trent, Bradford, Coventry or Leicester will give a very good picture of the wide range of firms which provide one component for, or carry out one process in, the manufacture of the products in which these areas specialise.

4. The educational institutions in centres of localised industry provide *special courses of training* geared to the needs of the industry. The technical colleges in Leicester have important Hosiery and Boot and Shoe departments, while those in Bradford and Manchester have highly developed Schools of Textiles. The existence of these specialised training facilities tends to reinforce and perpetuate the attraction of the supply of skilled labour available in the established centres of industry.

5. The *industrial and commercial environment* in such areas is likely to be more stimulating and conducive to technical progress than would be the case where an industry is widely dispersed. The opportunities for formal and informal contacts between members of different firms is much greater.

This creates many opportunities for the exchange of views and 'know how', and for a general cross-fertilisation of ideas. There is likely to be a constant awareness of the developments in the industry, which provides a stimulus to the individual firms.

This general account of the influences which bear upon the location of industry could be greatly extended by a list of the more specific factors. Restrictions on building and a grave shortage of sites in the existing centres might cause a firm to establish itself wherever it could find suitable accommodation. A firm (or an industry) might come to be established in a given area simply because the founder happened to live there (e.g. Morris in Oxford, or Rowntree in York). Firms which employ predominantly female labour might be tempted to move from areas where this kind of labour is in short supply (e.g. the Midlands) to areas where it is more abundant (e.g. South Wales). It may seem that, in some of these more specific examples, the decisions on location were not based on any careful calculation of alternative possibilities. But the fact that the firm has succeeded (and we do not hear very much about the failures) would indicate that the chosen site did not suffer from any serious economic defects. It may have been that the industry is of a type in which transport costs are relatively unimportant, or the entrepreneur, in setting up his enterprise locally, may have been able to raise finance more readily.

Although developments in transport and power have made possible a much wider choice of location this has not led to a greater dispersion of industry. The economies of concentration are formidable and the well-established centres of industry tend to attract new firms and new workers. The consequent development of vast conurbations has raised many serious social and economic problems.

Government Intervention

The increase in the extent of State control of industrial location is part of the general trend towards greater government intervention in the working of the economic system. In this particular case public policy may be justified on the grounds that the private decisions of the entrepreneur regarding the location of his factory may impose considerable costs on the public sector. The growth of industry in any region will involve public expenditure on housing, health, education, new roads, etc. The movement of industry away from any area could well result in the wastage of much social capital. A further justification for government intervention is the fact that the Government accepts the responsibility for maintaining a situation of full employment. It cannot discharge this responsibility adequately if it leaves the location of industry entirely to private decisions.

The Government was first prompted to act in this field during the great depression of the 1930s. Certain industries, which happened to be highly localised, suffered a more than average fall in the level of demand for their products. A permanent loss of export markets and a serious decline in the level of world trade seriously affected British industries such as coal-mining, cotton, iron and steel, and shipbuilding. The regions in which these industries were concentrated, South Wales, Lancashire, Clydeside, the North-East, and the North-West all suffered unemployment rates very much higher than the national average and were designated Depressed Areas, later renamed Special Areas. The problem was made particularly acute, because the newer developing industries, motor vehicles, electrical engineering, processed foods, and radio, tended to choose locations away from the Special Areas, and to settle in the South-East and the Midlands. The main attraction for these growing, and mainly consumer good industries were the mass markets of the Midlands and the London area.

The first legislation on the problem was the Special Areas Act of 1934, followed by further Acts in 1936 and 1937. Attempts were made, under these Acts, to induce labour to move from the depressed areas to the more prosperous regions, and to encourage private capital to move to the areas of very high unemployment. Although some migration, particularly from South Wales, did take place, the problem was so great that the net effect was very small indeed. The Government financed the building of factories on trading estates and let them at very favourable rentals to private firms. Government loans were made available to firms moving to the Special Areas and certain concessions were granted to these firms with regard to taxation and rates. More definite steps were taken by locating the ordnance factories, associated with the rearmament programme, in the depressed areas, and government pressure resulted in the location of a steel works in South Wales, after a site had first been chosen in Lincolnshire. But the problems of the Special Areas remained unsolved when the country went to war. During the war the problem disappeared,

Since the war, the level of unemployment has remained very low compared with the situation during the interwar period, but the problems of the Special Areas remain. The unemployment rates in these regions are still well above the national average.

The Distribution of Industry Act of 1945 aimed to produce a more diversified industrial structure in the Development Areas (formerly the Special Areas). The Board of Trade[1] was given power to acquire land and erect factories for renting, and loans and grants were made available to firms moving to the Development Areas. To these positive inducements was added a more powerful negative control. The Town and Country Planning Act of 1947 obliged firms seeking to erect industrial buildings

[1] The implementation of government policy on the location of industry is now the responsibility of the Department of Trade and Industry.

of more than 5,000 square feet, to obtain a Board of Trade Industrial Development Certificate before planning permission could be considered. These certificates were readily granted to firms wishing to build in the Development Areas, but were much more difficult to obtain in areas of low unemployment.

These controls on industrial buildings were supplemented, in November 1964, by restrictions on office building in the London area. These were later extended to the whole of south-east England.

In spite of these measures, which did, in fact, lead many firms to set up factories in the Development Areas, it became apparent that any slight recession in the level of economic activity, caused unemployment in some areas to rise more rapidly than the national average. The Local Employment Act of 1960 consolidated all previous legislation on the subject, and replaced the old Development Areas by a new list of Development Districts. This list could be varied, by the Board of Trade, to include any area which had a high or persistent unemployment rate. A large list of smaller, more closely specified districts replaced the smaller number of large Development Areas. The whole range of government aid applied to firms which were in the regions on the current list of Development Districts. The Government, it should be noted, has no power to compel, but relies on reinforced persuasion. It had a notable success in the early 1960s when it persuaded the major motor manufacturers to site new plants in central Scotland and on Merseyside.

More incentives came in the 1963 Budget. Aid for investment in the Development Districts was increased by a system of standard grants of 25 per cent of the cost of buildings, and 10 per cent of the cost of new plant and machinery. Major tax concessions were granted on the depreciation of plant and equipment. Grants to local authorities in these districts, for clearing derelict areas, were increased to cover almost the whole cost.

In January 1966 the Government announced new policies with regard to the location of industry. The development districts under the Local Employment Acts were replaced by new and wider development areas. They cover virtually the whole of Scotland and Wales, and, in England, the Northern Region, Merseyside, and almost the whole of Cornwall and North Devon. The existing system of investment allowances was cancelled and replaced by a system of cash grants. A cash grant equal to 20 per cent of the cost of new investment was paid to firms in specified industries, chiefly manufacturing and extractive industries. In the new development areas these grants were at the rate of 40 per cent. New industrial building did not qualify for the new grants, except in the development areas, where grants of 25 per cent or 35 per cent were paid if the Board of Trade was satisfied that there would be an adequate provision of employment.

An entirely new form of assistance was introduced in 1967 in the form of Regional Employment Premiums whereby firms in the development areas received a weekly grant of 150 pence for each full-time male employee and reduced rates for women, juveniles and part-time workers. The Government guaranteed that these payments would be given for a minimum period of seven years. Capital-intensive firms, many of whom benefited substantially from investment grants, had been induced to move to development areas, but such firms often provided relatively little employment. The R.E.P. was a scheme designed to attract labour-intensive firms to the selected areas.

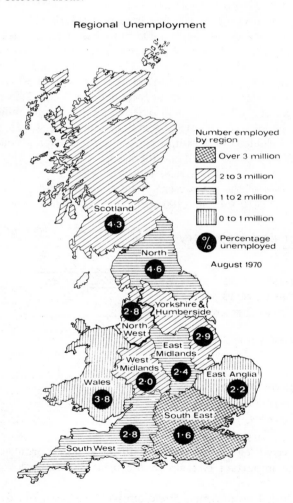

Regional Unemployment

Figure 12.

Source: *Barclays Bank Briefing No. 11.*

A variety of assistance is available for industrial training in the development areas which, in proportion to the numbers of male workers, have twice as many training places in Government training centres as in other parts of the country. Since 1967 a training grant of £10 per week, per worker, has been payable to firms which have moved into, or expanded in the development areas.

In the financial year 1968/69, total Government assistance to industry in the development areas amounted to £265 million.

SPECIAL AREAS AND INTERMEDIATE AREAS

In 1967 certain localities which had been particularly affected by colliery closures were designated Special Development Areas. These localities, situated in the coalfields of S. Wales, N.E. England, W. Cumberland, and Clydeside, qualified for extra help. The 1970 Local Employment Act authorised the designation of another type of area to which assistance might be given. These are known as Intermediate Areas. They are situated on the fringes of the Development Areas and suffer from similar problems although not in such an acute form. Intermediate Areas include the Yorkshire coalfield, north Humberside, the Notts/Derby coalfield, N.E. Lancashire, S.E. Wales, Leith and Plymouth.

Investment Incentives 1972

Some examples of the net present value of grants and tax savings from capital allowances for every £100 spent on investment.

THE 1972 INDUSTRY ACT

The most recent legislation dealing with the regional problem has introduced some important changes in the measures to deal with regional imbalance.

1. The Regional Employment Premium will be phased out over a period from September 1974.

2. The need to apply for an IDC is lifted altogether in Development and Special Development Areas. The IDC limit is raised to 10,000 square feet for S.E. England and to 15,000 square feet for the rest of the country.
3. Regional Development Grants

In 1970 the government abolished the use of investment grants and re-introduced tax allowances as investment incentives. These tax allowances are now made available to the whole country while investment grants (RDGs) are re-introduced for the Development Areas at a rate of 20 per cent for plant and buildings, and, for the Special Development Areas, at 22 per cent. The Intermediate Areas qualify for the 20 per cent building grants.

These grants are expected to amount to something like £300 million per annum by 1975.

Regional Policies

Regional policy is a twentieth-century development. All industrialised countries are now grappling with regional economic problems. These have three basic forms.
(i) An excessive concentration of people in particular cities and towns.
(ii) Areas dominated by old and/or declining industries.
(iii) Regions depressed due to a dependence on low income extractive industries such as agriculture, forestry and fishing.

In the U.K. the major problem is the second one, but the problems of London and the South-East provide an example of the first type, and the problems of the Scottish Highlands and the S.W. peninsula are examples of the third type.

The nature and extent of the regional problem is revealed by variation in unemployment rates. In the development areas these have been substantially above the national average for a long time. In November 1970, the unemployment rate for Great Britain was 2·6 per cent. The rates for the different regions were:

	%		%
London and the S.E.	1·5	North Western	2·7
Eastern and Southern	1·9	Yorks/Humberside	3·0
Midlands	2·1	Scotland	4·6
South Western	3·0	Wales	3·9
		Northern	4·6

This uneven distribution of unemployment gives rise to several problems:
1. The unemployment in the development areas represents a serious

waste of economic resources and the national income is lower than it might otherwise be.

2. The drift of population to the more prosperous areas leads to housing shortages, congestion, and general overcrowding in these areas. There are added social costs incurred in trying to relieve the problems of the overcrowded areas. In other areas, the community life may be damaged by the loss of population and there are social costs in the form of wasted social capital.

3. When total demand for goods and services is high, there is an excess demand for labour (and other factors) in the prosperous areas giving rise to upward pressures on incomes and prices. Inflationary pressures are generated while manpower resources are under-utilised elsewhere.

Regional policy measures fall into three main groups:

(a) Development of the infrastructure by improving roads, railways, airports, increasing the availability of fuel and power, and providing the necessary social capital and amenities.

(b) Schemes to improve the occupational and geographical mobility of labour so that labour can move more readily to the new jobs provided by any new industries established in or near the areas with surplus labour.

(c) Measures to stimulate industrial expansion and industrial diversification in the selected areas together with restrictions on expansion elsewhere.

The measures adopted in Britain have already been outlined. They have tended to concentrate on the object of 'taking work to the workers', although a great deal is being done to improve infrastructures and labour mobility. The building of new towns may be seen as part of the general strategy to relieve congestion in the great conurbations, although some of these new towns were designed to provide growth points in certain depressed areas.

It is extremely difficult to assess the extent to which Government policy has been successful. In spite of the very substantial financial inducements, the discrepancies in regional unemployment rates still remain. It is possible, of course, that without Government intervention, the divergencies might have been very much greater. The policies have been criticised on several grounds.

1. A policy of diversification may result in a substantial loss of external economies of scale. The motor-car industry appeared to be very reluctant to forego the significant economies of concentration they derive in the established centres of the industry.

2. The policy of taking work to the workers may have been pushed too far. Firms which have been refused permission to expand their existing

plant in the prosperous areas may have cancelled their plans for expansion rather than accept the alternative of operating a branch factory in a development area.

3. Labour availability is only one criterion for industrial location and areas with surplus labour may well be high cost areas in other respects. If so, pressures to locate firms in these areas might reduce their competitiveness – especially in export markets.

4. It should be recognised that some areas are 'economically exhausted' and no amount of financial inducement will persuade firms to move into such areas on a scale sufficient to rehabilitate them.

As against these arguments it must be said that such criticisms are largely based on an assumption that firms, left to themselves, will always choose the least-cost location. It is difficult to prove this, and all sorts of personal factors seem to be involved in location decisions. Again, some economists believe that many modern industries are 'footloose' in the sense that their costs of production are not significantly affected by the location of the enterprise.

More recently Government policy has recognised that areas with high unemployment are not the only regional problems. The prosperous areas have problems of traffic congestion, overcrowded schools and hospitals, acute shortages of skilled manpower and so on. A broader approach to regional planning to ensure balanced growth in all regions has led to the establishment of regional planning organisations. The whole country has been divided into ten regions each with its own Regional Council consisting of representatives from industry, local government, and the universities together with a Regional Planning Board consisting of civil servants from the ministries concerned. These groups are intended to carry out regional studies, to identify problems, and to formulate and implement regional plans.

Chapter 12

How Prices are Determined

Price and Value

In this chapter we discuss the basic determinants of price. *Price* is not the same thing as *value*. Things are 'valuable', because people think they are, and for no other reason. The 'value' which an individual places on a commodity cannot be measured, its value will be different for different people. This kind of intrinsic value is not the concern of the economist, who is only interested in 'value in exchange'. The economic worth or value of a good can only be measured in some kind of market transaction, which reveals the value of the good in terms of what is offered in exchange for it. If 5 lb of potatoes will exchange for 1 lb of sugar, then the price of 1 lb of sugar is 5 lb of potatoes. Nowadays, practically all exchanges represent an exchange of goods for money, and price, in terms of money, is the market value of the commodity bought and sold.

Markets

Prices arise in exchange transactions, and this implies some kind of market arrangement. A market need not, necessarily, be a fixed place – a building, or a market place. We are all familiar with the open and covered markets in the centres of our towns, but in the modern world, the word 'market' has a much wider meaning. Any effective arrangement for bringing buyers and sellers into contact with one another, is defined as a market. For some commodities, notably fresh fruit and vegetables, the traditional market is still the normal arrangement, but for most commodities, the 'market' is a national one. In a modern economy, most consumer goods are bought and sold on a countrywide basis, and for the manufacturers of these goods, the market is the whole country.

For other commodities, the market is worldwide. This is particularly true of the more important raw materials such as rubber, tin, copper, leather, etc., and of the basic foodstuffs such as meat, wheat, rice, sugar, and coffee.

The price of any economic good, under market conditions such as we find in the capitalist world, is determined by the forces of supply and demand. Briefly, then, we have some kind of market arrangement, where buyers and sellers are in contact, and the forces of supply acting through the sellers, and the forces of demand acting through the buyers, determine the market price.

Demand

The first thing to understand is that demand is not the same thing as desire, or need, or want. We are looking for the forces which determine price, and the strength of the desire for the commodity will not, in itself, have any influence on the price. Only when a desire is supported by the ability and willingness to pay the price, does it become an effective demand and have an influence in the market. Demand, in economics, means effective demand, and may be defined as '*the quantity of the commodity which will be demanded at any given price over some period of time*'.

Consider the following statements:

1. The demand for the commodity X is 1,000 units.
2. The demand for commodity X, at a price of 6p per unit, is 1,000 units.
3. The demand for commodity X, at a price of 6p per unit, is 1,000 units per week.

Note that only the third statement is meaningful. The first statement is incomplete because the quantity demanded will, normally, be different at different prices. The second statement tells us the quantity demanded at a given price, but it does not tell us how long it will take to sell 1,000 units. Any definition of demand must say something about the quantity, the price, and the time period.

For the great majority of goods, experience shows that the quantity demanded will increase as the price falls. Such a *demand schedule* will be of the following form.

Price per unit	Quantity demanded (*per week*)
50p	50
40p	80
30p	130
20p	190
10p	300

The schedule may be represented graphically in the form of a *demand curve* which slopes downwards from left to right. (Fig. 13.)

DEMAND AND UTILITY

Why should demand curves slope downwards from left to right? Why should the quantity demanded increase as the price falls? One explanation of this aspect of consumer behaviour is based upon the notion of *diminishing marginal utility*. Utility is defined as the satisfaction which is derived from the consumption of some good or service. A customer buys a good because it yields him 'utility' or satisfaction. As he buys more of any good the total utility he derives, increases, but the increase in total utility is not proportionate to the increase in his consumption.

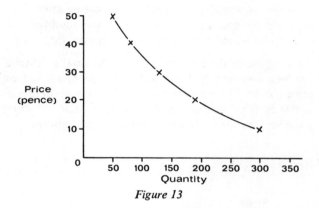

Figure 13

The additional utility, derived from the next unit purchased, we define as the *marginal utility* of the commodity, and marginal utility diminishes as consumption increases. After a strenuous session of work, the first cup of tea provides us with great satisfaction, the marginal utility of the first cup is very high. The second cup of tea might also be very welcome, but it will not yield so much utility as the first, while the third cup will provide an even lower level of satisfaction. If we continue to consume cups of tea we should reach a stage where it became positively distasteful and marginal utility would be negative.

Utility cannot be measured, because it is *a subjective valuation* and will vary from person to person according to individual tastes. Tobacco, to the smoker, has a high degree of utility, to the non-smoker its utility is negligible. Nevertheless, the law of diminishing marginal utility is a valid generalisation of human behaviour; the more of any commodity we consume, the less the utility derived from the consumption of a further unit. This relationship between consumption and satisfaction might be used to indicate the sacrifice which a consumer is prepared to make in order to obtain further units of a given commodity. A typical consumer, subjected to an experiment which extracted from him the maximum sacrifices he was prepared to make, might react as follows:

If he possesses none of the article he will pay 25p for 1st unit

If he possesses 1 unit of the article he will pay 19p for 2nd unit

117

If he possesses 2 units of the article he will pay 10p for 3rd unit
If he possesses 3 units of the article he will pay 5p for 4th unit.

This information can be re-arranged to show how this consumer would react to a range of market prices.

When price is 25p he would buy 1 unit of the commodity
When price is 20p he would buy 1 unit of the commodity
When price is 15p he would buy 2 units of the commodity
When price is 10p he would buy 3 units of the commodity
When price is 5p he would buy 4 units of the commodity

This is nothing more than a part of the individual's demand schedule for this particular commodity, for it shows us how much he would buy at different prices. It could be represented by a demand curve which would slope downwards from left to right. The total demand curve for the product is the summation of the individual demand curves.

THE DEMAND CURVE

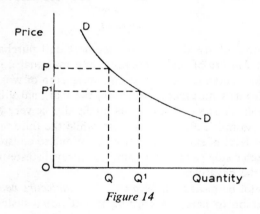

Figure 14

The demand curve tells us what quantities would be demanded at any given price. At a price of OP, the quantity demanded would be OQ; at a price of OP^1 the quantity demanded would be OQ^1. Alternatively the demand curve tells us the price at which any given quantity will be taken up by willing buyers.

The areas of the rectangles under the demand curve represent the Total Revenue forthcoming at different prices, since they are equal to Price × Quantity. If we use the figure to show the effect of changes in price, we can see that if price falls from OP to OP^1 the result of this change in price is an *increase in the quantity demanded* from OQ to OQ^1. There is no overall change *in demand*,[1] for the position of the demand curve has not altered. Changes in price bring about changes in the quantity demanded. The diagram above may be used to show the effect of an increase in price.

INCOME AND SUBSTITUTION EFFECTS

The shape of the typical demand curve may be explained in terms of the income and substitution effects of price changes. Other things being equal, when the price of a commodity changes, the real income of the consumer changes. The purchasing power of his money will be greater if the price of the commodity has fallen, it will be less if the price of the commodity has risen. When the price of a good falls, therefore, we would expect consumers to buy more because they can afford to buy more (the income effect). Existing buyers will probably increase their purchases and new buyers, who did not purchase at the higher price, will enter the market.

A fall in the price of a commodity will make it *relatively* cheaper when compared with its rivals. There will probably be some 'switching' of purchases away from the now relatively dearer substitutes towards the commodity which has fallen in price. This is the substitution effect.

The opposite effects will apply when price rises.

CHANGES IN DEMAND

A change in demand implies a shift in the basic conditions of demand and the whole of the demand curve moves. An *increase in demand means that more is now demanded at each and every price.* Such a change in demand is illustrated below.

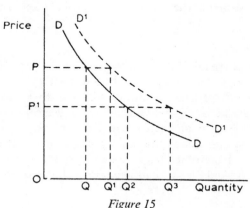

Figure 15

[1] It is most important to understand this distinction between a 'change in the quantity demanded' and a 'change in demand'. A change in the quantity demanded which implies a movement along an existing demand curve is sometimes referred to as an 'extension of demand', or a 'contraction of demand.'

The diagram may be used to illustrate either an increase in demand or a decrease in demand. An increase in demand would mean that the curve D^1D^1 has replaced the curve DD. We can see that the change in demand has resulted in an increased quantity being demanded at any given price. At a price of OP the quantity demanded has increased from OQ to OQ^1; at a price of OP^1 the quantity demanded has risen from OQ^2 to OQ^3. A fall in demand would mean that the demand curve had shifted from D^1D^1 to DD and less would now be demanded at any given price. There are many kinds of changes which would lead to an increase or decrease in demand. The following are the more important of these changes.

(a) Changes in Income

The most important general influence on the level of demand for most commodities is the level of incomes. If incomes are rising the demand for most goods, particularly the more expensive and better quality goods, will tend to increase. A striking example of this tendency has been the steady increase in the demand for motor cars in Western Europe which has accompanied the general rise in incomes since the end of the war. Rising incomes will also lead to falls in the demands for some commodities such as the cheaper types of clothing, or the cheaper basic foodstuffs (the demand for bread has gradually declined over the past decade in Europe). A fall in incomes would have the opposite effects to those outlined above.

It is *disposable income* that is the major determinant of demand. Disposable income is the income remaining after direct taxation (e.g. income tax). Changes in demand, therefore, may be brought about by changes in direct taxation.

(b) Changes in Other Prices

If two commodities are fairly close substitutes (e.g. butter and margarine), a *change in the price* of one of them will lead to a *change in the demand* for the other. A rise in the price of butter will lead to an increase in the demand for margarine. An increase in the price (wages) of some types of labour may well lead to an increase in the demand for labour-saving machinery. Where two goods are jointly demanded – the use of one requiring the use of the other (e.g. cars and petrol) – then a fall in the price of one (cars) would lead to an increase in the demand for the other (petrol).

(c) Changes in Tastes and Fashions

The demand for some goods is very susceptible to changes in taste or fashion. Particularly affected are the clothing trades, but the industries producing furniture, foodstuffs, entertainment, and beverages are all subject to movements in taste and fashion. The changing public taste in entertainment has led to the closing down of thousands of cinemas in recent years. Changes in taste with regard to beverages and entertainment have brought about the opening of thousands of new coffee bars during the same period.

(d) Changes in the Distribution of Wealth

A person's ability to buy depends upon the level of his income and the extent of his wealth. The government, by their ability to levy taxation, can change the distribution of wealth by reducing the inequality of incomes and reducing the amounts which people may inherit.

Public expenditure in the form of pensions, national assistance grants, and other welfare payments can raise the purchasing power of the poorer sections of the community. In both cases the pattern of demand for various commodities will change. Heavy, progressive taxation will reduce the demand for Rolls Royces and luxury yachts, while higher pensions will raise the demand for foodstuffs, coal, electricity, and less expensive clothing and furniture.

(e) Changes in Population

The influence of this factor will be of a longer term nature, unless the change comes about by large-scale migration. Changes in the total population and changes in the age distribution will affect the demands for various goods and services (see Chapter 2).

ELASTICITY OF DEMAND

So much for the position of the demand curve. Another important aspect of demand concerns the effect of a change in price on the quantity demanded. When price changes, the quantity demanded usually changes, but what will be the extent of the change in quantity in relation to the change in price? Will a small change in price bring about a large change, a small change, or no change in the quantity demanded? The degree to which quantity demanded responds to a change in price is known as the *elasticity of demand*. If a small change in price causes a relatively large change in the quantity demanded, we say that demand is elastic. If the change in the quantity demanded is relatively small, then demand is said to be inelastic. It is important to note that we are concerned with *proportionate* changes in price and quantity, and not with *absolute* changes. Elasticity will, therefore, be different at each and every price, and it can only be meaningful when related to small changes in price. *Elasticity of demand is the relationship between proportionate changes in price and the resulting proportionate changes in quantity demanded.*

$$\text{Elasticity of Demand} = \frac{\% \text{ Change in Quantity Demanded}}{\% \text{ Change in Price}}$$

Where this ratio is *greater* than 1, demand is *elastic*
Where this ratio is *less* than 1, demand is *inelastic*
Where this ratio is *equal* to 1, demand has *unit elasticity.*

The easiest method of ascertaining whether or not demand is elastic is to examine the changes in Total Revenue. If a 5 per cent reduction in price leads to a 10 per cent increase in the quantity demanded, then demand is elastic. It should be apparent that such changes will increase total revenue. Examine the following demand schedule.

Price	Quantity demanded	Total revenue	Demand elasticity	
50p	100	5000p	$E > 1$	elastic
45p	120	5400p	$E > 1$	elastic
40p	140	5600p	$E = 1$	unity
35p	160	5600p	$E < 1$	
30p	180	5400p	$E < 1$	inelastic
25p	200	5000p	$E < 1$	
20p	240	4800p		

If demand is elastic, (a) an increase in price will cause total revenue to fall; (b) a fall in price will increase total revenue.
If demand is inelastic, (a) an increase in price will increase total revenue; (b) a fall in price will reduce total revenue.

If the elasticity of demand is unity, a change in price will not lead to any change in total revenue.

These relationships may be illustrated graphically. In Fig. 16a the area OP^1YQ^1 (total revenue) exceeds the area OPXQ, and illustrates a situation where demand, in this price range ($OP - OP^1$) is inelastic.

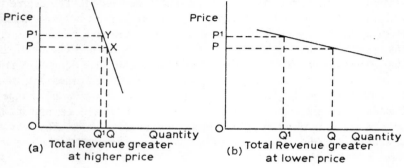

(a) Total Revenue greater at higher price

(b) Total Revenue greater at lower price

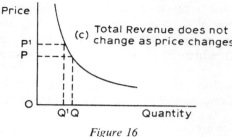

Figure 16

Figure 16b shows a situation where demand is elastic in the price range OP – OP[1]. Figure 16c illustrates the interesting case where the elasticity of demand is unity and total revenue will be the same at all prices.

Elasticity of demand must not be confused with the slope of the demand curve. Normally, elasticity will be different at every price. The exceptions to this are:

(1) Where the demand curve is a rectangular hyperbola (Figure 16c) – elasticity is unity at every price.

(2) Where the demand curve is perpendicular to the quantity axis – elasticity of demand is zero.

(3) Where the demand curve is perpendicular to the price axis – elasticity of demand is infinite.

What determines the degree of elasticity? The major influence is the availability of close substitutes for the product. *Where a close substitute is available in the relevant price range, demand will be elastic.* If the producer of such a commodity were to raise his price, consumers would turn to the substitute. The demand for cigarettes will be inelastic because there is no close substitute, but the demand for a particular brand of cigarettes will be elastic because there are a number of very effective substitutes in the relevant price range.

The proportion of a consumer's income which is spent on the commodity will be an important determinant of the elasticity of demand. Where this proportion is very small, demand will tend to be inelastic. Matches account for a very small part of our total spending, and a relatively large increase in their price would not have any great effect on the quantity demanded.

It is sometimes held that the demand for necessities is inelastic and the demand for luxuries elastic. The demand for necessities such as bread, potatoes, water, and clothing is certainly inelastic, but is this not another aspect of the availability of substitutes? There are no close substitutes for these articles in the relevant price ranges. The demand for luxuries will be elastic, it is argued, because if their prices rise we can manage without them. But the demands for motor cars, petrol, cigarettes and alcoholic drinks have proved to be extremely inelastic. These are hardly 'necessities' in the strict sense of the word. The use of words such as 'luxury' and 'necessity' raises many problems. In an economy where incomes are steadily rising, the luxuries of one generation become necessities for the next.

Some commodities are habit-forming – tobacco and alcohol are good examples – and the demand for such goods will tend to be inelastic.

EXCEPTIONAL DEMAND CURVES

All our demand curves have sloped downwards from left to right, obeying the general law which says that more is demanded at a lower price than at a higher price. There are, however, some unusual demand curves which do not obey this 'law', and which represent conditions where 'more will be demanded at a higher price'. This situation might well apply when a price has moved upwards, but people are convinced that the price of this commodity will rise still further.

Examples of this kind of behaviour are found on the Stock Exchange when the prices of stocks and shares are particularly unstable during periods of uncertainty in the business world. A further example of exceptional demand curves would be the case of ostentatious buying, where people buy more of the good, *because* its price is high, in order to display their wealth.

Probably the most important exceptions to the general law of demand are provided by the staple foodstuffs such as potatoes, bread, rice, and corn, in conditions where living standards are very low. Where income per head is very low and expenditure on such basic foodstuffs comprises the greater part of people's incomes, a rise in price may well lead to more being demanded. If the prices of other goods remained the same and consumers' incomes were unchanged, but they were obliged to buy the same quantity of bread or potatoes or rice as before, then less would remain to be spent on other commodities. Consumers may well prefer to spend more on the staple foodstuffs rather than buy much reduced quantities of other less essential goods.

Supply

The demand curve showed the relationships between prices and the quantities which consumers were prepared to buy. *The supply schedule and supply curve show the relationships between market prices and the amounts which producers are prepared to bring to the market.* Supply means the quantities supplied at given prices over some particular period of time. Thus, a complete statement on supply might read: 'At a market price of 5p, 1,000 units would be supplied each week.' Supply curves normally slope upwards from left to right, indicating that more is supplied

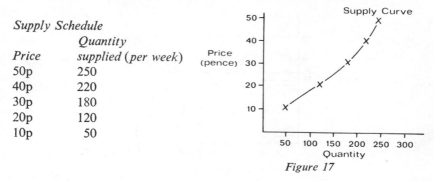

Supply Schedule

Price	Quantity supplied (*per week*)
50p	250
40p	220
30p	180
20p	120
10p	50

Figure 17

at the higher price. The basis of the demand curve was explained in terms of marginal utility. The basis of the supply curve lies in the costs of production. In considering how much of a commodity a firm is willing to supply, it is evident that its costs of production will be the vital determinant. We have already discussed the various types of costs in an earlier chapter; the most important types to be studied in relation to supply, are marginal cost and average cost. Marginal cost represents the cost of producing one more – the addition to total cost resulting from the expansion of output by one unit. The entrepreneur will continue to expand his output as long as the receipts from the sale of extra units exceed the cost of producing them. We assume that entrepreneurs always attempt to earn maximum profits. If further additions to output add more to revenue than they add to costs, then total profits must be increasing. *Maximum profits will be earned when production is expanded to the point where marginal cost is equal to marginal revenue.* Marginal revenue represents the change in total revenue which results from the sale of one more unit. *If price does not change as the number sold increases, then marginal revenue must be equal to the price.* In the earlier work on costs it was shown that marginal and average costs of the individual firm were assumed to behave as shown in the diagram Fig. 18.

OP, OP^1 and OP^2 are given prices, and OQ, OQ^1 and OQ^2 are the respective outputs which would result if the entrepreneur produced quantities which made Price = Marginal Cost. Since we are assuming that the price remains constant over the range of output, price will be equal to marginal revenue; each additional unit sold will add to the total revenue a sum of money which is equal to its price. We could, therefore, rephrase the above equation as follows:

Price = Marginal Revenue = Marginal Cost.

125

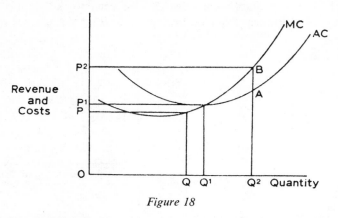

Figure 18

At a price of OP² we note that an output of OQ² is forthcoming. Why is output not greater? or smaller? At any level of production smaller than OQ² profits are not maximised, because additions to costs will be smaller than additions to revenue (M.C. is less than M.R.) and the entrepreneur would gain by expanding his output. At production levels greater than OQ² the additions to costs are greater than additions to revenue, and it would pay the businessman to reduce his output. Only at output OQ² would maximum profits be realised. Note that an output of OQ² is produced at an average cost per unit of Q²A, but each unit is sold at a price of Q²B (= OP²), hence profit per unit is equal to AB.

At a price of OP¹, maximum profits are obtained when production is at OQ¹. Again, the reason is that only at this output is Price (= M.R.) = Marginal Cost. In this particular case, price is also equal to average cost. Since revenue only just covers costs, is production worth while? The answer is 'Yes', because the economist includes what is known as *normal profits* in his average cost curve. Normal profit is defined as that level of profit which makes it just worth while for the firm to stay in its present line of business. Since this minimum level of profit is needed to keep the firm in production, it is legitimate to regard these profits as a cost of production. Thus, the profit per unit AB, which is earned when the price is OP² must be regarded as surplus or *abnormal profit*.

When the price per unit is OP, then price is equal to marginal cost when output is at OQ. At this level of production, however, price is below average cost. In such a situation production could only be carried on at a loss and we must assume that the firm would not, in the long run, produce at this price. Our rule for determining the output which gives maximum profit, i.e. MR = MC, still applies, but in this case 'maximum profits' must be read as 'minimum losses'.

If we now ask the question, 'What quantities would this firm supply at any given price?' the answer must lie in the marginal cost curve, but only that part of the marginal cost curve which lies above the average cost curve. If we choose any price above OP^1, then the quantity supplied at the chosen price is determined by the intersection of the price line and the marginal cost curve. Here we have the supply curve of the individual firm; it is that part of the marginal cost curve which lies above the average cost curve. The total (market) supply curve for the product will be obtained by adding the supply curves of the individual firms.

Existing firms will supply more if the market price increases (this is evident from the diagram above) and at higher market prices supply will also be increased by the entry of new firms. Higher prices will enable less efficient firms to enter the market. In the diagram Fig. 18 on page 126 a rise in price from OP to OP^1 would enable this particular firm to enter the market.

THE SHAPE OF THE SUPPLY CURVE

A change in price will bring about a change in the quantity supplied. *The relationship between the proportionate change in the quantity supplied and the proportionate change in price is known as the Elasticity of Supply.* The formula for the elasticity of supply is similar to that for the elasticity of demand.

$$\text{Elasticity of supply} = \frac{\%\ \text{change in quantity supplied}}{\%\ \text{change in price}}.$$

If this ratio is greater than 1 then supply is said to be *elastic*
If this ratio is less than 1 then supply is said to be *inelastic*
If this ratio is equal to 1 then supply is said to have *unit elasticity*

When the supply curve is perpendicular to the quantity axis, the elasticity of supply is zero
When the supply curve is perpendicular to the price axis, the elasticity of supply is infinite.

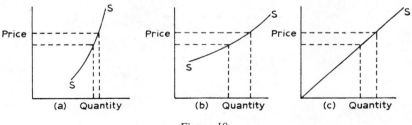

Figure 19

Diagram Fig. 19 (*a*) illustrates a situation where supply is inelastic – the

127

proportionate change in the quantity supplied is quite small relative to the proportionate change in the price. Diagram (*b*) illustrates a situation where the elasticity of supply is greater than 1. In diagram (*c*) we have the interesting case of supply having an elasticity of unity – the proportionate changes in price and quantity being equal.

The extent to which supply is elastic depends upon the flexibility of the productive resources. If production, with existing capacity, can be expanded easily and quickly in response to changes in demand, then supply will be elastic. An increase in the demand for many manufactured products could be met by employing more men, bringing into use stand-by equipment, and by working overtime. This would no doubt be true in the case of products such as footwear, hosiery and razor blades.

On the other hand, the supply of agricultural products must be fairly inelastic, because the quantity supplied in any one year is governed by acreage planted in the sowing season. Some natural raw materials and some foodstuffs have supply curves which are extremely inelastic; rubber trees take five to seven years to reach maturity, and a significant increase in the size of dairy and beef herds would take several years.

CHANGES IN SUPPLY

Elasticity is concerned with movements along the existing supply curve, but increases and decreases of supply are represented by movements of the whole supply curve. An increase in supply means that the whole supply curve has moved to the right. A reduction in supply is represented by a movement of the supply curve to the left.

An increase in supply means that more is now supplied at each and every price. The figure (20) demonstrates the effect of an increase in supply. A new supply curve S¹S¹ has replaced the original curve. At a price of OP producers are now supplying the larger quantity OQ¹. The same diagram may be used to demonstrate a reduction in supply.

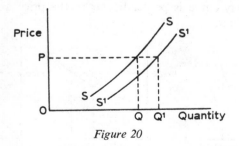

Figure 20

Causes of Changes in Supply
Weather. The output of agricultural products (and some other industries such as building) is seriously affected by variations in weather conditions.

An excellent growing season will produce a bumper crop; an unfavourable season will mean a poor harvest. Total output in agriculture is subject to variations from year to year which are independent of the acreage planted. *Technical progress.* Technical progress takes the form of more efficient machines, improved materials, better organisation, and superior techniques of production. Such changes mean a greater output per unit of input and they will move the supply curve to the right.

Changes in the prices of the factors of production. The supply curve, as we have seen, is based upon the costs of production. Any changes in the prices of the factors of production, therefore, will bring about a change in supply. In a labour intensive industry, an increase in wages, not matched by an increase in productivity, will move the supply curve to the left. A fall in the prices of raw materials would have the opposite effect.

Changes in the prices of other commodities. Changes in the prices of other goods will affect the supply of any given commodity whose price does not change. If the prices of other goods increase, the production of these things will become more profitable (if the price rise were due to an increase in demand) and resources would tend to move to the production of these higher-priced goods. Less of a commodity, whose price is unchanged, would now be produced.

Taxation. The imposition of indirect taxes will bring about changes in supply. As explained later on page 137, a tax on a commodity or service may be regarded as an increase in the costs of supplying that good or service.

Expansion of Capacity

Where the industry is growing, new firms will be coming in, and existing firms will be undertaking extensions of their existing capacity. This expansion of productive potential will give rise to economies of scale. The supply curve for the product of the industry will be moving to the right. When firms are closing down, or transferring their resources to other uses, then the supply curve will be moving to the left.

Changes in supply are brought about by changes in the scale of production, or by the introduction of new methods and techniques of production. In each case the changes will mean that the costs of production have altered. An increase in scale, or an improvement in methods will mean a lowering of costs and new cost curves become applicable.

The diagram (Fig. 21) is intended to show the effects of a firm expanding and modernising its production facilities. In the original situation, its average and marginal costs of production are represented by the curves AC and MC. Its modernisation programme results in greater efficiency and a lowering of its cost curves. The new cost conditions are represented by the curves AC¹ and MC¹. Its supply curves are the heavier-lined sections of the marginal cost curves. Note that the result of the increased efficiency is the movement of the supply curve to the right.

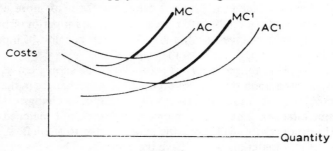

Figure 21

CETERIS PARIBUS

The elementary supply and demand theory used in this chapter makes use of *ceteris paribus* arguments. In other words, whenever we examine the effects of some change in one of the determinants of supply and demand we make an assumption that '*other things remain equal*'. The use of this particular technique enables us to isolate the effects of changing *one* element in supply and demand relationships. The phrase 'other things remaining equal' should precede the statements we make about the effects of changes in supply, or demand, or price. So far then we have established two important economic 'laws'.

(i)   *Other things remaining equal, more of a commodity or service will be demanded at a lower price than at a higher price.*

(ii) *Other things remaining equal, more of a commodity or service will be supplied at a higher price than at a lower price.*

The reader must be aware of the limitations of this procedure, because, in the real world, other things do not remain equal. It is true that lower prices will cause demand to extend *if* there are no changes in income, taste and fashion, and the prices of other goods. It is true that higher prices will cause more to be supplied *if* there are no changes in the prices of the factors of production, the techniques of production, and the prices of other goods.

The effects of changes in these other determinants of supply and demand are discussed in the next section.

Interaction of Demand and Supply

We are now familiar with some of the more important aspects of demand and supply, the two market forces which determine prices. For each commodity and service there is a demand schedule and a supply schedule.

If the two are brought together, the quantity demanded and the quantity supplied will be found to be equal at one, and only one price. This is the *equilibrium price.*

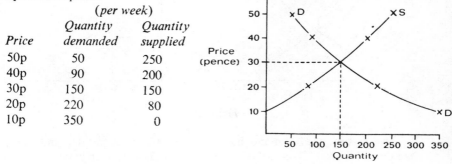

	(*per week*)	
Price	*Quantity demanded*	*Quantity supplied*
50p	50	250
40p	90	200
30p	150	150
20p	220	80
10p	350	0

Figure 22

The equilibrium price is given by the intersection of the demand and supply curves. In this example, the equilibrium price is 30p, for only at this price are the quantities demanded and supplied equal; the amount brought to the market by willing sellers, is exactly balanced by the amounts taken off by the market by willing buyers. This balancing or equating of demand and supply at the market price can be seen in the diagram (Figure 22). At prices higher than the market price (e.g. 40p) the quantity supplied exceeds the quantity demanded, and this excess supply will mean that sellers will be obliged to lower prices in order to dispose of their output; a situation sometimes referred to as *a buyers' market*. At lower prices (e.g. 20p) the quantity demanded will exceed the quantity supplied and competition between buyers will force up the price giving rise to conditions known as *a seller's market*. Only at a price of 30p are there no forces at work which are tending to change the price.

EFFECTS OF CHANGES IN DEMAND AND SUPPLY

Changes in price are brought about by changes in demand and/or changes in supply.

Other things being equal, an increase in demand will raise the price and increase the quantity supplied.

Other things being equal, a decrease in demand will lower the price and reduce the quantity supplied.

These statements are economic laws. They are generalisations based on studies of human behaviour and since they indicate what happens in the very great majority of cases they are normally identified as 'laws'. The diagrams (Fig. 23) show the effects of changes in demand, and may be used to illustrate either an increase or a decrease in demand.

131

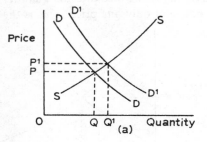 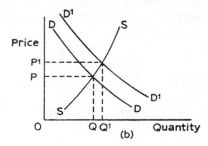

Figure 23

If we assume that demand has increased and that the demand curve has moved from DD to D¹D¹, then the effect has been to raise the price from OP to OP¹ and to increase the quantity supplied from OQ to OQ¹. The extent to which price and quantity are affected depends upon the elasticity of supply. In Fig. 23 (*b*) supply is relatively inelastic and the change in demand has led to a large proportionate increase in price but only a small proportionate increase in the quantity supplied. In Fig. 23 (*a*) the supply curve is relatively elastic in the price range OP – OP¹, and the change in demand has caused a proportionate change in price less than the proportionate change in quantity supplied. Diagram (*b*) would be a fairly realistic interpretation of the situation in the markets for many agricultural products, whereas diagram (*a*) would be appropriate to the markets for many manufactured goods. The reader should use the diagrams to reason out, for himself, the consequences of a fall in demand.

An increase in supply, other things being equal, will lower the price and increase the quantity demanded.

A fall in supply, other things being equal, will raise the price and reduce the quantity demanded.

The above statements are two more fundamental laws of supply **and** demand, the operation of which is illustrated below.

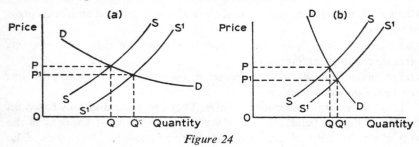

Figure 24

In this example we assume that supply has increased and the supply curve has moved from SS to S^1S^1. The change in supply has caused price to fall from OP to OP^1 and the quantity demanded has increased from OQ to OQ^1. The extent of these changes in price and quantity is dependent upon the elasticity of demand. In Fig. 24 (a) where demand, in the price range $OP-OP^1$, is relatively elastic, the proportionate change in the quantity demanded is greater than the proportionate change in price. Figure 24 (b) illustrates a situation where an increase in supply has a proportionately greater influence on price than on quantity. A decrease in the costs of production of margarine would be an example of the changes shown in diagram (a), and diagram (b) shows what might be the consequence of reduced costs of production for commodities such as petrol.

THE INFLUENCE OF TIME

Changes in demand can be very significant even over the short period, especially where they are due to changes in taste and fashion, or where they are due to the introduction of a new product. Changes in supply normally take a much longer time to take effect. Time plays a very important part in determining the degree to which price is affected by changes in demand and supply. It is useful to distinguish three time periods in demand and supply analysis.

1. *The Momentary Period* (or the very short-term period)

This is defined as the period of time during which supply is restricted to the quantities actually available in the market. Supply is fixed for the momentary period, and the supply curve will be a straight line parallel to the Y axis. Normally this period will be very short; in the case of perishable goods such as fish, fruit, and vegetables, it will be one day. In local markets, the supply for the day is the quantity delivered in the early morning.

2. *The Short Period*

The short period is the interval which must elapse before more can be supplied with the existing capacity. More fish can be supplied by the trawlermen fishing longer hours or fishing farther afield. More fruit can be supplied by speeding up the harvesting, or by using up existing stocks more quickly. More houses can be built by working overtime and speeding up procedures. The short period in some industries (e.g. manufacturing) may be only a matter of days, but in others it may be many months (e.g. housebuilding).

3. *The Long Period*

This is the time interval which is long enough for fundamental changes to take place in the structure of the industry. Existing firms may expand (or contract) their capacity; they may adopt new methods and instal more efficient machines. New firms may enter (or existing firms may leave) the industry. The fishing industry may expand by bringing new boats into use; the production of fruit may be increased by the planting of more trees, and the building industry may take on more workers and increase its stock of capital equipment. The long period may be a matter of months in the case of manufacturing industry, or several years in the case of fruit-growing where trees have to reach maturity. The changes described here involve a series of shifts in the short period supply curves. These movements give rise to the long period supply curve.

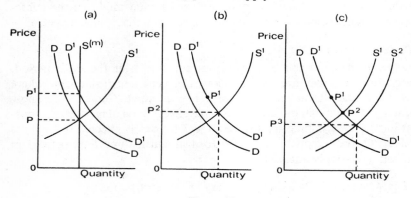

Figure 25

Figures 25 (*a*), (*b*), and (*c*) illustrate the short- and long-run effects of a change in demand. S^1 is the existing short run supply curve, and $S^{(m)}$ illustrates the fixed supply available in the very short or momentary period. When demand increases to D^1D^1, the immediate effect is to raise the price from OP to OP^1. Price rises by the full extent of the shift in demand since supply is perfectly inelastic. In Figure 25 (*b*) we have the situation after sufficient time has elapsed for some adjustments to be made to output using the existing resources of the industry. The quantity supplied has increased and this is represented by a movement along the short period supply curve S^1. In the short run the price will be OP^2, somewhat lower than the price in the momentary period. This higher price, if sustained, will lead to changes in the productive capacity of the industry. Existing firms will be encouraged to expand their capacity and new firms may enter the industry. The new supply conditions are represented by an entirely new short run supply curve S^2 (Fig. 25c), and price falls from OP^2 to OP^3, as the quantity supplied increases. Price OP^3 may be higher or lower than the original price OP depending upon the extent of the economies of scale derived from the increase in the productive capacity.

DEMAND AND SUPPLY – RELATIONSHIPS AND APPLICATIONS

Joint Demand

Some commodities are jointly demanded; they are complementary in the sense that the use of one implies the use of the other. The demand for petrol is associated with the demand for motor cars; the demand for tennis balls is linked to the demand for tennis racquets. An increase (or decrease) in the demand for one of these goods will be accompanied by an increase (or decrease) in the demand for the other. An increase in the demand for tea might well cause an increase in the price of sugar. The reader should trace out the developments implied in the last sentence.

Competitive Demand

The demand for margarine varies inversely as the demand for butter. Where two commodities are associated in this manner, they are said to be in competitive demand. An increase in the demand for one will cause a fall in the demand for the other. An increase in the demand for butter

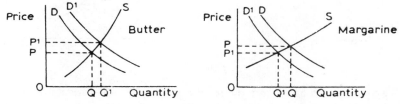

Figure 26

will cause an increase in its price and an extension of the supply. A consequence of the increased demand for butter will be a fall in the demand for margarine leading to a fall in its price and a reduction in the quantity supplied. The reader should be able to show the effects of an increase *in the supply* of butter, *on the price of margarine.*

Composite Demand

Commodities are said to be in composite demand when they are required for several different uses. The demand for such goods is the aggregate of the demands of the various users. Wool will be demanded by the textile industry, carpet manufacturers, blanket manufacturers, hosiery manufacturers and many others. An increase in the demand for any one use, say clothing, will raise the price of wool and affect the prices of all other commodities made from wool. Another good illustration of a commodity for which the demand is a composite of many separate demands would be nylon.

Joint Supply

An interesting relationship, and one which gives rise to a number of economic problems, is that of joint supply. The production of coal gas entails the production of coke. The production of petrol leads to the production of benzine and fuel oil. We cannot produce beef unless we also produce hides. Where the production of one commodity necessarily leads to the production of another, then the commodities are in joint supply. One very important, but not so obvious, example of this relationship, is to be found in the transport industry. Haulage contractors, bus companies and the railways cannot, normally, supply an outward journey without also supplying an inward journey. This gives rise to the obvious and costly problem of 'empty running'. Where commodities are in joint supply, an increase in the demand for one of them will cause a fall in the price of the other.

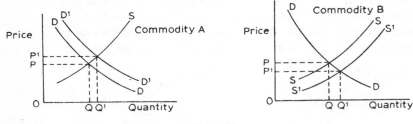

Figure 27

Two commodities A and B are jointly supplied. The demand for A increases, causing the price to increase from OP to OP¹, and the quantity supplied to increase from OQ to OQ¹. But *this increase in the quantity supplied of A, means an increase in the supply of commodity B.* The price of commodity B will fall from OP to OP¹ and the quantity demanded will increase from OQ to OQ¹.

Price Fixing

It sometimes happens that prices are not allowed to find their level through the free working of the forces of supply and demand. In wartime, when many necessities are in short supply, and the 'market' price would put them out of the reach of the poorer classes, the Government determines a statutory price which is often well below the price which would obtain in a free market. In peacetime, too, we have examples of price fixing, the most important illustration being that of rent control. Supply and demand diagrams make clear the consequences of price fixing. The figure (28) below shows the price fixed at OP, well below the price which would obtain in a free market (OP¹). At the controlled price, the quantity demanded (OQ) exceeds the quantity supplied (OQ¹). If no further action were taken, this would lead to firstcomers satisfying their wants, leaving nothing for the less fortunate latecomers. It would mean queues forming outside the shops as soon as information was received that supplies had arrived, and, in the case of some goods, it might mean that shopkeepers would introduce waiting lists. Since price control is normally imposed on the basic necessities of life, it is usually accompanied by some system of rationing. During and after the last war, goods were rationed by means of coupons which entitled the owners to specific quantities of those goods which were subject to price control.

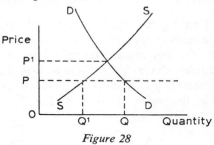

Figure 28

Taxes on Commodities

When a tax, such as purchase tax, is imposed on a commodity, it has the same economic effect as an increase in the costs of production; the whole supply curve moves upwards and to the left. The cost of bringing the good to market is now increased by the amount of the tax being levied. Such taxes are normally levied at the wholesale stage. The effect of the tax becomes clear when we examine the supply schedule, both before and after the imposition of the tax (5p per unit). The first column shows the prices; the second column shows the quantities supplied at these prices before the imposition of the tax. The third column shows the quantities supplied after the tax has been imposed. The fourth column shows the quantities demanded. The imposition of the tax changes the supply situation completely. A market price of 50p now represents a *supply price* of 45p. Producers selling goods in the market at a price of 50p only receive 45p, and, at this supply price, they are only prepared to offer 775 units per week.

	BEFORE TAX	AFTER TAX (5p per unit)	
Price	*Quantity supplied (units per week)*	*Quantity supplied*	*Quantity demanded*
50p	825	775	475
45p	775	735	520
40p	735	675	545
35p	675	625	580
30p	625	560	625

137

Price	BEFORE TAX Quantity supplied (units per week)	AFTER TAX (5p per unit) Quantity supplied	Quantity demanded
25p	560	480	670
20p	480	365	720
15p	365		775

When the market price is 45p, the producers will only supply 735 units per week, because a market price of 45p represents a return to the producer of only 40p, the government taking 5p in taxation. When the details in the schedules above are converted into graphical form, the levying of the tax is seen as a movement of the supply curve, which moves vertically upwards by the amount of the tax. (Fig. 29.)

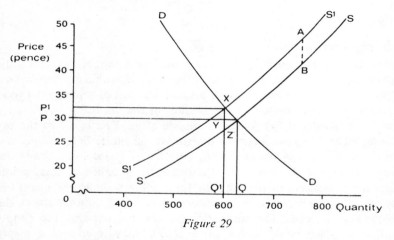

Figure 29

The supply curve has moved (SS to S¹S¹) by the extent of the tax (AB=5p). This can be checked by looking back at the supply schedule. Producers will now require a higher market price in order to bring forward any given quantity of the commodity.

Let us examine the influence of the tax on the market price. Price has risen from OP to OP¹, and quantity supplied has fallen from OQ to OQ¹. But the price has not risen by the full extent of the tax. The tax is equal to the amount XZ, but the price has risen by the amount XY. The burden of the tax has been shared, the consumer bearing the amount XY (=the increase in price), and the producer is obliged to bear the amount YZ. Although the price is now OP¹ (=XQ¹), the producer only receives ZQ¹, while the government takes XZ in taxation.

Figures 30 (a), (b) and (c) show the effects of the tax under differing

138

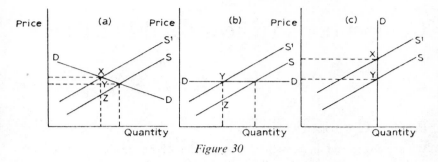

Figure 30

demand conditions. In Fig. 30 (*a*) the demand is elastic and the producer has to suffer a fall in price greater than the price increase borne by the consumer (YZ > XY). In Fig. 30 (*b*) demand is perfectly elastic and the whole burden of the tax is borne by the producers who experience a fall in price equal to the amount of the tax (YZ). Figure 30 (*c*) illustrates the situation where the consumer must experience a price increase equal to the full amount of taxation (XY). In this latter example demand is perfectly inelastic and the producer is able to pass on to the consumer the full effects of the tax.

But the elasticity of supply also plays its part in deciding how the tax burden is distributed. It would be an instructive exercise if the reader now used supply and demand diagrams to show that the more inelastic the supply curve, the greater is the proportion of the tax borne by the producers.

The distribution of the tax burden between consumer and producer is determined by the relationship between the elasticity of supply and the elasticity of demand. If demand is more inelastic than supply, then the consumer bears the greater share.

Subsidies

Subsidies may be regarded as negative taxes. A subsidy normally takes the form of a payment by the Government to the producers. The normal procedure is to make the payment a specific one, hence, on agricultural products, it takes the form of 'so many pence per ton'. In the case of housing subsidies it will be a payment of '*x* pence per week' in respect of a house qualifying for the subsidy. Producers now receive a payment greater than the market price. The supply curve moves downwards by the amount of the subsidy. There is a fall in the price and an increase in the quantity demanded.

Chapter 13

Competition in Theory and Practice

Perfect Competition

We are concerned here with the operation of an unplanned economy, where the basic decisions on the uses which a society makes of its economic resources, and the way in which its wealth is distributed, are taken by the individual citizens, each deciding for himself how he shall earn and spend his income. In such a society, it is the movements of prices which help to shape the courses of action taken by producers and consumers. In a planned society the basic economic decisions are taken by some central authority acting on behalf of the citizens. But in the real world there is no such thing as a completely planned or completely unplanned society. There is no economy where *all* decisions are taken by the central authority just as there is no country where the government does not take some part in deciding the course of economic affairs. The unplanned society is often referred to as a capitalist society, a free enterprise system, or simply a competitive system.

In the last chapter it was pointed out that prices were determined by the forces of supply and demand operating in the markets for goods and services, markets being some kind of arrangement whereby buyers and sellers were brought into effective contact. We have a picture of buyers competing with one another in demanding the product, and sellers competing with one another in supplying the product. We must now turn to the subject of competition and try to understand its importance in the operation of the economic system.

Economists have a model, or concept, known as Perfect Competition. Although the conditions necessary for a state of perfect competition are not to be found in the real world, the notion is nevertheless a very useful tool of economic analysis.

The economist tries to construct an 'ideal' competitive system and to find the conditions which are necessary for the operation of such an ideal system. He then compares and contrasts this ideal with the real world. The real world is much too complicated to be understood all at once. It is necessary to examine one feature at a time, and the model of perfect competition will prove a great aid in this kind of analysis. Perfect competition will obtain only when certain conditions are satisfied. They are:

1. All units of the commodity must be homogeneous (i.e. one unit exactly like another). If this is so, then buyers will be completely indifferent as to the seller they approach, and sellers will be indifferent as to the buyer to whom they sell.

2. There must be many buyers and many sellers, so that the behaviour of any one seller, or any one buyer, will have no influence on the market price. Each buyer comprises such a small part of the total demand for the commodity, and each seller such a small part of the total supply that any change in their plans will have no influence in the market place.

3. There must be perfect knowledge in the market. All buyers and sellers must be fully aware of market conditions. Buyers are fully informed as to the strength of the demand from other buyers and of the intentions of the sellers. Sellers are fully informed as to the intentions of buyers and they know exactly what other sellers are doing.

4. There must be perfect mobility of factors of production, and of consumers. Everyone will try to maximise his returns. Customers will switch from one shop to another, workers will move from one employer to another, and entrepreneurs from one industry to another, if by doing so they could increase their returns or satisfaction.

When a state of perfect competition exists, it means that one price, and only one price, for the commodity will be established; perfect knowledge ensures that buyers will not pay different prices. Perfect mobility ensures that consumers and factors of production will move to equalise any price differentials which may arise. Homogeneity of product ensures that preferences will not arise which might be converted into price differences.

All of this means that an equilibrium price will be established which is due entirely to forces of supply and demand which cannot be influenced by individual buyers or sellers, and there will be no associations of buyers or sellers which might, by their actions, affect the market conditions.

The Individual Firm under Perfect Competition

Under conditions of perfect competition the individual firm supplies but a tiny fraction of the total supply. It is powerless to exert any influence on the price of the commodity, and it sees the market price as 'given', that is, a price established by forces beyond its control. It sees itself as selling in a market where there is an externally determined market price. The demand curve for the products of such a firm must therefore be a horizontal line, or, more precisely, the demand curve is perfectly elastic. No matter how many units the firm sells it cannot change the price. It can sell its entire output at the ruling market price. If it tries to sell at any higher price, there will be no demand for its products, and there is no incentive to sell at any lower price. The market price for the product will be determined by the total demand and supply curves, which will be of the normal shape, but the demand curve for the products of the individual firm will be a horizontal line, drawn at the ruling market price.

If the demand for the output of the firm is perfectly elastic, how is the output of the firm determined? Remember that *the most profitable output is always that output where Marginal Revenue = Marginal Cost.* Where the demand curve is horizontal, Average Revenue = Marginal Revenue. The most profitable output must, therefore, occur where the demand curve (AR = MR) cuts the Marginal Cost Curve. The demand curve is in fact the price line or average revenue curve. Under perfect competition the individual firm will be earning maximum profits when it produces that output where AR = MR = MC.

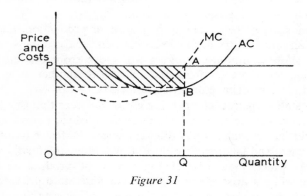

Figure 31

At a market price of OP, the firm will produce an output of OQ. Figure 31 shows the firm producing at a price which exceeds average cost, and making abnormal profits equal to the shaded area. Price is equal to QA, while average cost per unit equals QB. Abnormal profit per unit must be equal to AB and total abnormal profits will be AB × AP. But if there is perfect mobility of the factors of production, this state of affairs cannot persist, because the abnormal profit will attract new firms to the industry. Total supply will increase causing the price to fall until only normal profit is being earned, as in Fig. 32.

Price has now fallen due to the increased market supply, and the firm is making normal profits, producing the output OQ. At this output the firm is producing at its minimum average cost, at the point where the marginal cost curve intersects the average cost curve. Under perfect competition the individual firm is in equilibrium, earning normal profits, when

$$AR = MR = AC = MC$$

If we assume that all factors of production are equally efficient, and there

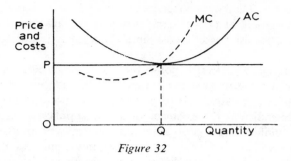

Figure 32

is perfect mobility of factors, then all firms will have identical cost curves and the industry will be in equilibrium when *all firms* are in the position shown in Fig. 32, that is, *earning normal profits*, and producing the optimum output. It is more realistic to assume that factors of production will not be homogeneous, and certainly entrepreneurial efficiency is likely to vary as between firms. This will mean that the cost curves of the more efficient firms will be lower than those of the less efficient. If this is so, then at any given price the more efficient firms will be earning abnormal profits (as in Fig. 31). Equilibrium of the industry will now obtain when the least efficient, or *marginal firm is just making normal profits* (as in Fig. 32).

Perfect competition is not to be found in the real world, although it is possible to point to some markets where there is some rough approximation to this 'ideal'. There are hundreds of thousands of wheat producers scattered all over the world and no one of them is large enough to influence the world market price of wheat. The world markets for a number of agricultural products do contain many of the features of a perfect market. There are many producers and many buyers; modern methods of communication make knowledge of market conditions almost perfect, and the grading of commodities means that the products in any one grade can be considered as homogeneous. Another, often quoted, example of a market which bears some resemblance to the model of a perfect market is the Stock Exchange, the market in stocks and shares.

Monopoly

The classical economists, Adam Smith, David Ricardo and John Stuart Mill, wrote of, and analysed, the working of a competitive system. Later economists, during the course of the nineteenth century, developed from these earlier views the 'ideal' system of perfect competition. Whereas the earlier economists, like Smith, described and commented on what they observed, many economists since that time have tended to be more interested in theoretical perfection than in the actual developments of the capitalist system. They were concerned to show how an economic system based on the model of perfect competition would always mean (1) production at the lowest possible cost, and, (2) consumer satisfaction at its maximum.

The only exception to perfect competition which seemed to merit serious attention during the nineteenth century was the concept of monopoly, which is, in fact, the antithesis of perfect competition. Monopoly in the market place indicates the existence of a sole supplier. It may take the form of one unified business organisation, or it may be an association of separate firms which combine, or act together, in the business of marketing their products. In either case the market is dominated by one seller. A monopolist has the power to determine either

(*a*) *the price at which he will market his product*, or

(*b*) *the quantity he is prepared to sell.*

He cannot determine both, because he cannot control the demand. If he decided on the price at which he is prepared to sell, then the demand curve will determine the quantity sold at this price. If he is determined to market a given quantity per month, then the demand curve will decide the price at which this quantity can be disposed of.

The monopolist's power to influence price depends upon two factors,

1. *the availability of close substitutes*

2. *the power to restrict the entry of new firms.*

If there are a number of reasonably close substitutes available, the prices of which compare favourably with the price of the monopolist's product, then he will not be able to vary his prices upwards to any significant extent, and his monopoly power will not be very great. Monopoly power has been defined as the ability to earn long run surplus profits without attracting competition. If, in some way, the entry of new firms is restricted, then the monopolist's power is increased. The more effective the restrictions on the emergence of new competitors, and the fewer the close substitutes for his product, the greater will be the power of the monopolist to exploit the consumer by raising his prices.

Since the monopolist is the sole supplier of the commodity, the demand curve for his product is also the market demand curve. This is a very different state of affairs from that which obtains under perfect competition where the individual firm's demand curve is a horizontal line, representing an infinitesimal fraction of the total demand curve.

We assume that the monopolist will always attempt to earn maximum profits. Can we say how the most profitable output will be determined? Earlier, we showed that maximum profits are gained when output is at the point where Marginal Cost = Marginal Revenue. This is true of all forms of markets, but there is one very important difference between the monopoly situation and the situation facing the firm operating under perfect competition. The monopolist's demand curve slopes downwards (it is the total demand curve); to sell more he must cut his price. When the demand curve slopes downwards from left to right, *marginal revenue is no longer equal to price*. The sale of one more unit now adds to the total revenue something less than the price at which it is sold. An examination of the table below will make the relationship between price and marginal revenue quite clear.

Price (p)	Quantity demanded per week	Total revenue (p)	Marginal revenue (p)
40	1	40	40
35	2	70	30
30	3	90	20
25	4	100	10
20	5	100	0
15	6	90	−10
10	7	70	−20

Column 4 shows the additions to total revenue brought about by the sale of one more unit. When the price is reduced from 40p to 35p the number of units sold increases from 1 to 2 and total revenue rises by 30p. The extra unit has been sold for 35p but revenue has not increased by this amount, because price has been cut in order to sell the extra unit. The net gain in revenue is equal to the extra 35p from the sale of the additional unit less the loss of 5p due to the reduction in price on the first unit. If the demand curve slopes downwards then marginal revenue will always be less than price, and the demand curve and marginal revenue curve will take the forms shown in Fig. 33.

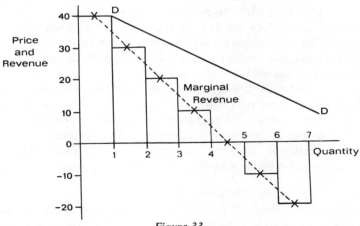

Figure 33

If we combine demand and marginal revenue curves with the conventional cost curves we have the following diagram. (Fig. 34.)

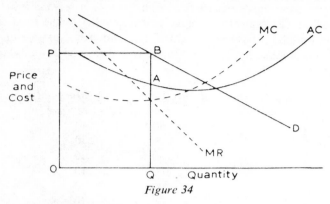

Figure 34

These are the points to note.

1. The most profitable output (OQ), is determined where MC = MR.
2. The price at which this output can be sold (OP) is determined by the demand curve.
3. When output is equal to OQ, the average cost per unit is QA.
4. Since each unit is sold for QB (= OP), the abnormal profit per unit is AB.
5. Total surplus profits are equal to the surplus profit per unit multiplied by the number of units sold (i.e. PB × AB).

Economic theory seems to indicate that output under monopoly will be restricted to less than what it would be under perfect competition. Output is restricted in order to earn maximum profits, and this is achieved when prices are higher than they would be under perfect competition. There are, in fact, three main features which distinguish the monopolist from the producer operating under competitive conditions.

1. The monopolist does not have to take the price as given – he can fix the price of his product (as an alternative to fixing output).
2. The demand curve for his product is less than perfectly elastic.
3. His marginal revenue is less than price.

It is possible to identify certain *causal factors* in connection with the development of monopoly situations. Remember that the essence of monopoly is the ability to 'restrict entry'. Effective monopoly power must, therefore, depend upon some measures which debar potential competitors from that particular industry. These *restrictions on entry* which make monopoly power possible may arise in a number of ways.

(a) Concentration of raw materials

The geographical distribution of natural resources is very uneven, and the known deposits of some materials are concentrated into very small regions.

Most of the world's nickel is obtained from a certain area in the Rockies. A very large proportion of the total supply of gold and diamonds comes from the Union of South Africa. Until the development of artificial fertilisers, Chile had a virtual monopoly of the world supply of nitrates. Where the known deposits of materials are highly concentrated in a given geographical area, there is a great incentive for producers to form a monopoly, in order to control the market, by manipulating the supply. Of a rather similar nature is the monopoly position acquired by certain regions in the supply of products such as wine or whisky. The climatic and soil features of some areas have enabled them to produce wines or spirits or beers with characteristic flavours and qualities. Hence we have Champagne, Burgundy, Moselle and many other drinks whose names are associated with the places where they are produced.

(b) Technical Barriers

In modern capitalist states there are a number of industries which are now dominated by a few giant firms. This is especially true of the science-based industries where firms have been able to reap very great technical economies of scale. Tyre manufacture, oil processing, chemicals, and the motor car industry may be cited as typical examples. Where the existing firms are already operating on a vast scale, and making use of expensive indivisible units of capital, the entry of new firms is almost impossible. There is very little prospect of any new entrant starting in a small way and then growing larger by increasing his share of the market. The small producer could not compete with the existing large firms because his average cost of production would be so very much greater. Only by commencing operations on a scale comparable to that employed by existing firms would a new entrant be able to compete effectively. Firms already operating are in a protected position, and this is always an inducement to form a monopoly.

(c) Legal Barriers

Probably the most formidable restraints on the entry of new firms are legal barriers, where the law of the land operates to prevent the emergence of competing firms. This particular form of restriction has a long history. The great overseas trading companies formed in the late fifteenth and early sixteenth centuries were granted monopoly trading rights in specified geographical areas. These rights were granted by the Crown in the form of Royal Charters. The Hudson's Bay Company and the East India Company are two of the more famous of these trading companies which were granted the sole right to trade in given areas. Much later, public utility companies, formed by Act of Parliament to provide water, gas and electricity, were granted local monopoly powers, but were subject to some degree of public regulation.

More recently, we have the examples of the nationalised industries where the controlling boards have complete control over the supply of the goods and services produced by these industries. The National Coal Board, for example, has a complete monopoly of the production and wholesaleing of coal in the United Kingdom. The granting of patent rights is a further example of competition being limited by law. The firm holding the patent rights is protected from the threat of competition from new firms (or existing firms) making identical products, at least for the period of time which is the life of the patent, usually 16 years.

(d) Transport Costs and Tariffs

Although two or more firms may be making identical products and operating at similar costs, it is possible for one or more of the firms to enjoy local monopolies. Firm A will be able to sell more cheaply, in its own locality, than Firm B, if Firm B is producing in a location which is some distance removed from the local market of Firm A. Firm A will thus be able to raise its price in its local market by the amount of the transport costs which Firm B would incur, should it try to sell in Firm A's local market.

Tariffs operate to protect a home market against the competition of foreign firms. They have the same economic effect as transport costs, for they raise the price in the home market above the foreign producer's costs of production. Tariffs tend to facilitate the formation of monopolies in the home market, for the home producers can raise their market prices by the extent of any differential between their own costs of production and the artificially high price of the foreign good.

(e) Competition

It may seem paradoxical that competition should be instanced as an example of a factor which might give rise to monopoly. The existence of unrestricted competition, or 'cut-throat' competition as it is often termed, might well lead to a monopoly situation. Where entrepreneurs and factors of production are not homogeneous, the more efficient firms will eliminate the less efficient, and capture their shares of the market. The logical end to such a sequence of events is the emergence of one dominating firm – the most efficient firm. It was, indeed, this pattern of events which led to the anti-monopoly legislation in the United States towards the end of the nineteenth century.

DISCRIMINATING MONOPOLY

One of the criticisms of monopoly is based upon the fact that a monopolist is able to discriminate in his pricing policy – he can charge different prices in different markets for the same product. Three basic conditions are necessary for such a policy to be effective.

(i) In order to charge different prices the seller must be able to control the supply.

(ii) The seller must be able to prevent those paying lower prices reselling the goods to those being charged higher prices.

(iii) The demand conditions in the separate markets must be different so that total profits may be increased by charging different prices. (It is really a matter of equating MC and MR in each market, but the proof of this point is not appropriate to this text.)

The monopolist, then, can practise profitable price discrimination if the markets can be effectively separated, and we have plenty of evidence from our everyday experience to show that these conditions can be met. Markets may be separated by a time barrier. Most passenger transport undertakings charge cheaper rates for off-peak journeys. A seat on the 09.40 train to London cannot be 're-sold' to someone wishing to travel at 08.00. Electricity and telephone charges are varied according to the time at which they are consumed. Again this is a service which cannot be transferred from the cheaper to the dearer market.

Markets may be separated by transport costs and tariffs. This is evidenced by the practice of dumping, where exports are sold at much cheaper prices than those charged on the home market. The price difference, of course, cannot exceed the costs of transport plus any tariff on imports.

A third type of price discrimination is based upon differences in the type of demand. Before the National Health Service was established doctors commonly charged lower fees to poorer patients than to their wealthier clients. Milk is sold more cheaply to industrial users. Electricity charges are also varied according to the type of consumer.

Price discrimination means that some groups pay more than others, and whether we think it is an 'unfair' practice depends upon whether we think there will be a net gain or a net loss. It is possible for price discrimination to be beneficial. Where it leads to a great expansion of output and a significant fall in average costs of production, even those in the higher-priced market may be obtaining the goods at prices lower than would be charged in a single market (e.g. export markets may lead to economies of scale which benefit home consumers although the home price may be higher than the export price).

FEATURES OF MONOPOLY

Economic theory, as we have seen, indicates that, under monopoly, prices would be higher and output lower than they would be under perfect competition. Restricting output in order to raise prices means that the

149

firm is operating at less than the optimum output and will have some excess capacity. This may be regarded as a waste of economic resources. At lower prices more would be demanded and more would be produced – at prices which would still cover average costs.

It is also argued that since the monopolist is not operating under competitive conditions he will not be so efficient as the producer who is constantly under pressure from competing firms. The monopolist does not have the same incentive to improve his products and methods of production as does the firm in a competitive market. Since he can restrict the entry of new firms the monopolist is not under a continuous threat from rivals who are seeking to produce something better than their competitors.

The fact that a monopolist is earning profits does not necessarily indicate that the firm is efficient. A monopolist can use his market power to raise prices in order to cover costs. The competitive firm has to get its average costs below a market price which it cannot determine itself.

On the other hand, it is often pointed out that much of the 'waste' of competitive advertising is eliminated when there is one supplier. Competition may lead to an excessive variety of product which prevents the achievement of the economies of scale which are possible when products are standardised. There is no doubt that, in certain circumstances (e.g. motor-car and electrical components) greater standardisation has made possible great economies in production. Monopoly would tend to encourage such standardisation.

In some industries it is undoubtedly the case that monopoly is the most efficient type of organisation. This is true of the public utilities supplying gas, electricity, water, and telephone services. In such industries fixed costs form a very great proportion of total costs and competition would mean a wasteful duplication of fixed capital. A number of competing firms would each have similar fixed costs but only a fraction of the total output over which to spread these fixed costs. Average costs would be much higher in a competitive situation than in a monopoly.

It may be the case that the size of the total market is just sufficient to support one firm of optimum size (e.g. making individual components for cars, shoes, or television sets). In this case several competing firms would each have higher costs per unit than the single firm.

A monopoly may provide greater stability. Since it is supplying the entire market, it will be much more aware of market trends than any one individual firm competing with many other firms. The single supplier will be able to adjust supply to changes in demand more effectively and monopoly price is likely to be more stable than a competitive price. Since it is a larger firm, a monopoly is more likely to weather a trade recession than a smaller competitive firm.

150

Competition and Modern Capitalism

Perfect competition is not to be found in the real world, and absolute monopoly is, likewise, almost impossible to achieve, for it implies a firm operating in the total absence of competition. No competition whatsoever would require the absence of substitutes. This is unrealistic, because all goods are competitive in the sense that they compete for our limited incomes. A more realistic definition of monopoly would be 'a sole supplier of a commodity for which there is no very good substitute'. The effectiveness of the substitutes limits the extent of the monopolist's power, and modern capitalism is characterised by a large number of 'limited' monopolies.

MONOPOLISTIC COMPETITION (*Imperfect Competition*)

These terms are used to describe the market situations found in modern capitalist states, the basic features being a large number of firms selling differentiated products. The commodities produced by any one industry are not homogeneous; the technique of *branding* differentiates the product of any one firm from the products of other firms in the same industry. The individual firm has a monopoly of its own product, but it faces keen competition from firms making very similar products, and it does not have the power to restrict the entry of new firms. Product differentiation, made possible by the technique of branding, is further emphasised by the practice of *competitive advertising*, perhaps the most striking feature of monopolistic competition. Advertising is employed to heighten, in the consumer's mind, the differences between Brand X and Brand Y. It is important to realise that we are concerned with the differentiation of goods in the economic sense and not in the technical sense. Two branded products may be almost identical in their technical features or chemical composition, but if advertising and other selling practices have created different images in the consumer's mind, then these products are different, from our point of view, because the consumer will be prepared to pay different prices for them.

Although each producer is a monopolist, and the demand curve for his product will slope downwards, the availability of close substitutes will mean that the demand for his product will be elastic. His ability to exploit, by charging high prices, will be further limited by the constant threat of new firms coming into the industry. Competition may well be so keen that only normal profits are being earned.

OLIGOPOLY

Some industries, as noted earlier, have come to be dominated by a small number of very large firms. Where great economies of scale are possible, the process of fierce competition, or, more likely nowadays, amalgama-

F

tion and merger, have served to eliminate many rival producers, leaving a small number of large firms producing branded products. This means market conditions where the individual firm can, by its own actions, affect the level of prices. Each firm supplies a significant proportion of the total market. If one firm cuts its prices, then its rivals are obliged to follow suit, or they will lose much of their business to the price-cutter. If one firm cuts its price then it seems inevitable that a price war will ensue, leaving all the firms worse off. If, under oligopoly, one firm considers raising its prices then it must take account of the likely reaction of its rivals – will they follow suit or not? The degree of uncertainty in this type of competition, coupled with the constant danger of price warfare, usually leads to some kind of price agreement between the oligopolists. Once the firms agree not to compete on the basis of price, often by accepting the price leadership of some dominant firm, then competition shifts to other forms, competitive advertising, elaborate packaging, after-sales service, special offers and the like.

The real world presents us with a picture of imperfect markets. Commodities are not homogeneous; they are differentiated by advertising and branding. In some markets there are not many sellers, but, rather, conditions of near monopoly and oligopoly. In other markets we find there are a few very large buyers. The Post Office Corporation is virtually the only major buyer of certain types of telephone equipment; the Electricity Generating Boards are the only buyers of certain types of cables and generating plant, and, to an increasing extent, the great chain stores and supermarkets are attaining powerful positions as the major buyers of consumer goods. Large and powerful sellers are now being faced by large and powerful buyers. This is also true of the labour market where strong trade unions occupy near-monopoly positions as suppliers of labour.

The immobility of factors of production and of consumers is another serious imperfection in the markets of the real world. This immobility is sometimes due to lack of knowledge (we do not know *all* the relevant facts about sellers, commodities and prices), and sometimes due to inertia (we cannot be bothered to find out all the possible alternatives before we make our purchases).

Advertising might be said to have made markets more perfect in the sense that it increases the knowledge of buyers and sellers. As against this, it increases the imperfections of a market by differentiating the products.

Chapter 14

Monopoly and Public Policy

Monopolistic Elements in British Industry

There appears to be a general presumption that monopoly, oligopoly, and imperfect competition are against the public interest, and that public policy should be directed towards removing restrictions on competition. Certainly, the economist's case against monopoly has helped to mould a hostile public opinion. But monopoly is also seen as a restriction on personal freedom, the freedom of an individual to enter a trade and carry on a business. Much of the opposition to monopoly has a political basis. Many people think it wrong that major sectors of our economy should be controlled by a few powerful private interests, and they would like to see, where great size is necessary to efficiency, the monopoly converted from private ownership to public ownership.

For centuries the common law, in Britain, has held that 'agreements in restraint of trade' are against the public interest, but the courts have tended, in this century at least, to interpret this law very leniently. Only since the last war has Britain seen legislation specifically designed to deal with the restriction of competition in the business world.

Before proceeding to study the problems of controlling monopoly it is necessary to examine briefly the extent and effectiveness of monopoly power in Britain. We are now using the word 'monopoly', in a much more general sense, to mean 'the power to restrict competition' or 'the ability to restrict entry'. What kinds of monopoly do we have in Britain today? There are very few absolute monopolies outside the nationalised industries, but there are several examples of fully unified near-monopolies, where one firm or business unit exercises a dominant influence in an industry. Pilkingtons hold a dominating position in the flat-glass industry, Wallpaper Manufacturers Ltd. in the supply of wallpaper, Associated Portland Cement in the cement industry and Imperial Tobacco in the manufacture of cigarettes. The position of such firms is dominant in relation to the home supply of the commodities but they may face keen competition from imported products.

More common is the oligopolistic position where two or three firms share the greater part of the market. Several recent studies have revealed a high degree of concentration in some important British industries (see page 72).

Monopolistic elements were mentioned in a number of official reports published between the wars and in the years following the Second World War. The elements referred to generally take the form of *restrictive trade practices* employed by the existing firms to reduce (or eliminate) the degree of competition in the industry. A report by the Monopolies Commission in 1955 indicated that restrictive trade practices were a common feature in the business world. There are many such practices; only a few are explained below.

EXCLUSIVE DEALING AND COLLECTIVE BOYCOTT

Producers agree to supply only recognised dealers, normally only one dealer in each area, on condition that the dealer does not stock the products of any producer outside the group. Should the dealer break this agreement, all members of the group agree to withhold supplies from the offender. This practice has proved a very effective restriction on competition, for it means that any new firms would find it very difficult to secure market outlets.

PRICE AND OUTPUT AGREEMENTS

The most common restrictive practice is the agreement on prices. Member firms fix common prices and agree not to compete on the basis of price. The agreed price (or prices) is normally well above the average costs of the more efficient firms, and it is often held at this higher level by a complementary agreement to limit output; member firms accepting agreed output quotas.

CARTELS

In its most developed form a cartel comprises a selling syndicate, formed by a group of firms, through which the products of the member firms are marketed. The syndicate, or selling agency, pays the producers a fixed price for their outputs and markets the products as a single seller. Profits are distributed to member firms in proportion to outputs.

COLLUSIVE TENDERING

There are many commodities which are not produced 'in anticipation of demand', but are made 'to order'. The buyers announce their requirements by publishing a specification, and producers are invited to tender for the contract to supply. This is the normal procedure in the building industry, the civil engineering industry, the shipbuilding industry, and in the heavy sectors of the engineering industry. The preparation of a tender, for a large building, the building of a bridge or a ship, or for the erection of a large industrial plant, can be a very expensive operation. There is much survey-ing, estimating and costing involved. Since only one firm can succeed in getting the contract, the unsuccessful bidders incur heavy non-recoverable expenses. In some industries producers have combined to eliminate competition between themselves by means of schemes which ensure that the available contracts are shared out between the co-operating firms. This may be done by the various firms agreeing not to submit lower tender prices than the firm which is entitled to the next contract.

RESALE PRICE MAINTENANCE

This is the practice, extremely common until the recent (1964) legislation, whereby the manufacturer fixes the price of his product at each stage of distribution. Although the goods are being distributed by independent wholesalers and retailers, they are obliged to charge prices which are laid down by the manufacturer. Hence the profit margins at the retail stage are determined by the manufacturer. These fixed margins may be enforced collectively or individually. Collective resale price maintenance applies when a group of manufacturers agree to withhold supplies from any distributor who sells an article below the agreed resale price. Individual resale price maintenance applies where the individual manufacturer is left to enforce the agreed price by the threat of withholding supplies from any dealer infringing the agreement. Manufacturers believe that resale price maintenance is advantageous because prices are fixed and known (since they can be included in the advertisements). This leads to stable markets. They also maintain that shoppers prefer the system because they do not have the inconvenience and trouble of 'shopping around' for the cheapest buy. On the other hand, the practice has undoubtedly led to the mainten-ance of an excessive number of small retail outlets. Manufacturers, anxious to preserve the maximum number of market outlets for their products, have fixed retail prices at levels which give satisfactory profits to the less efficient retailers.

The Control of Monopoly

There are some restraints on the abuse of monopoly power which are the result of natural developments rather than the consequence of legislation. A monopolist will hesitate to practice extreme exploitation of consumers because such a policy can only lead to an intensified search for a substitute. The ability of modern technology to provide a continual multiplication of new products and new materials is a constant threat to the monopolist. The increasing publicity and attention given to the subject of monopoly means that the monopolist must constantly take into account the effects of his actions on public opinion. With the possibility of investigation by the

Monopolies Commission an ever-present factor, and frequent calls for nationalisation being made by some political bodies, the monopolist is not likely to take undue advantage of his position.

Although, in the past, Acts of Parliament gave the State certain controls over monopolies in industries such as railway transport and electricity (when these were privately owned), the first general legislation on this subject came with the *1948 Monopolies and Restrictive Practices Act*. In the U.S.A., the Sherman Act of 1890 and the Clayton Act of 1914 declared monopolies to be illegal, but British legislation did not take this line. Although it was felt that monopolies were injurious to the economic development of the country, it was recognised that there might be circumstances where monopoly organisation could be justified, and the procedure adopted was to investigate and treat each case on its merits.

The Act of 1948 established a *Monopolies Commission*, the function of which is to investigate and report. The Commission receives its instructions from the Secretary of State for Trade and Industry, who directs the Commission to inquire into the workings of sectors of the economy where monopoly elements are thought to prevail. It is the duty of the Commission to prepare a report on their findings, and to say whether they consider the practices investigated are against the public interest, and what action they think is appropriate. For the purposes of the Act, a monopoly situation is defined as one where one third or more of a class of goods is supplied in the United Kingdom by one 'person', or group of persons, acting in such a way as to restrict competition. But the Commission was also given power to investigate the general effects of monopolistic practices as well as the situation in given industries.

Although the Commission was given legal powers to call for any evidence they required, it has no executive power to enforce its recommendations. Any action subsequent to its report is left to the Department of Trade and Industry, which is given authority to make orders declaring any agreements or arrangements to be illegal. The great problem in implementing public policy in this matter is that of defining 'the public interest'. The Act attempted to give some guidance, but only in very broad terms. It said that it was in the public interest to stimulate the efficient and full utilisation of resources; to encourage new enterprise and innovation and to provide goods of such types and in such quantities and at such prices as will best meet the requirements of home and overseas markets. The reports of the Commission are very detailed and give a first-class, authoritative account of the economic structure of those industries which have been the subject of investigation (some twenty-four up to the present time). The reports have shown that restrictive practices, price arrangements, and general restraints on competition were very prevalent in British industry and commerce.

The ministerial order, making practices illegal, was very rarely used, but, in most cases, the industries concerned gave assurances to the Board of Trade (now the Department of Trade and Industry) that practices condemned by the Commission would be abandoned or modified. The main criticism of the Commission was that it worked very slowly, and in 1965 the government enlarged the Commission from ten to twenty-five members so that it could do its work in small groups, investigating a number of industries simultaneously. But the general feeling that progress was too slow persisted, and as a result of the Commission's report in 1955 on the widespread nature of collective discrimination, further legislation followed. The basic features of *collective discrimination* are:

1. There is a list of buyers and sellers who are members of a restricted trade association.

2. Members of the association give each other special terms which are not granted to outsiders.

3. In some cases, no sales on any terms may be made to outsiders.

The Commission strongly condemned such practices; the majority thought they should be banned, with exceptions only in special cases. The minority agreed that they were, in general, against the public interest, but thought such agreements should be registered and investigated individually. *The 1956 Restrictive Trade Practices Act* which followed this report was something of a compromise. It accepted the investigation proposal, but declared that restrictive trade practices were, *prima facie*, against the public interest and the defending party had to prove that they were not.

The 1956 Act established a *Registrar of Restrictive Trade Practices* whose duty it is to maintain a register of such agreements and to submit them to the *Restrictive Practices Court* for consideration. The Court is a judicial body composed of High Court judges and laymen. It has the responsibility of conducting an inquiry into the effects of restrictive practices and pronouncing whether or not the practice is against the public interest. The judgment of this court is binding on all the parties.

Over 2,500 practices have been registered and in the first two years after the Court started work at least a third had been abandoned or replaced by agreements which were within the law. The firms or trade associations which choose to defend their agreements must select a form of defence which is laid down in the Act. There are seven such grounds for defence, generally referred to as 'the seven "gateways"'.[1] The defendants must, in addition, show that any gain from the operation of the practice is not outweighed by any damage to persons not party to the agreement. For

---

[1] See Appendix to this chapter (p. 161)

example, in the case of the Lancashire Yarn Spinners, the defendants proved, to the satisfaction of the court, that the abandonment of their practice would lead to increased unemployment in South Lancashire. They succeeded in getting through one of the gateways. But they did not satisfy the court on the second requirement. The court decided that the nigher prices which were the result of the restrictive practice did more damage to the public interest than the gain which was obtained by a section of the cotton trade.

The number of cases heard by the Court has not been very great, but each contested case has been of great significance. By carefully selecting the particular restrictive agreements to be judged by the Court, the Registrar has been able to make each case a test case for a large number of similar agreements. If a particular case is lost, it is very likely that a large number of similar agreements will be voluntarily abandoned. Only those agreements which seem to have a reasonable chance of meeting the necessary criteria laid down by the Act will be defended. Of the first thirty-four cases contested eleven were successful in obtaining the approval of the Court. This may seem a high proportion, but the Registrar pointed out that it meant that less than 1 per cent of the *registered* agreements had been found consistent with the public interest.

The Court has tended to be severe in upholding the general principle that restriction of competition is against the public interest. It has generally taken the view that agreements which restrict the entry of new firms are unfair and harmful since they create rigidities in the structure of industry and provide a brake on the pace of innovation. But in several cases the Court has upheld existing arrangements where price and output agreements have been shown to provide positive benefits. For example, a common price agreement between manufacturers of metal windows was approved because the producers demonstrated that the freedom from price competition had encouraged the firms to co-operate in increasing efficiency and in reducing the variety of windows produced.

The effects of its judgments have varied. In some cases the breaking of the agreements has led to keen price competition, but in other cases the registrable agreements seem to have been replaced by 'information' or 'open-price' agreements. These are agreements where firms exchange information, mainly about prices. They involve no restrictions and were not registrable under the 1956 Act, but they could be used as a means of avoiding price competition. It has been suggested that the breaking of effective restrictive agreements has tended to encourage mergers. Firms having become accustomed to working closely together in matters of price fixing may be reluctant to indulge in fierce competition when their agreements are abandoned. They may choose the alternative of amalgamation.

A second part of the 1956 Act declared collective resale price mainten-ance to be illegal, but made individual resale price maintenance legally enforceable. The individual manufacturer could now prosecute any dealer who broke his resale price maintenance agreement.

A third section dealt with the future of the Monopolies Commission. The Commission was reduced to its former size of ten members and its role was restricted to the investigation of single firm monopolies, and to the control of restrictive agreements which are specifically concerned with foreign trade.

In the years following the 1956 Act the Government had second thoughts about resale price maintenance, and legislation in 1964 declared this practice to be contrary to the public interest. *The Resale Prices Act 1964* prohibited resale price maintenance with provision for suppliers to claim exemption for their products. Claims for exemption had to be registered with the Registrar of Restrictive Trading Agreements. The law became effective on 30 April 1965, but firms which had claimed exemption were allowed to continue price maintenance until the Restrictive Practices Court had decided their case. The Act laid down 'five "gateways"'[1] which might be used as justification for resale price maintenance. The Act follows the 1956 legislation with the presumption that the practice is harmful and the onus of proof is on the suppliers. By February 1965 about 500 classes of goods had been registered for exemption.

It was noteworthy that no applications for exemption were received from important industries such as motor-cars and accessories, paints and wallpaper, and sports goods. Some of the larger firms had abandoned R.P.M. even before its legal prohibition. In view of these developments, the Registrar anticipated, correctly as it happened, that very few cases would be contested. The great majority of R.P.M. agreements have been voluntarily abandoned; only two industries, confectionery and footwear took their cases to Court and both lost. In the cases of only two com-modities, books and proprietary medicines, have the R.P.M. agreements been upheld.

The effects of the abolition of R.P.M. has not been, as was anticipated, to drive hordes of small shopkeepers out of business. Price cutting has appeared, most noticeably in the grocery trade, and severe price competition became a feature of the retail trade in wines and spirits and electrical goods. But in the cases of some consumer goods (furniture, watches, clocks, stationery and toys) there has been very little change.

In 1965 the Government introduced further legislation in the form of the *Monopolies and Mergers Act*. This legislation gives the Monopolies Com-mission power to enquire into the supply of services – the previous

[1] See Appendix to this chapter.

legislation had been restricted to the supply of goods. Where there has been an adverse report by the Monopolies Commission, the Department of Trade and Industry is given power to require the publication of price lists and to control prices. The Act empowers the Department to refer to the Commission a merger within six months of its completion, or any proposed merger, where it would lead to, or strengthen a monopoly, or where the value of the assets taken over would exceed £5 million. The Department may, if necessary, prohibit or dissolve the merger. There are special provisions for the control of newspaper mergers.

To enable the Monopolies Commission to carry this extra load, its membership was increased to twenty-five. After the Act was passed a large number of mergers were considered by the then Board of Trade, but very few of these were referred to the Commission (only nine out of the first 170). The cases in which the Monopolies Commission declared a proposed merger to be against the public interest attracted a great deal of attention and, in some cases, charges of inconsistency. The union of the National Provincial and Westminster banks was approved while the proposed merger between Barclays and the Midland was not supported. The refusal to allow the mergers between Montague Burton and United Drapery Stores, and between Rank and De La Rue also attracted criticism on the grounds that the reasons given were not fully convincing and the fact that mergers creating much more formidable monopolies (e.g. G.E.C./A.E.I./English Electric) had been allowed without any reference to the Commission).

But it must be pointed out that British legislation is not so much anti-monopoly as an attempt to eliminate the disadvantages of monopoly. Monopoly will be approved and may well be encouraged where it can be shown to be in the public interest. It was not necessarily inconsistent therefore for the I.R.C. to be actively encouraging mergers whilst at the same time the Commission was vetoing mergers. The refusal of a merger, however, is a rather negative approach which may result in the loss of an opportunity to carry out some more efficient regrouping of the various parts of the firm concerned.

There was some change in the economic climate in the later 1950s and in the 1960s. The presumption that monopoly is against the public interest is not so strongly held as it was. The increasing competition in world and home markets as the barriers to trade come down, has led to a greater realisation that, in many industries, a very large firm may be better able to withstand foreign competition both at home and abroad. Some amendments were made to the existing legislation by *The Restrictive Practices Act 1968*. One major change gives the Department for Trade and Industry the authority to exempt from registration certain restrictive agreements where such exemption would promote an important industrial or commercial project. It had been discovered that certain desirable investment projects were being inhibited by the 1956 Act. In some industries the economic size of new plant is extremely large and very costly. Firms are reluctant to undertake such large-scale investment without some assurance that competition will be restricted. A good illustration of this point was provided by Shell's decision (early in 1970) to undertake massive invest-ment in new petro-chemical plant. Basic chemical plants have grown to such a size that it is simply not possible for every producer in Britain to invest in them without flooding the market. Shell's decision was made possible because its principal competitors I.C.I. and B.P. agreed to integrate their own investment plans so as not to compete directly with this project. Such agreements were made possible by the 1968 Act.

A further modification introduced by the 1968 legislation gives the Department of Trade and Industry power to order the registration of information agreements. Such agreements are no⁺ automatically registrable – they only become so when the Department f Trade and Industry chooses to make an order to that effect. The 196 Act also introduced a further gateway into the 1956 Act (see below).

In 1970 the Government announced that it intended to abolish the I.R.C. At the same time it created a super-ministry, the Department of Trade and Industry, by merging the Ministry of Technology and the Board of Trade. Administration of the policies on monopolies and restrictive practices was transferred to the new ministry from the former Department of Employment and Productivity.

APPENDICES

The Restrictive Trade Practices Act 1956

The Seven 'Gateways'[1]

The respondents must show that the agreement confers benefits in one or more of the following ways.

1. By protecting the public against injury in connection with the installa-tion, use, or consumption of goods;

2. By making available other specific and substantial benefits to the public;

3. By counteracting restrictive measures taken by any one person who is not a party to the agreement;

4. By permitting the negotiation of fair terms for the purchase or sale of goods with buyers or sellers who represent a preponderant part of the trade;

---

[1] The 1968 Act introduced an eighth 'gateway'. Any restriction may be held by the Court not to be contrary to the public interest so long as it does not restrict or discourage competition to any material degree.

5. By preventing the occurrence of serious and persistent unemployment in an area heavily dependent upon the particular trade;

6. In maintaining the volume or earnings of the export trade in the commodity where this is substantial in relation to the export trade of the United Kingdom as a whole, or in relation to the whole business of the particular trade;

7. In maintaining some other restriction which the Court holds to be justified on its own merits.

The Resale Prices Act 1964

The Five 'Gateways'

Exemptions to be granted if, *through the ending of price maintenance*, the public suffered detriment by reason of:

1. Substantial reduction in the variety or quality of goods,
2. Substantial deterioration in after-sales service,
3. Substantial loss of retail outlets,
4. Goods being sold under conditions likely to cause danger to health and safety by misuse,
5. The possibility that retail prices might rise in the long term.

The Fair Trading Act 1973

In 1973 the government carried out a major reorganisation of the administrative machinery for keeping competition policy under review. The Fair Trading Act introduced new measures for dealing with consumer protection, monopolies and mergers, and restrictive practices.

i. A powerful new official, *The Director-General of Fair Trading*, is given wide powers to implement government policy on trade practices, and to protect the consumer against malpractices. He will take the lead in making references to the re-named Monopolies and Mergers Commission; take on the function of the Registrar of Restrictive Trade Agreements; and he may refer consumers' complaints to a new body—the Consumer Protection Advisory Committee. The Director-General may obtain a court order against firms who persistently indulge in conduct detrimental to consumers.

ii. The Monopolies and Mergers Commission are given powers to investigate the nationalized industries. Local as well as national monopolies may now be subject to scrutiny. The qualifying marker share for a monopoly reference is reduced from one third to one quarter.

Chapter 15

The National Income

Up to this point most of the subject matter which we have discussed has been concerned with various aspects of production. The factors of production, the laws of production, the types of business organisation, the location and finance of industry, and prices are all important facets of the problem of producing wealth. It is time, now, to examine the product of economic activity – the aggregate of all the goods and services produced by the various agents of production. Our problem is to find some means of totalling the bewildering variety of goods and services produced. The only possible solution is to use money as our measuring rod, and to total the money values of these goods and services. This is not an ideal solution, as we shall see later. The next question is one of time. The output of goods and services is a continuous process so that any measurement of the volume of output must be restricted to some interval of time. It is normal to take one year as the accounting period.

Gross National Product and Net National Product

If we aggregate the money values of all the goods and services produced during a period of one year, we shall have a total which is known as the *Gross National Product*. This total will include all the consumption goods, all the capital goods, and all the services produced during the period. We must include services, for we are concerned here with *production*, and this is defined as any economic activity which *satisfies a want*, and for which people are prepared to pay a price. The Gross National Product includes all the capital goods produced, an item which is defined as Gross Investment. Some part of the output of capital, does not, however, represent any net addition to the nation's stock of capital equipment, but is required to replace worn out and obsolete equipment. That part of the output which is required for this purpose is known as depreciation.

Thus   Gross Investment – Depreciation = Net Investment
                                         (additions to capital stock)
and   Gross National Product – Depreciation = Net National Product.

Net National Product consists, therefore, of all the goods and services available for consumption, together with the net additions to our stock of capital goods. This total is generally known as the *National Income* of the country concerned.

The National Income may be looked at in three different ways.

1. *The Output Method*

The National Income is the money value of goods and services becoming available to the nation from economic activity.

2. *The Income Method*

The National Income is the total value of the incomes received by the agents of production as payments for their services in producing the national product.

3. *The Expenditure Method*

The National Income is the total expenditure on goods and services during the given period of time.

Whichever method is used in estimating the national income, the same total will result. The three different definitions given above, are nothing more than three different ways of measuring the same thing – i.e., *a flow of income over time.*

The value of any economic good is exactly equal to the total of the incomes generated in its production. All the expenses of production consist of wages, rent, interest, and profits. Wages are paid for the services of labour, rent for the use of land, interest for the use of capital, and profits are the return to the entrepreneur for bearing risks. We can regard prices as 'bundles of incomes'. This statement may be verified by tracing the various stages of production of some commodity, say, bread. The prices paid to the retailer for bread become income to the retailer, and comprise his profits, the wages paid to his employees, rent for his shop, interest on his capital and the payments he must make for his materials. The latter item will consist of baked bread purchased from the bakery. The retailer's payments to the baker can be broken down in exactly the same way, as can the baker's payments to the miller, and the miller's payments to the farmer.

Figure 35 illustrates these relationships. It can be seen that the finished product of one stage of production forms the raw material for the succeeding stage, and the sum of the heights of the shaded areas is exactly equal to the money value of the loaf of bread. This is a highly simplified example, for we have only gone back to the farmer, and assumed that the whole process of producing bread starts there. In fact there are several more stages, but the basic principle outlined above remains true.

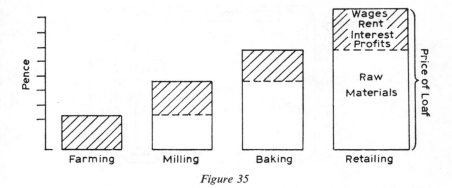

Figure 35

(At the initial stages of production – extraction – the whole value of the output consists of income payments to factors of production.)

Hence *National Income = National Output*

The expenditure method of computing the National Income relies on another very simple economic truth, namely, that the expenditure of one person becomes the income of another. When I purchase a textbook, my spending becomes income to the bookseller. When the bookseller buys petrol his expenditure becomes income to the garage proprietor. Incomes from production are only earned because someone has purchased the goods and services produced. Unless there is expenditure on these commodities, no income will be received. In any given time period, the total of factor incomes may not equal the value of the goods and services sold. There will be some additions to stocks and a certain amount of work in progress for which incomes have been paid but which have not been sold to final buyers. In such cases we assume that the firm itself has 'bought' the goods. For purposes of the national income accounts the expenditure on such items is an imputed expenditure.

Measuring the National Income

There are a number of serious difficulties to be faced in measuring the National Income by each of these three methods. We shall examine each method in turn, but before doing so, it might be useful to study the following diagram which helps the understanding of the National Income as a *flow* of goods and services not as a stock of goods and services. The National Income is the total flow along the upper 'pipe' during a period of one year.

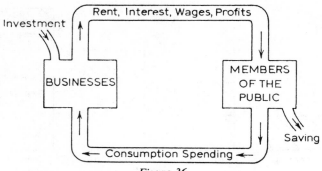

Figure 36

THE INCOME METHOD

The obvious starting point is to find the total of all personal incomes, the great majority of which are obtainable from the returns made by taxpayers to the Inland Revenue. A complete coverage of all personal incomes, however, is not possible, and some estimate must be made of those incomes not officially recorded. But all personal incomes are not included in the National Income. We are only concerned with those incomes earned in productive activity. A large group of incomes which must be excluded are known as Transfer Payments, and comprise, in the main, those incomes received from the State in the form of Old Age Pensions, Unemployment Pay, National Assistance Payments, Sickness Benefits and so on. The test to apply in deciding whether an income is, or is not, included in the National Income, is to ask: 'Is this income a payment for services rendered by a person (or by his property)?' Only payments for services rendered must be taken into account. A further problem arises in respect of the taxation levied on incomes. The relevant figure is the gross income (i.e. the income before tax), because this is the factor payment which is included in the value of the commodity or service produced.

Some of the income generated in production is not received by persons and the sum of personal incomes would leave us with a total less than the true National Income. Part of the profits earned by companies is not distributed to shareholders, but is retained by the company. This is true of the surpluses earned by public enterprises. Public authorities also receive considerable income from property in the form of interest and rents. Since this income is not received by individuals, it will not appear in the total of personal incomes. Figure 37 illustrates the income method of computing the National Income.

The final total is the National Income 'at factor cost', and represents the sum total of all the incomes received as payments for the production of goods and services. It is equal to the value of the goods and services produced, less depreciation.

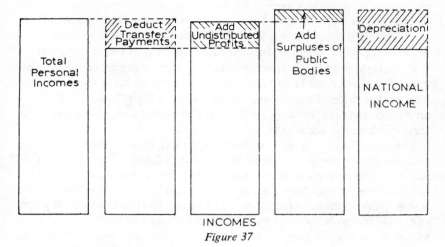

INCOMES

Figure 37

THE OUTPUT METHOD

The major problem, here, is that of 'Double Counting'. If we sum the values of the total outputs of all enterprises, both public and private, the final total will greatly exceed the true National Income. The total we require is the value of the output of 'final' goods and services, plus any net increase in the stocks held by producers. Reverting to the example used earlier, bread is the *final* good; wheat, flour, and baked dough are all 'intermediate' goods. The value of the loaves of bread includes the value of the wheat output of the farmer, plus the value of the miller's output, plus the value of the baker's output. If we added the values of the outputs of all these separate stages we should be guilty of double counting. There are two methods of deriving the National Income by the output method, (*a*) by using the value of final goods, plus additions to stocks, and (*b*) by summing the 'values added' at each stage of production.

	Value of output	Goods bought out	Value added
Farmers	10	0	10
Millers	15	10	5
Bakers	25	15	10
Retailers	30	25	5
			30

Note that the sum of all the values added at each stage of production is exactly equal to the value of the final goods.

We must also take account of the 'output of property' owned abroad which leads to income in the form of dividends and interest. British owned property abroad creates income for its owners in this country, and foreign owned property in Britain leads to interest and profit payments to foreigners. It is usual to set one payment against the other and include the net amount in the National Income (this may be positive or negative).

If the total production is being valued at market prices, certain adjustments have to be made to take account of indirect taxes and subsidies. The market price of many goods is greater than their 'factor cost' by the amount of the taxation they bear, while some goods are sold at less than their factor cost, because they are subsidised.

The statisticians engaged in the compilation of the National Income can only take account of 'market transactions', that is, they can only deal with the output which is bought and sold at some recorded price. But there is much production which does not have a market price, and for which it is impossible to make any satisfactory estimate. The most obvious example of this difficulty, is the work of housewives whose enormous contribution to economic welfare goes unrecorded in the National Income. The food grown in the domestic garden, and the 'do-it-yourself' repair and construction work, are further examples of unrecorded output. The output method is illustrated in Fig. 38.

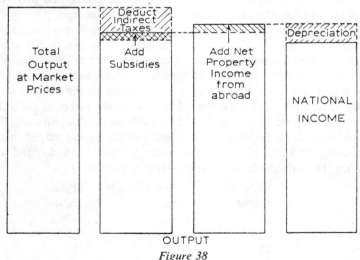

OUTPUT

Figure 38

THE EXPENDITURE METHOD

The whole of the national output must be bought for use, or added to stocks, and in attempting to measure the National Income by this method, the total which we must try to obtain is the total expenditure on final goods plus any increase in the value of stocks held by producers and merchants. Government expenditure forms an important part of total expenditure, but only what the government spends on goods and services is relevant here. Government expenditure on pensions and other transfer payments must be excluded. There must be adjustments for indirect taxes and subsidies, and account must be taken of foreign trade. Expenditure on exports must be included since much spending generates income at home, but the value of imports must be deducted from total expenditure since this spending does not create factor incomes at home.

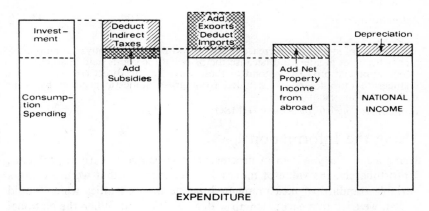

Figure 39

Table 14. *The National Income – United Kingdom – 1972* (£ million)

The expenditure aspect	£	The income aspect	£
Consumers' expenditure	39,263	Income from employment	37,138
Public authorities' consumption	11,702	Income from self-employment	4,764
Gross fixed investment	11,214	Gross trading profits of companies	6,584
Value of physical increase in stocks[1]	−440	Gross trading surpluses of public corporations	1,612
Total domestic expenditure at market prices	61,739	Gross trading surpluses of other public enterprises	178
Exports and property income from abroad	16,694	Rent	4,182
less Imports and property income paid abroad	−16,347	*Total Domestic Income*	54,458
less Taxes on expenditure	−9,279	*less* Stock appreciation[1]	−1,319
		Residual error	345

Subsidies	1,133		

Gross Domestic Product at factor cost	53,484
Net property income from abroad	456

Gross National Product at factor cost	53,940	Gross National Product	53,940
less Capital Consumption	− 5,824	*less* Capital Consumption	− 5,824
National Income	48,116	*National Income*	48,116

[1] The value of stocks can increase in two ways: because the physical amount of stocks becomes greater, and because the prices of the goods held in stock go up (stock appreciation). The second of these ways has no direct connection with changes in output, and is excluded from gross domestic product by being deducted from incomes.

Source: *National Income Book* (HMSO)

Using the Information

Using a monetary system of measurement gives rise to certain problems. Unfortunately, the value of money itself changes so that we are using a variable standard of measurement. Imagine the difficulties which would arise if we tried to measure length with an elastic yard. When the National Income of one year is compared with that of another year, account must be taken of any changes which have occurred in the value of money. The normal practice is to use an index number of prices (explained in Chapter 22), which provides a measurement of changes in the general price level. A simple example will help to make clear the manner in which the National Income of one year may be compared with that of another.

	Year 1	Year 2
National Income (£s million)	10,000	12,000
Index of prices	100	105

National Income of Year 2, expressed in terms of the prices ruling in

$$\text{Year 1} = \frac{12,000}{1} \times \frac{100}{105} = £11,428 \cdot 57 \text{ million.}$$

This type of calculation enables us to compare movements in the *real* National Income. In the example above, we see that National Income in monetary terms had increased by 20 per cent, but in real terms the increase was only about 14·3 per cent.

The measurement of the National Income by official sources was first carried out in 1941, and the information is now published annually in the *National Income Blue Book*. National Income statistics are presented in

170

great detail and are important for several purposes.

1. Since income is a flow of wealth, movements in the National Income give some indication of economic welfare. The total figure, however, can be misleading, since account must be taken of the changes in the value of money, and of changes in the total population. Income per head is the indicator which is generally used for this purpose. It is also necessary to take note of the nature of the output, since a large increase in the National Income may be due to a large increase in the output of capital goods or military equipment which will not represent any immediate increase in economic welfare. The total figure may also be misleading because it does not tell us how the income is distributed. This information may be obtained from supplementary tables in the Blue Book.

2. National Income per head is used to compare standards of living in different countries (see Chapter 30). Again, this can be misleading because such figures tend to exaggerate the differences. In poorer countries most people perform services for themselves which, in richer countries, are carried out for money payments. Domestic service, restaurants, laundry services, and dressmaking are typical examples. In underdeveloped countries, most people live in largely self-sufficient villages where they do not have to pay transport costs in order to get to work. A large number of poorer countries are in the tropics where there is less need to devote economic resources to the provision of fuel for domestic heating, of warm clothing, or of solidly built houses. Because the National Income figures are expressed in different currencies they have to be compared by using the foreign exchange rate which might not be a good measure of the internal purchasing power of the currencies.

3. Economic growth (see Chapter 31, p. 359) is measured in terms of National Income per head, and the National Income figures (in real terms) are used to measure the rate of growth.

4. The information is now presented in a manner which makes possible an analysis of the behaviour of the different sectors of the economy. The Blue Book gives details of changes in consumption and investment spending, in the level of savings, in the outputs of the different branches of industry, in the expenditure of the public authorities, and in the distribution of income among the different income groups. These details are essential if any attempt to plan the economy is to be successful.

Chapter 16
Wages

This section deals with the distribution of the National Income. The individual's share of the National Income depends upon the level of his income. The economist, as such, is not concerned with the question of whether the National Income is shared equitably, but with the forces which determine the size of the shares accruing to the different factors of production.

Incomes may be classified as (1) those incomes which are the rewards for personal service (e.g. wages and salaries) and (2) those paid to the owners of property for the use of their property in production. In this category are rent (the payment for the use of land) and interest (the payment for the use of capital). A third category of income includes transfer payments.

All incomes, except transfer payments (see Chapter 15, p. 167), are the earnings of the factors of production; labour earns a wage or salary, capital earns interest, land earns rent and the entrepreneur earns profits. These incomes can be regarded as prices. There are markets for labour, land, and capital just as there are markets for the things they produce. Like other prices, incomes are determined by demand and supply. A study of incomes, then, must be an analysis of the forces which influence the supply of, and the demand for, the factors of production.

A wage is a payment, normally made under contract, for *the services of labour*. We are all aware of the fact that there are very great differences in wage rates as between different occupations and the common sense explanation for this would be that labour is not a homogeneous commodity. There are very great differences in the skills and abilities, and in the demands for different workers giving rise to not one labour market, but many different markets each with its own supply and demand conditions. The variations in the conditions of supply and demand as between these markets will give rise to different prices, hence the existence of wage differentials.

This is all very true, but we have to explain why these differentials persist. Why is there no rapid movement of workers from the lower paid jobs to those more highly paid? Such a movement would tend to equalise wages, for the movements out of the lower paid jobs would reduce the supply of this type of labour and raise its price, while the movements into the more highly paid jobs would increase the supply and tend to lower the price. Adam Smith asked the question, 'If labour were perfectly mobile would wages in all occupations then be equal?' In fact they would not, because some jobs are more attractive than others. If wages were equal in all occupations, the dirty and disagreeable jobs would attract little labour, most people would seek the jobs with pleasant and congenial conditions. Smith pointed out that under such circumstances it would be the *net advantages* of occupations which would tend to equality. There would be differences in money wages and these differentials would measure, in money terms, the non-monetary[1] differences between the occupations.

If we turn to the real world again, we find that dirty and disagreeable jobs are often paid less than the more pleasant and attractive jobs. It is apparent that existing wage differences do not equalise the attractiveness of different occupations. To explain why one job pays £x per week while another pays £y per week, we must examine the supply and demand conditions to find out what makes them equate at different price levels in the different markets.

The Demand for Labour

There are four basic propositions regarding the demand for labour.

1. *The demand for labour is a derived demand.* No one employs labour for any immediate satisfaction obtained from its employment. Labour is required not for itself, but for what it will produce. The demand for labour derives directly from the demand for the product of labour. The greater the demand for the product, the greater the demand for labour. No matter how skilful the worker, no matter how long his period of training, if what he produces is no longer in demand, his services will no longer be required.

2. *If the demand for the product is inelastic, then the demand for the labour which produces it will tend to be inelastic.* An increase in the price of the product will not produce a large fall in the quantity demanded, and will, therefore, not cause a significant fall in the demand for labour. This means that where the effects of wage changes are passed on in the form of price changes, they will have a less than proportionate effect on the demand for labour.

3. *Where labour costs form only a small part of the total costs, the demand for that type of labour is likely to be inelastic.* Some industries are labour-intensive, that is, they use a high proportion of labour relative to land

[1] e.g. the degree of security, the element of danger, the nature of the surroundings, etc.

and capital. Building is such an industry. Other industries are capital-intensive, using a high proportion of capital. Such industries are chemicals, oil refining, and electricity generation. If wages form 50 per cent of total costs and are increased by 10 per cent, then total costs will increase by 5 per cent. But if wages only make up 20 per cent of the total costs, a wage increase of 10 per cent will only increase total costs by 2 per cent. The smaller the percentage of wage costs in total costs, the smaller will be the impact of wage changes on the price of the product.

4. *One of the determinants of the demand for labour is the ease with which capital, in the form of machinery, may be substituted for it.* An increase in wage rates will increase the cost of labour relative to the other factors. There will come a point where it is economic to replace labour with machines. In low wage countries like India, China and Hong Kong it is more economic to use labour rather than capital. It is notable that the country with the highest wage level in the world, the U.S.A., is also the country which makes the maximum use of labour-saving machinery. Where it is possible to substitute machines for labour, the demand for labour will become more elastic as wage rates rise.

These are important aspects of the demand for labour. They indicate some of the influences which help to determine the shape of the demand curve for labour, but they do not tell us why the demand curve for labour is what it is.

Marginal Revenue Productivity

The demand for labour is a derived demand – the entrepreneur employs labour for what it produces. Although he is concerned with the physical productivity of labour, his major interest will be in the revenue yielded by labour's efforts. He will have no interest in the efforts of the most industrious operative if his output cannot be sold or can only be sold at a loss. It is the value of labour's output (the revenue product) which really matters. In assessing the determinants of the demand for labour our particular concern is the *marginal revenue product* (M.R.P.) of labour which may be defined as the revenue resulting from the sale of the output of an additional worker. If the firm is operating under conditions of perfect competition, where it cannot affect the price of the product, then the marginal revenue product of labour will be equal to the marginal physical product (M.P.) multiplied by the price of the product.

M.R.P. of labour = M.P. of labour × Price of product

In Chapter 6, Table 6 (p. 47) and Fig. 5 (p. 48) illustrate the changing values of the Average and Marginal Products of labour when a fixed amount of capital and land is combined with varying amounts of labour. The law of diminishing returns tells us that the A.P. and M.P. of labour will, sooner or later, begin to decline. If these average and marginal products are multiplied by the price of the product (we are assuming the price to remain constant as output changes), then it should be clear that we will obtain the marginal revenue and average revenue products. If these are represented diagrammatically the M.R.P. and A.R.P. curves will be the same shape as the M.P. and A.P. curves in Fig. 5. In Fig. 40 we have the marginal revenue product and average revenue product curves for an individual firm.

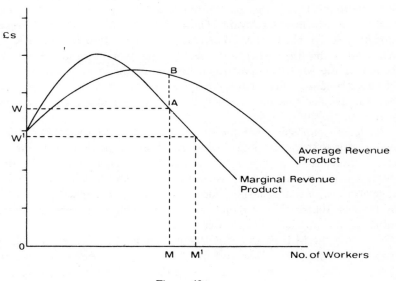

Figure 40

If we assume the firm cannot influence the wage rate, the supply of labour to the firm is perfectly elastic. It can obtain as many workers as it wishes to employ at the ruling wage rate. How many workers will it employ? The equilibrium condition should be familiar to us since it has already been encountered when discussing the optimum output of the firm. The profit maximising firm will employ additional workers as long as these workers are adding more to the firm's revenue than to the firm's costs. In other words, labour will be employed up to the point where the marginal revenue product of labour is equal to the wage rate. Since the wage rate is constant this equilibrium may be written,

Marginal Revenue Product of Labour = Marginal Cost of Labour

Thus, in Fig. 40, when the wage rate is OW, the firm will employ OM men. At this wage, as employment increases up to OM, each additional man is adding more to the firm's revenue than to the firm's costs. Beyond OM the employment of extra men adds more to costs than to revenue. If the wage rate falls to OW^1 employment will rise to OM^1– it becomes worthwhile to employ MM^1 extra workers since the marginal revenue products of these men are higher than the new lower wage rate.

The marginal revenue product curve, then, tells us how much labour will be demanded at any given price (i.e. wage). Since this is the function of a demand curve, *the M.R.P. curve is the firm's demand curve for labour*. But note that it is only that part of the M.R.P. curve which lies below the A.R.P. curve which is relevant. The A.R.P. curve indicates the average monetary return per worker. When OM men are employed, the A.R.P. is MB so that the firm is earning a surplus per worker equal to AB. The section of the M.R.P. curve which lies above the A.R.P. curve has no relevance because a firm will not employ labour when the wage is higher than the average revenue product – it would be making a loss on each worker employed.

We have established that the firm's demand curve for labour will be of the normal shape, sloping downwards from let to right. Although we have assumed a state of perfect competition the same conclusions apply to imperfect competition. In this case the A.R.P. and M.R.P. curves would slope downwards more sharply, since, in addition to the effects of diminishing returns, the revenue product would also decline because the greater output could only be sold at lower prices.

Note that the M.R.P. and A.R.P. curves will be influenced by changes in *the productivity of labour* and by changes in *the price of the product*. These are the two determinants of revenue productivity. An increase in the productivity of labour and/or an increase in the price of the product will move the curves upwards. The reader should be able to see that such a movement amounts to an increase in the demand for labour.

The industry's demand curve for labour will be of the same general shape. It is not the summation of the individual firms' demand curves since, if the price of labour changes, all the firms will change the number of workers they employ. This will alter the total supply of the product and hence its market price. The change in the market price of the product will affect the M.R.P. curves of all the firms in the industry. This does not affect the conclusion that the industry's demand curve for labour will be downward sloping; it must be so, since as more units of labour are employed, the marginal physical product of labour declines and so does the price of the product.

Although we have confined this very brief outline of the marginal productivity theory to the factor labour, exactly the same reasoning can be applied to land and capital to show that the demand for factors of production depends upon their prices and their marginal productivity.

We now have some preliminary notions of the forces which determine the demand for labour. They should help our understanding of the variations in the demand conditions in the different labour markets; of why, for instance, the demand for civil engineers is likely to be very different from the demand for railway porters. But we are seeking an understanding of the price of labour, and demand is only half the story; supply plays an equally important role.

The Supply of Labour

In examining some of the characteristics of the factors of production in Chapter 4, the question of the total supply of labour was dealt with in some detail. It was pointed out that the supply of labour refers to the number of hours of work which is offered by the labour force. This depends upon such facts as the size of the total population, the age composition of the population, the numbers in full-time education, the retiring age, and the numbers of married women who go out to work. It depends too, on the length of the working week, and the number of holidays. In this study of wages we are concerned not so much with the total supply of labour as with the forces which determine the supply of labour to different occupations. This will be governed by the numbers willing and able to enter the particular trade and the hours they are prepared to work.

In many occupations, the number of hours worked by the individual cannot be varied. He works an agreed number of hours (e.g. 40 or 42 hours) each week, most trades having a recognised working week. The average worker can only work when the facilities (machines, materials, and power) are made available to him. It is true that those people who are self-employed, such as taxi drivers, can vary the number of hours they work, and very often the employed person has the option of working overtime. But the choice of work or leisure is, indirectly, available to the individual worker by virtue of the part he can play in deciding union policy. When Trade Unions press more strongly for a shorter working week than they do for higher pay, we can say that workers are choosing more leisure in preference to more income. The supply curve of labour from the individual worker will be of the normal shape for only part of its length. A higher price will call forth a greater supply up to a point. Beyond this point a higher price will lead to a reduced supply. When the worker's income is sufficient to buy all the necessities of life and an adequate supply of semi-luxuries he will tend to place a greater value on leisure. As one's income rises so does the necessity for more leisure. Much of what one buys with extra income requires extra leisure in order to enjoy the consumption of the additional goods and services. One has only to think of motoring, canoeing, sailing, and foreign travel to appreciate the increasing preference given to leisure.

The individual's supply curve of labour, therefore, will bend backwards at some point (Fig. 41).

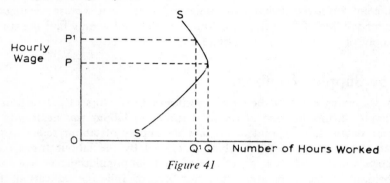

Figure 41

As the hourly wage increases up to the level OP the worker is tempted to work longer hours. At higher wage rates, however, the worker chooses more leisure rather than a higher income. When the wage rate is OP^1 the number of hours worked falls to OQ^1. What we are saying, in fact, is, that as wages increase, there comes a point when *the marginal utility of leisure exceeds the marginal utility of income.* But the total supply curve of labour to an industry will not bend backwards, because higher wages will call forth more workers.

SUPPLY OF LABOUR TO A GIVEN OCCUPATION

Occupationally, labour is not perfectly mobile. There are many restrictions on the supply of labour to any particular occupation. Most of these barriers to entry have been discussed under 'the Mobility of Labour' in Chapter 5. Where the restrictions on entry are very severe, the supply of that type of skill will be inelastic. For example, an increase in the demand for surgeons, under competitive conditions, would lead to a large increase in the price of that particular ability. The supply of surgeons is very inelastic in the short run because it would take several years of training to bring forward an increased number of them, and the number of recruits must be limited by the level of natural ability required. The supply of unskilled labour or semiskilled labour in an industry is likely to be elastic. An increase in the demand for builders' labourers or assembly line operatives would not lead to a very great increase in price. A relatively small rise in pay is likely to attract workers from unskilled or semiskilled work in other industries.[1]

One occupation is not paid at a much higher rate than another *because* it requires a much longer period of training, or a much higher level of education, or a greater degree of natural ability. The possession of skills and knowledge for which there is no demand is of no economic significance. *Knowledge, skill and training are important influences on the level of wages, but only in so far as they affect the supply situation.* Wage differences can only be explained by an examination of the supply and demand conditions in the different occupations.

The Wage Rate in a Particular Occupation

We can now summarise the position. The wage rate will be determined by the supply and demand conditions in the market for the particular grade of labour. The demand for labour depends, as we have seen, on the physical productivity of labour and the price of the product. These two facts determine the marginal revenue productivity of labour and hence the position of the demand curve. If the price of the product increases, or the productivity of labour increases, the demand for labour will increase and the demand curve will move to the right.

The elasticity of demand for labour will depend on:

1. the elasticity of demand for the product;
2. the possibility of substituting other factors for labour (e.g. labour-saving machinery);
3. whether labour forms a large or a small proportion of total costs.

The supply of labour to any given occupation depends upon:

1. the extent of the mobility of labour (discussed on pp. 44–46 and p. 282);
2. the amount of work offered by each individual worker at different wage rates.

The wage rate will be determined by the interaction of demand and supply as illustrated in Fig. 42.

As mentioned earlier, there are many different markets for labour, with different demand and supply conditions giving rise to different wage rates. There is not a separate market for each type of skill or occupation but rather separate markets for groups of occupations. Within these groups it is possible for labour to move from one occupation to another (e.g. bus driver to lorry driver).

[1] In some cases unions can restrict the supply of labour by the operation of various restrictive practices (e.g. controlling recruitment).

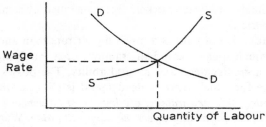

Figure 42

Real Wages and Nominal Wages

This is an important distinction. *Nominal wages* are the actual sums of money received by the worker in return for his services. Of more interest to the worker is the level of his real wages. *Real wages* consist of the goods and services for which his money wages will exchange. Real wages are a measure of the purchasing power of the wage packet. It is possible for nominal wages to increase while real wages are falling. This would happen if the percentage rise in consumer prices exceeded the percentage rise in money wages. Everyone in Britain, and in most other countries too, must be aware of the fact that an increase in pay does not necessarily lead to an increase in the standard of living.

Real wages must depend on the output of goods and services. If money wages increase, but no more goods and services are produced, then real wages cannot increase. The only exception to this rule would be if labour increased its share of the national income at the expense of profits, interest or rent. (There is a further exception, discussed in Chapter 27, which relates to changes in the terms of trade.) In fact, the share of wages and salaries in the National Income has changed very little since the war. It is true to say, therefore, that the level of real wages depends primarily on the movements in productivity. This is borne out by the statistics of wage, output, and price movements in recent years (Table 15).

Another aspect of real wages, which has tended to increase in importance, is the existence of so-called 'fringe benefits'. Many money wages are now supplemented by 'payment in kind'. Some jobs carry the right to subsidised meals in the firm's dining rooms, others provide travel warrants to cover the costs of travelling to work, while some jobs, such as coal-mining, carry the right to coal (or other goods) at very low prices. Many persons, such as commercial travellers, have motor cars provided by the firm for the purposes of their official duties, but which they are able to use, to some extent, for private purposes.

Table 15. *Income, output, prices – U.K.*

Year	Income (per head) from employment	Output per person	Retail prices
1963	100	100	100
1964	106·8	104·4	103·3
1965	114·1	106·2	108·2
1966	121·8	107·9	112·5
1967	128·8	111·1	115·3
1968	139·0	116·2	120·7
1969	149·5	119·4	127·2
1970	165·8	122·5	135·3
1971	189·7	126·8	148·1

Source: *National Institute Economic Review*

Table 15 shows that incomes have been rising faster than output causing prices to rise. The increase in prices has meant that real incomes have not kept pace with money incomes.

Between 1963 and 1970 (see Fig. 43):

The index of money incomes rose from 100 to 165·8, i.e. by 65·8 per cent

The index of prices rose from 100 to 136, i.e. by 36 per cent

The index of real incomes, therefore, rose from 100 to, $\dfrac{165 \cdot 8 \times 100}{136} = 121.9$,

i.e. by 21.9 per cent

Collective Bargaining and Trade Unions

The wages and salaries of the majority of the working population are settled by some kind of collective bargaining procedure. The individual worker is in a weak bargaining position, and the main purpose of a Trade Union is to strengthen the position of the worker in relation to his employer. Collective bargaining is the process whereby representatives of the employers negotiate with representatives of the employees in respect of wages and working conditions. The growth of trade unions has been paralleled by the development of employers' associations. Increasingly these negotiations settle wages on a national basis. In the early days of collective bargaining, most agreements related to local conditions of employment, and this gave rise to variations in wages as between regions. Nowadays, for most of the well organised trades, there is a national wage rate.

There are some 550 trade unions in Great Britain, the great majority of which are small. The movement is dominated by a small number of large unions; the Transport and General Workers' Union and the Union

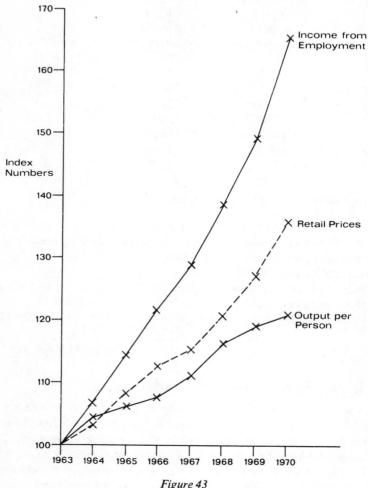

Figure 43

of General and Municipal Workers each have more than one million members. The sixteen largest unions have more than two-thirds of the total membership. Trade union membership numbers about 10 million workers, which is less than half the total working population. This is, perhaps, a rather surprising fact when one considers the power and influence of the trade union movement in our society. But there are very large numbers of employees belonging to associations which carry out trade union-type functions but which are not strictly classified as such. A much greater percentage of male workers than female workers belong to trade unions. Although large numbers of workers are not members of a trade union, it would be true to say that, in the great majority of cases, their pay and working conditions are settled by trade union negotiations. Such settlements are widely applied and are not normally confined to trade union members.

Trade unions have three major functions:

1. To provide friendly society benefits for their members. Before the development of the welfare state, trade unions were, very often, the only source of aid to the needy worker, providing unemployment and sick pay, and small pensions. Many of them still provide these services.

2. To persuade the Government to pass legislation in favour of the working class. Hence the prominent part played by the unions in the political life of the country.

3. To bargain, on behalf of their members, for better pay and working conditions.

It is this last function which concerns us here. How great is the power of the unions to influence wages? One thing is certain, they have great power to influence the level of money wages during periods of full employment such as Britain has enjoyed almost continuously for the past twenty-five years. When full employment exists, trade unions are very strong, their membership is high and their funds are in a healthy condition. This means that they are capable of staging effective and lengthy strikes. Under such conditions they have proved their ability to raise the money wages of their members. In Britain we have now become accustomed to the frequent wage claims and wage rises. Whether trade unions can exert a significant influence on the level of real wages is a much more difficult question to answer. We have noted that real wages depend upon productivity and there is much evidence to show that in recent years, real wages have tended to move in line with productivity (see p. 181). Trade unions could raise real wages, in excess of any increase in productivity, only by increasing labour's share of the national income. Where labour was being exploited, and not receiving the value of its marginal product, unions could raise real wages at the expense of profits.

But individual unions might well increase the real wages of their own members at the expense of some other income groups, especially at the expense of those groups which are less well organised or not so militant. We have a large number of unions in Britain and each union tends to direct its efforts to increasing the welfare of its own members. This, after all, is the main reason for its existence. The well organised and powerful unions might succeed in getting larger and more frequent wage increases. If the effects of these wage increases were reflected in higher prices, the workers receiving the more favourable wage increases would be gaining at the expense of other groups, particularly those on relatively fixed incomes such as pensioners.

It is often said that the determination of wages is now a matter for unions and employers to settle by negotiation, and the theory of supply and demand has little relevance. However, there is much evidence to show that market forces have a much more powerful influence on the level of wages than is generally appreciated. When the representatives of workers and employers are bargaining on wages, the supply and demand factors, which have just been discussed, must be taken into account in their deliberations. Employers must be conscious of the demand for their product and the likely effect of any wage increase on its price. They must also be thinking of the wage level which is required to recruit the type of labour they need. Unions must take into account the possibility of substituting machinery for labour if wages are pushed too high. The power of the unions rests ultimately on their ability to call an effective strike – to withhold the supply of labour, and employers must bear in mind the likely impact of such a strike on their production and sales.

The working of market forces is revealed quite clearly when wage movements over the past twenty years are studied. There have been years when wages have risen appreciably although no major union wage claim has been submitted. The shortage of labour caused employers to bid up the price.

The Department of Employment publishes details of the movements of agreed wages rates and the movements of *earnings*, that is, the 'take home' pay. A feature of the postwar period has been the discrepancy between the two indexes. Earnings have tended to rise faster than wage rates. In many industries the excess demand for labour has tended to 'pull up' the price of labour faster than trade unions have been able to 'push up' the wage rate. Employers short of labour have been forced to raise their 'bids' in order to attract labour from others firms and industries. Some of the excess of earnings over wages is due to overtime payments, but, in the figures given below, this has been allowed for. Wage drift[1] represents the extent to which average hourly earnings, exclusive of the overtime element, have tended to exceed the increase in average hourly wage rates.

Table. 16. *Wage drift (percentage change on preceding year)*

Year (1)	Average hourly earnings (excluding effects of overtime) (2)	Average hourly wage rate (3)	Wage drift (4) (2–3)
1960	7·3	5·5	1·8

[1] Wage drift is associated with demand inflation. More recently cost-push inflation has been experienced (see Chapter 23).

1961	6·9	6·4	0·5
1962	4·4	4·2	0·2
1963	3·6	2·3	1·3
1964	8·1	5·7	2·4
1965	9·5	7·3	2·2
1966	6·5	5·6	0·9
1967	5·0	5·3	−0·3
1968	7·0	6·7	+0·3
1969	8·0	5·5	2·5
1970	16·0	12·4	3·6
1971	13·7	11·6	2·1

Source: *Dept. of Employment Gazette.*

Trade union claims for higher wages are normally based upon one or more of three grounds:

(*a*) A rise in the cost of living has reduced the real income of their members.

(*b*) Workers in comparable occupations have received a wage increase.

(*c*) The increased profits in the industry justify a higher return to labour.

THE COST OF LIVING ARGUMENT

If the rise in the cost of living is due to a rise in costs of production, which itself is due to a previous wage increase, then the claim cannot be justified on economic grounds. This is the case where wages are rising faster than productivity. If the increased cost of living is due to an increase in the prices of imports, then again, the wage claim cannot be justified on economic grounds, since, unless there is an increase in productivity, a rise in wages will cause a further rise in prices. If the rise in prices is due to an increase in monopoly (or abnormal) profits then labour would feel quite justified in claiming a compensating wage increase, although the community as a whole would benefit from lower prices and the elimination of the excess profits.

THE DIFFERENTIAL ARGUMENT

The basis of the wage claim is that workers in a comparable occupation have received an increase in pay. This argument has a strong emotional appeal because there is a widespread belief that it is *fair* that workers doing similar jobs should get the same reward. A claim which has for its basis the differential argument is felt to accord with popular ideas of social justice. One of the problems here lies in the meaning given to the term 'comparable occupation'. There are so many aspects of a particular job; the length of training, the degree of skill, the measure of responsibility, the security of tenure, the degree of danger, the prospects of promotion, the nature of the working conditions and so on. While two jobs may be comparable on one or more of these grounds it would, in most cases, be difficult to establish strict comparability. Is there a job which is strictly comparable to, say, that of a policeman or an engine driver?

In a free society, labour cannot be directed where it is most needed, yet economic growth requires a high degree of labour mobility. How do we get workers to move from declining or less 'essential' industries to the expanding industries? The only practical way in which such a movement may be brought about is by using wage differentials. If the growth industries offer higher rates of pay they will attract workers from other industries. But if these higher rates of pay lead immediately to compensating awards in other industries, the differentials will remain unchanged, and there will be no monetary incentive for labour to move. Unless we are prepared to accept wage differences, then we will have to resort to the direction of labour.

THE PROFITABILITY ARGUMENT

This has already been touched upon in the discussion of the cost of living argument. The individual union, seeking the interests of its own members, feels completely justified in pressing for an increase in wages whenever the profits of the industry are increasing. When we recognise the imperfections of the product markets and the labour markets, it is difficult to say that the unions are not justified in such circumstances. Yet it appears, from the point of view of the community as a whole, that certain privileged groups (the shareholders and workers in these industries) are gaining at the expense of the general public. If the degree of competition were not restricted, and if the markets were more perfect, more labour and capital would move into these more profitable industries, more would be produced, prices would be lower and the excess profits would be eliminated.

The long period of full employment, and the existence of an excess demand for labour in many markets, have led to a situation where the national agreed wage rate has tended to become a minimum wage for the occupation. Regional differences in the supply and demand conditions for labour, and the wide variations in productivity movements between industries have led to the growth of factory-level wage agreements which use the nationally agreed wage rate as a 'floor'.

The agreements made by collective bargaining procedures are not legally binding on the unions; they depend for their observance on the good faith of the parties to the agreement. In certain industries where there is a lack of voluntary arrangements for the settlement of terms of employment, or where such arrangements are ineffective, there are statutory bodies known as *wages councils* (e.g. in the catering industry). They are made up of equal numbers of employers' representatives and workers' representatives with some independent members. The councils submit proposals on wages and working conditions to the Minister of Labour who then makes an order giving legal force to the agreement. Wages and working conditions in agriculture are determined by a similar body known as the Agricultural Wages Board.

Trade Unions and the Law

The growth of unofficial strikes has become one of the most disquieting features of the British system of industrial relations. Approximately 95 per cent of all strikes occurring in recent years have been in breach of existing collective agreements. Table 17 gives an indication of the trends in recent years.

Table 17.

	1960–66 Average	1967	1968	1969	1970
No. of stoppages	2,407	2,116	2,378	3,116	3,888
Workers involved (000s)	1,238	732	2,256	1,656	1,784
Total working days lost	3,032	2,787	4,690	6,846	10,970

Source: *National Institute Economic Review*

These figures do not give a complete picture of the economic effects since they do not record the effects of the 'go-slow' and 'work-to-rule' types of dislocation, neither do they include the numbers laid off as the result of a strike.

The causes of the deterioration are numerous and complex, but one undoubted contributory cause is the growth of the practice of collective bargaining at the plant and company level. Official agreements between employers and unions decide national standards in respect of working conditions and rates of pay, but these, as mentioned earlier, tend to become minimum standards which provide a basis for further negotiations at the local level. Bonus rates, piece work rates and various other allowances are increasingly settled in negotiations between the company and worker representatives (usually shop stewards). Disputes and disagreements, mainly about wages, at this local level, are now the most common form of industrial stoppage.

As a result of advancing technology, capital costs are rising relative to labour costs so that any major stoppages are becoming increasingly costly to bear (fixed costs remain high as output drops to zero). The increasing extent of specialisation and the continuing movement to large-scale production make the economy more and more interdependent so that a strike of even a relatively few workers can have an extremely widespread effect.

Growing concern with this problem has led to some support for measures to bring industrial relations far more within the framework of the law. The 1906 Trades Disputes Act provides legal protection for unofficial strikers and the majority of collective agreements are not legal contracts. In January 1969 the Labour government proposed to introduce an Industrial Relations Bill which would have given the Government statutory powers to intervene in industrial disputes. This Bill was not proceeded with although one of the proposals, the creation of a Commission for Industrial Relations, was carried out. The role of the C.I.R. is to investigate disputes, to offer advice and to recommend and actively encourage the reform of existing labour-management agreements.

In 1970 the Conservative government introduced an Industrial Relations Bill. This was passed through the House of Commons early in 1971. It is a complex measure which aims, under certain circumstances, to make the collective agreement a legally binding contract. It calls for the establishment of a Registrar of Trade Unions and only those unions whose rules meet certain requirements will be registered. Unions whose rules do not accord with certain basic principles will not be registered and hence will not acquire legal status and the legal privileges which go with it. A National Industrial Relations Court is proposed. This court would have wide powers to make collective agreements legally binding and to award damages against those responsible for strikes in breach of contract and against employers who are in breach of contract. The Government would be able to apply to the Court for an order requiring a cooling off period in a national emergency or for a compulsory ballot in certain strike situations. It is also proposed to establish an Industrial Relations Tribunal to act as an extra buffer between the company and the law. An individual employee would be able to use this tribunal to insist upon his rights against his union or against his employer. The C.I.R. retains its role as an investigating and advisory body and it must be consulted by the Industrial Relations Court.

Chapter 17

The Rate of Interest

We have already noted that interest is the price of capital. In a monetary economy it may be regarded as the price of the funds required to purchase the capital goods.

If the rate of interest is a price, then it must be determined by the forces of supply and demand, and it is to these forces that we now turn our attention.

The Demand for Capital

It is the possibility of a greater future output which leads to a demand for capital. More strictly, it is its *net productivity* which is the basis of the demand for capital. Let us take a very simple example.

Country A and Country B have the same quantity of economic resources. Country A devotes them all to the production of consumption goods and produces 1,000 units per annum.

Country B devotes half her resources to the production of capital goods (e.g. ploughs, fertilisers and drainage) and produces only 500 units of consumption goods per annum.

But subsequently, using capitalistic methods of production, Country B is able to produce 2,000 units of consumption goods per annum.

Country B is now producing 1,000 units per annum more than Country A, but the net productivity of her capital equipment is less than this. Allowances must be made for the sacrifices experienced during the period of capital creation and also for the fact that each year Country B must devote some resources to maintaining her stock of capital (i.e. for depreciation). The amount by which Country B's output exceeds Country A's output, after all these costs have been met, is the net productivity of her capital.

Why do we need to measure the net productivity of capital? It is necessary, because we must have some means of comparing the efficiency of capital in different industries. In a modern economy there are many different types of capital equipment producing a great range of goods and services. It would be possible, as in the foregoing example, to express the net productivity of capital, in any one industry, in terms of the extra units of output. But this would not help us to evaluate the alternative uses of capital. How can we compare an increase in output in agriculture of say, 1,000 tons of potatoes, with an increase in output in the footwear industry of 1,500 pairs of shoes? We need some measure which would help us to decide whether new capital would be more productive in one industry than in another. Our economic resources are limited and we can only have more of one thing by having less of another. It is necessary to choose between alternatives, at any given moment of time one industry can only have more capital at the expense of another industry.

The only way to compare the net productivity of capital in such diverse projects as agriculture, coal-mining, chemicals or the motor industry is to measure the percentage changes in output in value terms. It is necessary, therefore, to use money values for the inputs and outputs of the different industries. The total costs are expressed in terms of money and so are the total receipts. The annual excess of receipts over costs can then be expressed as a percentage yield on the capital employed. This is a measure of the productivity of capital.

The demand for capital depends upon (1) *its net productivity, and* (2) *the price of the funds required to purchase the equipment.* If the productivity of capital increases and the price of funds remains unchanged, we should expect the demand for capital to increase. The price of funds is the rate of interest, which is also expressed in percentage terms, so that the price and productivity of capital can be readily compared. For example, if the expected return on the proposed investment is $4\frac{1}{2}$ per cent and the rate of interest is 5 per cent, then the project will not go forward. The cost exceeds the expected return. If, however, the rate of interest falls to something less than $4\frac{1}{2}$ per cent, the proposition now becomes a profitable one.

It should be noted that the example uses the expression '*the expected return*'. This draws attention to an important characteristic of capital and one which tends to complicate matters. Most units of capital are durable, they are long-lasting. The businessman who is contemplating the purchase of capital assets is trying to assess the productivity of these assets over a period of time which lies in the future. His decision whether to buy or not rests upon his estimates of the likely profitability of the investment. In other words, the demand for capital is really determined by the *expected* net productivity of capital. These estimates of the expected future yield on new capital can be, at best, only an inspired guess.

Like other factors of production, capital is subject to the Law of Diminishing Returns. Any increase in the amount of capital, relative to the other factors of production, will lead to a fall in the marginal productivity of capital. Successive equal additions to the stock of capital will result in smaller and smaller additions to the total output. When the marginal productivity of capital is diminishing it means that the demand curve for capital will slope downwards from left to right. *The entrepreneur will employ capital up to the point where the price he has to pay for the loan is equal to the expected yield (the net productivity) on the capital.* Only if he is able to borrow at a price which is less than the expected return, will he demand capital.

The demand for capital will be governed by similar influences to those which applied to the demand for labour. The demand for capital is a derived demand, and changes in the demand for the goods produced with capital will cause changes in the demand for capital. Changes in the productivity of capital will also cause the demand to change. If technical progress results in greatly improved and more efficient machines, the productivity of capital is increased and this will lead to a greater demand for it. The increased productivity will lower the price of the products and increase the quantity demanded causing more capital to be demanded. The improved performance of capital relative to other factors will encourage the substitution of capital for labour (and possibly for land), again leading to an increased demand for capital. The development of an efficient paint-spraying machine has led to a substitution of capital for labour in industry. A few men with these machines can do the work of a large number of men using the traditional paint brush.

The demand for capital arises because it is productive, and people are prepared to pay a price for this productive potential. This price is the rate of interest.

The Supply of Capital

Society can only invest (i.e. accumulate capital) by the process of saving. Saving requires consumption to be less than output, for *saving is the process of abstaining from consumption.* In an advanced economy, the link between saving and capital creation is not easy to see. A person receives his income in the form of money. His money income represents a claim to goods and services. He could choose to spend the whole of his income on consumption goods and services, and if everyone chose to do exactly the same thing, there would be no saving. Suppose this person decides to save £3 per week. He is giving up his power to command resources to the value of £3; he is sacrificing current consumption. By lending this sum of money he confers on the borrower the ability to employ resources to the value of £3. The borrower could now use this purchasing power to employ resources to make capital goods. He would purchase the services of factors of production to the value of £3. This £3 would be received as income by the owners of the factors of production, who could then purchase consumer goods of this value. The consumer goods thus obtained are available by virtue of the abstention of the savers. The men who build ships, roads, machines, houses, and factories are adding nothing (directly) to the output of consumer goods, but they are all consumers. They require food, clothing, entertainment, and other services and since they are not producing consumer goods and services, others must provide for them. It is because some people save (i.e. forego consumption) that it is possible for others to be employed in the production of capital goods.

It would be very convenient if we could now say that the rate of interest is the price which equates the demand for capital and the supply of savings. The older theories of the rate of interest did say something very like this. They regarded interest as being a reward for saving, a reward for the sacrifice entailed in abstaining from consumption. The supply of savings, they held, obeyed the accepted laws of supply – at a higher price (interest rate) more would be saved. The intersection of the demand curve for capital and the supply curve of savings gave us the price of loans, or the rate of interest.

Unfortunately, the rate of interest is not determined in quite this way. As we shall see later, the supply of funds is not solely dependent upon the current level of savings, and the supply of savings does not necessarily vary directly with the price offered for loans. We cannot assume that a higher interest rate will bring forward more savings. It is necessary, therefore, to examine the nature of savings in a modern society and to look at the relationship between savings and the rate of interest.

Savings

Table 18 provides background data to the subsequent discussion:

Table 18. *Savings in the United Kingdom, 1972*
Total savings in the U.K. in 1972 were estimated to be £12,031 million – about one quarter of the Gross National Product.

	£ million	% of total
Personal savings	4,090	33·9
Company savings	4,872	40·5
Central government	1,305	10·8
Local authorities	884	7·4
Public corporations	880	7·3
	12,031	100·0

It is possible to identify some of the principal factors which influence the level of savings.

(a) Income

The most obvious requirement is the ability to save, and this depends upon the level of income. No one can save until the level of his income is more than sufficient to cover the necessities of life. As income rises, so does the ability to save. As we earn more, so we spend more, but the *proportion* of our income which is devoted to consumption expenditure tends to fall. A man earning £15 per week might spend £14 on consumption goods, whereas a man earning £30 per week might spend £24 on consumption goods and services; a greater sum of money, but a smaller proportion of his income. What is true of the individual is also true, in this case, of society; the rate of savings in rich countries is much higher than that of poor countries.

(b) Social Attitudes

The prevailing attitude towards thrift has a significant influence on the rate of saving. Where thrift is regarded as a virtue, more will be saved. In Victorian times, hard work and careful saving were regarded as admirable characteristics, and were important contributors to the rapid industrial progress of that period. Other communities place a higher value on leisure and consumption, and, in such a society, the thrifty man might be regarded as a mean man. In such a society the level of saving would be much lower.

(c) The Financial Framework

In the developed countries, all kinds of institutions for the safe deposit of savings are available. Savings banks, commercial banks, insurance companies, building societies, government securities, and company shares are all widely known, easily accessible, and have the confidence of the people. This range of opportunities for saving not only stimulates saving, but ensures that most of the potential savings are actually made available to borrowers. In less developed countries there are few such institutions, they are not widely known or easily accessible, neither do they have the confidence of the majority of the people, who lack knowledge and experience of such bodies. Hence money is hoarded not lent.

We have not included the rate of interest in these influences on the level of savings; it is better to deal with the subject in a separate section.

SAVINGS AND THE RATE OF INTEREST

Interest may be regarded as a reward for 'waiting', i.e. as a payment for the postponement of consumption. Most people, given the choice, would prefer purchasing power *now*, to the promise of purchasing power *in the future*. Would you rather have £100 now, or the promise of £100 in one year's time? The stronger your preference for present satisfaction over future satisfaction, the stronger is your *time preference*. Interest may be regarded as the payment which is necessary to overcome people's time preference. If you are presented with the choice of £100 now, or £105 in one year's time, and you feel that £5 is only just sufficient compensation for waiting, a rate of interest of 5 per cent is required to overcome your time preference.

But it is doubtful whether changes in the rate of interest have any great influence on the level of savings under the conditions which obtain in an advanced capitalist society. As the rate of interest rises, it may be that people with a stronger time preference may be persuaded to save, and people already saving may be persuaded to save more. But when we examine the nature of savings in our type of economy, we can see why there is great uncertainty about the influence of the rate of interest on saving.

(*a*) *Much saving is habitual.* Many people firmly believe that saving is a good moral habit, that is, people *ought* to save. Others like to have the feeling of security which comes with the possession of 'something in the bank'. Changes in the rate of interest are not likely to affect this type of saving.

(*b*) *A large part of presentday saving is contractual.* This kind of saving is carried out through insurance companies, pension funds and building societies. The individual saver puts himself under a contractual agreement to pay a fixed annual sum (e.g. the insurance premium or the superannuation contribution). Variations in the rate of interest will not have much effect on existing contracts, though they might alter the nature of future contracts.

(*c*) *Many people save in order to achieve some definite objective,* such as the deposit for a new house, or the purchase price of a motor cycle, or to cover the cost of a holiday abroad. Saving in order to accumulate a fixed and known sum of money is not likely to be influenced by changes in the rate of interest, although an increase in the rate of interest might well *reduce* the level of such saving since, at the higher interest rate, the required sum will accumulate at a faster rate.

(*d*) *Almost half the total saving in the United Kingdom is carried out by companies.* Companies save in order to build up reserves which will act as a cushion against future business fluctuations, and in order to have funds which will serve to finance expansion. Company savings are not likely to vary with changes in the rate of interest, since the purpose of such saving is not to achieve income in the form of interest.

(*e*) *A part of total saving is made up of government saving.* When government revenue from taxation exceeds government expenditure, we have a form of public saving. This will occur when the Government feels that the purchasing power of the community is excessive. Public saving of this nature will not be varied to take account of any changes in the rate of interest.

The motives for, and the nature of saving provide sufficient evidence to support the view that the rate of interest and the rate of saving are not linked in any simple straightforward manner. Very high and very low rates of interest might well have some marked effects on the level of saving, but any 'normal' changes in the rate will probably have very little effect.

Investment and the Rate of Interest

The demand for new capital (investment), as noted earlier, will be affected by the rate of interest, since this is the price which must be paid for borrowed funds. It is also a cost (i.e. opportunity cost) which must be taken into account when a firm uses its own funds for the purchase of capital equipment. But, once again, we cannot assume that the relationship can always be depicted by the normal demand curve, for higher prices do not necessarily mean a reduction in the quantity demanded. It all depends upon the state of businessmen's expectations. If there is a boom in progress and sales prospects are very bright, entrepreneurs are not likely to be deterred by moderate increases in the rate of interest. If there should be a slump and the business outlook is very bleak, a reduction in the rate of interest will not tempt businessmen to borrow and invest. All we can say is that very high interest rates will cut back investment spending and, if the future sales prospects look very promising, a reduction in the rate of interest will stimulate investment.

We have now gained some understanding of the determinants of the demand for capital and of the level of savings. This knowledge is sufficient to cast serious doubts on the classical theory which viewed the rate of interest as the price which equated the demand for loans and the amounts which people were prepared to save.

Liquidity Preference and the Rate of Interest

Lord Keynes presented a monetary theory to explain the determination of the rate of interest. He saw the rate of interest as being determined by the demand for money and the supply of money. He pointed out that the demand for loans comes not only from those who wish to purchase capital goods, but also from (1) those who wish to purchase consumer goods, (2) those who wish to purchase existing securities and (3) those who wish to hold larger money balances. The demand for loans, therefore, is not related solely to the demand for capital goods. The supply of loans does not depend solely on the current rate of saving, it can be augmented by new money created by the banking system and by people who are prepared to reduce the amount of money they are holding. If individuals holding large money balances are prepared to release some of this money to borrowers, the supply of loans has been increased, but there has been no increase in saving from current income.

We have concentrated on the rate of interest as a reward for *saving*; more accurately, it is the reward for *lending* (although saving must precede lending, except where the banks are creating credit).[1] It is the act of lending which involves the loss of the ability to spend. When Keynes spoke of the demand for money, he meant the demand for 'money to hold'. In everyday speech, the expression has a different meaning; in desiring money, people are really desiring the things which money will buy. We do not go to work for money, but for food, clothing, entertainment and other goods and services. The money we are paid for our labours is only a claim to these things. In economics the term 'the demand for money' must be interpreted literally; it refers to the desire to hold wealth in the form of money. This preference for money over other kinds of assets is known as *liquidity preference*, because money is the most liquid asset. Liquidity describes the readiness with which an asset can be converted into other forms of wealth without any significant loss in value. Money gives us the greatest freedom of action because it can be freely exchanged for other types of asset, and it has a constant money value. A blast furnace is an example of a very illiquid asset. The great advantages of holding wealth in the form of money are, therefore, *its liquidity, and the certainty of its money value*. If we exchange money for, say, a share in a company, the money value of our asset is now uncertain, but we have secured an income-yielding asset. The disadvantage of holding money is that it does not earn any income, it is a sterile asset.

Keynes defined the rate of interest as *the price which must be paid to overcome people's liquidity preference*. The public has to be persuaded to surrender the advantages of holding cash and the rate of interest is the necessary inducement. Since money, as such, yields no direct satisfaction to its holder and earns no income, why do people hold money? Surely money is only desired for what it will buy? Apart from the morbid satisfaction obtained by the miser, those small pieces of paper and cheap metal coins are not desired for their own sake. Why do people hold money instead of exchanging it for goods and services which will render them some pleasure? There are three motives for holding money.

1. *The Transactions Motive*

Practically all our daily wants are obtained by some act of exchange. We do not, and usually cannot, provide our requirements directly. We buy

[1] See Chapter 21.

what we need. If we knew in advance exactly how much we were going to spend each day, we might keep all our wealth in the form of income-earning assets and sell, daily, enough shares or securities to give us the cash requirements for one day. But this is not a practical proposition. For one thing we do not know our future daily requirements, and secondly, it would be extremely expensive and inconvenient to operate a daily exchange of securities for cash. It is necessary for everyone to hold cash during the period from one pay day to the next to finance day-to-day transactions.

2. *The Precautionary Motive*

In addition to the cash holdings required to see us through the normal everyday pattern of spending, it is normal to hold additional cash for emergencies, or for the unexpected bargain which may appear. We may have an unexpected journey to make, or unanticipated visitors may appear, involving additional entertainment expenditure; something catches our eye in a shop window, or the tube in the television set might fail – such are the contingencies requiring sudden expenditure which lead people to hold money balances for precautionary purposes.

The amount of money held for transactions and precautionary purposes will depend upon the level of the national income and the habits of the people. In the short run it will tend to be very stable.

3. *The Speculative Motive*

Money held in excess of the requirements outlined above must be held for speculative purposes. Individuals prefer to hold money rather than securities when they fear that the prices of securities are going to fall. A bond bought today for £100 would bring in, say, £5 in interest over the next year. But if the price of the bond were to fall to £90 during the year, the bondholder would lose £5 (capital loss £10 minus interest received £5). If this person had preferred to hold money, the value of his assets would not have changed. An expectation of falling security prices will increase liquidity preference, while a belief that security prices are about to rise will reduce liquidity preference.

The total demand for money is made up of these three elements. The supply of money is controlled by the monetary authorities (the Treasury, the Bank of England and the commercial banks), and will be fixed in the short run. The rate of interest equates the demand for money and the supply of money as illustrated in Figure 44.

LL represents the liquidity preference schedule (the demand for money). MM is the supply of money. OR is the market rate of interest. Changes in the liquidity preference schedule or in the supply of money will cause changes in the rate of interest. Note that LL levels out at a positive rate

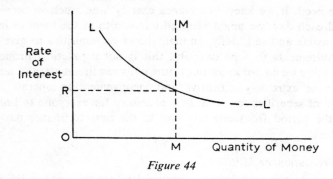

Figure 44

of interest, indicating that there is a rate (perhaps in the region of 2 per cent) below which people do not regard the reward for giving up the advantages of liquidity to be worth while.

The Pattern of Interest Rates

Throughout this section we have been discussing *the rate of interest* as though there were one, and only one, rate of interest. In fact, the slightest of contacts with the real world reveals not one, but very many rates of interest. The National Savings Bank may offer 2½ per cent on deposits; building societies may tempt us with offers to pay 4½ per cent for our savings; we are asked to pay, perhaps, 7 per cent on a mortage; local authorities may be prepared to pay 7 per cent for short-term loans, and so on.

The existence at any given moment of time, of many different rates of interest does not invalidate the preceding analysis of the forces which determine the rate of interest. There is a particular structure of interest rates which is affected by the supply and demand conditions which have been outlined above. Changes in liquidity preference and in the supply of money will affect all these interest rates. An increase in liquidity preference will tend to increase rates of interest in general; the government, building societies, banks, local authorities, and companies will all be obliged to offer higher rates of interest in order to obtain the funds they require. The major reasons for so many rates of interest prevailing at any given time are as follows:

1. *The Duration of the Loan*
The longer the period for which the money is borrowed, the greater is the risk of default by the borrower. The future is uncertain and the longer the period, the greater is the uncertainty. Short-term loans, therefore, will normally carry lower rates of interest than long-term loans. The lender

will accept a lower price because he feels more capable of estimating the course of events over the next few months than over the next few years. Note that a current account in a commercial bank carries no interest because these funds are subject to instant withdrawal, whereas a deposit account earns interest because the money is loaned for at least seven days.

2. *The Credit-worthiness of the Borrower*

Lending is a risky business and the degree of risk varies according to the evidence of the borrower's ability to repay. The loans with the greatest degree of security are those made to the government (hence the expression 'gilt-edged' securities). The risk of default is negligible because the government has the power to tax the whole of the nation's wealth in order to meet its liabilities. Borrowers with a credit standing almost as high are the great industrial and commercial companies. Lenders will demand a much lower rate of interest from such borrowers. Individuals or companies with a low credit rating (probably because they are unknown quantities) will be charged higher rates of interest.

3. *The Marketability of the I.O.U.*

Loans are made to the government by purchasing a government security (a defence bond, a premium bond, or perhaps, a national savings certificate). Loans are made to companies by purchasing a share or a debenture. These certificates (or I.O.U.s) may, or may not, be easily marketable. Most government securities are marketable and may be bought and sold daily on the Stock Exchange. This is also true of the shares of most public companies. Where the ownership of the security can easily be transferred, the lender has a liquid asset. He can, if he wishes, 'change his mind' about lending his money and recover his cash. If he does decide to sell his security, however, he cannot be sure of recovering the full amount of his loan, because the market price of his security is subject to change. He may recover more than he loaned or he may receive less, it all depends upon the movements in the market prices of his bonds or shares. Where the acknowledgement of the loan is in the form of a marketable security, the loan will attract lower interest rates, because the loan is a liquid asset.

The structure of interest rates rests upon a basic market rate of interest. This is the rate at which the Government is able to borrow on undated securities. Here, the risk of default is at a minimum, and the loan has a guaranteed market on the Stock Exchange. Undated securities are those which carry no definite date for repayment – most securities now issued by the government have dates for repayment. It is possible to calculate the current long-term market rate of interest from the market price of these securities. Take the quoted price of, say 2·5 per cent Consols (government bonds) from the Stock Exchange daily list. The quoted price is the price at which £100 (face value) of this stock is selling, e.g. 2·5 per cent **Consols** at 45·5. This means that £45·50 will buy £100 nominal value of this particular government stock, and will earn an income of £2·50 per annum.

The yield on this investment will be:

$$\frac{2\cdot5}{45\cdot5} \times 100 = \frac{500}{91} = 5\cdot5\% \text{ (approx.).}$$

This will be the rate of interest at which the Government will be able to borrow funds on a long term basis. If the public are only prepared to pay £45·50 for an income of £2·50 per annum, it means that they require a rate of interest of 5·5 per cent in order to be persuaded to part with liquidity.

The short-term market rate of interest may be calculated in a similar manner from the current market price of Treasury Bills. These are a very liquid type of government security and have a life of three months.

Other market rates of interest will differ from these basic rates according to the relative importance of the three factors outlined above, namely, duration, creditworthiness and marketability.

The rate of interest is an important influence on economic activity. It will be referred to many times in subsequent chapters and it was necessary, therefore, to spend this time in trying to understand some of the rather difficult ideas concerning the determination of this particular price.

Chapter 18

Rent

Everyone is familiar with the process of renting, a procedure which has undergone rapid development in recent years. It is now possible to rent land, factories, machines, houses, offices, cars, television sets, washing-machines and almost any durable good. Rent, in ordinary speech, simply means the periodical payment which is made for the use of some particular object. Rent is a contractual payment, fixed in terms of money, and normally arranged on an annual basis. The type of payment ordinarily known as rent, the rent payable for the use of a car, for example, contains an element of wages (labour is employed in providing the service), an element of interest (money has been invested in the business) and an element of profits.

Ricardo and Economic Rent

Economists have given a much more restricted meaning to the word Rent. It is used to describe the payments made for factors of production which are inelastic in supply. When the theory of economic rent was first propounded, it was applied specifically to land. Ricardo, who formulated the theory, said that rent was the payment for 'the original and indestructible powers of the soil'. Although the concept of economic rent is now applied to all the factors of production, it is best to outline the theory in relation to the earnings of land.

Ricardo believed that the value of a commodity was determined by its costs of production and that this was equally true of the value of the factors of production. The price of labour, he held, would tend towards a subsistence wage level – a wage level which was just sufficient to maintain the labourer and his family. The level of wages could not, in the long run, rise above what was just necessary to maintain the supply of labour. If wages fell below this level, workers would starve, marriages would be postponed, the supply of labour would fall, and its price would rise. If wages rose above this level, larger families and earlier marriages would increase the supply of labour and its price would fall. He applied his theory to the price of capital; its price would equal its 'cost of production', since it must be high enough to persuade savers to produce the amount required.

But he could not use a 'cost of production' theory to explain the earnings of land, because land cannot be produced. He had to develop another theory to deal with the determination of economic rent. The explanation he offered was that rent payments arose because land was limited in supply and different regions varied in fertility. When the demand for land increases, its supply cannot be increased and hence its price must increase. *Basically, his theory rests upon two facts* (a) *the supply of land is inelastic, and* (b) *the law of diminishing returns.* Ricardo's ideas can best be understood by taking a simplified, historical example of economic development.

In the earliest stages, with abundant land and small numbers of people, land will be free and the people will cultivate the most fertile areas. As the population grows, so the demand for food will increase. More will be produced, but there will come a point where the law of diminishing returns will begin to take effect on the most fertile land (Grade 1 land). Eventually a point will be reached where the employment of further men on the Grade 1 land will yield less output than the employment of these men on the less fertile (Grade 2) land. The rising demand for food will cause its price to increase and so make profitable the cultivation of less fertile land. Grade 2 and Grade 3 land will gradually be brought into use.

Areas of differing fertility will be cultivated up to the point where the marginal product of labour is the same on all grades of land. When this is achieved, the employment of an extra man on Grade 1 land will yield the same increment in output as would the employment of this man on Grade 2 or Grade 3 land. Total output cannot be increased by any redistribution of the labour force. This situation is illustrated in Fig. 45.

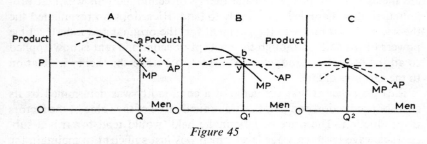

Figure 45

A, B and C are three grades of land, A being the most fertile and C the least fertile. Total employment is equal to $OQ + OQ^1 + OQ^2$. The marginal products of labour on each type of land are equal (OP), but the average products of labour are not equal. On Grade A land the average product of labour is Qa, on Grade B land it is Q^1b and on Grade C land it is Q^2c. If we assume perfect markets, the commodity produced, say wheat, will all be sold at one given market price, and all workers will receive the same wage, which will be equal to the value of their marginal product. Since the average product of labour is higher on Grade A land than it is on Grade B or Grade C land, the cost of production per bushel is correspondingly less. One shillingsworth of labour produces more wheat on Grade A land than it does on Grade B or Grade C land. Another way of looking at this is to regard A and B landowners as receiving a surplus.

Rent as a Surplus

In this example Grade C land is just worth cultivating; the returns are just equal to the cost. If labour is receiving the value of its marginal product there can be no surplus from Grade C land, because output is at the point where the average product of labour is equal to the marginal product. Only if producers receive the whole value of the output is Grade C land worth using. But on Grade A land labour is producing Qa units per man, and only receiving Qx units (measuring wages in terms of output). There is a surplus accruing to the owners of land A which is equal to $(ax \times OQ)$ and the owners of Grade B land will receive a surplus equal to $(by \times OQ^1)$.

These surpluses are economic rent. If Grade C land is just worth cultivating, then the owners of Grade A and Grade B land are receiving rewards greater than the amounts strictly necessary to bring their land into use. *When factors of production are receiving payments in excess of what is necessary to keep them in their present employment, the surpluses are known as economic rent.* Why do we use the term 'economic rent' to describe these surpluses? Because the owners of the more fertile land could charge a rent equal to the value of the surplus. Wheat growers would be indifferent as to whether they used the marginal land (i.e. no rent land) free, or paid a rent for the better land. Note that as more wheat is produced, the lower become the average and marginal products of labour. Falling productivity means increasing costs. More wheat will be produced only if its price rises to cover the higher costs. A rising demand for wheat will lead to higher prices and cause the margin of cultivation to move outwards. More will be produced on the land already in cultivation, and the extramarginal land will be brought into use. As the margin moves outwards, the surpluses earned by the more fertile land will increase. Hence the view of the classical economists that the group which stood to gain most from an expanding population was the landlord class.

Capital and Labour and Economic Rent

All this may seem rather complex, but the basic idea is a relatively simple one. The supply of land of any given grade of fertility is fixed in the short period. If the demand for the products of this land increases, the price of the product increases, less fertile and higher cost land will come into use.

The lower cost, more fertile land, will now earn a surplus which we call economic rent. Economic rent arises because of the fixity of the supply of the more fertile land. Looking at the problem from another angle, if the law of diminishing returns did not apply, we could increase the output from the more fertile land without incurring increasing average costs, and no use would be made of the inferior land. We would take the most fertile piece of land and apply more and more labour and capital to it. The increases in output would be proportionate, average costs would be constant and theoretically, therefore, the world's food supply could be obtained from one acre of the most fertile land!

The theory of economic rent has been much refined since Ricardo's time. It has been shown that economic rent is not peculiar to land; labour, capital, and entrepreneurship can also earn this kind of surplus. Any earnings of a factor of production which are in excess of its supply price are classified as economic rent. The supply price of a factor of production is that price which is just sufficient to attract it to its present employment. Thus the supply price of land (i.e. the *total* supply of land) is zero, because if the price of land dropped to zero, the supply of land would be unchanged. But this is not true of the supply of land for a particular purpose, since most land has alternative uses. The supply of land for wheat-growing is not fixed, for land can be taken from other uses and used for the cultivation of wheat. The supply price of land for any particular purpose is its earning power in its next most profitable use or 'occupation'. The supply price of wheat land, for example, might be what that land could earn when used to grow barley. The supply price of land for the building of office blocks, might be the earnings of that same land when used as a site for a cinema or a bowling alley. *The highest income which a factor of production could earn in alternative employment can be regarded as its transfer earnings.* To retain that factor in its present use, it must receive a reward at least equal to its transfer earnings. Any payment above its transfer earnings represents a surplus, since this part of its income is not strictly necessary to keep the factor in its present employment. Payments in excess of transfer earnings are regarded as economic rent. *Economic rent arises when the demand for the factor increases and the supply is not perfectly elastic.*

If there is a large increase in world trade, the demand for shipping will increase. Ships take a long time to build, and the supply of shipping-space cannot be increased in the short run. Freight rates will increase and the earnings of existing ships will rise quite sharply. The extra income now being received by ships which were formerly working at the lower rates can be regarded as economic rent. The example in Fig. 46 shows how economic rent might accrue to labour.

At a wage of OW, OM workers are employed. The demand for this type

204

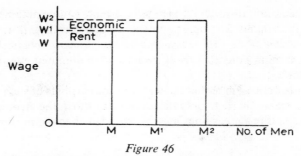

Figure 46

of labour increases, but more workers can only be attracted to this type of work by offering a higher wage in order to tempt them away from their present jobs. The wage is raised to OW^1 and MM^1 additional workers are engaged. Since all workers in this occupation receive the same wage, the original labour force OM is now receiving economic rent equal to $WW^1 \times OM$. If there is a further increase in the demand for this grade of labour then the element of economic rent will increase. The first group of workers will receive rent payments equal to $WW^2 \times OM$ and the second group will receive economic rent equal to $W^1W^2 \times MM^1$.

Probably the most striking example of earnings which contain a very large proportion of economic rent is to be found in the payments made to popular entertainers. The 'pop' groups of recent years are good illustrations. The transfer earnings of such groups would be but a tiny fraction of their earnings as popular entertainers. The greater part of their income, represented by that part which is in excess of what they might earn in the most remunerative alternative employment, must be classified as economic rent.

Site Value

The concept of economic rent can be used to explain *the site value of land*. In recent years quite staggering sums have been paid for sites in the centres of our cities. Extremely high rents are paid for buildings occupying central positions in the large towns. Such sites are strictly limited in supply – a site in the suburbs is no substitute for one in the High Street. The supply of sites in the High Street cannot be increased. The demand for city-centre sites is high because people prefer to shop in the centre of the city and do so in large numbers. They also seek their entertainment in the centre of the city. It is the great demand for goods and services in these central areas which leads to the high demand for sites there. It is this high level of demand for goods and services in the centres of cities which gives rise to the high rents in these areas. It is not the high rents which *cause* high prices, but the high prices which make possible the charging of high rents. The high prices of cinema and theatre seats in the West End of London are not due to the high rentals in this area; the high rents can be obtained because of the high demand for entertainment in this locality. *It is the great earning potential of the sites which enables the owners to obtain high rents.* This great earning potential arises because of the limited supply and the great demand.

But we must not assume that the whole of the earnings of such sites takes the form of economic rent. Only the amount by which the income from the site exceeds its transfer earnings may be regarded as economic rent.

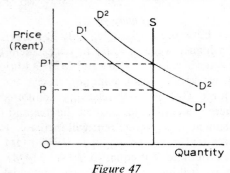

Figure 47

Suppose D^2D^2 in Fig. 47 represents the demand for a particular plot of land as a site for a supermarket and D^1D^1 is the demand for the same plot in its next most profitable use as a site for a block of offices. Then OP^1 would be the price or annual rental of this site if it were occupied by a supermarket, and OP is the annual rental it would command as a location for a block of offices. PP^1 then is economic rent, whereas OP must be regarded as a cost payment. This is so because a payment at least equal to OP must be made in order to change the utilisation of this land from a site for an office block to a site for a supermarket. But PP^1 is a payment in excess of this cost (or supply price) and is, therefore, economic rent.

Chapter 19

Profits

Measuring the Rate of Profit

Once again we find ourselves using a word which has a number of different meanings. Profit is commonly understood to be 'the difference between receipts and costs'. In the business world, however, the word is used in a variety of contexts.

1. The businessman will note that *the profit margin* on a particular line of goods is 10 per cent per unit. This is the kind of relationship found in the examples in an arithmetic textbook.

e.g. Cost Price 50p   Selling price 55p   Profit 5p

$$\text{Percentage profit} = \frac{1}{10} \times 100 = \underline{10\%}$$

2. A more common view of profit is that of *a percentage return on turnover*. In this case the profit is calculated as a percentage of the total revenue.

e.g. Sales receipts £1,000,000   Profits £150,000

$$\text{Rate of profit} = \frac{150,000}{1,000,000} \times 100 = \underline{15\%}$$

3. Another aspect of profit is as *the rate of return on the capital employed*. The profit is expressed as a percentage yield on the value of the capital employed in the business.

e.g. Sales receipts £1,000,000   Total costs £800,000   Capital £1,200,000

$$\text{Return on capital} = \frac{200,000}{1,200,000} \times 100 = \underline{16\cdot66\%}.$$

In any discussion of profit it is important to be aware of the particular view of profit which is being employed. A crude rate of profit, without any further analysis, can be very misleading. In the following example we have two firms, one making a very small profit on each unit sold, but having a large turnover, the other making a large profit on each unit, but having a smaller turnover. Each firm has the same amount of capital employed in the business. Profit margins are expressed as a percentage of the selling prices.

Firm A. Capital employed £1,000,000   Sales £5,000,000
      Profit margin 5%   Profit £250,000

$$\text{Return on capital employed} = \frac{250,000}{1,000,000} \times \frac{100}{1} = \underline{25\%}.$$

Firm B. Capital employed £1,000,000   Sales £500,000
      Profit margin 20%   Profit £100,000

$$\text{Return on capital employed} = \frac{100,000}{1,000,000} \times \frac{100}{1} = \underline{10\%}.$$

Although Firm B is operating with a profit margin four times as great as that earned by Firm A the return on its capital employed is very much less than that earned by Firm A.

Economists are concerned with profit as an income and not as a percentage differential on individual transactions. In most firms the profit margins per unit sold will be different on the various products in which they deal. We are interested in *the profit earned over time, as a flow of income*, and hence it is the rate of profit on capital employed which is the relevant view of profit.

Gross Profit and Net Profit

Another reason for the confusion which arises in many discussions on the subject of profit is the distinction between gross profit and net profit. *Gross profit* is defined as the excess of selling price over the buying or cost price. *Net profit* is the excess of gross profit over the selling and management expenses. It is normal for companies to prepare their accounts so that both gross and net profits are revealed. The following account is a very simplified example.

Trading Account
(year ending 31.12.67)

	£		£
Opening stock	5,000	Sales	23,000
Purchases	10,000	Closing stock	5,000
Transport	1,000		
Wages	5,000		
Fuels	200		
Balance (Gross profit)	6,800		
	£28,000		£28,000

Profit and Loss Account	£		£
Salaries	1,500	Gross profit	6,800
Insurance	100		
Rates and taxes	150		
Depreciation	500		
Interest on capital	1,000		
Balance (net profit)	3,550		
	£6,800		£6,800

It will be seen that gross profit is the figure obtained by deducting direct costs from total receipts. The true, or net profit, is arrived at by deducting *all* expenses from the total receipts. This is all very clear when the accounts of joint stock companies are examined, but in the case of the one-man business or small partnership the distinction between gross and net profit is often blurred. The small proprietor will declare that he has made say, £3,000 'profit' during the past year. This figure will usually be the gross profit which he obtains by deducting his purchases from his sales receipts. His true profit will be much less, because the declared profit contains an element of wages since he has employed his own labour in the business. An amount equal to what he could have earned doing similar work as a paid employee should be deducted from the gross profits. The entrepreneur will almost certainly have invested his personal savings in the enterprise and some part of his gross profit is made up of interest on capital. The interest which might have been earned by lending this money on good security should be deducted from gross profit. This deduction represents the opportunity cost of using his savings in his own business.

Profit differs from other forms of income in three ways. First, *profit may be negative*, that is, the company may make losses, whereas wages, rent, and interest are most unlikely to be negative payments. Secondly, *profit fluctuates* far more than other forms of income. Rent, interest and wages are, normally, established at agreed rates for some fixed period of time (e.g. a wage of £20 per week, or interest at 5 per cent per annum), but profit cannot be agreed in advance. Quite mild fluctuations in business activity can have very great effects on the rate of profit, but cause little or no change in wages, rent, and interest rates. Thirdly, *profit is a residual item*, it is what remains after all expenses have been paid out of receipts. The amount is uncertain. Wages, rent, and interest, on the other hand, are contractual payments fixed in advance of the performance of the services for which they are payments.

Risk-bearing and Profits

It has just been pointed out that profits are a residual item and therefore uncertain in amount. Entrepreneurial activities are motivated by *expectations* of profits, but the realised rate of profit may be very different from that which was anticipated. Profit is the reward for bearing the burden of uncertainty. When all costs have been allowed for, and, in the case of the small firm, these must include allowances for the proprietor's labour and capital, the residue or net profit represents the return to the function of risk-bearing. A man will not risk his capital in a business venture unless there is some prospect of making profits. It is the expectation of profit which encourages men to embark upon production in anticipation of demand.

The risks incurred in the running of a business organisation are of many kinds. Some of these, such as the risk of loss due to fire, or flood, or burglary, are insurable, but the businessman must face other risks which are not insurable. Future business losses cannot be insured against, because the risks are not subject to a statistical calculation which will give the likelihood of losses being incurred. In the examples given above of risks which are insurable it is possible to calculate the chances of these losses being incurred; this is not so with questions of success or failure in the business world. Uncertainty arises because we live in a world of change. The outcome of events can be very different from the estimates which persuaded the entrepreneur to undertake his business venture. So many things, which cannot possibly be foreseen, can affect the future demand for the product and the future costs of production. We can only guess what the future will hold, we can never be certain. Success in the business world would seem to require a combination of hard work, organising ability, good luck, and the comparatively rare ability to sense, before others, changes in the market situation, or the potentialities of a new product or new technique.

Mention of this rare ability to guess correctly more often than your competitors leads us to another view of profit. Some economists believe that profit is merely another form of economic rent. It arises because some special ability is limited in supply, or because some favourable situation is limited in supply. In other words, profit arises because there is some degree of monopoly, either of ability, or market situation. The store which occupies an extremely favourable site in the city, and the manufacturer who has a secret process, are examples of monopoly-type situations where abnormal profits might be earned. It is also argued that profits earned by the entrepreneur who has more successful 'hunches' than his competitors are, in part, economic rent. In the latter case the economic rent is referred to as a 'rent of ability'. In all these cases the profits earned are greater than the return necessary to keep these enterprises in their present line of business.

There are, then, four different aspects of profits. In the first place, reported profits might be regarded as implicit factor earnings and are a compound of wages, interest, rent and profits. The second view of profits sees them as a reward for bearing the uncertainty and risks of a competitive and changing world. Thirdly, profits are identified as the necessary inducement required to bring about innovation; to stimulate the discovery and adoption of new products and techniques. The fourth view of profits tends to regard them as a kind of monopoly return or economic rent.

If the future were known, if all future changes in population, tastes, incomes and technology could be accurately predicted, then profit would disappear. All risks would then be capable of actuarial calculation and would be insurable. All firms would earn *normal profits*, which would comprise the wages of management and interest on capital.

Chapter 20

Money and Banks

The Nature and Development of Money

Money is one of man's greatest inventions, and the fact that all but the simplest of human societies have used money proves that it is an essential tool of civilisation. Societies which do not have money must make use of a system known as barter, the direct exchange of goods and services for goods and services. Barter is a system which will serve man's requirements when he provides most of his needs directly and relies upon exchange for a very limited range of requirements. As the degree of specialisation increases, the methods of barter will prove inefficient and frustrating. In a simple agricultural society each family may produce most of what it needs and a little of what it does not need. A farmer can exchange small surpluses of food crops, or wool, or wood, for the products of specialised artisans, such as blacksmiths. The first specialists can, if necessary, exchange again the things they take in trade.

The great disadvantage of barter is the fact that it depends upon the 'double coincidence of wants'. A hunter who wishes to exchange some of his skins for corn, must find, not merely a person who requires skins, but a person who requires skins *and* has a surplus of corn for disposal. The alternative is to exchange his skins for some other article and then carry out a series of subsequent exchanges until he finally obtains his corn.

Quite early in his history man discovered a much more convenient system. The use of some commodity as a medium of exchange made exchange triangular and removed the difficulties of the barter system. Goods and services are now exchanged for money, a universally acceptable commodity, and the money is then exchanged for whatever goods and services are wanted.

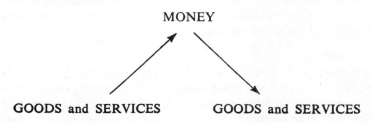

MONEY

GOODS and SERVICES   GOODS and SERVICES

The essential characteristic of money is that it should be generally acceptable in the society in which it circulates. If a commodity is freely acceptable
in exchange for goods and services, then that commodity is serving as
money. An immense variety of things has been used as money at one time
or another; shells, feathers, sharks' teeth, tobacco, salt, and many others.
Almost anything will serve as money if there is general confidence in its
acceptability. But as the extent of the division of labour and trade
developed, money acquired other functions and certain commodities were
seen to possess special attributes which made them particularly suitable to
serve as money. Let us now examine the functions of money in a modern
economy and then proceed to outline the evolution of the modern
monetary unit.

The Functions of Money

1. A MEDIUM OF EXCHANGE

As we have already explained, the use of money as a medium of exchange
makes it possible for man to specialise to a much greater extent than would
be possible under the system of barter. In a highly developed economy we
can so easily exchange one hour's labour for a haircut, a packet of
cigarettes, a meal in a café, a train journey, or an almost unlimited variety
of other goods and services, that we rarely, if ever, stop to consider the
wonderful service which money renders in making these transactions
possible, or how difficult – in most cases impossible – such exchanges
would be without the use of money.

2. A MEASURE OF VALUE

It is probable that one of the first steps in the use of money was the
adoption of some commodity as a unit of account or standard of value.
Money probably came into use alongside the use of barter as a means by
which the values of the various goods could be compared. The direct
exchange of goods for goods would raise constant problems of valuation;
for example, 'How many bushels of corn are equal to one sheep, if twenty
sheep are equal to three cows and two cows exchange for twenty-five
bushels of corn?' This problem of exchange ratios is easily solved when all
commodities are valued in terms of one given commodity which then acts
as a standard of value. When all commodities have money prices we know,
immediately, the value of one good in terms of another.

3. A STORE OF VALUE

Once a commodity has become universally acceptable in exchange for
goods and services it is possible to store wealth by holding this commodity.
Hence whatever is used as money must not be subject to deterioration,
neither must it be costly to store. The great advantage of storing wealth

in the form of money is that its possessor has immediate command over resources of any kind; he has a complete freedom of choice whenever he chooses to consume his wealth. Consider the disadvantages of holding wealth in the form of wheat. It may deteriorate; it is costly to store; it must be sold before the owner can consume his wealth in forms which are attractive to him. It should be apparent that money can only serve effectively as a store of value if its own value is stable.

4. A MEANS OF DEFERRED PAYMENT

An important function of money in the modern world, where so much business is conducted on the basis of credit, is to act as a standard of deferred payment. Contracts are made now which will be fulfilled at some future date. The manufacturer buys raw material promising to pay in three months' time; a company borrows money which it promises to repay in, perhaps, ten years' time; a man buys a car on hire purchase terms by which repayments are spread over three years; these are all examples of transactions which require *future* payment for goods and services which are transferred in the *present*. A complex trading organisation based upon a system of credit is only possible in a monetary economy. A seller could not accept a promise to pay, expressed in terms of some specified commodity, at some future date, because he cannot foresee his future wants in terms of that commodity. He will be prepared to accept future payment in terms of money, because, no matter what the pattern of his future wants, they can be satisfied if he possesses money.

The Media of Exchange

The commodity which is chosen to serve as money must possess certain qualities if it is to carry out, in a satisfactory manner, all the functions which have just been outlined.

Except in the most advanced societies, the commodity must be desired for its own sake, that is, it must have a commodity value as well as a money value. For use as a medium of exchange, people would only accept a good which they thought would be acceptable to others, and the best guarantee of acceptability was that the commodity should have an intrinsic value. So, for a very long period in the history of money, the commodity in use as money had to be desired for its own sake, and not merely as a medium of exchange. Gold met these requirements admirably.

An efficient medium of exchange must be *portable* and have a high ratio of value to weight. Traders, in early days, would be obliged to carry with them their receipts, and sellers, the means of making their payments. It would be very inconvenient to carry large, heavy or bulky objects to act as a medium of exchange.

H

215

The substance must be *divisible*. It must be possible to divide the material into smaller units without loss of value so that various quantities of any good can be bought and sold. This is another great disadvantage of the barter system. Suppose two sheep are worth one hide, how does the man with the hide buy one sheep? When the hide is cut into two halves, the value of the two halves is not equal to the value of the whole.

A most necessary characteristic is that of *durability*. Money cannot serve as a store of value unless it is capable of storage for long periods without any deterioration.

Finally, the commodity must be *limited in supply*. Unless there is some limitation of supply, natural, or artificial, people will have very little confidence in the value of money.

This list of desirable characteristics provides an explanation for the almost universal adoption, as civilisation develops, of the precious metals as the commodities to serve as money. In almost all societies, and at all times, men have placed a high value on gold and silver, and even today, gold still serves as the international standard of value. Gold and silver were used as money by the Babylonians as early as 2000 B.C.

Gold and silver are portable since they have a very high value relative to weight; they are divisible without loss of value; it is fairly easy to produce gold and silver of uniform fineness; they are easily recognisable and can be stored without deterioration. The limitation of supply is a natural limitation, for these metals are not easy to obtain. The annual additions to the existing stocks are relatively very small and will have no effect on the value of the metals.[1]

COINS AND BANK-NOTES

The precious metals were first used as money on a basis of weight. We read in the Bible: 'And Abraham weighed unto Ephron the silver' (Gen. 23:16). Our word 'pound'[2] serves as an indication of a unit of money and a unit of weight. The inconvenience of weighing out the metals each time a commodity was bought and sold led to the development of coinage. It was appreciated that exchange would be greatly facilitated if each piece of metal, used as money, carried some clear indication of its weight and fineness and hence of its value. Coins are shaped pieces of metal bearing some government imprint which certifies their value. The earliest known coins were used by the Greeks and were minted in Lydia about 700 B.C. A people suspicious of money or of the integrity of their rulers will only

[1] There have been some periods when the supply was increased sharply and caused some subsequent fall in value. This happened in the sixteenth century following the Spanish exploitation of the American gold and silver deposits and in the nineteenth century following the Californian, Australian and South African discoveries.

[2] i.e. one pound sterling silver.

accept coins if they are certain that the commodity value of the coin is equal to its money value. There is always a temptation for rulers to enrich themselves by reducing the commodity value of the coinage, that is, by putting less of the precious metal into the coins. This means that any given weight of gold or silver could be used to produce more coins. Many rulers, in the past, have attempted to raise funds by 'debasing' the coinage (e.g. issuing pennies which did not contain one pennyworth of silver). There was a long series of such debasements in England beginning in 1343. The silver content of the penny in the year 1300 was twenty-two grains troy, but by 1544 it had fallen to ten grains. Debasement during this period seriously affected the acceptability of money and led to a series of crises until the reform of the coinage under Elizabeth I. The events of the period led to the formulation of *Gresham's Law*, which states that *bad money drives out good*. Where a variety of coins are circulating, some of which have a higher gold or silver content than others, people will tend to hoard the coins with the greater commodity value and to use the debased coinage as currency.

The next great step in the development of money was the introduction of paper money. Bank-notes first came into use, in Britain, during the seventeenth century. The history of the bank-note shows how what was originally a claim to money, came to be used as money itself. Metallic money, although having the advantage of being easily carried, suffered the disadvantage of being easily stolen. The habit of leaving gold and silver in a place of safety (the embryonic bank) led to the issuing of deposit receipts, or some written evidence of 'a promise to pay' issued by the person who had been entrusted with the safe-keeping of the precious metal. If these certificates were stolen no loss was suffered because the gold or silver could not be withdrawn without the depositor's signature. In time these I.O.U.s came to be used as money. The banker's promise to pay came to be accepted in settlement of debts, a procedure which eliminated the time, trouble, and danger involved in withdrawing and transporting the bullion. The debtor merely endorsed his 'notes', making over his claim to the deposit to his creditors. The banker would act on these instructions whenever a claim for payment was made. Then followed a further simplification of this procedure. Bankers began to make out their deposit receipts, or promises to pay, as payable 'to bearer' (i.e. anyone having possession of the document) instead of to a named person. The 'notes' were issued for convenient round sums of money (e.g. £1, £5 or £10) instead of being a single receipt for the full amount of the cash deposited. The persons in possession of these promissory notes were deemed to be the rightful owners. Thus developed the fully-fledged bank-note.

FRACTIONAL BACKING

Initially the bank-note would be accepted as a claim to money, being

INTRODUCTORY ECONOMICS

used for one transaction and then 'cashed'. But, in time, the bank-note itself came to be regarded as money and was passed on from hand to hand, financing numerous transactions. As long as people were certain that they could convert the note into gold or silver they were prepared to use it as money. The increasing use of the bank-note as money had very important consequences. Bankers, originally, issued notes equal in value to their deposits of gold and silver, in other words, their note issue had a 100 per cent 'backing' in the form of precious metal. When these notes began to circulate freely and the public acquired confidence in them, it became apparent that the greater part of the bankers' holdings of gold and silver were lying idle. Each day some notes would be presented for conversion into cash (i.e. specie), but each day other people would be coming in to deposit cash. Only a small proportion of the metal 'backing' would be required to meet the daily demands for cash. Bankers began to adopt the practice of issuing notes well in excess of the value of their holdings of gold and silver. Suppose a banker found, by experience, that, over a period of time, only one in ten of his bank notes were presented for payment. This would mean that he could issue notes to a value equal to ten times the value of his cash. A careful banker, conscious of the fact that he might have to meet unexpected demands for cash, might well issue notes equal to five times the value of his cash. We have now reached the stage where bankers are creating money, a practice which developed during the seventeenth and eighteenth centuries. This particular stage in the evolution of money was marked by a long series of crises and bank failures – 'crises of confidence' as they were called. Bankers were tempted to issue notes excessively and they tried to operate with reserves of cash which proved inadequate to meet unexpected demands. Failure to meet demands for cash destroyed confidence in the bank, holders of notes rushed to recover their deposits and the bank, unable to meet these demands, was forced into liquidation with consequent serious losses being incurred by depositors. Bank-notes fell into disrepute and the State was obliged to regulate the note issue. *The Bank Charter Act of 1844* placed a statutory limit on the *fiduciary issue*, (that part of the note issue which was not backed by gold or silver).

So far all the bank-notes issued had been fully convertible and the next step in the history of the bank-note came with the acceptability, by the public, of notes which were not convertible. Until 1914 English bank-notes were convertible, on demand, into gold, except for a temporary suspension of convertibility during the Napoleonic Wars. Convertibility was again suspended in 1914, resumed in a limited form in 1925, and finally abandoned in 1931. Since this latter date Bank of England notes have been wholly inconvertible and we have now reached the stage where paper money, carrying a 'promise to pay' which is utterly meaningless, is universally acceptable throughout the British Isles. Our notes and coins are

218

token money, since our coinage is now made of cheap metals, the commodity value of which is but a small fraction of the money value. The general acceptance of inconvertible notes follows á long period of familiarity with paper money. Early bank-notes were only accepted because they could be converted into gold, now they are accepted for their own sake.

Bank Deposits

Bank notes and coins, however, are not the major form of money in Great Britain, nor in most advanced countries. In Great Britain, about 90 per cent by value of all transactions are settled by the use of cheques. But cheques themselves are not money, they are merely orders to bankers to transfer money from one person to another. The money so transferred consists of bank deposits. The greater part of the money supply in advanced countries consists of bank deposits and the cheque is an instruction to the banker to transfer bank deposits from debtor to creditor. If there is no deposit in the account of the person drawing the cheque or if his funds are insufficient, then the cheque itself is worthless.

Cheques were used as early as the second half of the seventeenth century, but they did not come into general use until the second half of the nineteenth. The Bank Charter Act of 1844 put strict limitations on the note issue at a time when the production of goods and services was expanding rapidly. The need for an expansion of the money supply to keep pace with this increasing output greatly stimulated the use of bank deposits which were subject to payment by cheque.

We must now turn to a study of the banking system in order to understand how bank deposits come into existence.

The Functions of a Bank

1. The oldest banking function, but by no means the most important, is that of providing a safe deposit for valuables.
2. The most profitable activity of the banks is the lending of money. The banker's major source of income is the interest he earns on his loans.
3. One of the earliest of banking activities, as we have already seen, was the issuing of bank-notes. In England and Wales this right is now restricted to the Bank of England.
4. Modern banks provide, by means of bank deposits subject to movement by cheque, a very efficient means of settling debts.

In Great Britain there are several types of bank, only one of which now carries out all the functions listed above. These different kinds of bank are classified as follows:

1. SAVINGS BANKS

These banks, as their name implies, tend to concentrate on the oldest banking function. They were formed to encourage the saving habit among the poorer sections of the community and branches of the two largest savings banks, the Post Office Savings Bank and the Trustees Savings Bank are to be found in most towns in Britain. They do not provide a cheque system, but at the time of writing there are serious proposals for the introduction of such a system. These banks carry out the lending function, but their loans are restricted to the Government and other public bodies.

2. MERCHANT BANKS

Merchant banks are to be found principally in the City of London. Most of them are old-established businesses and among them we find such famous names as Rothschilds, Barings, Schroeders, Lazards, and Morgan. Some of them began as merchants trading in certain commodities, in certain parts of the world, while others were bankers from the start who tended to specialise in world trade.

One of the main functions of the merchant banks is to provide credit for the financing of world trade. The main instrument for this purpose was *the bill of exchange* and it was in dealings with bills of exchange that the London merchants achieved wealth and fame. The bill of exchange is still an important credit instrument but the telegraphic transfer of funds has tended to diminish its use.

When a trader sells goods he draws up a bill of exchange which he sends to the debtor for signature. The debtor signs (or *accepts*) the bill and returns it to the seller who now holds a legal acknowledgement of the buyer's indebtedness. Bills are normally drawn up for payment at some time in the future, the traditional period of credit being three months. This means that the buyer has three months' grace before payment becomes due, but the seller is often not prepared to wait three months before receiving payment. If the credit standing of the buyer is very good, the seller may be able to sell, or, more accurately, 'discount' the bill at his bank. He will not receive the full value of the bill because the banks will charge a discount[1] for their services. The bank will have to wait three months before the bill is due for payment, so that the 'discount' is, in fact, the interest payment on a three-month loan. In normal circumstances, however, the bank will not know the credit standing of the debtor and it will be necessary for the trader to have the bill 'accepted' by a merchant bank. Merchant banks maintain agents all over the world; they tend to specialise in certain commodity markets, so that they are able to check the financial standing of almost any firm of traders. In return for a commission they will accept the

[1] See page 229.

220

bill by endorsing it with their name, thus guaranteeing payment of the bill should the buyer of the goods default. Once the name of one of the great merchant banks appears on a bill of exchange it becomes 'eligible' paper and will be readily acceptable by a bank, or by one of the Discount Houses which specialise in discounting bills of exchange. The seller of the goods is thus enabled to receive immediate payment, while the buyer obtains three months' credit. In this way the acceptance houses and the discount houses provide the credit which makes international trade possible on a large scale.

But the merchant banks carry out several other important financial functions. They act as issuing houses for companies which are making share issues, and carry through all the complex procedures involved in the floating of share issues on the capital market. Another of their functions is to act as expert managers of investment trusts, and to manage the investment of pension funds and other trust funds. They operate in the foreign exchange markets and provide all the normal banking services for their customers. In recent years the merchant banks have obtained considerable publicity from the part they play in 'takeover' operations. The business firms concerned with amalgamations and mergers usually employ merchant banks to handle the financial aspects of these deals.

3. COMMERCIAL BANKS

The principal form of banking institution in this country is the commercial bank or joint stock bank as it is commonly called. A recent spate of mergers has reduced the number of the clearing banks (i.e. members of the London Clearing House) from eleven to six. The National Provincial merged with the Westminster to form the National Westminster Bank which also absorbed the District Bank. Barclays merged with Martins. Two Scottish banks, the Royal Bank of Scotland and the National Commercial Bank of Scotland amalgamated under the name of the Royal Bank of Scotland. Three subsidiaries of these Scottish Banks, Williams Deacons, Glyn Mills, and the National Bank were merged into a single bank under the title Williams and Glyns Bank.

The six clearing banks are: Barclays/Martins, the National Westminster, the Midland, Lloyds, Williams and Glyns, and Coutts. The first four of these banks (the Big Four) dominate commercial banking in this country and operate between them some 12,500 branches. One result of the rationalisation programmes which will follow the integrations will be a reduction in the number of these branches. Other economies will flow from the greater use of computers, data processing machines, and other advanced technological aids to computation and communications.

The commercial banks have traditionally offered a wide variety of services. Their major functions are the provision of loans to all sections of industry and commerce, and the operation of a mechanism for settling debts by the use of cheques. In addition, they provide foreign exchange, act as investment counsellors and trustees, act as agents for issuing houses by collecting applications and payments for share issues, carry out the duties of executors in the settlement of wills, and provide specialist information on such subjects as exporting and the setting up of new businesses.

In more recent times the banks have further extended the range of their services and activities. New machines allow depositors to draw small sums of cash at any time of the day or night; the provision of a credit transfer scheme enables the banks' customers to pay a number of separate bills by means of a single cheque, and a system of credit cards makes it possible for depositors to spend up to some specified sum at certain shops simply by producing the card and signing the bill. Most banks issue excellent little booklets which give full details of the various services provided.

The commercial banks now hold a controlling interest in several of the major hire purchase companies. A series of credit squeezes had diverted many potential customers of the banks to this form of borrowing and the commercial banks felt obliged to protect their interests by entering this market.

Several commercial banks have created links with leading merchant banks in order to extend their activities into other fields (e.g. longer term lending, share issuing and unit trusts).

4. CENTRAL BANKS

Most countries now have a central bank, the functions of which vary according to the level of economic development of the particular country. In Britain the central bank is the Bank of England, the functions of which are summarised below and will be dealt with in more detail later, in Chapter 21. The major duties of the Bank of England are to act as:

(a) a lender of last resort,
(b) the Government's bank,
(c) the bankers' bank,
(d) the bank which controls the note issue,
(e) the means by which the Government operates its monetary policy,
(f) the institution which handles the National Debt,
(g) the Government's agent in the foreign exchange market.

The Banking Mechanism and the Supply of Money

Bank Deposits

Our next step is to examine the nature of the money supply and the manner in which it is created and controlled. The supply of money consists of two elements, (i) notes and coin, and (ii) bank deposits. In the U.K., notes and coin are supplied by the state and issued through the Bank of England. The major part of the money supply consists of bank deposits held by the private sector of the banking system.

U.K. Money Supply July 1972	£ million
Notes and Coin in Circulation	3,744
Bank Deposits	19,491
	23,235

The bank deposits are created by the commercial banks. They come into being in two ways:

(*a*) When a person brings cash (notes and coin) into a bank he receives a bank deposit in exchange for his cash. The value of his personal supply of money has not changed, it has simply changed its form. He now possesses a bank deposit whereas previously he held cash of the same value. There has been no change in the money supply.

(*b*) The second and more important method in which bank deposits come into being is by means of a bank's lending operations. Bank lending may take two forms. The bank may purchase securities (normally government securities) with cheques drawn on itself. The sellers of these securities will pay these cheques into their bank accounts and acquire bank deposits of corresponding value. The greater part of bank deposits, however, is created when the bank makes a loan and credits the account of the borrower with the amount of the loan. In both cases the bank has created bank deposits without any prior deposit of cash. In this context it is useful to remember the maxim, 'Every loan creates a deposit'. What has taken place, in fact, is an exchange of claims.

223

The bank's liabilities and assets have increased by equal amounts. If you lend me 50p then I acquire an asset together with an equal and opposite liability to repay you the 50p. You, on the other hand, have exchanged one asset, the 50p, for a different asset, namely, my promise to repay.

The banker's deposits are liabilities because he is committed to meet all his depositors' demands for cash and to honour all cheques drawn on these deposits. His loans represent assets because they are claims against the borrowers and banks safeguard themselves by requiring borrowers to provide some kind of security to cover the value of the loan. This security may take the form of a legal charge on the borrower's property or some good evidence of the likely success of the business venture.

The two types of transaction outlined above will affect the banks' balance sheets in the following way:

(a) A person makes a deposit of cash (£100)

Liabilities		Assets	
Deposits	£100	Cash	£100

(b) The bank buys securities value £100

Liabilities		Assets	
Deposits	£100	Securities	£100

Bank deposits may be held in current accounts or as time deposits. Money held in current accounts is transferable by cheque, but does not earn interest. Time deposits are not transferable by cheque and can only be withdrawn after due notice. Interest is paid on the funds held in deposit accounts.

In order to understand the basis of the banks' ability to create deposits and the manner in which this ability is controlled, we must first examine the structure of the banking system.

The Bank of England

The Bank of England was brought into public ownership in 1946 and is directly under the control of the Treasury. The Bank is divided into two departments, the Issue Department and the Banking Department. The Issue Department is responsible for the note issue, and the Banking Department carries out all other banking functions. The Bank of England publishes a weekly return which gives details of the current assets and liabilities of the two departments. Table 19 consists of such a return.

Table 19. *The Bank of England: weekly return, 16 August 1972* (£ *million*)

Issue Department

Liabilities		Assets	
Notes in circulation	4,052	Government securities	3,534
Notes in Banking Department	23	Other assets	541
			4,075
	4,075		

Banking Department

Public Deposits	19	Government securities	337
Special Deposits	—	Discounts/Advances	32
Bankers' Deposits	204	Other Securities	130
Other Accounts	284	Notes and Coin	23
	507		522

(This account does not balance because some small items
have been omitted)

Source: *Bank of England Quarterly Bulletin September 1972.*

The statement from the *Issue Department* shows that the British note issue is wholly fiduciary, in other words, it is not backed by gold. The assets which are held to cover the liabilities of the department consist almost entirely of government securities. The Banking Department draws notes from the Issue Department as required, handing over in exchange government securities of equivalent value.

Turning now to the items in the return from the *Banking Department* we have, on the *liabilities* side:

(*a*) *Public Deposits.* This is the government's account, but the published figure of £19 million has little meaning. The inflow and outflow of funds on this account is very large, amounting to hundreds of millions of pounds each week. The balance is always kept to a minimum and any temporary surplus is used to reduce the government's borrowing.

(*b*) *Special Deposits.* These are funds which may be called from the commercial banks when the monetary authorities (the Treasury and the Bank of England) wish to reduce the liquid assets of the private banking sector. Their function is described later.

(*c*) *Bankers' Deposits.* These are the deposits of the commercial banks. They are current accounts and, since the deposits can be converted into currency on demand, they comprise part of the commercial banks' cash reserves.

(*d*) *Other Accounts.* This is a miscellaneous group of deposits and includes the accounts of overseas central banks and international monetary institutions.

The *assets* of the Banking Department are made up of:

(*a*) *Government Securities.* These are securities, both short- and long-term, issued by the British government.

(*b*) *Discounts and Advances.* This item consists of the bills discounted for the Banks' customers together with any loans made on the security of such bills. These transactions are described in the next section.

(*c*) *Other Securities.* These are all other securities of whatever sort and will include some commercial bills purchased in open market operations (explained later).

(*d*) *Notes and Coin.* This is the counterpart of the item on the liabilities side of the return from the Issue Department. These notes and coin are held in readiness to meet demands from the commercial banks.

The London Money Market

This is the market for short-term and very short-term loans and centres around the activities of a small number of discount houses which are members of the London Discount Market Association. A number of institutions play a part in the operation of the London Money Market. They include the Bank of England, the head offices of the commercial banks, the merchant banks, the discount houses, and the London branches of overseas banks. Their work involves dealings in certain important instruments of credit, namely Treasury Bills, bills of exchange, and short-dated government securities. The bill of exchange was described on page 220. *Treasury Bills* are government securities with a life of 91 days and are the instruments by which the government carries out its short term borrowing. Each week the government borrows large sums by offering Treasury Bills for sale to the money market. The system used is one of tendering and each week various financial institutions (e.g. discount houses and branches of overseas banks) are invited to submit offers for the following week's issue of Treasury Bills. The higher the bid-price, the lower will be the rate of interest paid by the government for its short term borrowing. For example, if the bid-price is £99 (per £100), the government will be paying slightly over 4 per cent for short term funds. Since the government redeems the bills at their face value, it is paying an interest rate of £1 on a loan of £99 for 3 months

i.e. $\dfrac{1}{99} \times \dfrac{100}{1} \times \dfrac{4}{1} = 4 \cdot 04$ per cent.

This procedure of buying a security at less than its face value is described as *discounting*. In the example above we assumed that the money market paid £99 for a security which had a face value of £100. The difference between the price paid for the security and its value when it becomes due for repayment may be expressed as a rate of interest.

The discount houses obtain only a part of the weekly issue of Treasury Bills, although they guarantee to take up the total issue at the prices they offer. Other financial institutions usually outbid them for part of the issue. Discount houses borrow from the commercial banks and use the borrowed funds to purchase Treasury Bills and commercial bills. These loans appear as 'money at call and short notice' in the banks' balance sheets (page 228). The discount houses make a profit (or a loss) from the difference between the rate of interest at which they borrow and the rate they charge on their lending (i.e. when discounting bills). As the bills near maturity the discount houses may sell them to the commercial banks. The banks tend to hold these bills until they mature. Like the discount houses they will earn interest on these loans since they rediscount the bills (e.g they may pay £99½ for the bill used in our example, after it has run for, say, six weeks).

In order to make a profit the discount houses are obliged to take the risks involved in 'borrowing short and lending long'. The funds they borrow are repayable at very short notice; some, in fact, are repayable 'at call', that is, on demand. They commit these funds to longer term loans – 91 days in the case of newly issued Treasury Bills. If the commercial banks run short of cash, they will normally call back some of their loans to the money market, and the discount houses must honour their obligations to repay these loans. Since the borrowed funds are 'locked up' in Treasury Bills and bills of exchange, the discount houses must turn to the lender of last resort – the Bank of England. The central bank will always come to the aid of the discount houses by buying (i.e. rediscounting) some of their bills, or by providing loans against the security of such bills. The Bank will only deal in first class bills[1] and its lending rate is higher than current money market rates of interest. The Bank's minimum lending rate[2] is fixed at a level slightly higher than the current market rate on Treasury Bills. This means that the discount houses, will be making losses on the loans they are repaying to the commercial banks. In order to obtain the money to repay, they will be obliged to pay a higher rate of interest than they have been earning on their own lending.

---

[1]First class bills are either (i) Treasury Bills or (ii) commercial bills which bear at least two signatures of persons of acceptable credit standing, (e.g. merchant banks).
[2]Formerly known as Bank Rate.

The Commercial Banks

The major commercial banks are the London Clearing Banks, that is, the members of the London Clearing House (see page 230). The business tends to be dominated by the Big Four and their subsidiaries. They are Lloyds, Barclays, Midland, and the National Westminster. There are some smaller clearing banks, and a large number of non-clearing banks.

The commercial banks are profit-seeking enterprises, making most of their profits from the interest they charge on their loans. Since lending is the most profitable of their activities, they have every incentive to maximise their loans. In addition to this obligation to their shareholders, however, the banks have obligations to their depositors which require them to meet all demands for cash (notes and coin). The banks must maintain an adequate supply of notes and coin and, additionally, some extremely liquid assets which can readily be converted into cash should depositors make unexpectedly heavy demands for currency.

These different obligations provide the banker with a dilemma since the demand for profitability conflicts with the demand for liquidity. The most liquid asset, cash, earns no income at all, and, generally speaking, the more liquid the asset, the lower its earning power. Very short term loans are more liquid than longer term loans, but they earn lower rates of interest. Just how the banks reconcile the conflicting aims of liquidity and profitability may be seen in Table 20 which shows the structure of bank assets and liabilities.

Table 20. *The London clearing banks: combined balance sheet, July 1972 (£ million)*

Liabilities		Assets	
Gross Deposits:		Coin, notes, and balances	
(i) in Sterling	13,681	with the Bank of England	848
(ii) in other currencies	1,000	Balances with other U.K.	
Other Accounts	459	banks	891
		Money at Call and Short	
		Notice	1,258
		Bills discounted	541
		Investments in U.K.	
		government securities	1,348
		Loans to Local Authorities	341
		Advances	9,332
		Other assets	563
		Special deposits	—
	15,140		15,122

(The two sides do not balance because some small items are omitted.)
Source: *Bank of England Quarterly Bulletin*, September 1972.

The left hand side of the balance sheet shows that the liabilities of the banks consist of their deposits.

The right hand side shows the distribution of the banks' assets, and it is here that we see the pattern of bank lending. Taking the items in order, we have:

(*a*) *Coin, Notes, and Balances with the Bank of England*. The coins and notes are held in the banks' tills in order to meet depositors' demands for cash. The deposits held at the Bank of England have already been explained. The total represents the banks' cash reserves and, until 1971, when new arrangements were introduced, the banks maintained cash reserves equal in value to 8 per cent of their total deposits. This was the traditional cash ratio. These assets earn no income.

(*b*) *Balances with other U.K. banks*. These are assets to the clearing banks since they are claims on other banks. For the whole banking system, however, such balances would cancel each other out. This may be verified by looking at Table 11 in the Bank of England Quarterly Bulletin.

(*c*) *Money at Call and Short Notice*. This is the total of bank lending to the London Money Market, principally to the discount houses. From the banks' point of view such loans represent very liquid assets since any loss of cash can be made good very quickly by calling in some of these loans. These loans, by virtue of their very short-term nature, earn relatively low rates of interest.

(*d*) *Bills Discounted*. This item is made up of the Treasury Bills and commercial bills which the banks have purchased from the discount houses. The bills have a maturity of three months, but the banks tend to buy them when they have about a half, or less, of their life to run. Since the banks are buying them continuously, they will have some bills maturing every day, and it would be possible for them to increase their holdings of cash by buying bills of less value than those currently maturing. The interest yield on these bills will be rather higher than that earned on money at call and short notice.

(*e*) *Investments*. This component of the banks' assets comprises longer-term government securities, although the banks will not normally buy such securities until they have five years or less to run. They earn a more favourable rate of interest than the short-term loans and can be sold at any time on the Stock Exchange. Heavy sales of such securities, however, would depress their prices and cause the banks to suffer capital losses.

(*f*) *Advances*. This is the most profitable but least liquid of the banks' assets. Bank loans provide a most important source of short-term capital to industry and commerce, and there is a large business in personal loans. Although banks prefer to make fairly short-term loans (six months or so), such loans can usually be renewed, unless the banks are under pressure to reduce their deposits. Interest rates on bank loans vary according to the creditworthiness of the borrower and the duration of the loan. Until 1971, the banks operated a cartel whereby they all charged the same rate of interest to the most creditworthy borrowers (the base rate). They now compete with each other on the basis of price (i.e. interest rates) and each bank is free to set its own base rate.

(g) *Special Deposits.* The functions of special deposits are explained on page 234.

Coins, notes, balances at the central bank, money at call and short notice, and bills discounted have been regarded as the traditional liquid assets of the banking system. Until September 1971 the banks were required to maintain a minimum liquid assets ratio of 28 per cent. Investments and advances are the less liquid but more profitable assets.

THE BANKERS' CLEARING HOUSE

The procedure for making payments by means of cheques requires some machinery to carry out the transfer of money from the drawer to the drawee. The person making the payment may keep his account in a different bank from that which holds the account of the person receiving payment. The final settlement of the debt, therefore, requires the movement of funds from one bank to another. In any one day there will be many thousands of such inter-bank transactions to be carried out; many of them will offset each other. There will be a large number of cheques drawn on accounts in Bank A payable to accounts in Bank B, but there will also be many cheques requiring a transfer of funds in the opposite direction.

Each separate bank in a multi-bank system will find itself in this kind of situation. It is an obvious solution for each bank to pay (or receive) the net amount owing after the banks have totalled their claims against each other. This is the function of the Bankers' Clearing House. Cheques drawn on one bank but payable to another bank are sent to the clearing house where the mutual claims are offset and the banks merely settle the outstanding amounts. These payments from one bank to another are carried out by movements in the bankers' deposits at the central bank. These are current accounts and the banks can use them to make payments to each other in the same way that members of the public use their current accounts in the commercial banks. It is very important to note, however, that when one bank makes payment to another, one bank will gain cash and the other bank loses cash. The reason for this, of course, is that their deposits at the central bank are part of the banks' cash reserves.

Reserve Assets

Deposit banking is based upon the principle that all depositors will not simultaneously exercise their right to withdraw their funds. It is an obligation of a bank to encash its deposits when called upon to do so. On any given day some customers will be withdrawing cash from the banks, but, at the same time, other customers will be paying it in. Since such receipts and payments of cash are not likely to balance each other exactly, banks will need to keep some reserves of cash. These reserves are the first item on the assets side of the balance sheet. The cash reserves of the banks will be kept to some safe minimum. Banks will not want to hold any more cash than is strictly necessary since it earns no income. The value of the cash reserves expressed as a percentage of total deposits is known as the *cash ratio*. In Table 20 this ratio is about 5·6 per cent, rather lower than the old traditional ratio of 8 per cent.

The size of the cash ratio is determined by experience. If there is a large measure of public confidence in the banking system, banks deposits will be the most important form of money and most payments will be made by cheque. Quite small cash reserves will then be adequate to meet demands for cash. This is the situation in most developed countries. A further reason why banks in such countries are able to operate with very small cash reserves is the availability of very liquid assets, which the banks hold as secondary reserves. Unexpectedly heavy demands for cash can be met by converting these reserve assets into cash. These liquid assets consist of the loans to the money market, Treasury Bills, commercial bills, and government securities which are very close to maturity.

THE RESERVE ASSETS RATIO

If, (i) the banks always maintain some fixed proportion between certain reserve assets and total deposits, and (ii) the central bank has the ability to control the banks' supply of reserve assets, it follows that the monetary authorities will be able to control the level of bank deposits. It will also be the case that any variation in the banks' holdings of reserve assets will have 'multiplier' effects on the level of bank deposits.

For example, suppose the banks maintain a reserve assets ratio of 10 per cent, then

$$\text{Total Deposits} = 10 \times \text{Reserve Assets}$$

If we assume the banks are holding reserve assets to the value of £10 million, the value of total deposits will be £100 million. Suppose now, the central bank is able to reduce the banks' reserve assets by £2 million. The banks will now be holding £8 million of reserve assets, but these will only support total deposits of £80 million. The banks will be forced to reduce their total deposits to this figure of £80 million. The total effect will be to reduce the money supply (bank deposits) by £20 million. The multiplier is 10.

The value of the multiplier is clearly $\dfrac{1}{\text{Reserve Assets Ratio}}$; in our case, $\dfrac{1}{\frac{10}{100}} = 10$.

An expansion of the money supply, in the form of additional bank lending, becomes possible when the banks obtain additional supplies of reserve assets. Again there will be multiplier effects. With a reserve assets ratio of 10 per cent, the banks would be able to expand deposits by an amount equal to ten times the value of any additional reserve assets they can acquire. (See also page 234).

The British banking system now operates with a reserve assets ratio of $12\frac{1}{2}$ per cent, so that the theoretical multiplier is 8. The assets which qualify for the status of reserve assets have been clearly defined by the Bank of England. They are:

(a) *The commercial banks' balances at the Bank of England.* Special deposits are not included in this figure, and it is important to note that the notes and coins held by the banks do not count as reserve assets.

(b) *Treasury Bills*

(c) *Company tax reserve certificates.* A company may not have to pay certain taxes until some time after the close of the financial year during which the tax liability was incurred. It is possible for a company to make provision for its tax liability by purchasing tax reserve certificates (from the government) which carry tax free interest. These certificates may be surrendered in payment of the tax when it becomes due, or they may be surrendered for cash beforehand.

(d) *Money at call with the London Money Market*

(e) *British government securities which have less than one year to run to maturity*

(f) *Local authority bills eligible for rediscount with the Bank of England.* These are short-term securities issued by the local authorities.

(g) Commercial bills eligible for rediscount at the Bank of England up to a maximum of 2 per cent of total deposits.

The reserve assets ratio applies to all banks in the U.K. with the exception of the National Giro and the discount houses. Finance houses, which provide funds for, e.g., hire purchase and hold deposits on a longer term basis, must maintain a reserve assets ratio of 10 per cent.

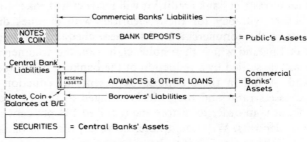

Figure 48

The Control of the Money Supply

The major part of the money supply consists of bank deposits created by the banks' lending activities. Measures to control the money supply must be effective in controlling the commercial banks' ability to lend.

In the strictest sense of the word, banks do not 'create'; it might be more accurate to say that they 'transform'. Bank lending is a process of exchanging claims. The banks tend to see their function as one of transforming an illiquid asset into a liquid asset. Borrowers must provide the banks with some form of acceptable security (i.e. illiquid assets) which the borrowers exchange for a liquid asset, money. One limitation on the banks' ability to lend, is the extent to which potential borrowers can supply collateral (i.e. security). The banks can only lend to the limit of their ability when there is an adequate supply of creditworthy borrowers.

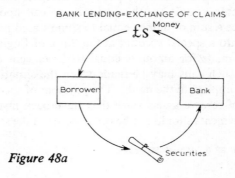

Figure 48a

CENTRAL BANK CONTROLS

The most important controls on bank lending (and hence on the money supply) are those operated by the Bank of England.

(a) Open Market Operations

The Bank of England, through its brokers, buys and sells securities (Treasury Bills and other government securities) in the open market. If it wishes to restrict bank credit,[1] it will instruct its broker to sell securities. The buyers will pay for these securities with cheques drawn on their accounts in the commercial banks. These cheques will be payable to the Bank of England which then holds claims on the commercial banks. The debts will be settled by a reduction of the bankers' deposits at the Bank of England. A fall in these deposits represents a reduction in the banks' reserve assets ratio and they will be obliged to reduce the level of their total deposits in order to restore the required $12\frac{1}{2}$ per cent ratio of reserve assets to deposits. We should note, however, that the banks will only be forced to take this action if they are operating with the required minimum of reserve assets. If the banks have a surplus of reserve assets, a reduction in their deposits at the central bank might still leave them with an adequate supply of reserve assets and they will not be obliged to reduce deposits.

When the central bank wishes to see an expansion of bank lending (i.e. an increase in the money supply) it will enter the market and buy securities, making payment for them with cheques drawn on itself. The sellers of these securities will pay the central bank's cheques into their accounts in the commercial banks. These banks now hold claims against the Bank of England which will settle its indebtedness by crediting the outstanding amounts to the bankers' deposits. An increase in bankers' deposits at the central bank amounts to an increase in their cash reserves and in their reserve assets ratio. They will be able to increase their deposits by a multiple of this increase in their reserve assets.

(b) Special Deposits

This particular instrument of monetary policy is fairly new – it was first used in 1960. The central bank has the authority to call upon the commercial banks to place a sum of money equal to some stated percentage of their total deposits into a special account at the Bank of England. Normally these 'calls' are made for amounts equal to 1 per cent of deposits, although a series of such calls may be made when the situation requires strong pressure to be applied to the banks. The payment of special deposits deprives the banks of reserve assets since they have been instructed that the funds for such payments should not be obtained from the sale of longer

[1]Sometimes referred to as a 'credit squeeze'.

term securities. A call for special deposits, therefore, has the same effect as open market sales of securities, but it is a much more direct instrument. If the monetary authorities wish to encourage bank lending they can release any special deposits they are holding. Special deposits earn interest but they cannot be counted as reserve assets and do not form part of the banks' cash reserves.

(c) *Funding*

Although open market operations and calls for special deposits may be successful in changing the banks' reserve assets ratio, they will not be an effective instrument for restraining bank lending when the banks are holding surplus reserve assets. One way in which the Bank of England may reduce the supplies of reserve assets is to carry out a policy of funding. This policy requires the central bank to change the structure of the national debt by issuing more long term securities and fewer short term securities (Treasury Bills). These short term securities are an important component of the banks' reserve assets and a reduction in the total supply will reduce the amount held by the banks. They will then be more vulnerable to open market operations and calls for special deposits.

(d) *Quantitative Controls*

In recent years the Bank of England has supplemented its controls over the money supply by making increasing use of direct requests to the banks. Each bank has been asked to limit the amount of its lending to some specified figure. These *ceilings* have not been confined to the clearing banks, but have been applied to a wide range of financial institutions. Quantitative directives have usually been accompanied by qualitative guidance, as when banks have been asked not to restrict loans to exporters, or to firms in development areas, but to be much more selective with requests for loans for personal consumption or speculation. Ceilings applied to advances became the most important instrument of direct control during the 1960s, but the new policy measures introduced in 1971 indicated that the Bank of England intended to make little use of such ceilings and would rely far more on special deposits and open market operations.

Monetary Policy

In pursuing its monetary policy, the government has usually given fiscal policy the leading role. Fiscal policy refers to the deliberate variation of government spending and taxation with a view to influencing economic activity. The major instrument of fiscal policy is the Budget. Major changes in fiscal policy cannot be carried out more frequently than once a year, because they involve a large amount of administrative work.

Monetary policy comes into the picture because the estimates and fore-casts on which fiscal measures are based are very uncertain. Monetary policy provides intruments of control which can be applied very quickly and in large and small degrees. Open market operations, for example, can be carried out on a day to day basis.

We have described the use of monetary controls as a means of influencing the supply of money through variations in the level of bank deposits. But monetary policy is also concerned with the price of borrowed funds that is, the rate of interest. The level of total spending is not only influenced by the availability of bank credit – the price of bank credit is also important. Even if the banks are able and willing to lend, some potential borrowers will not be persuaded to take up bank loans when the rate of interest is so high that the potential profits from the use of the loan, or the satisfaction from spending it on consumption, are scarcely higher than its cost. The monetary authorities can influence the level of total demand by acting on the market rate of interest. Chapter 17 explained the relationship between the supply of money and the rate of interest. We have seen how the central bank is able to control the supply of money. Provided the demand for money (liquidity preference) does not vary, changes in the supply of money will bring about changes in the rate of interest.

Figure 44 on page 198 indicates that the central bank is faced with something of a dilemma in the operation of monetary policy. It cannot control both the quantity of money and the rate of interest, since it cannot control the demand for money. This places the Bank of England in a difficult position because, in addition to its responsibility for operating the government's monetary policy, it also has the responsibility for manag-ing the national debt. In this role, it has the task of raising large sums of money for the government every year. The Bank of England must float new loans to finance additional government expenditure and in order to repay the loans which are maturing. The rate of interest is an important consideration since it affects the costs of servicing the national debt. The annual interest charges are a large element in the annual Budget. It will happen, therefore, that situations will arise when the monetary authorities wish to see higher interest rates in order to restrain private spending, but in carrying out the appropriate policy they will be increasing the cost of the national debt.

On the other hand the government may find itself having to borrow large sums of money by selling large quantities of securities. Substantial sales of such securities, however, will depress their prices and hence raise the rate of interest. The increase in the rate of interest could well conflict with current monetary policy which may be attempting to stimulate private spending.

MONEY AND NEAR-MONEY

We have defined money as being whatever is generally acceptable in exchange for goods and services. It is this particular characteristic which makes money the most liquid of assets. But there is a wide variety of assets which are very liquid. There is no clear cut line between liquid and non-liquid assets. If all assets are arranged in descending order of liquidity, where do we draw the line which separates liquid from non-liquid assets?

If money is strictly defined as those assets which can be immediately exchanged for goods and services, then it consists of notes, coins, and bank deposits held on current account. Time deposits in the banks cannot be transferred by cheque, but the banks will often transfer funds from deposit to current accounts without insisting on the usual seven days' notice. Some definitions will only accept the first group of assets as money, whereas others include all bank deposits as money.

There is, however, another group of assets described as *near-money* or *quasi-money* because they are extremely liquid. Building society deposits, National Savings deposits and similar assets can be exchanged easily and quickly for currency without loss. This is an important group of assets since a person's ability to spend depends not only on his holdings of money but also upon his holdings of near-money assets.

The Giro

In October 1968 the National Giro, managed by the Post Office, commenced operations. The aim of the giro is to provide a cheap, simple and quick money transmission service, by making use of the existing network of post offices. All records are kept, and the processing carried out, at the computerised giro centre at Bootle, Lancashire. People holding giro accounts are provided with three basic services.

1. *Transfers to other account holders*
The payee completes a giro transfer form, which already bears his name and account number, and posts it to the giro centre. The computer credits the payee's account and debits the payer's account. Slips are then posted to payee and payer telling them that this has been done. These transfers are free although there is a small charge for stationery.

2. *Deposits*
The account holder can pay into his account in cash (at a post office), or by cheque. Other people can also pay into his account in a similar manner when a charge of 4p is made. Deposits into one's own account are free.

3. *Payments*

An account holder can draw cash through post offices, or he can make payments to non-account holders by means of a postal cheque. In each case the cost is 4p. Payments into the bank accounts of non-account holders cost 3p.

No interest is paid on giro accounts and no overdrafts are allowed. Postage is free. The giro system is not new, most western European countries have been running such systems for many years.

The balances held in the system should provide investment income sufficient to cover all operating costs. Since the system consists mainly of a set of computers, the costs are largely fixed costs. It is estimated that rather more than one million accounts with an average balance of between £100 and £150 are required in order to break even. Giro in Great Britain started rather slowly and losses were made in the first two years, but the introduction of a loan scheme (in association with a finance house) has led to a significant increase in the number of accounts.

Chapter 22

The Value of Money

Money and Prices

The functions of money have already been dealt with in some detail, but one very important aspect of money remains to be discussed, namely, its value.

The intrinsic value of money may be negligible; the £1 note regarded as a piece of paper is practically worthless, and its only value arises from its acceptability in exchange. Units of money exchange for goods and services, and the rates at which money exchanges for these things are known as prices. But the price of any article is not the same thing as the value of that article. In economic writings the word 'value' always refers to 'value in exchange'. Even in the modern world we are doing exactly what is done under a barter system, exchanging goods and services for goods and services, and money only serves to facilitate such exchanges. If the price of a loaf of bread is 10p this only has meaning to the seller of bread because he knows what 10p will buy. The value of the loaf of bread is the goods and services for which it can be exchanged and the price merely gives us an indication of the exchange value of the loaf. In the same way the rate of pay which we receive for our work is expressed in terms of money, but what we are really interested in is the rate at which our hours of labour will exchange for goods and services. A system of money prices helps us to understand this rate.

But prices change and alter the rates at which goods and services exchange against other goods and services. If all prices were to double, values would not have changed. A ton of coal would be worth exactly the same number of pounds of meat. The only value which would have altered would be the value of money itself; the exchange value of the £1 note would have halved, while the exchange value of a loaf of bread would be unchanged. If the expression *the value of money* has any meaning, it can only be expressed in terms of what the unit of money will buy, and this is determined by the prices of the various goods and services. When prices rise, the value of money falls and likewise falling prices will indicate an increase in the value of money. This is all very well, but a most difficult question now arises – 'What prices?'. When the man in the street thinks about the value of money, he is considering the value of *his* money, and this can only be measured in terms of the prices of the goods which *he* buys. If the prices of beer and cigarettes increase, but no other prices are changed, then the value of money to the teetotaller and non-smoker will not have changed, but this would not be true of the money spent by the man who smokes and drinks. Changes in the prices of raw wool and raw cotton will affect the value of money used by the importer, the merchant and the textile manufacturer, but few others will be directly affected. Thus, if we wish to speak of the value of money in precise terms, then we have to admit that there are as many different values of money as there are spenders of money, for it is unlikely that any two individuals will spend their money in exactly the same manner. In spite of this difficulty it is necessary to attempt some assessment of the extent of movements in the value of money. People wish to know how the real values of wages, pensions, the National Income, investments and many other items, are changing over time. As we have already said, these problems would not arise if all prices moved proportionately and in the same direction, but prices do not move in this way. In any given period of time, some prices will rise, others will fall, and some will remain unchanged, and those prices which do move in the same direction do not all move to the same extent.

Changes in the Value of Money

Any attempt to measure changes in the value of money must use some kind of average measurement of price changes. The ordinary citizen is interested in changes in retail prices, while producers are affected principally by changes in wholesale prices and in the prices of labour (wages).

Attempts have been made to deal with this problem by measuring changes in the value of money in these different markets. In what follows we shall be concentrating on the value of money as reflected in changes in retail prices, but the same principles apply to the 'wholesale' value of money.

The measurement of price changes involves some arbitrary selection of the prices to be considered, for whether we take the whole range of retail prices (an impracticable objective) or merely a selection of retail prices, we must recognise that these prices, and subsequent changes in them, affect each individual in a different manner. Before proceeding further it is necessary to point out that we cannot, in fact, measure the value of money. It is impossible to give a meaningful answer to the question, 'What is the value of £1?' The only possible answer would be an almost endless list of the quantities of the various goods and services for which £1 may be exchanged. Even if the list were accurate it would have no meaning. Our task, however, is not to measure the absolute value of money, but the changes in its value, and this can be done by making use of a statistical device known as index numbers. It might be noted at this point that there is an interesting aspect of the relationship between the value of money and the level of prices. A fall in prices increases the value of money and a rise in prices reduces money's value, but the changes in prices and money value are not proportional. A rise of 20 per cent in the general price level does not mean that the value of money has fallen 20 per cent. If prices rise by 20 per cent, they have moved in the ratio 5:6, but the value of money has moved in the opposite direction in the ratio 6:5, this is a change of 16⅔ per cent.

INDEX NUMBERS

Index numbers deal with *percentage changes* rather than with absolute changes. The price change of each commodity is expressed in percentage terms and the average of these percentage changes is then calculated. The index number 100 is given to the price in the year on which we base our comparisons.

EXAMPLE

	Year 1		Year 2	
Commodity	Price	Index	Price	Index
A	5p	100	10p	200
B	12½p	100	15p	120
C	£1	100	75p	75
				3)395

$$\text{Price Index} = 131 \cdot 6$$

A simple average of the percentage changes in price indicates that prices in Year 2 are 31·6 per cent higher than they were in Year 1. Prices in subsequent years would be expressed as percentages of those in Year 1 (the base year) and averaged in a similar manner.

The index numbers resulting from these calculations would be somewhat misleading, since each of the commodities is assumed to be of equal importance. This is not likely to be the case, the price of bread, for example, is of much greater importance to the general mass of consumers than is the price of fur coats. It is possible to overcome this particular difficulty by using a system of 'weights' whereby each commodity is given a weight proportional to its importance in the general pattern of consumer spending. Referring back to the example above, let us suppose that 50 per cent of total consumer spending is devoted to commodity A, 30 per cent to Commodity B and 20 per cent to Commodity C. Weights are now allocated to these in the proportions 5:3:2. The price indices for each year are

241

multiplied by the appropriate weights and the average is obtained by dividing the total of these weighted indices by the total of the weights.

EXAMPLE

Commodity	Year 1 Price	Index	Weight	Weighted Index
A	5p	100	5	500
B	12½p	100	3	300
C	£1	100	2	200

10)1000

Price Index 100

Commodity	Year 2 Price	Index		Weighted Index
A	10p	200		1,000
B	15p	120		360
C	75p	75		150

10)1510

Price Index   151

The weighting of the commodities has produced a different result from that obtained in the earlier calculation. The average price movement is now revealed as an increase of 51 per cent, as against 31·6 per cent in the earlier example. This is due to the fact that Commodity A, which had the largest percentage price increase, was also the commodity which was most heavily weighted.

The Index of Retail Prices

In the United Kingdom, official attempts to measure movements in the cost of living have been made since 1914. The first Cost of Living Index, started in this year, was restricted in its coverage, since its construction was based upon a sample of 2,000 'typical working-class' households. It was compiled on the same basis until 1947, when the name was changed to the *Index of Retail Prices*. Subsequently the index has been revised at intervals of five or six years. The basic features of the construction of these indices are as follows:

1. A representative sample of the population is selected and asked to maintain a careful budget of their expenditure over some period of time, usually one month.
2. These budgets are analysed to provide a great deal of information on the pattern of consumer spending. From this information we derive a picture of the pattern of spending of the 'average family'.

3. Decisions are taken on the selection of goods and services to be included in the index and weights are allocated to the different goods and services according to the proportions of consumer spending which are devoted to them.

4. Some particular date is now chosen as the base date and the prices, at this particular date, are expressed as 100.

5. The prices of the goods and services are now checked at regular intervals and the new prices are expressed as percentages of those ruling at the base date.

6. The price index is now calculated as shown in the earlier examples.

The Index of Retail Prices began its life in June 1947; a new index was introduced in 1952 and this was replaced by a revised index in January 1956. At the time of writing the current index has a base date of January 1962. Each of these indexes, except the most recent, had weights which were based upon prior surveys of consumer spending. The latest index has weights which are revised each year during the life of the index and are based upon a continuous survey of family spending.

As time has gone by the samples used in the surveys have tended to become more and more representative of the entire population and it is held that the 1962 index is based upon an expenditure survey which is representative of 88 per cent of the whole population. Likewise the list of goods and services included in the index has been gradually extended and now includes more than 350 separate items, for many of which information is collected for several different varieties.

The Department of Employment, through its local offices, carries out price checks in some 200 towns of different sizes, distributed geographically according to population densities. Prices are collected from the whole range of retail outlets, small shops, super-markets, chain stores, department stores, mail order firms, co-operative societies and so on. The index of retail prices divides the goods and services covered into eleven main groups, each group containing a number of sections. There are ninety-two such sections. In addition to the index number for all items, indices are calculated for each of the main groups. Table 21 shows recent movements in (a) the index of retail prices, (b) the indices for the main groups, and (c) the weights allocated to the main groups.

The index is published monthly and has come to be regarded as one of the most important economic indicators. It is this index which is normally used when assessing changes in the value of money; changes in the index form the basis of many wage claims, and large numbers of workers now have wage agreements which allow for automatic changes in wages related to changes in the index.

The construction of the Index is no easy task. There are many difficulties to be overcome and we must be careful not to read into the index a degree of accuracy which it cannot possibly possess. Some of these problems are considered below:

1. The Index only attempts to measure changes in retail prices as they affect the 'average family', but are there any such families?

2. The pattern of consumer spending is constantly changing. As incomes, tastes and fashions change, so do the demands for the various goods and services. This raises problems with regard to weighting since the weights on which any one index is based become more and more unrealistic. It is for this reason that the weights of the current index are frequently adjusted.

Table 21. *The index of retail prices* (*Jan.* 1962 = 100)

	1968		1969		1970 (*June*)	
	Weight	*Index* (*monthly average*)	*Weight*	*Index* (*monthly average*)	*Weight*	*Index*
Food	263	123·2	254	131·0	255	141·6
Alcoholic drinks	63	127·1	64	136·2	66	143·2
Tobacco	66	125·5	68	135·5	64	135·8
Housing	121	141·3	118	147·0	119	158·6
Fuel and light	62	133·8	61	137·8	61	142·1
Durable household goods	59	113·2	60	118·3	60	125·1
Clothing/footwear	89	113·4	86	117·7	86	123·1
Transport and vehicles	120	119·1	124	123·9	126	131·0
Miscellaneous goods	60	124·5	66	132·3	65	141·7
Services	56	132·4	57	142·5	55	151·6
Meals bought and consumed outside the home	41	126·9	42	135·0	43	145·0
All items	1,000	125·0	1,000	131·8	1,000	139·9

Source: *Annual Abstract of Statistics*, 1970

3. Many commodities are subject to constant changes in design, or quality, or performance. Where the price change accompanies the introduction of a new model or an improved design, it is extremely difficult to interpret the real nature of the price change. Can we really say what has happened to the price of furniture, washing machines or motor cars over the past ten years? The price comparisons would not be related to the same products. If the price of a particular make of car has increased by 10 per cent but the quality

and performance of the recent model is much superior to that of the older model, has the exchange value of the car risen or fallen?

4. New materials, and new products are constantly coming into use and causing significant shifts in consumer demand. The introduction of television brought about a rapid movement in the nature of consumer spending on entertainment, the evidence of which is to be seen in the closing down of thousands of British cinemas during the 1950s and 1960s. In recent years a great variety of new plastics have been introduced making possible a whole new range of domestic products. This is particularly noticeable in the kitchen where polythene bowls, buckets, food containers, etc., have replaced galvanised and enamelled steel products.

5. Consumers' shopping habits change. In the 1950s and 1960s there was something of a revolution in the retail trade with the introduction and rapid growth of supermarkets. As the proportion of consumer spending in the different kinds of retail outlets changes so must the procedure for making price checks. Nowadays a greater weight must be given to the prices of goods sold by supermarkets and chain stores and a smaller weight to the prices in the small independent shops.

Price Movements

We have seen that it is possible, by means of index numbers, to obtain some approximate idea of the extent of the changes in the value of money. We now turn to the problems of explaining the nature and causes of these changes.

The forces which tend to change prices tend to change *all* prices although there will be deviations from the general pattern (e.g. a change of fashion leading to a temporary surplus and hence a lower price when other prices are moving upwards).

There are great differences in the flexibility of different prices. The most variable prices are those of raw materials and other primary products which are traded on world markets. A glance at any table of commodity prices (mining and agricultural products) will disclose just how extensive these price variations can be over relatively short periods of time. The explanation lies in the fact that both the demand for and supply of these commodities tend to be inelastic, so that quite small changes in demand or supply will cause large movements in price. It is significant that most of the major government schemes to stabilize prices are concerned with agricultural products.

The prices of manufactured goods tend to be much more stable. The prices of many of these goods are often controlled by very large firms or trade associations where stability of price is important from the points of view of advertising campaigns and production planning, but, quite apart from this, the supply is much more elastic and can readily be adjusted to meet changes in demand.

Long-term Price Movements

The long-term tendency is for prices to rise. Over the past seven centuries the average trend of British prices has been an increase of 1½ per cent per annum. But it would be misleading to interpret this statement as indicating a smooth steady upward movement in prices. There have been many periods when prices have been falling, and several periods of comparative price stability. The general picture seems to be one of a series of periods when there was a strong upward movement in the price level followed by periods of stable prices or periods when prices were falling, but where they did not fall by anything like the amount of the previous rise. The percentage changes between the main peaks and troughs of the price level over these seven centuries were as follows:

Table 21a. *British prices* (*consumables*)

Period	No. of Years	% changes in price level
1275–1525	250	+29
1525–1650	125	+550
1650–1744	94	−38
1744–1813	69	+263
1813–1893	80	−51
1893–1920	27	+183
1920–1932	12	−59
1932–1959	27	+322

Source: *R. G. Lipsey*, '*Does money always depreciate?*', *Lloyds Bank Review*, Oct. 1960.

The Quantity Theory of Money

When we come to the analysis of the causes of changes in the value of money, it is logical to refer back to the chapter on prices where we saw that the value of anything depends upon the relationship between the demand for it and the supply available. For a long time it was believed that the value of money bore a direct relationship to its supply. An increase in the supply, it was held, would cause a proportionate fall in the value of money and a fall in the supply would have the opposite effect.

The supply of money is simply the total quantity in existence and is made up of coins, plus banknotes, plus the total of bank deposits. The supply of money at any particular time is normally referred to as the *Quantity of Money* represented by the symbol M.

There is another aspect of the supply of money, namely, the supply over a given period of time, say one year. During a period of a year, each unit of money may be used several times – coins and bank notes passing through several hands. The term *Velocity of Circulation* (represented by the symbol *V*) is used to describe the rate at which money changes hands. If the total value of all transactions during one year was £20,000 million and the stock of money was £5,000 million, then the velocity of circulation would be 4, since, on average, each unit of money has changed hands 4 times, or, each £1 of money has purchased £4 worth of goods and services. Although the stock of money was only £5,000 million, total purchasing power was equal to £20,000 million.

The velocity of circulation of bank deposits may be measured by dividing the total value of all the cheques cleared by the average level of bank deposits during the year. Thus, if the average level of bank deposits was £10,000 million and the value of cheques cleared during the period was £100,000 million then the velocity of circulation of bank deposits would be 10.

We have, therefore, two views of the supply of money. It may be regarded as a physical stock (i.e. *M*), or as a flow, that is, as a stock of money moving at some given rate. It is this latter view which is relevant here, because we are concerned with the acts of spending. Whether it is a case of £1 being spent twice, or two different £1s being spent once, the effect of these acts of spending is the same. The flow of spending will be equal to *MV*.

This flow of spending must be equal to the total value of the goods and services sold by businesses. If we designate *P* as the symbol to represent the average price level and *T* to represent the total volume of transactions, then *PT* will stand for the value of the goods and services bought and sold.

M = the quantity of money
V = the velocity of circulation
P = the general price level
T = the total volume of transactions.

MV, as explained, is the amount of money 'handed over' or spent, and *PT*, is the value of the goods and services 'handed over' or sold. Hence,

$$MV = PT$$

P and *T* are quantities which are easy to imagine but difficult to measure. *P* is an average of all prices at which market transactions take place, and *T* is the total number of these transactions. $MV = PT$ is the well-known *Equation of Exchange* and represents a refinement of the famous Quantity Theory of Money which held that price changes were directly proportional to changes in the quantity of money, that is, $M \propto P$.

$MV = PT$ is not a theory, but a statement of fact, and, as shown, it must, by definition, be true. It is not a theory because it tells us nothing about the causes of the changes in the various quantities. The value of the Equation

I

of Exchange lies in the fact that it identifies and calls our attention to the different factors which may influence the value of money.

It draws our attention to the influence of V. If V were constant then a change in M would mean a change in P or T or both. If full employment conditions existed and V were constant, an increase in T is not possible in the short run and an increase in M would lead to an increase in P. It was this kind of direct relationship between M and P, based on the assumption that V and T were constant which was the basis of the crude Quantity Theory.

If, however, there were unemployed resources available, an increase in M, V remaining constant, would lead to an increase in output (and hence in T) and P would not change.

But V is not constant and there is evidence to show that it has increased very much in the years since the Second World War. If an increase in M is accompanied by an increase in V, as is very likely in inflationary conditions, then, if T is constant, an increase in M will lead to a more than proportionate increase in P. An increase in V is one of the causal factors in a situation of hyperinflation. When prices begin to rise rapidly people will be reluctant to hold money because it is losing value and will exchange it for goods and services as quickly as possible.

In the 1930s during the Great Depression, fears of unemployment and possible business losses greatly reduced the spending of consumers and businessmen. In other words there was a reduction in V. An increase in M in such circumstances would be offset by a fall in V and would have very little effect on prices or output.

The idea that changes in the value of money can be explained by changes in the quantity of money is no longer accepted. Modern thinking lays more emphasis on changes in incomes as the determinant of the price level and regards changes in the quantity of money as a consequence rather than a cause. It is spending which is the effective action as far as prices are concerned and an increase in the quantity of money does not necessarily lead to increased spending – the extra money may be held in idle balances (i.e. V falls).

But the Quantity Theory should not be dismissed as wholly misleading. Certain long-term trends can be partially explained in terms of this theory. The major changes in the price level during the nineteenth century bear a close correlation to movements in the supply of gold to which the supply of money at that time was immediately linked. The large increase in the level of prices during the two world wars was accompanied by very large increases in the supply of money and the great inflations in Germany during the early 1920s and in Hungary in the 1940s were both characterised by massive increases in the supply of money. We can conclude that big changes in the price level cannot come about without similar changes in the supply of money, but the problems of inflation and deflation cannot be explained solely in terms of the Quantity Theory.

CHAPTER 23

Inflation

Types of Inflation

There are several ways of defining inflation. In some contexts it refers to a steady increase in the supply of money. In others it is seen as a situation where demand persistently exceeds supply. It seems best, however, to define inflation in terms of its basic symptom – rising prices. Inflation is a situation where the general price level is persistently moving upwards. The excess demand definition hardly fits the recent British experience when prices were rising quite sharply at a time when unemployment was increasing.

In an extreme form of inflation, prices rise at a phenomenal rate and terms such as *hyperinflation*, galloping inflation, or runaway inflation have been used to describe these conditions. In 1923, Germany experienced this kind of inflation, and by the end of that year, prices were one million million times greater than their pre-war level. Towards the end of 1923, paper money was losing half or more of its value in one hour, and wages were fixed and paid daily. The price of a newspaper rose to 200,000,000,000 marks (one mark had been worth about one shilling in 1914). In 1924 the currency was withdrawn and new marks were issued at the rate of 1 Reichsmark = 1,000,000,000,000 marks. In 1944 Hungary experienced an even more severe inflation, the note circulation reaching a figure with 27 noughts.

Under conditions of hyperinflation people lose confidence in the currency's ability to carry out its functions. It becomes unacceptable as a medium of exchange and other commodities, such as cigarettes, are used as money. The only step is to withdraw the currency and issue new monetary units. So great was the loss of confidence in Hungary that the new currency had to be given a new name, the Forint replacing the Pengo. Although it had not reached anything like the proportions of hyperinflation, France, in January 1960, withdrew the existing franc and issued new ones at the rate of 100 old francs for 1 new franc.

Another type of inflation is described as *suppressed inflation* and refers to a situation where demand exceeds supply, but the effect on the price level is minimised by the use of such devices as price controls and rationing. We should note that price controls do not deal with the causes of inflation, they merely suppress the symptom.

The most common type of inflation is that experienced, since the war, by Britain and most other countries. This is *creeping inflation* where the price level rises at an annual average rate between 1 and 6 per cent. In Britain the average rate for the period 1939–1967 was about 4 per cent per annum, but in more recent years the rate of inflation has increased quite sharply.

It now appears that a moderate rate of inflation does not destroy the ability of money to fulfil its functions – people have learned to live with these conditions. Inflation, however, appears to have a built-in tendency to speed up, and governments have found it extremely difficult to hold inflation to rates of 3 or 4 per cent per annum.

The causes of inflation are now usually classified as demand-pull or cost-push.

Demand Inflation

Demand inflation may be defined as a situation where demand persistently exceeds supply at current prices, so that prices are being 'pulled' upwards. This type of inflation is usually associated with conditions of full employment. If there are unemployed resources in the economy, an increase in demand can be met by bringing these resources into employment. Supply will increase and the increase in demand will have little or no effect on the general price level. If the total demand for goods and services continues to increase, however, a full employment situation will be reached and no further increases in output are possible (i.e. in the short run). Any further increase in demand can only lead to an upward movement of prices.

Conditions of excess demand when there is full employment can arise in several different ways. Wartime conditions provide a good example. War brings full employment, a large increase in the numbers at work, and a great deal of overtime working. The net result is a large increase in total income and hence in potential demand. On the other hand, the supply of consumer goods and services will fall as resources are diverted to meet military demands. Total demand will exceed total supply at current prices and there will be a strong upward pressure on prices. During wartime, the excess demand is not allowed to exert its full effect on the price level. The government imposes price controls on foodstuffs and essential consumer goods and supports these price controls with a system of rationing. Large scale savings campaigns and heavy taxation are also used to remove some of the excess demand.

The dangers of inflation are probably at their greatest in the immediate post-war years. After years of austerity and rationing, people will be very anxious to return to the greater freedoms of peace-time conditions and to spend the savings accumulated during the war. They will have both a strong desire and a great ability to spend, but supplies of consumer goods and services will still be severely restricted, because it takes time to reallocate resources to peace-time needs, and a large proportion of economic resources will have to be devoted to reconstruction. The government will be in a difficult position. Restraints on demand will have to be imposed, but they will not be accepted so willingly as they were when the nation was at war. Measures such as increased taxation, hire purchase restrictions and higher interest rates cannot be pushed too far without having some disincentive effects on effort and enterprise. Price controls and rationing will be necessary for several years after the war has ended.

A situation of excess demand may arise when a country is trying to achieve an export surplus. Exports are inflationary because they generate income at home, but reduce home supplies. If exports are greater in value than imports there will be excess demand in the home market, unless taxes and savings are increased to absorb the excess purchasing power.

Inflationary conditions may develop when, with full employment, a country tries to increase its rate of economic growth. In order to devote more of its resources to capital accumulation it will be obliged to reduce the output of consumer goods. Incomes will not fall since the factors of production are still fully employed, but the supply of things on which these incomes may be spent has been reduced. Unless savings and taxation increase there will be excess demand and prices will rise.

Another possible cause of inflation under conditions of full employment is an expansion of government spending financed by borrowing from the banking system. In this case the expenditure is being financed by an increase in the money supply.

THE INFLATIONARY PROCESS

We have shown how excess total demand might arise at the full employment level of national output. Since national output cannot expand in the short run, the impact of excess demand must fall entirely on the price level. Prices will rise, but why should they continue to rise? An inflationary process of the demand-induced type is usually explained in terms of the conditions in the markets for the factors of production, especially the labour market.

When firms find that they can sell more goods and services than they are producing, they will increase their demands for labour and, since there is already full employment, the excess demand in the labour market will bid up wages and salaries. If, as is most likely, the rise in wages exceeds any rise in productivity, costs will rise and businessmen will pass these higher costs on to the consumer in the form of higher prices. But the increase in wages and salaries means that aggregate demand will also rise so that, once again, we have excess demand in the markets for goods and services – and so the process will go on. Prices in both the markets for goods, and the markets for factors of production, are being pulled upwards.

More recent experience of inflation, however, provides evidence of the pressures on prices coming from 'below' rather than 'above'. Prices have continued to rise under conditions where there has been excess supply rather than excess demand in the labour markets. Economists have been obliged to pay increasing attention to the problem of prices being pushed upwards.

Cost-Push Inflation

Cost-push inflation describes a situation where the process of rising prices is initiated and sustained by rising costs which push up the general level of prices. It is most commonly explained in terms of trade union pressures causing wage rates to rise faster than productivity, but it is important to distinguish the causes of the wage increases. If wages rise because of an excess demand for labour, and entrepreneurs, operating in a sellers' market, simply pass on these higher wage costs in the form of higher prices, the cause is really demand-pull.

Cost inflation arises when prices are forced upwards by increases in the prices of factors of production which do not arise from excess demand. It is usually regarded as a wage-inflation process because wages and salaries make up by far the greater part of total costs (about 70 per cent). Nevertheless, cost inflation can develop whenever any other item of costs increases independently of changes in demand. A rise in import prices or an increase in indirect taxation (i.e. taxes on goods and services) might originate a cost-push process. Focusing attention on wages may be justified not only because they are a most important element in costs, but because, if the other components of total costs increase, there seems no very good reason why an upward trend in prices should occur. An increase in import prices or indirect taxation could lead to a once-and-for-all increase in prices. An increase in wages designed to compensate for the increase in prices is likely to generate an inflationary trend because an increase in prices is one of the major causes of further wage increases.

The characteristic feature of cost inflation is the use of market power by wage-earners and profit recipients to increase their respective shares of national income in real terms. Once under way, cost inflation seems to generate 'an income-increase psychology' which is based upon expectations of regular increases in income regardless of the particular or general economic situation.

In modern capitalist societies the bargaining power of organised labour is extremely effective, and we must expect trade union leaders to use this bargaining power in the interests of their members, particularly in a society based upon the principles of free enterprise. Higher rates of unemployment have not had the effect of diminishing the pressure for higher wages. This may be due, in part, to improved unemployment and other social security benefits and to the introduction of the scheme of redundancy payments, all of which have tended to alleviate the financial hardship of unemployment. The strike weapon tends to become more effective as industry becomes more specialised and capital-intensive. Quite small stoppages can cause massive disruption in industries geared to mass production and dependent upon supplies of components from many sources. When output drops to zero because of a strike, the heavy fixed costs of capital equipment continue to be incurred, and this adds substantially to the financial penalties imposed by the loss of output.

A contributory factor in the sequence of wage-price increases is the strong attachment to existing wage differentials. An increase in pay in one sector of the economy leads to a 'chain reaction' of wage increases elsewhere as other groups try to restore the previous pattern of wage differentials. It may be that the originating wage increase was granted in an industry where productivity had increased so that wage costs did not rise. It is most likely, however, that wage increases in the other sectors, based on comparability arguments, will lead to an average increase in wages substantially greater than the average increase in productivity. Entrepreneurs obliged to concede wage increases in excess of improvements in productivity will raise prices in order to protect their profit margins. These price increases will provoke further wage demands.

One feature of cost inflation which seriously increases social tensions is the fact that existing wage and salary differentials are not maintained. Groups with more powerful bargaining positions will gain relative to those in weaker positions. It does not follow that wages are increased at the expense of profits since firms may have sufficient market power to maintain profits.

The distinction between the two types of inflation is important from the point of view of the appropriate policies to deal with inflation. Where the cause is excess demand, measures to reduce aggregate demand are called for. These are described on pages 291-2. If the problem is one of cost-push, some kind of incomes policy seems the most likely solution. Incomes policy is discussed in Chapter 31.

The Effects of Inflation

Inflation is regarded as undesirable because it produces some serious economic and social problems.

(a) *The Effects on Income*

Inflation leads to an arbitrary redistribution of real income. Although a rise in the general price level produces a corresponding rise in money income, all prices do not rise to the same extent and different income groups will be affected in different ways. There will be some 'gainers' and some 'losers'.

The losers are those whose incomes are fixed, or relatively fixed, in money terms. This group will include people whose income is derived from fixed interest securities, controlled rents, or some private pensions schemes. Income recipients in this category will experience a fall in their real incomes.

When incomes are directly related to prices, real income will remain relatively unchanged. The incomes of salesmen and professional groups such as architects, surveyors, and estate agents, where fees are expressed as a percentage of the value of work undertaken, fall into this category. A large number of wage earners also come into this group since many workers have agreements which link their money wages to the Retail Price Index.

The effects on income derived from profits depend largely upon the kind of inflation being experienced. During demand-pull inflation, profits tend to rise. The prices of final goods and services tend to be more flexible in an upward direction than many factor prices and the margin between the two price levels tends to widen because of the time lag. When there is cost-push inflation, profits may be squeezed. Since there is no excess demand some firms may find it rather difficult to pass on the full effects of rising costs in the form of higher prices.

Wage earners generally more than hold their own when the price level is rising. In the U.K. and most other industrial countries wages have risen faster than prices, (see page 181). But, as already mentioned, there tends to be some redistribution effect as those with superior bargaining power gain at the expense of weaker groups.

(b) Effects on Production

Demand-pull inflation is associated with buoyant trading conditions and sellers' markets where the risks of trading are greatly reduced. These easy market conditions might give rise to complacency and inefficiency since the competitive pressures to improve both product and performance will be greatly weakened. This is not likely to be the case in a cost-push inflation where trading conditions are likely to place a premium on greater efficiency. Where firms cannot absorb some of the higher factor prices by improving efficiency they may find it difficult to survive. It is possible that employers, seeking to hold down costs, will react to rapidly rising wage costs by devising means of economising in their use of labour, and hence raise the level of unemployment.

Demand inflation, it is sometimes argued, is conducive to a faster rate of economic growth since the excess demand and favourable market conditions will stimulate investment and expansion. The falling value of money, however, may encourage spending rather than saving and so reduce the funds available for investment. It may also lead to higher rates of interest as creditors demand some additional return to compensate for the falling value of money.

(c) Effects on the Balance of Payments

In economies such as the U.K. which are dependent upon a high level of exports and imports, inflation often leads to balance of payments difficulties. If other countries are not inflating to the same extent, home-produced goods will become less competitive in foreign markets and foreign goods will become more competitive in the home market. Exports will be depressed and imports will rise. If this process continues it must lead to a balance of payments deficit on the current account. The problem will be a particularly difficult one where inflation is of the demand-pull type, because, in addition to the price effects, the excess demand at home will tend to 'draw in' more imports. These balance of payments effects only apply where a country is operating a fixed rate of exchange. As we shall see in Chapter 28, a floating rate of exchange means that the rise in home prices does not have such unfavourable effects on exports and imports.

Chapter 24

The Income and Expenditure of Public Authorities

Public finance is that part of the subject matter of economics which is concerned with the income and expenditure of Public Authorities (the Government and local authorities). The collection and expenditure of money by the State is as old as the State itself. Whenever there has been some kind of organised political authority, that authority has levied taxes, in kind, or in money. In earlier times the lord of the manor, the church, or the parishes levied taxes in kind which usually took the form of some part of the peasant's crop or of so many days' compulsory labour. Nowadays taxes are calculated and collected in money terms.

The Growth of Public Spending

In Great Britain and in most other countries, the State is far and away the greatest spender, and the proportion of total spending accounted for by public authorities has grown enormously during the present century. In Great Britain, taxation amounts to about 30 per cent of the national income and total public spending is about 40 per cent of total spending. In 1971 total public expenditure was estimated to be about £22,396 million – about £420 per head of the population.

Until the end of the nineteenth century, public finance was concerned with raising the funds necessary to finance a very limited range of services, which, it was believed, could only be provided effectively on a collective basis. The main items of expenditure were for:

(*a*) the defence of the realm (i.e. the armed forces),
(*b*) the maintenance of law and order (i.e. the police and judiciary),
(*c*) the payment of interest on the National Debt,
(*d*) the necessary administration (i.e. the civil service).

During the present century there have been very great changes in the nature of public finance; the total has grown, the pattern of spending has changed, and the income and expenditure of the public sector is now used as a regulator for the whole economy. There are several reasons why these changes have come about:

1. Defence remains a major item of expenditure. Defence forces have been reduced over the years but modern weaponry is very costly.

2. There has been a great expansion in those services provided by the State which are required for the enforcement of regulations designed to protect the community as a whole or certain groups within the community. Life in a civilised society is extremely complex and calls for a vast range of regulations which impose and enforce certain standards of conduct on the industrial, commercial and civilian communities. The Factory Acts lay down minimum standards for working conditions in factories; the Public Health Acts and Clean Food Acts govern standards of hygiene in public and private premises; the Companies Acts enforce certain standards of commercial behaviour for registered companies; the Town and Country Planning Acts control the development of land for different uses; the Monopolies and Restrictive Practices Acts are intended to exercise supervision of trading practices in the business world. All these measures, and many more, involve public expenditure on a large scale in order to make them operative.

3. The State now intervenes extensively in economic life in order to achieve specific social and economic ends. It makes use of public funds to assist certain industries. Agriculture receives substantial subsidies, and, in recent years, financial assistance has been given to the cotton and ship-building industries. The State finances a large part of the industrial research in both the public and private sectors. It uses public expenditure to influence the location of industry and provides a great range of advisory services for industry. It goes into business itself by bringing certain basic industries into public ownership.

The most important single change in financial policy has been the deliberate use of government income and expenditure as a regulator, that is, as a means of persuading the economy to move in the direction the government wants it to go. Until relatively recent times, the Budget was regarded as little more than a balance sheet showing how the government proposed to raise the least possible revenue to meet expenses which had to be kept to a minimum. Nowadays the Budget is the most powerful single instrument of economic policy.

But the greatest change in the pattern of public spending during this century has been the growth of 'social expenditure' which now takes up about one-third of total public spending. The main subjects of this form of spending are education, health, unemployment and sickness benefits, pensions and national assistance. Some idea of the extent of these changes can be obtained from the following table.

Distribution of Government Spending

	1760	1860	1960	1971
Defence	75 per cent	40 per cent	17 per cent	11 per cent
Interest on National Debt	20 per cent	39 per cent	13 per cent	9 per cent
Civil government	5 per cent	20 per cent	34 per cent	41 per cent
Social services	—	1 per cent	36 per cent	39 per cent

The Budget

The Budget is the main occasion each year on which the Exchequer Accounts are reviewed. On Budget Day the Chancellor of the Exchequer presents a financial statement which forecasts government income and expenditure for the year to come and reports on the actual receipts and expenditure for the year which has just ended (1 April to 31 March).

Budget Day is usually between 1 April and 5 May. The powers to collect income tax and corporation tax have to be renewed within one month of the end of the financial year on 5 April. Although there is usually only one Budget each year, certain indirect taxes (purchase tax and excise duties) can be changed within a limit of 10 per cent between Budgets by the use of what is known as 'the regulator'.

The central government's accounts are centred on two funds, the *Consolidated Fund* which meets the expenditure from revenue (almost wholly derived from taxation) and the *National Loans Fund* which conducts the bulk of the Government's domestic lending and borrowing. Most of the expenditure from the Consolidated Fund is devoted to *Supply Services*. These items comprise:

(i) the direct expenditure on goods and services,
(ii) grants made by the Government to cover expenditure on the National Health Service and the National Insurance Scheme,
(iii) grants to local authorities to support their spending on such services as education, local health, and security,
(iv) agricultural subsidies,
(v) overseas aid programmes.

Estimates of these expenditures have to be submitted to and voted by Parliament annually. In addition to the supply services, other items of expenditure come under the heading *Consolidated Fund Standing Services*. These expenditures do not require an annual parliamentary vote. They include, an appropriation of funds to meet interest on the national debt, the salaries and pensions of judges, and payments to members of the Royal Family.

When the expenditure from the Consolidated Fund is set against revenue, there will be a surplus or deficit. If a surplus arises, it will be paid into the National Loans Fund and serve to reduce the amount which the Government will have to borrow in order to meet its outgoings on this account. If there is a Budget deficit, it will be financed by a loan from the National Loans Fund and this will increase the amount of the Government's borrowing requirement.

The National Loans Fund is operated as an official account of the Bank of England and is the account through which the Government conducts its lending and borrowing. These items are mainly of a capital nature while most of the items in the Consolidated Fund are of a current nature.

It is now quite normal for the Chancellor to budget for a surplus or a deficit depending on the economic situation at the time. When the prevailing situation has inflationary tendencies, he will aim to produce a Budget surplus. Government income from taxation and other sources will exceed its current spending and total demand will be reduced. A deflationary situation usually calls for a Budget deficit. The Government's expenditure will exceed its current revenue and total demand will increase.

Table 22. *The Budget: 1971* (£ *million*)

ESTIMATES 1971–72

REVENUE	£	EXPENDITURE	£
Inland Revenue		*Supply Services*	
Income tax	6,491	Defence	2,545
Surtax	360	Government and finance	216
Corporation tax	1,620	Commonwealth and	
Capital gains tax	165	foreign	312
Death duties	375	Home and justice	334
Stamp duties	108	Trade, industry, and	
Other	1	employment	2,394
		Agriculture	441
Total – Inland Revenue	9,120	Environmental services	3,643
		Social services	3,388
		Education and science	564
Customs and Excise		The Arts	25
Purchase tax	1,495	Other public departments	240
Oil	1,460	Miscellaneous	47
Tobacco	1,100		
Spirits, wine, beer	1,000	Supplementary provision[1]	−278
Betting, gaming	145		
Other revenue duties	10	Total – Supply services	13,871

Protective duties	265		
Import deposits	−116	*Consolidated Fund*	
		Standing Services	
Total – Customs & Excise	5,359	Payment to National	
		Loans Fund in respect	
Motor vehicle duties	440	of service of the	
Selective Employment		National Debt	225
Tax (gross)	1,298	Northern Ireland	320
		Other services	30
Total taxation	16,217		
		TOTAL	14,446
Broadcasting licences	120	Surplus transferred to	
Interest and dividends	105	National Loans Fund	2,316
Other	320		
TOTAL	16,762		16,762

THE NATIONAL LOANS FUND

Interest on loans, profits of Issue Dept. of Bank of England etc.	1,345	Interest on National Debt	1,525
		Management expenses of National Debt	45
Balance of interest on National Debt received from Consolidated Fund	225		
	1,570		1,570
Consolidated Fund surplus	2,316	Loans:	
Net borrowing	−264	to nationalised industries	982
		to other public corporations	157
		to local and harbour authorities	885
		to private sector	−3
		within central government	31
	3,622		3,622

[1] Adjustment to Supply Votes due to changes in S.E.T., pensions, and subsidiaries to Agriculture.

261

Government Income

Table 22 shows the sources of Government income and the main items of expenditure. The receipts fall under five headings: inland revenue, customs and excise, motor vehicle duties, selective employment tax, and miscellaneous items.

THE INLAND REVENUE DEPARTMENT

The taxes collected by the Inland Revenue are sometimes described as *direct taxes*. They are levied on persons and companies and must be borne by the persons paying the taxes. They are not usually passed on in the form of higher prices as is the case with indirect taxes. Direct taxes are levied on income and capital.

1. *Income Tax*

This is by far the most important direct tax. It is levied on individuals at a standard rate (38¾ per cent in 1971). The tax is not chargeable on the whole of a person's income since a variety of allowances serve to reduce the amount of the income subject to taxation.

2. *Surtax*

This is an additional tax on incomes and applies to incomes in excess of £5,000 per annum, or £2,500 in the case of unearned income (i.e. incomes derived from property). Surtax is a steeply progressive tax – larger incomes are taxed at higher rates.

3. *Corporation Tax*

Corporation tax is levied on the gross profits of companies. It is a proportional tax – the current rate (1971) being 40 per cent. Profits which are distributed as dividends are subject to further taxation in the form of income tax. To some extent this additional burden of taxation on distributed profits tends to encourage a company to retain profits within the enterprise.

4. *Capital Gains Tax*

Capital Gains Tax is levied on the increase in the value of assets between the time of their purchase and their sale. In 1971 the tax was levied at the rate of 30 per cent. Capital gains taxes are not applicable to owner-occupied houses or assets held for personal use such as cars.

5. *Death Duties*

These taxes are imposed on the value of property passing at death.

Estates of less than £12,500 are exempt from tax. Death duties are steeply progressive, the maximum rate being 80 per cent on estates of £1 million or more.

6. *Stamp Duties*
These duties are payable on various legal documents such as those which transfer the ownership of property (e.g. share transfers).

THE CUSTOMS AND EXCISE DEPARTMENT
The taxes collected by this department are usually classified as *indirect taxes* since the burden may not be borne by the person who pays the tax. For example, purchase tax[1] may be paid by the manufacturer or wholesaler, but the burden of the tax may be passed to the final purchaser in the form of higher prices.

Customs duties refer to the duties imposed on imports whereas excise duties are imposed on goods produced at home. Purchase tax is levied on both home produced and foreign goods, but it is not levied on goods subject to excise duties.

It is clear from Table 22 that the great providers of revenue are tobacco, oil-petrol, alcohol, and purchase tax. These four duties bring in well over 90 per cent of the revenue collected by the Customs and Excise and nearly 30 per cent of the total revenue from taxation.

In the case of petrol, tobacco, and alcohol, the tax represents a huge proportion of the price and these three commodities provide exceptionally appropriate subjects for heavy indirect taxation. They have demands which are extremely inelastic with respect to price, they have very large markets and account for a substantial proportion of total consumer expenditure, and, in the case of petrol, at least, there is a positive income elasticity of demand (i.e. percentage change in quantity demanded is greater than the percentage change in income).

Most of these indirect taxes are flat rate taxes and it is argued that such taxes are regressive in their effects. The poor man pays the same tax on his packet of cigarettes as the rich man. Purchase tax is a proportional tax and the purchaser of the more expensive model pays more in tax.

Duties are levied on a wide variety of gambling activities including football pools. There are also taxes on some other forms of entertainment. Motor vehicle duties include driving licence fees and the licence fees paid by all motor vehicle operators ('road tax').

In November 1968 the Government introduced an import deposit scheme whereby importers of certain goods (mainly manufactured goods) were required to place deposits equal to 50 per cent of the goods imported, with the Customs and Excise Departments. The deposit was refunded six months later. It was reduced to 40 per cent in December 1969 and to 30

[1] Now replaced by V.A.T., see page 265.

per cent in May 1970, and finally abolished in December 1970. The intention of the scheme was to reduce imports by imposing a penalty on the firms' liquidity positions. It was also, of course, a short-term, interest-free loan to the government.

The Selective Employment Tax

This tax was introduced in the 1966 Budget and is now a major source of Government revenue. The tax is paid by all employers in both public and private sectors. The current weekly rates (1971) are £1·20 per man, £0·60 for women and boys, and £0·40 for girls, in employment. Under the original scheme, employers in manufacturing industries received a refund of the tax plus an additional payment ($37\frac{1}{2}$p for each man, less for others). Transport, agriculture, local authorities and public corporations received a plain refund of the tax, but the service industries received no refund. The subsidy to manufacturers has now been withdrawn – they receive a simple refund of the tax paid. The original purposes of the tax were:

(*a*) to divert labour from services industries to manufacturing industries,
(*b*) to spread the indirect tax burden more widely – most of the burden had previously been borne by goods.

Both reasons have been heavily criticised. The idea that service industries are in some way 'unproductive' is not very convincing and critics were quick to point out that such services earn very substantial surpluses on the balance of payments. Secondly, not all goods were subject to indirect taxation, why, therefore, should *all* services be taxed? A further criticism points out that the tax does nothing to improve labour utilisation in manufacturing industries. It should be noted, however, that a recent study has indicated that one effect of the tax has been to improve labour productivity in the service industries.

Government Expenditure

About two-thirds of Government current spending is on goods and services and makes, therefore, a direct claim on the nation's resources. The remaining third consists of transfer payments such as social security benefits (pensions etc.) and various subsidies. A large part of this current spending is carried out by the local authorities who have the responsibility for the administration of a variety of services in respect of which they receive grants from the Government. They raise additional revenue by means of local taxes known as rates. The major items of Government spending are:

Defence

Britain has treaty obligations and international commitments which oblige her to maintain a modern defence organisation. Although in terms of manpower the forces have declined over the years, the cost of defence has remained high because modern military equipment is extremely costly. Until very recently defence was the largest single item of Government expenditure.

The Social Services
These services make up a major part of Government expenditure and comprise one of the fastest growing elements. They include the expenditures on education, health and welfare, and social security. Total *public expenditure* on these items is much greater than the figures shown in the Budget because these amounts are supplemented by funds from the national insurance scheme and from local rates.

Environmental Services
This is a very broad category which includes the expenditures on roads, transport services, housing, law and order, and a wide variety of local services (water supply, local health services, etc.)

Trade, Industry, and Employment
Under this heading are included assistance to private industry (grants and regional employment premiums), Government expenditure on research, and the employment services of government.

THE NATIONAL LOANS FUND
The main sources of funds in the N.L.F. consist of, interest payments on past loans made by the government, repayments of past loans, the standing charge on the Consolidated Fund to cover interest on the national debt, and the surplus on the Consolidated Fund. Outgoings from the fund include interest on the national debt, loans to the nationalised industries and loans to local authorities. There may also be some lending to other public bodies and to the private sector. Where receipts exceed payments the balances of the National Loans Fund may be used to repay some part of the national debt. If payments exceed receipts, the Government will have a borrowing requirement.

THE 1971 BUDGET
In the 1971 Budget the Chancellor announced some major reforms of the British tax system. In 1973 it is proposed to abolish the Selective Employment Tax and Purchase Tax. These taxes will be replaced by a Value Added Tax, similar to those now used in several European countries. Value Added Tax is a tax levied (usually at a standard rate) on the value added at each stage in the productive process (see page 167). It will apply to all economic activities including services, but certain industries such as food will be excluded. This will mean that the present selective system of indirect taxation will be replaced by a comprehensive system. One advantage of a V.A.T. is that such a tax is rebatable on exports.

It is also proposed to merge the existing income tax and surtax into a single graduated tax. This change will also take effect in 1973. The Budget statement also contained a proposal to alter the method of taxing companies so that the present discrimination against distributed profits will be removed.

Public Expenditure

The Budget is concerned with the income and expenditure of the central government as far as it relates to the two great funds, the Consolidated Fund, and the National Loans Fund. It is important to realise that the

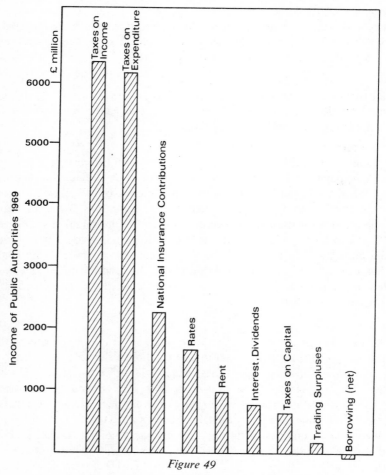

Figure 49

Source: *National Income and Expenditure 1970* (H.M.S.O.).

total income and expenditure of the public sector are very much greater than the totals shown in the Budget.

Total public expenditure is equal in size to nearly half of the national output and includes all spending by Government departments and local authorities together with the capital expenditures of the nationalised industries and other public corporations.

In recent years about 60 per cent of all public spending has been undertaken directly by the central government, about 30 per cent by local authorities and about 10 per cent by the public corporations. Public expenditure is financed with funds drawn from several sources. About two-thirds is derived from taxation. The national insurance contributions from employers and employees is also a major source of funds. Other income is derived from publicly owned property (in the form of interest, rents, and dividends) and a considerable income is obtained from local taxation in the form of rates. If this income falls short of total expenditure the remainder must be obtained by borrowing. Figures 49 and 50 show the main items of public expenditure and income.

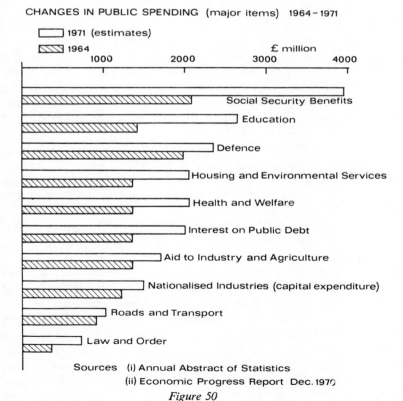

CHANGES IN PUBLIC SPENDING (major items) 1964–1971

☐ 1971 (estimates)
▧ 1964

£ million
1000   2000   3000   4000

Social Security Benefits
Education
Defence
Housing and Environmental Services
Health and Welfare
Interest on Public Debt
Aid to Industry and Agriculture
Nationalised Industries (capital expenditure)
Roads and Transport
Law and Order

Sources (i) Annual Abstract of Statistics
         (ii) Economic Progress Report Dec. 1970

Figure 50

The National Debt

Some part of total government spending may be covered by borrowing. This is particularly the case during wartime when the massive outlays required cannot be wholly covered by taxation. The greater part of the British National Debt has been accumulated during wars. It originated in 1694 with a loan of £1,200,000 from the newly formed Bank of England. The following brief details of its growth show how successive wars increased its size.

The National Debt (£ million)

1800	200
1815	800
1914	640
1918	8,000
1945	26,000
1965	29,000
1970	34,000

The debt is made up of a variety of loans which are represented by a wide variety of Government securities. A large part of the debt is held in the form of long and medium term securities with fixed maturities (i.e. they carry some date on which the Government promises to repay). Another part is in the form of undated stocks – the government having no obligation to repay. About 18 to 20 per cent of the debt is in the form of short-term loans (Treasury Bills). All these securities are marketable and ownership can be freely transferred.

A further 18 to 20 per cent takes the form of non-marketable securities, and is made up of National Savings Certificates (and Stamps), Development Bonds, Defence Bonds, Premium Bonds and the like. Nearly 20 per cent of the debt is held overseas by governments, international institutions (e.g. the I.M.F.) and individuals.

These securities are widely held, a large proportion of them by institutions such as banks, insurance societies, trade unions, pension funds, building societies and local authorities.

It is often said that the financing of government spending by means of borrowed funds is 'unfair' since it means transferring the liability for present spending to future generations who will be called upon to repay 'our' debts. This is not true. The financing of war, by accumulating a debt to be repaid in the future, does not transfer the real burden. The sacrifices are made by those who have to go without consumer goods so that war materials can be produced. The future interest payments and capital repayments really amount to a redistribution of income at the time when these payments are made. The generation making these payments is the same generation which is receiving these payments. They are paying taxes out of one pocket and putting interest payments and capital repayments in another. We cannot increase the amount of road-building and school-building in 1971 by reducing it in 1981. The real burden of the National Debt is borne by those who are living at the time when the debt is incurred.

Since the National Debt is simply a debt owed *by* the people collectively i.e. the State), *to* the people individually, the community as a whole is neither richer nor poorer. If one brother borrows from another brother, the wealth of the family is unchanged. But Britain's National Debt was incurred during wars so that there are very few productive assets to set off against the debt. Where borrowing is carried out in order to build railways, factories, docks, or roads, the creation of assets balances the creation of the liabilities, and the assets will produce revenue which will help to repay the debt. Britain's debt is, then, largely a deadweight debt.

That part of the debt held by foreigners is a real burden, because the payments of interest and capital must be made in foreign currencies. Exports will be required in order to earn these foreign currencies which might otherwise have been used to buy necessary imports.

Principles of Public Finance

TAXATION
Taxes may be of several kinds.

1. *Progressive Taxes*
A tax is progressive when the marginal rate of taxation is greater than the average rate of taxation. The wealthier not only pay more tax than the less well off, they pay proportionately more. A progressive tax is structured so that the rate of tax increases as the taxable income increases. Thus a person might pay, say, 10 per cent of his income in tax when he is earning £1,200 per annum, but 40 per cent of his income when he is earning £6,000 per annum. For many years the British income tax was progressive, but the 1970 Budget reduced it to a standard rate tax. Surtax and Death Duties are examples of progressive taxes.

2. *Proportional Taxes*
The tax is proportional when the rich pay more than the poor, but the proportions of income or wealth taken in taxation are the same for all taxpayers. If income tax were at a uniform rate of, say, 10 per cent of income, it would be a proportional tax. In Britain,. corporation tax provides an example of a proportional tax.

3. *Regressive Taxes*

Taxes are regressive when the poor are called upon to make a greater sacrifice than the rich. If the first £100 of income were taxed at 40p in the £, and the second £100 at a rate of 25p in the £, taxation would be regressive. Although the *rates* of taxation may not be regressive, the *effects* of taxation may well be so. It appears that indirect taxation operates in a regressive manner, for a specific[1] tax will take a greater proportion of the poor man's income than the rich man's income. This is evident when we consider the tax on a packet of cigarettes. But *ad valorem*[2] taxes will be less regressive.

4. *Flat Rate Taxes*

Where everyone subject to the tax pays the same amount in money terms, the tax is of the flat rate type. The basic National Insurance contribution is the same for all employed workers whatever their income, so is the tax on a gallon of petrol or a bottle of whisky.

Almost every kind of taxation will be unpopular, and it is almost impossible to devise a system of taxation which will be politically acceptable, capable of raising the required revenue, difficult to evade, and equitable. Adam Smith laid down certain *Canons of Taxation*; they are still generally acceptable as principles for a modern system of taxation. They are:

1. *Equity*

There must be equality of sacrifice. This implies that the people will be called upon to pay according to their ability to pay. There is now general acceptance of this 'ability to pay' criterion as being the 'fairest' basis for a tax system. Smith thought that proportional taxes would meet this requirement, but today it is almost universally accepted that a progressive tax accords best with the principle of equality of sacrifice. It is sometimes defended on the grounds that the principle of diminishing marginal utility applies to income. Taking £10 per week away from the man earning £40 per week only causes him to lose the same amount of satisfaction as would the removal of £1 per week from the man earning £15 per week – so runs the argument. On the same grounds it is possible to attack the system of indirect taxes as being inequitable since they act in a regressive manner.

The capital gains tax was introduced largely on grounds of equity. It was felt that a capital gain obtained by speculative activity in share or commodity markets should be subject to the same taxation as income earned by working in a factory or an office.

---

[1] A specific tax is levied on some physical unit (e.g. 18p per gallon).
[2] An *ad valorem* tax is levied on value (e.g. 5p in the £.)

2. *Certainty*

The taxpayer should know how much tax he has to pay and when and how it must be paid. Ideally the taxpayer should be able to assess his tax liability from information provided, and not be subject to tax demands made in an arbitrary fashion. The British tax system, in theory, fully meets this requirement, but legislation in respect of taxation has now become so voluminous and so complex that it is extremely difficult for the average man to check his tax assessments.

3. *Convenience*

Taxes must be collected in a convenient form and at a convenient time. The Pay As You Earn (P.A.Y.E.) system of income tax collection is extremely convenient. Under the previous system, taxes were paid in arrears – the tax on income earned in one period was payable in the following period. This method laid the onus of building up a tax reserve fund upon each individual taxpayer. Taxes are paid in money and, generally speaking, this is the most convenient form of payment, but difficulties often arise with regard to taxes on wealth such as death duties. These are levied on the deceased person's estate. Much of the wealth will be held in the form of land, buildings, works of art, and stocks and shares. First, there is the problem of making accurate valuations of these assets, and secondly, there is the task of realising these assets so that payment can be made in the form of money. This will often entail the breaking up of estates or private collections. Where shares are held in a private firm it might well mean the dissolution of the firm, since the shares cannot be sold on the open market.

4. *Economy*

The costs of collection and administration should be small in relation to the total revenue. This requirement usually conflicts with that of equity, for the 'fairest' tax system may involve casting the net so wide and so carefully that collection costs would be disproportionately high.

The Economic Effects of Taxation

1. ON THE DISTRIBUTION OF INCOME

Taxes will reduce the disposable income of individuals and, if they do not do this proportionately, they must change the distribution of income. When the tax is progressive, the incomes remaining after tax deductions must be less unequally distributed than incomes before tax. Only a proportional tax would leave the distribution of incomes relatively unchanged.

Indirect taxes which are regressive in their effects will also affect the distribution of income, in this case, the distribution of real income. Those

271

commodities which are heavily taxed (e.g. alcoholic drinks and tobacco) are very widely consumed and have demands which are inelastic with respect to price. If, as some surveys seem to show, the lower income groups spend a greater proportion of their income than the higher income groups on these commodities, there is a redistribution of real income in favour of the better-off households.

Indirect Taxes may be Regressive

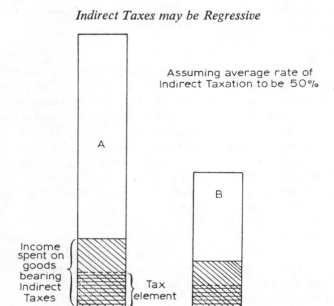

Assuming average rate of
Indirect Taxation to be 50%

Figure 51

(i) High-income family (A) spends $\frac{1}{4}$ of income on taxed commodities.
(ii) Low-income family (B) spends $\frac{1}{3}$ of income on taxed commodities.
If average rate of tax is equal to 50 per cent of the value of the goods:
High-income family will pay $\frac{1}{2} \times \frac{1}{4} = \frac{1}{8}$ of income in indirect taxation.
Low-income family will pay $\frac{1}{2} \times \frac{1}{3} = \frac{1}{6}$ of income in indirect taxation.

2. ON CONSUMPTION

Direct and indirect taxation will affect both the total and the pattern of consumer spending. Direct taxation reduces disposable income and hence will lead to a reduction in spending. The extent of the change in spending will depend upon the rate at which the community saves. In an affluent society with a high rate of saving, an increase in direct taxation might lead to a fall in saving and have little effect on the level of spending.

Indirect taxation also reduces the demand for goods and services since it is normally imposed on goods which have inelastic demands. Consumers will spend more on these goods in order to obtain the same or slightly smaller quantities and, hence, will have less to spend on other goods.

Indirect taxes, however, may have a marked effect on the pattern of consumer spending, since they may be used to discourage or encourage spending on different goods and services. During the serious shortage of electricity generating capacity in the early postwar years, a purchase tax of 100 per cent was placed on electric heaters in order to reduce the sales of these appliances. Sir Stafford Cripps in 1947, anxious to reduce the outflow of dollars, almost doubled the taxation on tobacco in an attempt to reduce the consumption and, hence, the imports of Virginia tobacco.

3. ON INCENTIVES

Every time the Chancellor has to take the unpopular course of increasing taxation, voices are raised to proclaim the fact that the new levels of taxation will mean less effort, less investment, and less enterprise from the members of the community, because the new rates of taxation make the *net* returns from extra toil, trouble, and responsibility seem very unattractive.

Direct taxation makes an immediate impact, because the workers receive 'lighter' pay packets. With a progressive system of taxation *additional* income is taxed at higher rates so that the *net* rewards from overtime, or from a rise in pay due to promotion, or from extra efforts by piece-workers, will be much less than the *gross* rewards. Since workers' efforts are related to their *net* rewards (i.e. their 'take home' pay), an increase in the rates of taxation may persuade them that the extra net reward is not worth the extra effort or the extra responsibility.

There is, obviously, some level at which these disincentive effects will come into operation, but this level is very difficult to determine. It might be argued that taxation will increase efforts. A person becomes accustomed to a given level of disposable income and a certain standard of living. Taxation will reduce his disposable income and he might react by working harder, or longer, in order to raise his disposable income to its former level.

4. ON SAVINGS AND INVESTMENT

Heavy and steeply progressive taxes might reduce both the ability and willingness to save and invest. Death duties might discourage the accumulation of wealth, since one of the incentives to save is the desire to pass on the results of one's efforts to one's children and grandchildren. An increase in taxation might lead to a reduction in savings by people who are determined to maintain their present level of expenditure. It is difficult to determine the strength of these influences since the increasing weight of taxation has been accompanied by a steady increase in real incomes. As mentioned earlier, savings have risen sharply in recent years.

In Britain, at the present time (1971), company profits are subject to corporation tax at the rate of 40 per cent. Does this level of taxation act as a disincentive to enterprise and investment? Again, it is not possible to give a definite answer to such a question, because so many other factors, which influence investment decisions, are at work. It might be that heavy taxation does act as a disincentive as far as the more risky projects are concerned, i.e., new inventions, new methods and new products. Let us take, as a simple example, two possible projects, one fairly safe and one very risky, and assume taxation of profits at a rate of 50 per cent.

	Estimated profits	
	Before tax	*After tax*
Project A (fairly safe)	£1,000 p.a.	£500 p.a.
Project B (very risky)	£3,000 p.a.	£1,500 p.a.

After tax, project B is still three times as profitable as project A, but the difference between the amounts of profit has fallen from £2,000 to £1,000. Is it worthwhile undertaking the much greater risks for a *net* gain of £1,000 as against the £2,000 gain which might be forthcoming without the tax?

The Effects of Government Spending

1. ON INCOME DISTRIBUTION

In the modern state, government spending has a very significant influence on the distribution of income since a large part of the total is devoted to transfer payments. Unemployment pay, sickness benefits, old age pensions and national assistance payments all raise the disposable incomes of the recipients. The redistribution effects depend upon whether the bulk of the taxes are paid by the more affluent members of society. This is true of direct taxation, but is it true of indirect taxation? Indirect taxation in Britain accounts for about 42 per cent of total tax revenue.

2. ON INCENTIVES

A large part of government spending may be regarded as an investment in people. The expenditures on the health services and on education will lead to the development of a more skilled, more efficient and healthier labour force. Public spending on education and training will lead to a greater widening of opportunities. The various national insurance benefits will provide a feeling of security and prevent a loss of health and morale when workers are unemployed. Government spending on research will help to raise the levels of performance in industry and commerce.

Government assistance to industry in the form of subsidies, grants and loans should help to stimulate investment in these industries. The

Government also provides funds to assist in the development of new products and new techniques so that new inventions should not be still-born for lack of finance. For example, the Government financed much of the early development work on the Concorde.

The pressure for more public spending is likely to go on. We are demanding more and more of those things provided by the State – more schools, more universities, more roads, more hospitals. The fundamental problem is to get the 'right' balance between public and private spending. We allow the State to spend 'on our behalf' about 40 per cent of our incomes, on the assumption that, to this extent, public spending is wiser than private spending.

Chapter 25

Unemployment

Unemployment in Britain between the Wars

In the modern world the most important responsibility of government is the maintenance of a high and stable level of employment. It is only comparatively recently that the provision of 'work for all who seek it' has been accepted as a responsibility of government and yet it has quickly come to be regarded as the government's principal task. In Britain it was the publication of the famous White Paper on *Employment Policy* (Cmd. 6527), in 1944, which gave the first official acknowledgement that the Government was prepared to accept this responsibility.

The widespread and prolonged unemployment of the interwar years led to a great deal of research and new thinking on the problems of employment and unemployment. Unemployment represents a waste of economic resources – a permanent waste, since the potential output is lost to the community for ever. One of the greatest puzzles of the capitalist world has been the existence of want and unemployed resources in the same places and at the same time.

Unemployment, in the sense that willing seekers of work were unable to obtain jobs, has certainly existed since the early days of the Industrial Revolution, but our knowledge of its extent in earlier times is not complete. In Britain we have comprehensive details of unemployment since 1948, when it became compulsory for all employed and self-employed persons to join the National Insurance scheme. Prior to this only part of the labour force had been covered (since 1911) by the National Insurance Acts, although trade unions had kept records of the incidence of unemployment among their members for much longer periods.

The most important contribution to our knowledge of the underlying determinants of the level of employment was made by Lord Keynes in his book *The General Theory of Income, Employment and Money*, published in 1936. Another leading writer in this field was Lord Beveridge whose book, *Full Employment in a Free Society*, published in 1944, is a standard work on government policy in this field. Beveridge, using such records as were available, carried out an extensive survey of the extent and variability of unemployment during the nineteenth century. Trade union returns, covering the period from 1856 up to the outbreak of the First World

War, show employment in Britain fluctuating in a succession of waves of unequal length. Unemployment varied from crest to trough in the range 2 per cent to 8 per cent, approximately, of the labour force.

More details are available on the situation between the wars when unemployment rates varied from a minimum of just under 10 per cent to a maximum of over 22 per cent and averaged for the period 14·2 per cent. In the 1930s, unemployment was much more severe than anything experienced earlier, and, at the lowest point of the depression, in 1932, there were 2,800,000 unemployed persons in the United Kingdom.

But these national averages cover a great variety of facts for they do not tell us how the unemployed were distributed geographically, or by industry, by duration, or by age. In the period between the wars unemployment varied greatly from one industry to another as Table 23 demonstrates.

Table 23. *Unemployment rates in various industries, U.K. 1937 (percentages)*

Scientific instruments	2·8
Electrical engineering	3·1
Professional services	4·3
Motor vehicles and aircraft	4·8
Pottery	14·6
Coal-mining	14·7
Linen	18·5
Shipping services	21·9
Shipbuilding	23·8
Docks and harbours	25·8
Jute	26·8

Source: Beveridge, *Full Employment in a Free Society*, Table 33.

As the employment rate differed from industry to industry, so it varied as between different parts of the country. (Table 24.)

Table 24. *U.K. unemployment rates 1937 (percentages)*

London	6·3
South-East	6·7
South-West	7·8
Midlands	7·2
North-East	11·0
North-West	14·0
North	17·9
Scotland	15·9
Wales	22·3
Great Britain	10·8

Source: Beveridge (Table 5).

The chronic nature of the unemployment problem at this time is revealed by details showing the duration of unemployment. In September 1929 nearly 90 per cent of the applicants for unemployment pay had been unemployed for less than six months, but in August 1936 only 64 per cent had been out of work for less than six months and 25 per cent had been unemployed for more than twelve months.

Unemployment in Britain remained at a high level until the outbreak of war in 1939, when the demands of the armed forces and the factories cured the problem. Fortunately the spectre of large-scale unemployment has not returned since the war and the unemployment rate has averaged about 2 per cent or less during the post-war period, although the figure had crept up to more than 3 per cent by mid-1971.

This brief survey, and the statistical details of the interwar unemployment problem, help to draw our attention to the basic features of unemployment. There is not one problem but a complex of related problems.

Types of Unemployment

1. SEASONAL UNEMPLOYMENT

The demands for several products have a seasonal variation. Many workers are needed on the farms during harvest time but not so many during the winter months. There is a great demand for labour in the holiday resorts during the summer months but very few workers will be needed out of season. Industries such as agriculture, building, ice cream manufacture, footwear, and motor cars are subject to seasonal variations in demand due to climatic conditions or to fashion. The peak demand for motor cars comes in the early spring; the demand for footwear rises sharply in the spring (the buying of new summer fashions) and again around Christmas when slippers and bootees are purchased; the demand for labour in the building industry reaches its peak during the summer months due to the more favourable weather and the longer hours of daylight.

This problem is not so acute nowadays as it was before the war. The growth of multiproduct firms means that labour can be used more effectively in meeting the variations in demands for any one product. Technical developments in the form of prefabricated units and anti-freeze mixtures have enabled building operations to proceed throughout the winter months. The motor car industry has developed large overseas markets which greatly reduce the impact of the seasonal variations in home demand. There is now a large body of student labour to meet some of the peak demand of the holiday industry, and mechanisation has greatly reduced the demand for labour on the farms. Nevertheless it is difficult to eliminate seasonal unemployment completely.

K

279

2. FRICTIONAL UNEMPLOYMENT

Beveridge defines this as being: 'Unemployment caused by individuals who make up the labour force not being completely interchangeable and mobile units, so that, though there is an unsatisfied demand for labour, the unemployed workers are not of the right sort or in the right place to meet that demand.'[1]

Even where the total demand for labour creates enough jobs to absorb the whole working population there will be, at any given time, a number of unemployed workers consisting mainly of people who are in the process of changing their jobs. Frictional unemployment arises because the demands for different types of labour are constantly changing. The development of new fashions, new products, and new techniques of production means a constant process of growth and decline as some industries expand and others contract. To meet this constantly changing pattern of demand, resources must move from one industry to another, but, because of the immobilities of labour (see Chapter 5), this transfer of resources involves some degree of unemployment. The new jobs created by the growing demands for the newer goods and services may be of a different type and in different places from the jobs which are being lost. Fewer men may be needed on the railways and more men required in the motor car industry and in garages, but such a transfer of labour is not easy to accomplish.

3. STRUCTURAL UNEMPLOYMENT

To quote Beveridge again: 'Structural unemployment means the unemployment arising in particular industries or localities through a change in demand so great that it may be regarded as affecting the main economic structure of the country.'[2] Where a major industry is experiencing a permanent decline in the demand for its products there might well be a serious unemployment problem, especially when, as in the case of many older industries, the industry is heavily localised.

It is not easy to distinguish structural from frictional unemployment. Where the fall in the demand for the products of one or more industries is accompanied by a compensating increase in demand for labour in other industries, then such unemployment as arises should be regarded as frictional, but, where there is no such compensating increase in demand, the unemployment is of the structural type. It may be justifiable to regard the distinction as one of degree rather than of type. If contracting industries are losing labour to expanding industries and the transfer involves short periods of unemployment as workers seek and move to new jobs,

[1] Beveridge, p. 408.
[2] Beveridge, p. 409.

this is unemployment of the frictional type, but where the movement is much more difficult because job opportunities are not being created quickly enough, or in sufficient volume, to absorb the displaced workers, this is structural unemployment. Both types have the same basic cause – the imperfect mobility of capital and labour.

Structural unemployment was very severe in Britain between the wars because it was imposed on a situation of general unemployment. The older basic industries of coal-mining, cotton, and shipbuilding were in decline, having lost their major export markets due to increased competition from other manufacturing nations and to the fact that many former importers had developed their own industries. Shipbuilding was also hit by the drastic fall in world trade and coal had also to face increasing competition from oil. The areas where these industries were concentrated, South Wales, Lancashire, the North-East, the North-West, and Scotland, experienced unemployment rates well above the national average.

Although the unemployment situation is now vastly different, the problem of structural unemployment in Britain remains unsolved, as the following table shows:

Table 25. *Unemployment rates (percentages)*

	N. Ireland	Scotland	Wales	N. England	U.K.
1953	8·2	3·0	3·0	2·4	1·8
1958	9·1	3·7	3·8	2·4	2·2
1965	5·7	2·7	2·6	2·5	1·4
1970	7·0	4·6	3·9	4·6	2·6

Measures which are intended to alleviate structural and frictional unemployment must be directed towards increasing the mobility of capital and labour. Where the problems are concerned with *geographical immobility* (where there are significant discrepancies in the regional rates of unemployment as illustrated in the table above), the task is to increase the geographical mobility of capital, or labour, or both. In Britain, the Government has tended to concentrate on a policy of 'taking work to the workers', aiming to increase the mobility of capital by persuading firms to set up new plants in the areas where unemployment is higher than the national average. Details of the kinds of measures used for this purpose are given in Chapter 11, pages 106–113. In the early 1960s there was some change of emphasis in government policy as the result of a number of detailed regional studies. Instead of trying to resurrect *all* the depressed districts by piecemeal measures, the aim is now to concentrate government assistance on selected 'growth points' which have a better chance of serving as a base for industrial expansion, and hence of being more attractive to businessmen.

But some recent studies have been critical of a policy which has placed the whole emphasis on the movement of industry and have suggested giving more attention to the possibilities of increasing the geographical mobility of labour. There is evidence to suggest that workers' unwillingness to move from one area to another is nothing like so great as had been supposed. Increased publicity and better information services would help to remove the ignorance of available opportunities which is still a barrier to movement. Greater financial assistance to cover the costs of movement and re-settlement would help matters, but the housing shortage is likely to be the major difficulty in the years ahead.

Where the problem is one of *occupational immobility* – and this is probably the greatest barrier to rapid economic change – the solution lies in improved methods of training and retraining. In addition, measures have to be taken to remove much of the reluctance to change. A large number of well-equipped retraining centres are required where workers can be quickly retrained in new skills, and it is necessary to pay the workers attending these courses a grant which bears some relation to their former earnings. It may also be necessary to revise the older ideas of industrial training which were designed to provide an extended period of training in *one* particular craft and to introduce a new system of concentrated training in *several* crafts. Multicraft training would provide a much more mobile labour force, but it would require a modification of trade union attitudes (and probably trade union structure) which are conditioned to fairly rigid demarcation lines identifying the kinds of work to be done by their members.

The reluctance to change one's job, especially where it means changing one's skill or craft, might be overcome by a system of redundancy payments. Britain, anxious to raise her rate of economic growth, and to overcome the barriers to change, has introduced two important measures to help achieve these objectives. The *Industrial Training Act*, 1964 gives the Minister of Labour powers to set up statutory training boards for each industry with the responsibility for instituting and supervising adequate training schemes in these industries. The boards also have a responsibility for retraining schemes. They are responsible for seeing that the quality and quantity of training is adequate to meet the needs of the industries for which they are established.

In December 1965 a *Redundancy Payments Scheme* came into effect. Under this scheme, people whose jobs disappear through technological or organisational change, or through industrial decline, are entitled to payments on dismissal. The payments are 'wage-related' and vary with age and length of service. These payments should remove some of the immediate financial worries associated with dismissal and help to remove some of the obstacles to labour mobility.

4. CYCLICAL UNEMPLOYMENT

The history of industrial capitalism is one of a succession of 'booms' and 'slumps'. Output per head has grown enormously since the Industrial Revolution, but economic growth.has not taken the form of a steady, smooth, upward movement, but of a succession of upward surges followed by recessions. Growth has taken place because each boom reached higher levels of economic activity than previous booms. The pattern was something like this:

This pattern of fluctuations in the level of national income, which from the end of the eighteenth century occurred in fairly regular nine-year cycles, is known as the *trade cycle*. The pattern was broken by two world wars. The years following the first world war witnessed a depression much longer and deeper than anything experienced before, while the years following the second world war have been free of any kind of serious recession. Cyclical is the most serious type of unemployment; all industries to varying degrees are affected by the fall in demand. It was to this type of general unemployment that Keynes and Beveridge directed most of their attention. The next chapter contains a brief survey of their ideas.

Chapter 26

Full Employment

The first step is to examine the forces which determine the level of employment. The demand for labour is derived from the demand for goods and services, so that the first condition required to ensure full employment is a level of demand for consumer goods, services and capital goods which will keep labour fully employed. Aggregate demand comprises the total spending on goods and services and this spending, in turn, is equal to total income (see Chapter 15 on National Income) – 'one man's spending is another man's income'. There will be a certain level of income which represents a full employment level of demand, but a capitalist economy does not automatically generate this level of income. Keynes showed that it is possible to reach an equilibrium situation where the level of spending (and hence income) was insufficient to keep all the workers employed.

It is not only necessary to achieve a *high level* of employment, it is also most desirable that this level of employment should be *stable*. Great hardship, misery, and waste is caused by the periodic fluctuations in employment which have been mentioned earlier. Economists have devoted much of their attention to the task of discovering the causes of these fluctuations.

Aggregate Demand and the Level of Employment

Expenditure is planned by four broad groups, private individuals, firms, public authorities and foreigners (i.e. the demand for our exports). It is necessary to examine these different types of expenditure in order to understand why aggregate demand may be both deficient and variable.

1. PRIVATE CONSUMPTION SPENDING (C)

As individuals we have two choices in the disposal of our income: we can either spend it on consumption goods and services or save it. At any given level of income, consumption spending is likely to be very stable, because it is governed by custom and habit. People do not change their way of life very readily and, assuming their income does not change, their spending will vary little from week to week.

As incomes rise, people will spend more on consumption goods and services, but *the proportion* of their income so spent tends to fall. That proportion of any *extra* income which is spent on consumption goods is known as the *Marginal Propensity to Consume*. If I were to receive an increase in my income of £1 and spent 75p of this on consumption goods and services, my MPC would be ¾. That part of any increase in income which is saved is known as the *Marginal Propensity to Save*, so that MPC + MPS = 1. As income increases, MPC tends to fall. The rich man's MPC may be ½ whereas the poor man's MPC may well be 1. In this particular case what is true of the individual is true of the community – a wealthy society will have a lower MPC than a poor society. Consumption behaviour may be shown graphically. (Fig. 52)

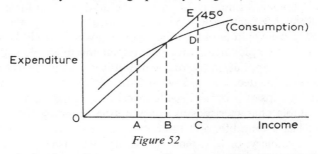

Figure 52

The vertical axis represents expenditure and the horizontal axis represents total income. The 45° line, therefore, will represent all points of equality of income and expenditure. The consumption line shows the levels of consumption spending at different levels of income. It rises as income rises, but *less than proportionately*, since MPC is falling. When income = OA, consumption spending is greater than income. At this low level of income the community must be spending its savings or borrowing. When income = OB the community is spending the whole of its income on consumption. When income = OC the community is spending CD on consumption and must, therefore, be saving ED (since income = OC = EC). If this state of affairs exists it means that businesses are paying out more in the form of incomes than they are receiving in the form of sales revenue. Now, income is equal to the total of payments made to the factors of production for services rendered and, hence, is equal to the value of total output. When income is equal to OC, therefore, supply is greater than demand; that is, the value of output (= income) is greater than the level of spending.[1] Businesses react by reducing output, incomes fall, and so does the level of employment. Income falls to the level OB, because, only at this level of income do we have a situation of equilibrium where business receipts are equal to their payments to factors – where, in fact, the spending of the community is equal to the value of total output. The

[1] i.e. Consumer spending. There are other types of spending to be considered later.

285

reader should be able to explain why OA is not an equilibrium level of income, and why income would rise from OA to OB.

But suppose that OC is the level of income required to maintain full employment. This particular income can only be achieved and maintained if expenditure is increased to cover the gap ED. There are a number of ways in which this might be achieved, since consumption spending is only one of the components of total demand. The others are discussed below.

2. PRIVATE INVESTMENT SPENDING (I)

Investment means the creation of new capital equipment and this demand for capital goods is an important part of the total demand for goods and services. Referring back to Fig. 53, if investment spending were equal to savings (ED), we would have a level of spending which would be sufficient to maintain full employment. Investment spending might be sufficient to close the saving gap, but, in the real world, it is just as likely not to do so. This is because the decisions to save and the decisions to invest are taken by different groups of people.[1] Private investment spending does not have the same stable characteristics as consumption spending. Much capital equipment has a long life, and the entrepreneur's decisions to buy new plant and machinery, or to extend his factory, are based on estimates of what is likely to happen over the next five or ten years (in industries such as the steel industry it might be twenty or thirty years). He must make intelligent guesses as to the probable economic life of his equipment, the future trends in the demand for his product, possible changes in his costs of production, likely changes in government policy, future developments in world trade, and many other possible developments which could affect the prospective profitability of the proposed investment. Any likely changes, or rumours of changes, in business prospects will have a marked effect on investment spending. An increase in the rate of interest might change the whole aspect of what had seemed an attractive proposition at the lower rate of interest. A businessman who was contemplating expansion in an industry which was highly protected by tariffs would probably change his plans if Britain decided to seek entry to the Common Market, whereas firms in highly competitive industries might be stimulated to undertake more investment by such a proposal.

Since investment decisions are based on calculations which are fraught with uncertainty, investment spending is likely to be extremely volatile. It is this component of total spending which contains the major elements of the variability of aggregate demand. Investment spending is determined by the expected profitability of capital which, in turn, is based upon estimates of future revenue and costs.

[1] Except in the case of retained profits.

3. GOVERNMENT SPENDING (G)

Public authorities account for a very large part of the total spending in most advanced countries. In Britain the spending of government and local authorities is about two-fifths of total spending. Public spending covers expenditure on both consumption and investment goods and the total is so large that relatively small percentage changes can have significant effects on total demand.

About one half of the investment in Britain is now carried out in the public sector, a very large part of it by the nationalised industries. Public investment is much more stable than private investment since it is not subject to the same kinds of tests with regard to profitability. Much of it is determined by the social and political desirability of the project and tends to be of a long-term nature. Road building programmes, school building programmes, defence projects and the like may be speeded up or slowed down, but they are not likely to be changed in any drastic fashion unless there is a serious economic crisis.

Public authorities' current spending is also fairly stable, most of it going in the form of payments for the current services of such people as civil servants, teachers, police and doctors.

4. EXPORTS (X)

Part of the demand for goods and services produced at home comes from foreigners. The spending by foreigners on British goods constitutes part of aggregate demand and part, therefore, of total incomes in Britain. Exports, we should note, are inflationary since they generate income at home but reduce the supply of goods on the home market.

5. IMPORTS (M)

Some part of the spending by consumers, businesses, and Government will be for the purchase of foreign goods. Imports do not generate income at home – they do not create any demand for domestic factors of production. In order to arrive at a figure for aggregate demand, therefore, it is necessary to deduct that part of total spending devoted to imports.

Income and Employment

Total demand may now be expressed in the form $C+I+G+X-M$ and changes in any of these components will lead to changes in income, production and employment – unless there is already full employment, when an increase in one or more of these forms of spending will only lead to price increases.

The relationships between total demand and the level of income may be seen more clearly by making use of the flow diagram which was introduced in the chapter on the National Income.

In Fig. 53 income is represented as a flow along the upper channel and the volume of this flow, during a period of one year, is equal to the National Income. It is this stream of income which determines the level of employment, because it is made up of payments to the factors of production. These income payments are made by businesses in return for the services of factors. The greater the total of factor payments, the greater is the demand for factors and, hence, the higher is the level of employment. But these factor payments are also equal to the value of the total output of goods and services (see Chapter 15).

The total demand for the output of businesses is shown as two separate flows. Along the lower channel there is represented the demand by the public for consumer goods and services. This is only part of the total demand for goods and services, because, as already explained, businesses have to meet demands from other firms (I), from the government (G) and from foreigners (X). These other components of total demand are shown as 'injections'.

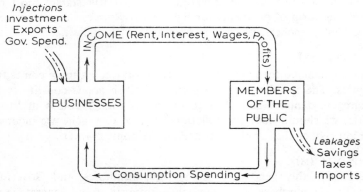

Figure 53

It must be noted that all incomes received by individuals do not flow back to businesses in the form of consumer demand; a part will be saved, a part will be taken in taxation and a part will be spent on imports. These three items are shown as 'leakages' since they do not make up, directly, any part of aggregate demand. It should be obvious, however, that savings and taxation may help to finance the demand for investment goods and Government spending after they have passed through various financial institutions and Government departments.

The requirement for a stable level of income and employment is that *Injections = Leakages*. If the leakages are greater than the injections, income and employment will fall. If injections are greater than leakages, incomes and employment will rise.

There is a very important relationship between the changes in the level of spending and the resultant level of income. It is known as the Multiplier. The diagram makes it clear that any change in the level of spending by consumers (C), by firms (I), by government (G), or by foreigners (X) will change the flow of income in the upper channel, and so increase employment. But the eventual change in the level of income will be a multiple of the change in the rate of spending, and the relationship,

$$\frac{\text{Eventual Change in Income}}{\text{Original Change in Level of Spending}} = \text{The Multiplier}$$

If an increase in the rate of spending of, say, £1,000, raises the level of income by £4,000, the multiplier is 4. Let us suppose that the Government raises its spending on school building by £1,000 per week, and the MPC of the community is $\frac{3}{4}$. The first group to receive the increase in spending will have their incomes increased by £1,000; they will spend £750 of this and so raise the incomes of a second group by this amount. This second group will spend £562·5 of their extra income and raise the incomes of a third group by the same amount. The process will continue until the increments are exhausted. Total income will rise by an amount equal to the sum of these successive rounds of spending.

It is not possible to develop the theory of the multiplier any further at this stage and it is sufficient, for our purpose, to appreciate the nature of the multiplier process.

It is not only necessary to have a level of income which is stable, it must be sufficient to maintain full employment. These requirements are by no means easy to satisfy. The government has taken upon itself the responsibility for maintaining the required level of demand. If demand falls below the required level, the Government must take steps to raise the level of spending by acting upon one or more of the components (C, I, G, and X). How it does this is discussed below. But demand may rise *above* the required level. How can this be? What happens is that total spending on the output of businesses exceeds the factor payments of businesses when they are already at full employment level. As indicated in Fig. 54, the effect will be to raise incomes, but if incomes are equal to the value of output, and we already have full employment, how can output possibly rise? It cannot. The adjustment takes place by a movement of prices. Incomes and output rise, but only in monetary terms, in other words, prices rise.

There are two possible situations, therefore, which call for some kind of government action.

(a) *Where demand is not sufficient to maintain full employment, the deficiency of demand is referred to as a Deflationary Gap.*

(b) *Where demand is greater than the level needed to maintain full employment, the excess demand is known as an Inflationary Gap.*

In pursuing a full employment policy, the government has a number of instruments available for the purpose of influencing the level of economic activity.

Deflationary Gap Policies

MONETARY POLICY

By making use of the central bank controls which were described in chapter 21, the Government may increase the supply of money and encourage borrowing and spending. An increase in the supply of money will tend to reduce interest rates. Special deposits held by the central bank may be released to the commercial banks in order to increase their ability to lend; open market operations may be used to increase the banks' liquidity, and directives can be used to increase the banks' willingness to lend. Easier and cheaper credit will help to stimulate investment by reducing costs and removing difficulties in raising finance. Easier personal loans will encourage more consumer spending. Since hire purchase is financed by borrowed funds, lower interest rates should make hire purchase terms more attractive, especially if these moves are accompanied by a reduction in the amount of the deposit required and an extension of the period for repayment.

FISCAL POLICY

Fiscal policy means making use of changes in the Government's revenue and expenditure in order to influence economic activity. When it is necessary to raise the level of expenditure the methods used would be:

(a) A Reduction in Taxation

Lowering the rates of income tax and profits tax will leave more purchasing power in the hands of the public, while a reduction in purchase tax and customs and excise duties will lower prices and lead to an increase in the quantities demanded.

(b) Increased Government Spending

This may take many forms. The Government may decide to increase the rate of investment in social capital by 'stepping up' road building, school building or hospital building programmes. It may decide to increase the rate of investment in the nationalised industries by building more power stations or by expanding the modernisation programmes of the railways or the docks. Another possibility is the expansion of government spending in the form of increased social security payments – higher pensions, more generous national assistance allowances and more unemployment pay. Practically the whole of these increased benefits would be spent, since the MPC of the recipients will be almost equal to 1.

It should be carefully noted that an increase in government spending will only raise the level of demand if it is not accompanied by a corresponding increase in taxation, otherwise the expansionary effect of the greater government spending will be largely offset by a reduction in private spending. Fiscal policy operates through the budget, and, in a deflationary situation, the Government will aim at a budget deficit (see Chapter 24 on Public Finance).

Another important point to note is that the increase in government spending will have a multiplier effect. If the Government wishes to raise the level of income by £100 million and the multiplier is 3, it will only need to raise the level of its spending by £33⅓ million.

(c) Taxation Allowances and Grants

Fiscal policy may be used to encourage a higher rate of investment by granting generous tax allowances on the purchase of new equipment. Britain used this system until January 1966 when a new method of making outright cash grants to purchasers of new capital equipment was introduced. There was a return to the system of tax allowances in 1970.

Inflationary Gap Policies

To achieve price stability expenditure must equal real income at the current price level, that is, expenditure must be reduced to the full employment level of income at the current prices. Demand may be reduced by 'reversing' most of the measures used to cure deflation.

MONETARY POLICY

The traditional policy is known as a *credit squeeze*. Interest rates will be raised in order to discourage borrowing and hence spending. Open market operations will be used to reduce bank liquidity and special deposits may be called for the same purpose. The central bank will issue directives to the commercial banks requesting them to curb their lending. Hire purchase restrictions will be increased by raising the level of deposits and reducing the periods allowed for repayment.

FISCAL POLICY

Taxation on income and expenditure will be increased in order to reduce total purchasing power, and government spending might be reduced. A cut in government expenditure, however, might not be easy to accomplish. Much government spending is regarded as desirable from social and political standpoints and is tied to long-term projects which do not allow a great deal of flexibility – it would be unacceptable to leave a hospital half-finished. A major item of public expenditure is defence, and it would need a strong mandate from the people before a Government would risk any major cuts in this item. Again, it would be extremely difficult for the Government to reduce its outlays on social security benefits since this would be interpreted as placing the burden of reducing demand on those groups least able to bear it.

Investment might be reduced by a withdrawal or a reduction in the taxation allowances or grants on new capital goods, although, if business prospects are very bright, this might not be much of a deterrent.

EXHORTATION AND PERSUASION

In a free society, the Government is subject to serious limitations in its ability to control the economic situation. If the population insists on a substantial amount of freedom in the choice of jobs, geographical movement, the manner in which wages are determined, and in the ways in which incomes are spent, the Government will be obliged to resort to persuasion.

One approach is to launch an extensive savings campaign with a variety of securities (e.g. savings stamps, development bonds, premium bonds, etc.) in an attempt to persuade people to save a greater proportion of their income. The Government must also try to get people not to press for increases in pay which exceed the movements in output per head. This measure implies the operation of some kind of *incomes policy*, the features of which are discussed in Chapter 31.

One of the greatest difficulties in the operation of a policy to ensure full employment is the task of trying to interpret the major economic trends. When demand is falling, the Government must try to raise the level of spending, but it is not easy to read the trend accurately. Is it merely a small temporary deviation or the beginning of a fairly serious depression? If it is the former, but the Government is led to believe that it is the latter, it may introduce measures which increase purchasing power excessively so that it only succeeds in creating an inflationary situation.

Another serious problem is that of the politically acceptable level of unemployment. In Britain, it now appears to be something in the region of 2 per cent. If the Government maintains demand at a level which does not allow unemployment to rise above this figure then the situation appears to be an inflationary one. The great power of the unions, the immobilities of labour and the excess demand which appears in many labour markets[1] will all operate to raise incomes faster than productivity.

[1] When the *average* rate of unemployment is in the range 1–1½ per cent, the demand for labour will greatly exceed the supply in many occupations. This will cause employers in these occupations to bid up wages in order to attract labour.

There is no completely satisfactory definition of *full employment*. Beveridge thought that it meant 'having more vacant jobs than unemployed men'. It does not mean that no one will be unemployed. As already explained, there will be some frictional unemployment, some seasonal unemployment and variations in world trade will probably give rise to some structural unemployment, so that, even when the number of job opportunities is adequate, there will be some unemployed. Beveridge estimated that in a full employment situation the number of unemployed would be about 3 per cent of the labour force.

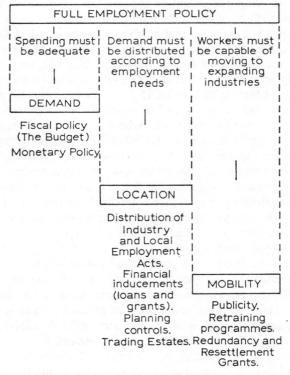

FULL EMPLOYMENT POLICY

Spending must be adequate

DEMAND

Fiscal policy (The Budget)
Monetary Policy

Demand must be distributed according to employment needs

LOCATION

Distribution of Industry and Local Employment Acts.
Financial inducements (loans and grants).
Planning controls.
Trading Estates.

Workers must be capable of moving to expanding industries

MOBILITY

Publicity.
Retraining programmes.
Redundancy and Resettlement Grants.

Figure 54

Automation and Employment

Originally used to describe the automatic linking of a succession of separate production processes, the word *automation* has now come to be used in a wider context to describe the production process as a whole. When a production process is redesigned and integrated so as to achieve a very high degree of mechanisation of all the operations, both the actual manufacturing processes and the transfer between operations, the assembly

293

is described as automation. Some of the most spectacular examples of automation are-found in the motor industry, where as many as 600 separate machine operations may be carried out on an engine block by fully automatic processes. The steel, chemical, oil refining and food processing industries have now adopted automation to a very great extent. These 'continuous process' industries are able to make use of control devices which can automatically control the various processes by responding to changes in temperature, pressure, rates of flow, levels of liquid, and composition of materials. These control devices can 'report' any undue variations and bring into operation the necessary corrective measures.

The possible effects of automation on the demand for labour is a subject on which there is a wide variety of views. The first task is to bring the problem into perspective and examine the possible scope for automation. It has been estimated that the industries in which automation might be economically applied account for about 40 per cent of Britain's manufacturing labour force; this is about 15 per cent of the working population. A further point is that the spread of automation may be relatively slow. Most of the necessary re-equipment schemes will be very expensive and only justifiable where there is a large market for a standardised product.

The experience of the past 150 years does not suggest that the introduction of 'labour-saving' machinery and increased mechanisation will bring any permanent decline in the demand for labour. Britain is now using more machinery (more capital-intensive methods of production) than ever before, and yet the numbers in employment are greater than at any time in her history. Mechanisation has brought higher standards of living and a shorter working week.

Automation will bring some problems of labour displacement but that does not necessarily mean that no jobs will be available elsewhere. Employment will be created in those industries making automated equipment. Since automation will mean lower costs of production and lower prices, the demand for the products of the industry which is applying the new techniques may well increase sufficiently to expand employment rather than reduce it. The reduction in the length of the working week will probably be one of the consequences of automation, and this will mean a greater demand for labour in the service industries such as entertainment, distribution, catering, motoring services and so on.

There will be problems of labour mobility arising from the changing pattern of demand for labour skills (e.g. fewer machine operatives will be required but more supervisors and technicians). These problems of labour mobility have been examined earlier (p. 282).

The disputes on the effects of automation arise mainly because of the uncertainty as to the pace of its introduction.

In America, where automation has proceeded much further than elsewhere in the world, some serious problems of employment have arisen. In 1966 the American Government estimated that automation was putting about 50,000 people out of work each year. The following details[1] illustrate the problem.

In the Appalachian coalfields, automation allows 142,000 miners to do the work once done by 530,000 miners. Automated equipment can now assemble entire electric typewriters in twenty minutes under the supervision of 48 workers. It used to take 400 men forty minutes to do the job.

A United States Government agency has cut its clerical staff from 13,000 to 3,000 with the purchase of a multipurpose computer.

Technical progress is making the matching of 'job creation' and 'job destruction' increasingly difficult. The pressure for a shorter working week is one aspect of this necessity to create more jobs.

[1] *The Sunday Times*, 6 March 1966.

Chapter 27

International Trade

In the earlier chapters of this book we saw how specialisation increases productivity and raises the standard of living. Within a country, individuals specialise, factories specialise, and regions specialise. In Coventry, for example, workers specialise on a tiny part of the total process of producing a motor car, factories specialise on producing one, or a very small number, of the components for the motor car, and the whole area specialises to a very great extent on the manufacture of motor cars.

The exchange of goods and services across national boundaries has enabled this principle of the division of labour to be extended to the international sphere. International trade originated on the basis of nations exchanging their products for others which they could not produce for themselves (or which they could produce only at an exorbitant cost). The obvious example is the exchange of commodities between Europe and the Tropics. Europeans could exchange manufactures for the foodstuffs and minerals from Africa, India, South-east Asia and South America. Adam Smith pointed out that Scotland might well produce its own wine by creating artificial hothouse conditions for the vine, but it would be a most inefficient use of resources. Scotland could obtain her wine much more cheaply by using her resources to produce engineering products and exchanging these for the wine produced in Mediterranean countries. In the case of minerals, of course, nations which do not have any deposits must rely on international trade for their supplies.

International specialisation is advantageous because:

1. The production of different kinds of goods requires different kinds of resources used in different proportions.

2. The various kinds of economic resources are unevenly distributed throughout the world.

3. The international mobility of resources is extremely limited.

Land (including climate) is obviously immobile in the geographical sense and there are very great barriers to the international movement of labour. Capital, although much more mobile geographically, only crosses international boundaries when particularly favourable conditions are present (e.g. political stability, no threat of confiscation, no barriers to taking profits out of the country, etc.).

297

Since it is difficult, or impossible, to move resources between nations, the goods which 'embody' these resources must move. Nations which have an abundance of land relative to labour will tend to concentrate on 'land-intensive' products such as agricultural commodities and will exchange these products for the 'labour-intensive' goods, such as manufactures, made by countries which have an abundance of labour relative to land. Just as our individual abilities and training fit us for different occupations, so the different resources and the historical developments of nations equip them for the production of different products.

Since different regions of the world have different factor endowments, they will tend to specialise in those industries which are appropriate to their natural and acquired resources (e.g. special skills). But unlike individuals, nations do not specialise in one process or in one product. They tend to concentrate on certain types of activities, but even the greatest importers of food grow some of their requirements, and importers of manufactures have some domestic manufacturing industries.

Gains from International Trade

We know that, in the real world, international trade is carried on by a large number of countries in a vast range of goods. This is a very complex situation, but it is possible to gain an understanding of the principles which underly this complicated economic structure by using a very simplified example, namely, an imaginary world with only two countries (A and B), and two products (wool and tractors).

Since the greater part of world trade now comprises the exchange of goods which countries could produce for themselves, we have to show how a country may gain by importing goods which it could produce domestically.

1. WHERE EACH COUNTRY HAS AN ABSOLUTE ADVANTAGE

We shall first consider the fairly realistic situation where each country is more efficient than the other in the production of one of the commodities. Country B produces wool more efficiently than country A, and country A produces tractors more efficiently than country B. We begin by assuming that each country produces both commodities and there is no international trade.

	Tractors Output per worker p.a.	Wool (bales) Output per worker p.a.
Country A	50	15,000
Country B	25	20,000

If, in country A, we moved a worker from the tractor industry to the woollen industry – we are assuming perfect mobility of labour – the output of tractors would fall by 50 units and the output of wool would rise by 15,000 bales. *The opportunity cost of 1 tractor is 300 bales of wool* (50 : 15,000 = 1 : 300).

In country B the movement of 1 worker from the production of tractors to wool production would cause tractor output to fall by 25 units and wool output to rise by 20,000 bales. *The opportunity cost of 1 tractor is 800 bales of wool* (25 : 20,000 = 1 : 800).

It should now be apparent that *the total output of wool and tractors could be increased by a re-allocation of resources.* The reader should put this statement to the test. What would be the effect on total output, if three men in country A were moved from the woollen industry to the tractor industry and four men in country B were transferred from the tractor industry to the woollen industry?

Let us now suppose that each country has 1,000 workers and, in the absence of the opportunity to trade with other nations, each country devotes half of its labour force to each industry.

	Tractors	*Wool (bales)*
Country A would produce each year	25,000	7,500,000
Country B would produce each year	12,500	10,000,000
Total output	37,500	17,500,000

Now if international trade were possible, there would be an incentive for each country to specialise; resources in country A would move from the production of wool to the production of tractors and in country B they would move from the production of tractors to the production of wool. If specialisation were complete, the following situation would arise:

	Tractors	*Wool (bales)*
Country A would produce each year	50,000	0
Country B would produce each year	0	20,000,000
Total Output	50,000	20,000,000

Specialisation thus leads to an increase in the world output of each commodity, but it must be accompanied by the exchange of commodities. Tractors and wool will exchange for one another at some rate which benefits *both* countries. The rate of exchange of wool for tractors (i.e. *the terms of trade*) must lie somewhere between the opportunity cost ratios in each of these countries. Why is this? Country A will wish to exchange tractors for wool, but she will not accept anything less than 300 bales of wool for her tractors since she can obtain wool at this 'price' by moving workers, at home, into the wool trade. Country B will wish to exchange wool for tractors but she will not offer more than 800 bales of wool for a tractor since she can obtain a tractor at this 'price' by using her own resources. Hence, the terms of trade must lie somewhere between:

1 tractor: 300 bales of wool and 1 tractor: 800 bales of wool

Let us assume that the rate settles at 1 tractor = 500 bales of wool, and, at this rate, 20,000 tractors are exchanged for 10,000,000 bales of wool. Then, after trade, the countries will be in the following position:

	Tractors	Wool (bales)
Country A has an annual supply of	30,000	10,000,000
Country B has an annual supply of	20,000	10,000,000

If we compare this situation with that which obtained before the countries decided to specialise and trade, we see that both are much better off.

2. WHERE EACH COUNTRY HAS A COMPARATIVE ADVANTAGE

It is perfectly reasonable to expect gains from trade and specialisation where each country has an absolute advantage in the production of one of the commodities. What is not so obvious, however, is the fact that, where one country has an absolute advantage over the other in the production of *both* commodities, there can be gains to both countries from specialisation and trade.

The principle which is involved here is known as the *Principle of Comparative Costs*, which indicates that both parties can gain from using their resources in a more specialised manner and exchanging goods as long as each country has a *comparative advantage* over the other in the production of one of the commodities. The principle is best explained by using, once again, the very simplified situation with two countries and two commodities. Let us assume that the output per worker, per annum, in each of the countries is as follows:

	Tractors	Wool (bales)
Country A	50	20,000
Country B	25	15,000

We shall further assume that the workers in each country are, occupationally, perfectly mobile; the movement of one worker in Country A from the tractor industry to the wool industry will reduce tractor output by fifty units and raise the output of wool by 20,000 bales.

Country A has an absolute advantage in the production of both commodities, she operates more efficiently in both industries, but she has *a comparative advantage* in the production of tractors. She is more efficient at producing both commodities, but the difference in efficiency is relatively greater in tractor production. Country B has a *comparative advantage* in the production of wool. In Country A the opportunity cost of 1,000 bales of wool is $2\frac{1}{2}$ tractors. In Country B the opportunity cost of 1,000 bales of wool is $1\frac{2}{3}$ tractors. Although the absolute cost of wool will be less in Country A, in terms of the alternative foregone, wool is cheaper in Country B. As long as the opportunity cost ratios are different in the two countries, specialisation will raise total output.

The gains to be obtained from specialisation and trade may be seen by carrying out a re-allocation of resources in the two countries. Suppose country A moves two men from the wool industry to the tractor industry and Country B moves three men from the tractor industry to the wool industry. The result of these changes in the distribution of labour would be:

Tractor production $+100$ units -75 units $= +25$ units
Wool production $+45,000$ bales $-40,000$ bales $= +5,000$ bales.

It is apparent that a movement of resources towards a greater degree of specialisation would benefit both countries providing there were facilities to exchange goods on favourable terms. Since the opportunity cost ratios are different in the two countries. it is possible to derive favourable terms of trade.

The gains from international trade are modified by the existence of transport costs and tariffs. The economic effects of these are virtually the same; in both cases the movement of the goods raises their costs of production. In the case of transport costs, the increase in the price is unavoidable whereas in the case of the tariff the increase in the price is 'artificial', because it is an 'administered' cost which causes the good to be dearer.

There is a further unrealistic simplification in the theory as outlined above. We have assumed that the opportunity costs of tractors in terms of wool did not change as resources were moved from one industry to another. Each time a worker, in Country A, was moved from the production of wool to the manufacture of tractors, it was assumed that the output of wool would fall by 20,000 bales and the output of tractors rise by fifty units. This is not very likely. Some resources will be more efficient at producing tractors and some more efficient at producing wool. Countries will only move their economic resources from one use to another up to the point where the opportunity cost ratios become unfavourable when compared with the international exchange ratios. Country A, for example, will only move her resources out of the woollen industry and into the tractor industry if the sacrifice she has to make in her woollen production is more than compensated by the rate at which she can exchange her tractors for wool in the world market.

The Terms of Trade

The rate at which one nation's goods exchange against those of other nations is referred to as the Terms of Trade. In the examples used earlier the concept can be seen very clearly, because we made use of a very simple example and the terms of trade could be expressed as 'so many bales of wool per tractor'. The actual rate at which tractors will exchange for wool, as demonstrated earlier, must lie somewhere between the domestic opportunity cost ratios of the two countries concerned. Just where the terms of trade will lie depends upon the conditions of supply and demand for both tractors and wool in A and B. The exchange ratio might favour both countries equally or it might favour one country more than the other.

In the real world the picture is much more complex. Countries such as Great Britain import and export a great variety of goods and services. It is not possible to express such a country's terms of trade in the form of a simple ratio between physical units of commodities. Nevertheless, the terms of trade is a very important relationship and it is necessary to obtain some idea of the movements in the terms on which a country is exchanging its goods for those of other countries. The method adopted makes use of two important index numbers – the Index of Import Prices and the Index of Export Prices. Although the reality of international trade is the exchange of goods and services for other goods and services, all these items have prices and it is only possible to measure their exchange values in terms of relative prices.

The terms of trade are given a numerical value which is equal to:

$$\frac{\text{Index of Export Prices}}{\text{Index of Import Prices}} \times 100.$$

In the base year, each of the two index numbers will be 100 so that the terms of trade will be 100. If, subsequently, export prices rise relative to import prices the numerical value of the terms of trade will rise. If import prices rise relative to export prices the terms of trade will fall. There are a number of possible ways in which such changes might come about.
1. Export prices and import prices could be moving in opposite directions.
2. One of them could be stable while the other is changing.
3. They could both be moving in the same direction but one of them could be rising or falling faster than the other.

A rise in the numerical value of the terms of trade is regarded as a 'favourable' movement since it indicates that any given volume of exports is now exchanging for a greater volume of imports. Similarly a fall in the terms of trade is regarded as 'unfavourable'. If the price of British exports rises by 5 per cent and the price of British imports falls by 5 per cent, this would be referred to as a 'favourable' movement, because any given volume of exports will now buy approximately 10 per cent more imports. (See reference to real wages, page 180.)

But we must be very careful not to interpret the words 'favourable' and 'unfavourable' too literally. While the price movements may be favourable, the effects on the country's trading position may be unfavourable. Similarly an unfavourable movement in the terms of trade may have favourable effects on the balance of trade. This point may be illustrated by using the example given above. If Britain's export prices rise by 5 per cent, she will only earn more foreign currency if her export sales-volume does not change, or falls by less than 5 per cent (i.e. if demand is inelastic). If her import prices fall by 5 per cent she will spend less foreign currency on imports only if she does not expand the quantity she buys by more than 5 per cent (i.e. if demand is inelastic). If the demands for exports and imports were elastic, the 'favourable' movements in the terms of trade would make Britain worse off since her expenditure abroad would rise and her income from abroad would fall.[1]

There is also the income effect to consider. Lower prices for imports means that foreign countries are earning less from *their* exports and hence their ability to buy from other countries will be correspondingly reduced. In the case we have considered, Britain might find that she is selling less abroad not only because the prices of her exports are higher, but also because other countries are less able to pay for imports.

For countries which engage in world trade on an extensive scale, as Britain does, movements in the terms of trade are of great significance. When the volumes of imports and exports are very large, quite small changes in the terms of trade make a very large impact on the trading position. With imports running at about £7,000 million per annum (in 1970) even a 1 per cent fall in import prices could mean, for Britain, a saving of some £70 million in foreign currency, or, alternatively, the existing level of exports could buy additional imports worth, approximately, £70 million.

Table 26. *The terms of trade – United Kingdom (1961 = 100)*

Year	Export prices	Import prices	Terms of trade
1967	114	109	105
1968	123	121	102
1969	127	126	101
1970	141	132	107
1971	150	139	108
1972[2]	163	157	104

[1] Not true in every case, e.g. a rise in export prices may be due to a rise in demand for exports.
[2] December.

Free Trade and Protection

Our theoretical account of the gains to be obtained from international trade seemed to be fairly conclusive, yet the facts are, that every major trading nation in the world, operates some form of restriction on international trade. It is true that in the years since the Second World War there has been a substantial reduction in the barriers to trade, but those which remain are still formidable. Before examining the reasons for these restrictions on international trade, it is necessary to describe the types of restriction most commonly used.

Restrictions on International Trade

QUOTAS

A quota is the most serious kind of restriction since it generally takes the form of a physical limit to the quantity of the commodity which is allowed to enter the country. Quotas bring in no revenue to the State, and foreign producers cannot overcome them by reducing their prices, as they might do in the case of tariffs.

TARIFFS

The tariff is the most common form of restriction on trade. It acts in exactly the same way as a tax by artificially raising the price of the foreign product as it enters the country. Tariffs may be used for revenue purposes, or as a means of protecting home industries from foreign competition.

EXCHANGE CONTROL

Importers require foreign currencies in order to make their purchases. American firms will require payment in dollars, German firms in marks and so on. A country obtains its supplies of foreign currencies by means of the efforts of its exporters. A thoroughgoing system of exchange control will require the foreign currencies earned by exporters to be surrendered to the central bank which will pay for them in the home currency. Importers requiring foreign currency must apply to the central bank which can thus, very effectively, control the variety and volume of imports by controlling the issue of foreign currency.

SUBSIDIES

A nation may decide to subsidise certain domestic industries as a means of protecting them from the competition of lower-priced foreign goods. The subsidy will reduce the prices of the products of these industries by lowering (artificially) the costs of production and hence make it more difficult for foreign producers to sell similar products in the home market. The community as a whole will not be better off, because they will have to pay taxes in order to finance the subsidy. Subsidies are an artificial means of reducing the differences in comparative costs between home and foreign producers.

The next question to be answered is: 'Why are such restrictions so commonplace?' There are many reasons for erecting barriers to international trade. They are often classified into economic and non-economic reasons, but this can be misleading since they will all have economic effects. Some of the principal arguments for protection are discussed below.

ARGUMENTS FOR PROTECTION

1. *For Revenue Purposes*

The use of customs duties as a means of providing the State with revenue has a very long history (more than 300 years in Britain). The budget statement on page 260 reveals that this is no longer a major source of revenue as far as the U.K. is concerned. Although not primarily intended to be protective, such duties will probably have some such effect unless the articles subject to duty are not produced at home.

2. *To Counter the Effect of a General Depression*

During the Great Depression of the 1930s, most countries greatly increased their protection in an attempt to maintain employment at home by reducing expenditure on foreign goods. Money spent on home produced goods creates employment in domestic industries but that spent on imports does not. But the imports of one country are the exports of another, and restrictions on imports create unemployment and distress in exporting countries. They are very likely to retaliate by protecting their own industries. A cumulative effect is inevitable, and world exports will decline – all trading nations will be, to some extent, worse off.

3. *To Protect Particular Industries*

(*a*) The best-known argument for the protective tariff is the 'infant industry argument'. A nation may be relatively late in developing a particular industry and yet be favourably endowed with the basic economic requirements for the establishment of such an industry. If this industry were to be established on a small scale, it would not survive the competition from fully developed, large-scale, foreign firms producing at much lower prices. It is necessary, therefore, to protect the infant industry until it reaches a scale of operation large enough to allow its costs to fall to a level which is competitive with its foreign rivals. The Germans were the first Europeans to establish an efficient large-scale chemical industry. The amalgamation of much smaller British firms in 1926 was preceded by the introduction of a protective tariff in order to allow the industry time to 'grow up'. Unfortunately these tariffs are difficult to remove. Industries, even when they have achieved large-scale production, do not welcome the removal of the protective wall.

(b) The comparative advantages enjoyed by different countries in the production of various commodities are constantly changing. The discoveries of new deposits of minerals, new methods of production, new methods of transport and the elimination of the requirement for great skill in the hands of the operative, all tend to shift the balance of advantage from one region to another. The country which was first to establish a major cotton industry, because she led the world in technical skills, may find that new methods of production, or a faster rate of technical advance in other countries, has moved the advantages she formerly enjoyed in cotton manufacture to other parts of the world. Other producers may be nearer to the source of raw materials, or to the major markets (which themselves may change), or they may have much cheaper supplies of labour.

These changes in the comparative costs of production will mean that particular industries will be declining in some countries and expanding in others. Ideally, a country should be moving its resources from those industries where it is losing its advantages to those newer industries where it is enjoying cost advantages, but economic resources are usually not mobile enough for this to take place without some hardship. Capital and labour cannot be moved quickly and easily from, say, cotton manufacturing to the computer industry. When such industries come under pressure from the lower-priced goods of the more efficient foreign competitor, there is a strong demand for some degree of protection. Britain's coal industry is protected from the imports of cheaper foreign coal. Tariffs are advocated as a means of protecting an industry while some adjustment to the new situation takes place. Lancashire has asked for protection from the low-priced cotton goods of India, Pakistan and Hong Kong while the industry is scaled down in size and the remaining firms are merged into much larger units of production so that they can take advantage of greater economies of scale.

4. To Safeguard the Interests of Workers

The basis of this particular argument is that imports from countries where wages are low represent 'unfair' competition and threaten the standard of living of the more highly paid workers in the home industries. But this is not very sound reasoning. Keeping out the low-wage imports will reduce the demand for these products, cause a reduced demand for labour in these countries, and drive the wages of the workers there even lower. It will increase the cost of living by reducing the imports of these cheaper goods and lessen the incentive to move resources out of the protected industries. It is, indeed, a dangerous argument, because it could well be used against the country imposing the restrictions. For example, the U.S.A. could use such an argument to restrict the entry of British goods, since, relative to the U.S.A., Britain is a low-wage country.

5. *For Strategic Reasons*

Certain industries such as iron and steel, agriculture, chemicals, and scientific instruments are regarded as strategic industries which are absolutely essential to a nation at war. It is regarded as most desirable that such industries should be preserved, since a nation dependent upon foreign supplies of strategic materials would be extremely vulnerable in the event of war. These industries, where they have not been competitive in world markets, have normally been protected by means of tariffs.

6. *To Prevent or Eliminate a Deficit on the Balance of Payments*

A country may find that it is persistently spending more on foreign goods and services than it is earning from the sale of its exports. When it has made every effort, without success, to eliminate this deficit by increasing its exports, it has little alternative to restricting its imports by means of tariffs, quotas or exchange control. Britain, in 1964, was obliged temporarily to increase its tariff on manufactured goods by 15 per cent for this very reason.

On purely economic grounds, it is difficult to support most of these arguments for the restriction of international trade. Tariffs distort the true cost relationships and reduce the differences in comparative costs. The extent of international specialisation is reduced and so is the possible level of world output. Consumers in the home country are obliged to pay higher prices for protected home-produced goods and for the imported goods which have artificially high prices. A further argument against the erection of trade barriers is that such actions invite retaliation by other countries and lead to a general reduction in world trade.

But we can be too enthusiastic in advocating *any* move towards freer trade, particularly where the gains are heavily weighted in favour of a particular group of countries. It seems that liberalisation of world trade has generally benefited the wealthier industrialised countries, and the gap between the rich and the poor countries is growing wider. Some limitation on free trade may be necessary in order to assist the developing countries.

G.A.T.T.

In 1947 some twenty-three major trading nations made an agreement on certain rules for trade policy and began a series of conferences with a view to reducing tariffs and dismantling other restrictions on trade. This arrangement has survived and is known as *The General Agreement on Tariffs and Trade*. Member nations meet at regular intervals to negotiate agreements to reduce quotas, tariffs and other restrictions. There are now more than sixty members – most of the trading nations in the non-communist world. At the heart of the G.A.T.T. agreement is the 'most-favoured nation clause', which provides that every tariff concession, agreed between any group of countries, must be extended to all members of G.A.T.T. If Britain agrees to make tariff or quota concessions to the U.S.A. on the import of motor cars in return for an American concession on the import of British cloth, these reductions must be allowed to all other countries which are members of G.A.T.T. Although the work of the organisation has increased, the rate of progress is relatively slow. There are many difficulties to be overcome. The G.A.T.T. rules forbid any discrimination among members, but members are allowed to use quotas when suffering from balance of payments difficulties, and developing nations are allowed to protect their infant industries. A nation which is prepared to strike bargains with some other nation may be dissuaded from doing so, because it is obliged to allow any concessions so granted to all other member nations.

A major achievement of G.A.T.T. was a series of six major tariff conferences terminating in the Kennedy Round, which, in 1967, secured agreement on substantial tariff reductions. Over two-thirds of these tariff cuts were of 50 per cent or more. The U.K. agreed to tariff cuts averaging about 33 per cent on all industrial goods originating outside the Commonwealth Preference Area and E.F.T.A. The cuts were planned to take effect over a five-year period.

Chapter 28

International Payments

Foreign Exchange

Different countries use different currencies. In Britain, the unit of currency is the pound sterling, in the U.S.A. it is the dollar, in Germany, the mark. These different currencies circulate freely within the different national boundaries, but they are generally unacceptable in another country. The French firm selling equipment to the U.S.A. will require payment in francs and not in dollars. The American buyer will ask his bank to supply the necessary francs and make payment for them with dollars drawn from his account at the bank.

There is a highly organised *foreign exchange market* which deals in this business of exchanging currencies. Most of the commercial banks have foreign exchange departments which are in direct contact with the great financial centres such as London, New York, and Zurich where much of the business is transacted. The merchant banks, foreign banks and foreign exchange brokers all deal in the foreign exchange market, buying and selling foreign currencies in response to the needs of traders and travellers.

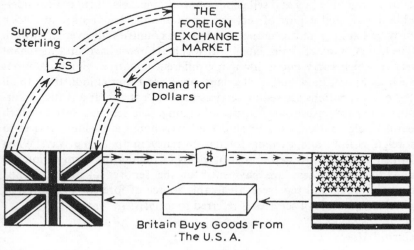

Figure 55

The important feature of these transactions is that the demand for foreign goods is represented, in the foreign exchange market, by a supply of the home currency and a demand for foreign currency. The British firm seeking German goods is supplying pounds and demanding marks.

The diagram on page 309 shows *the directions* in which funds will move. Dollars and pounds will not move in the physical sense implied in the diagram – the transactions will take the form of movements in bank deposits in the great financial centres.

The Balance of Payments

A country engaging in foreign trade will be making payments to foreign countries and receiving payments from them. Each nation keeps an account of its transactions with the rest of the world which it presents in the form of a balance sheet known as the *balance of payments*. In Britain, full details of the country's transactions on international account are given in the annual balance of payments' statement, while estimates of the balance of payments' situation are given quarterly.

International payments arise from a variety of transactions.

The Purchase and Sale of Goods

The export and import of goods is referred to as *visible trade,* and the difference between the values of exports and imports of commodities is known as the *balance of trade.*

The Purchase and Sale of Services

Nations not only buy and sell goods on world markets, there is a considerable import and export of services. London and New York and Zurich provide banking and insurance services for countries all over the world. The U.S.A., Great Britain, Japan, Norway and Greece have large merchant navies which carry goods for many different countries. Some countries such as Spain, Italy, and Switzerland have great tourist industries. In all these cases, nations are selling services to other nations. If a British insurance company insures an American building, it is selling a service which earns foreign currency for Britain. The Swiss hotels are selling services to foreign visitors and earning foreign currency in the same way. When British capital is invested abroad it yields income in the form of interest and dividends—these are payments for the services of British-owned capital abroad and represent a valuable source of foreign currency. The purchase and sale of services is referred to as *invisible trade.*

Capital Movements

Another type of transaction which gives rise to international payments is

310

the movement of capital from one country to another. Such movements take place when a resident in the home country buys shares in a foreign firm, or when one Government makes a grant or a loan to another. These transfers of capital are classified as *overseas investment*, a common form of which is the establishment of factories in foreign countries or the setting up of a foreign-owned company in the home country. Immigrants often send money to the families which they have left behind in their home country; these are capital transactions, but they normally appear in the current account of the balance of payments, because they do not give rise to future payments of interest or dividends.

Capital transactions are classified as short-term or long-term investments. Typical long-term capital movements are:

(*a*) Long-term loans between Governments or between Governments and international institutions.

(*b*) The purchase of stocks and shares in foreign companies, or the purchase by foreigners of shares in home companies. (In 1961 the American Ford Company purchased all the British-held shares in the British subsidiary company.)

(*c*) The setting up of plantations, mines, factories or trading enterprises abroad, (e.g. the great overseas investment of the British and American oil companies), or the establishment of foreign firms in the home market (e.g the many American-owned companies operating in Britain).

(*d*) The purchase of long-term securities issued by foreign governments, or the sale, to foreigners, of securities issued by the home government.

Short-term capital movements reflect the transfer of liquid assets from one country to another. The funds are held in bank accounts or in very liquid assets (e.g. Treasury Bills) and, hence, can be withdrawn at very short notice. Britain, as an international banker, holds very large funds of this type. Since sterling is a 'key' currency and is used to finance a large part of world trade, many nations maintain working balances in London. In recent years such short-term funds have been attracted to London by the relatively high short-term rates of interest in the London Money Market.

When all transactions between one country and the rest of the world, during the course of one year, have been recorded, we have that country's balance of payments for the year. The balance of payments is an accounting record and, like all balance sheets, it must balance. All those dealings which lead to an outflow of foreign currency (imports) are placed on the debit side, and those transactions which lead to an inflow of foreign currency (exports) are placed on the credit side.

It is very puzzling to read that the balance of payments always balances when we are constantly made aware of the fact that nations are often in balance of payments difficulties, or that they have a balance of payments

L

deficit. In 1968 Britain had a very heavy deficit on her balance of payments, but the balance of payments balanced! The problems do not arise because the total of the items on the debit side exceeds the total of the items on the credit side, but from the manner in which the two sides are brought into equality. It is *how* the two sides are balanced which is critical.

If the total payments made to foreigners exceed the payments which foreigners have made to us, there is a gap which must be filled. Just as a family may spend more than its income, so may a nation spend more than it earns on international account. The family will have to finance its 'deficit' by obtaining loans or gifts, selling some of its possessions or by using up some of its savings. A nation will have to use very similar methods in order to cover a deficit on its balance of payments. This is explained later.

U.K. Balance of Payments

The official presentation of the British Balance of Payments has recently changed its form. Traditionally it has been drawn up in four sections covering: Visible Trade, Invisible Trade, Long-Term Capital, and Monetary Movements. The newer formulation is nearer to recommended international practice and tries to show more clearly the interrelationships between the different parts of the balance of payments account. Table 27 illustrates the main sections of the current presentation.

Table 27. *Summary of the U.K. balance of payments: 1969 (£ million)*

SECTION A

Current account	£
Visible trade	−141
Invisible trade	+557
Current balance	+416

SECTION B

Currency flow and official financing:	
Current balance	+416
Investment and other capital flows	+48
Balancing item	+279
Total currency flow	+743
Financed as follows:	
Official borrowing (+) or repayment(−)	−699
Changes in official reserves additions (−), drawings (+)	−44
	−743

Section A of the table comprises the *Current Account*. It is made up of two parts, visible trade and invisible trade. The difference between the values of visible exports and visible imports is usually known as the *Balance of Trade* and is made known each month. Invisible trade, as explained, deals with transactions in services, details of which are made available on a quarterly basis.

Visible and invisible trade are aggregated to give the Balance of Payments on Current Account. The current balance is of great importance, because it shows the nation's profit and loss in its day-to-day dealings with the rest of the world. Just as a private citizen must keep a check on whether he is spending more than he is earning so must a nation. Expenditure may exceed income but the 'cost' will be revealed in borrowing from abroad, using up reserves of foreign currency, or selling overseas assets. A current account surplus on the other hand will enable a country to build up its investment abroad, add to its foreign currency reserves, or repay its overseas debts.

Section B of the balance of payments summary includes the capital transactions. These are flows of capital coming into Britain for investment or other forms of lending, either for a short period or a long one, and going out for similar purposes. When the total of these capital movements is added to the current balance, we have the net amount of foreign currency which the nation has gained or lost on its international trading activities. Unfortunately the *recorded* items never give the complete picture. It is impossible to get a complete and accurate account of the millions of transactions which affect the balance of payments. Since the Bank of England knows exactly the *net* effect of all these transactions, the total discrepancy in the records can be ascertained. This is the *Balancing Item*. When this is included, Section B gives us the total currency flow. This is the money available for adding to the reserves, paying off foreign debts, or investing abroad. When there is a loss – a minus currency flow – the nation will be obliged to borrow from abroad, run down its reserves, or sell some of its foreign assets.

The manner in which the surplus or deficit is dealt with is shown under the heading '*official financing*'. In 1968, for example, the British government were obliged to borrow nearly £1,300 million from the I.M.F. and other sources and ran down the reserves by £114 million. In 1969 the Government was able to repay nearly £700 million and to add £44 million to the reserves.

Table 28 gives a more detailed picture of the U.K. Balance of Payments.

Table 28. *The U.K. Balance of Payments – 1970 (£ million)*

A. CURRENT ACCOUNT

Visible trade

Exports	7,885
Imports	7,882
Visible balance	+3

Invisible trade

	£	£
Shipping	+1,073	
	−1,087	
		−14
Civil aviation	+313	
	−278	
		+35
Travel	+433	
	−388	
		+45
Other services	+1,114	
	−532	
		+582
	+182	
Private transfers	−254	
		−72
Interest/Profits/Dividends	+1,374	
	−842	
		+532
Government	+51	
	−531	
		−480
Invisible balance		+628
Current balance		+631

314

B. CURRENCY FLOW AND OFFICIAL FINANCING

(i) Current balance		+631
(ii) Capital flows:		
Foreign private investment in U.K.	+665	
U.K. private investment abroad	−735	
Official long term capital	−205	
U.K. banks foreign currency transactions	+313	
Other capital flows	+461	
	+499	
		+499
(iii) Balancing item		+157
Total currency flow		+1,287
Allocation of special drawing rights		+171
Gold subscription to I.M.F.		−38
TOTAL		+1,420
Financed as follows:		
Repayments to I.M.F.		−134
Repayments to other monetary authorities		−1,161
Additions to official reserves		−125
		−1,420

Visible Trade

1970 was an exceptional year in that visible trade showed a surplus. Britain normally has a deficit on visible trade. The 1970 figure indicates a continuing favourable situation following the 1967 devaluation.

Invisible Trade

The item 'Other services' includes the substantial earnings of the City of London in the provision of banking, insurance, and other financial services for overseas customers. Britain now earns a very substantial surplus on income from property; the receipts from investment abroad greatly exceed the interest and dividends earned by foreigners on their investments in Britain. The item 'Government' comprises mainly the payments for current goods and services consumed by British troops overseas, together with the costs of other government services abroad (e.g. diplomatic and commercial services). This latter item, of course, will be largely offset by foreign governments providing similar services in Britain. The deficit on government account is due to the military commitment.

Current Account and Currency Flow

The very favourable balance on Current Account in 1970 was due to the fact that no part of the large surplus on invisibles was required to offset a deficit on visible trade (as is normally the case). There was a net inflow of currency on the capital transactions and the balancing item was also in Britain's favour so that the total currency flow for the year provided the large surplus of £1,287 million. This was also the year in which Britain received the first allocation of Special Drawing Rights from the I.M.F. (see page 325). The foreign currency resources becoming available to the nation in 1970 amounted to £1,420 million.

In allocating these resources, the authorities made net repayments of previous borrowings amounting to £1,295 million and added £125 million to the reserves. Under the heading of 'official financing', the use of the minus and plus signs often causes confusion. 'Additions to reserves' for example appears with a minus sign, while 'borrowing from abroad' would appear with a plus sign. This particular usage is made necessary by the current practice of presenting the Balance of Payments as a single table. Since the balance of payments must balance, the final result must be zero. Hence if we have a surplus, the items which show the disposal of this surplus must carry minus signs. Alternatively, the minus signs may be taken as indicating 'money going out' either to pay off debts or into the reserves.

RECENT DEVELOPMENT IN THE U.K. BALANCE OF PAYMENTS

In the 1950s the British balance of payments maintained a fairly small surplus on current account and long-term investment overseas continued to grow at an average rate of about £170 million per annum. The current balance was achieved by the traditional surplus on invisibles more than offsetting the deficit on visible trade.

In the 1960s the balance of payments situation seriously deteriorated into fundamental disequilibrium (see Fig. 56). A major element in this worsening situation was the increase in the government deficit on invisible account which was more than offsetting the improvement in the other items on the invisible account. A further contributory factor was the average increase for the period 1963–68 in the deficit on visible trade; although the value of exports continued to increase, imports grew much more rapidly. A partial explanation of this increase in imports is provided by the gradual relaxation of the restrictions on international trade.

In spite of a series of measures directed at reducing the deficit (e.g. deflationary measures at home and a temporary import surcharge), the situation deteriorated further and, after heavy borrowing abroad, the Government, in November, 1967, decided to devalue the pound. It was felt that a major cause of the imbalance in international payments was the fact that the pound sterling was over-valued in relation to other major

316

currencies. In other words the pound was 'too expensive' in terms of dollars, marks, francs and so on. British exports were too expensive to foreigners and imports were, therefore, relatively cheap. Devaluation reduced the value of the pound from £1 = 2·8 dollars to £1 = 2·4 dollars, with the aim of increasing exports and slowing down the growth of imports.

In fact 1968 saw a further deterioration in the visible account. This is explained partly by the fact that although the sterling price of imports rose, their volume continued to increase, revealing a disturbingly strong propensity to import. Exports increased in volume but to a large extent this was offset by the fall in their foreign currency prices. The competitive advantages of devaluation take time to become effective and the 1969 figures reveal a transformation in the British Balance of Payments account.

There was a steep rise in exports due to an increase in volume and in their prices. The volume of imports grew, but at a much slower rate. There was also a marked improvement in the invisible earnings. The provisional figures for 1970 reveal another substantial current account surplus. In this year, however, the favourable movements were due more to favourable price movements than to volume movements. In fact, the volume of imports rose more than the volume of exports – but export prices rose much more than import prices.

It has been estimated that Britain needs to earn a current account surplus of around £500 million for several years, in order to repay the debts incurred in the 1960s, and build up her reserves to an adequate level.

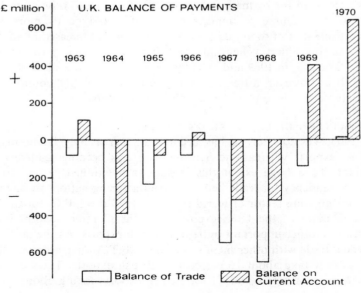

Figure 56

U.K. Current Balance 1965–1972 (£ million)

	1965	1966	1967	1968	1969	1970	1971	1972
Balance of trade	−237	−73	−557	−648	−143	+12	+317	−692
Invisibles	+188	+157	+242	+377	+586	+677	+730	+729
Current Balance	−49	+84	−315	−271	+443	+689	+1047	+37

The Structure of U.K. Foreign Trade

EXPORTS

Figure 59 shows that manufacturers dominate the export trade of the United Kingdom. Semi-manufactures and finished manufactures now account for about 85 per cent of the total value of exports. Although exports of manufactures have continued to increase, the U.K.'s share of the world trade in manufactures has continued to decline, from about 20 per cent in 1955 to about 11 per cent in 1971. The more important categories in the U.K. exports of manufactures are machinery, transport equipment and chemicals.

IMPORTS

During the last twenty years imports have grown in volume more rapidly than exports, but, in value, they have grown less rapidly. This difference is explained, of course, by favourable movements in the terms of trade over this period. There has been a most marked change in the commodity composition of imports in recent years. An increasingly large proportion is now accounted for by manufactured goods (see Fig. 57). Between 1960 and 1970, the volume of imports of manufactured goods more than doubled while that of food and raw materials hardly increased at all. The imports of machinery, chemicals and fuels have been growing particularly fast, and, in 1969 and 1970 the imports of vehicles also increased sharply. It is, however, a trend common to most developed countries for manufactured goods to take a larger share of imports.

AREA PATTERN OF U.K. FOREIGN TRADE

Since 1960 Western Europe has become an increasingly larger market for U.K. exports whereas the Sterling Area has become relatively less important. To a large extent this is due, as mentioned earlier, to the increasing tendency for trade between manufacturing nations to be much the fastest growing sector of world trade. In 1970 the E.E.C. for the first time took more of the U.K. exports than the Commonwealth. North America is another important outlet for British exports. As the tariff cuts proceeded, trade with other members of the E.F.T.A. increased and these countries now take about 16 per cent of British exports. The Commonwealth remains a major market for British exports taking about 20 per cent of the total.

The change in the area import pattern is very similar to those outlined for exports. Between 1960 and 1970, the share of the U.K. imports from the Sterling Area fell from 34 per cent to 27 per cent, while the share coming from Western Europe increased from 29 per cent to 38 per cent. The U.S.A. has also increased its share of the U.K. market.

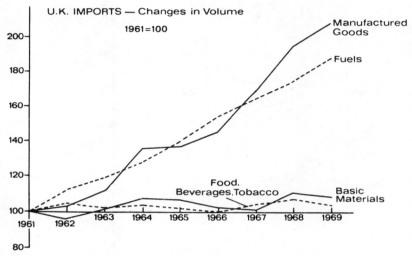

Figure 57

Source: *Annual Abstract of Statistics.*

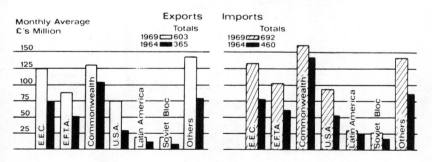

Figure 58

Source: *Barclay Bank Review*, February 1971

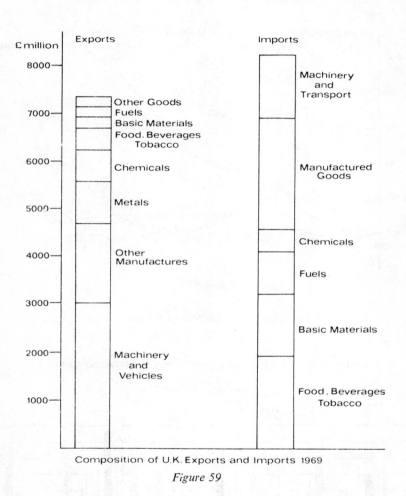

Composition of U.K. Exports and Imports 1969

Figure 59

Source: *Annual Abstract of Statistics.*

Exchange Rates

Currencies are exchanged in the foreign exchange market, but what determines the rates at which they exchange for one another? This is really a question of prices, for we are asking what it is that determines the prices of pounds, dollars and marks, etc., in terms of other currencies. There are a number of different systems by which exchange rates may be determined.

EXCHANGE CONTROL

The value of a currency in terms of other currencies may be fixed by government decree. The declared rate of exchange is maintained by a rigid system of exchange control which involves the careful rationing of foreign currency. This is merely another example of price control which was explained in Chapter 12.

FREE OR FLUCTUATING EXCHANGE RATES

If the foreign exchange market were completely free, prices would be determined by the forces of supply and demand. The value of the pound sterling would be determined by the strength of the foreigner's demand for pounds relative to the strength of the British demand for foreign currencies (= the supply of pounds). The demands for foreign currencies are derived, principally, from the demand for goods and services. If the British demand for foreign goods and services were to increase, while the foreign demand for British goods fell, the demand for pounds would fall relative to the supply, and the price of the pound, in terms of foreign currencies, would fall. In addition to the demand for goods and services, the demand for, and supply of, foreign currencies is affected by capital movements and speculation.

Free exchange rates provide a kind of automatic mechanism for the elimination of surpluses and deficits on the balance of payments. If Britain is importing goods and services of greater value than her exports, her demand for foreign currencies (= the supply of pounds) is greater than foreigners' demand for pounds. The price of the pound, on the foreign exchange market, will fall. Let us suppose that the exchange rate falls from £1 = $3 to £1 = $2.5. British goods will become cheaper in overseas markets (because £s are cheaper), and exports will rise. Foreign goods will become more expensive in the home market (because foreign currencies are dearer), and imports will fall. These trends will prevent a balance of payments deficit.[1]

But flexible exchange rates create a further element of uncertainty in world markets. Variable exchange rates will alter the prices of goods to

[1] The reader should try to reason out the adjustment process when there is a balance of payments surplus.

foreign buyers who will have to watch two price levels – the producers' prices *and* the prices of foreign currencies. Fluctuating exchange rates also encourage speculation in the foreign exchange market – this might help to stabilise prices, but it might also amplify the fluctuations. A further point regarding free exchange rates is the fact that continual shifts in the *external* prices of home produced goods would involve continual shifts of economic resources between production for the home market and production for export – such movements are difficult to carry out.

FIXED EXCHANGE RATES

Before the First World War, the major trading nations were on the *Gold Standard*. Their currencies were all given a fixed value in terms of gold, and were freely convertible into gold at this declared parity. Since the currencies were convertible into gold, the domestic money supply was closely linked to the supply of gold, and the export and import of gold was not subject to any restrictions.

Since each currency had a fixed value in terms of gold, the exchange rate between any two currencies was automatically established. For example, if the dollar were equal in value to $\frac{1}{16}$ ounces of gold and the pound contained $\frac{1}{4}$ ounces of gold, the rate of exchange would be £1 = $4. Exchange rates can only vary within very narrow limits, otherwise it becomes cheaper to use gold, rather than the currency units, to pay foreign debts.

The Gold Standard, like free exchange rates, provides a self-correcting mechanism for balance of payments problems. If a country had a balance of payments surplus, gold would be flowing into the country as payment for the excess exports. An inflow of gold would lead to an expansion of the domestic money supply; this would lead to more spending and an increase in demand. Home prices would rise and cause a fall in the demand for exports, while imported goods would become relatively cheaper in the home market. Exports would fall and imports would rise until the surplus on the balance of payments had been eliminated. The reader should have little difficulty in showing how a deficit would be eliminated.

But the Gold Standard proved difficult to work in the 20th century. It requires prices to be flexible, but in advanced economies they are not flexible in a downward direction. A fall in demand will lead to unemployment rather than a significant fall in prices. It requires governments to surrender control over the money supply to external forces (i.e. to changes in the balance of payments' situation) and they are not prepared to surrender this control while they have the responsibility for maintaining full employment.

Fixed exchange rates, however, do remove a great deal of uncertainty from the business of trading in world markets, and they encourage the negotiation of long term contracts and the granting of longer credits.

MANAGED EXCHANGE RATES

When the nations left the Gold Standard in the 1930s they sought a system which had the advantages of fixed exchange rates without the disadvantages of the Gold Standard. One system adopted was that of managed exchange rates. In 1932 Britain established the *Exchange Equalisation Account* with the object of operating in the foreign exchange market in order to stabilise the value of the pound. The account is operated by the Bank of England and consists of a large fund of foreign currencies, gold, and pounds. The aim is to maintain the exchange value of the pound at some agreed parity. When the value of the pound is falling, the account will enter the market and buy pounds, using, for this purpose, its stock of foreign currencies. The increased demand for pounds will raise the exchange value of the pound back to the required value. When the value of the pound rises above this level, the account will sell pounds, and replenish its stock of foreign currencies, as the value of the pound falls to the required level.

Britain still operates the Exchange Equalisation Account and its funds are, in effect, the nation's foreign currency reserves. When we read that 'the £ had to be supported' the Account has been buying pounds and the reserves will have fallen.

The International Monetary Fund and Multilateral Trade

In 1944 representatives of the Allied nations met at Bretton Woods in the U.S.A. to discuss plans for promoting world recovery after the war. The conference led to the establishment of two very important institutions, The International Monetary Fund, and The International Bank for Reconstruction and Development (the World Bank).

The I.M.F. was designed to promote world trade by helping countries to keep their exchange rates stable and by working for the full *convertibility* of national currencies. Currencies are fully convertible when they can be freely exchanged for other currencies. When currencies are convertible it means that nations do not have to trade on a bilateral basis – they do not, in other words, have to strike a trade balance with each separate nation. Country A, for example, may have a surplus with country C and a deficit with country B. So long as she is free to exchange her surplus of country C's currency for that of country B, she need only be concerned about balancing her total trade. This is *multilateral trade*, which can only be conducted when currencies are convertible. Bilateral trade requires each nation to balance its trade with each of its trading partners (see Figs. 60 and 61 on page 324).

Each member of the I.M.F. is required to contribute a quota to the

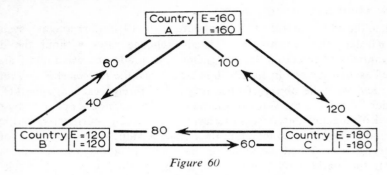

Figure 60

Multilateral Trade

Each country's trade is in balance (exports = imports), but no pair of countries have balanced trade. Balance is achieved because currencies are convertible, e.g. Country B will exchange her surplus of country A's currency for that of country C in order to finance her deficit with C.

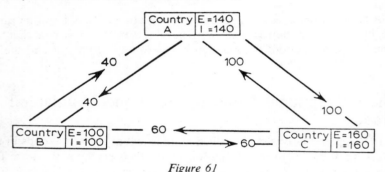

Figure 61

Bilateral Trade

Currencies are not convertible – the lower of the two demands will determine the volume of trade between any pair of countries, e.g. Country A can only purchase 100 from country C, because country C only wishes to purchase 100 from country A.

Fund's pool of foreign currencies and gold. These quotas, which vary in size according to the size of the member's national income, must be paid at 75 per cent in the member's own currency, and 25 per cent in gold. The quota represents the member's financial participation in the Fund (i.e. its subscription) and it largely determines its voting rights and its drawing rights. All members[1] must announce the value of their currency in terms of gold in order to fix the relative exchange rates. They must agree not to vary these parities (i.e. values expressed in terms of gold) without giving notice to the Fund. A variation of up to 10 per cent is permitted merely upon notification to the Fund; larger variations require the permission of the Fund. The aim of the Fund is to encourage members to maintain fixed

[1] In 1971, there were 118 members.

exchange rates, and permission to change the parity of a currency would only be granted where it was thought that other measures would not be effective (see later note on devaluation p. 326).

When a member incurs a balance of payments deficit, the normal course is for it to use its reserves to bridge the gap while it takes remedial action. If the reserves are not adequate for this purpose, it may purchase foreign currencies from the Fund in exchange for its own currency.

These drawing rights are divided into 'tranches' or slices. The first tranche, known as the gold tranche, is automatically available and is equivalent to the value of the member's gold subscription. There are a further four credit tranches each equal to 25 per cent of the member's quota. If these tranches were all fully drawn, the I.M.F. would hold the currency of the borrowing member equal to 200 per cent of its quota. Drawings must be repaid within three to five years, and the use of the credit tranches normally requires the borrower to supply the I.M.F. with some assurances that steps will be taken to rectify the imbalance which has led to the borrowing. Repayments will involve the member country in repurchasing its own currency from the I.M.F., using gold and foreign currency for this purpose. Interest is payable on I.M.F. loans.

The purpose of the Fund is to provide a member with *temporary* assistance. A nation experiencing a balance of payments' deficit, in the absence of any such help, might well be forced to impose restrictions upon imports. This could lead to retaliation and a general increase in the barriers to trade. The resources of the Fund can be used to prevent this kind of development, but they cannot be used to provide any permanent support – the nation must take steps to remedy the basic causes of its deficit.

The Fund's resources have been supplemented by the *General Agreement to Borrow* (G.A.B.) under which eight industrial members together with the central banks of two others undertook to lend their currencies, up to specified amounts totalling $6,000 million, if the Fund required assistance to cope with a serious crisis.

The I.M.F. system has been in serious disarray since the crisis of 1971 when massive movements of short-term capital (mainly sales of dollars) caused several countries to float their currencies rather than resort to devaluation or revaluation. It was hoped that a period of floating would establish realistic exchange rates which could then be stabilised according to I.M.F. rules.

International Liquidity

A nation's international reserves are made up of gold, convertible foreign currencies and its automatic drawing rights with the I.M.F. These reserves are necessary in order to finance its foreign trade and to deal with any temporary imbalances in this trade. World trade has been growing very rapidly during the past twenty years, much more rapidly than world reserves. There has been some concern that total reserves of convertible currencies, gold, and I.M.F. drawing rights (i.e. international liquidity) may become inadequate to support the size of imbalances which will arise at the newer, higher, levels of world trade.

In order to meet the demand for more liquidity, the I.M.F. has, on several occasions, increased the level of members' quotas, but the supply of international liquidity as a proportion of world imports has fallen by more than 50 per cent since the early 1950s. This situation has led the I.M.F. to create an entirely new reserve asset in the form of *Special Drawing Rights*. The scheme became operational on 1 January 1970.

S.D.R.s have been described as 'paper gold.' since a unit of S.D.R.s is defined as a certain quantity of gold. In fact, they are simply claims or rights which are honoured by members of the I.M.F. and by the I.M.F. itself. In January 1970 a total of 3·5 billion dollars was allocated among members of the I.M.F. in proportion to their quotas and a further 3 billion dollars will be distributed in each of the years 1971 and 1972. This scheme will add about 12 per cent to existing world reserves over the three-year period.

Members of the scheme may use S.D.R.s to 'purchase' (or exchange for) other members' currencies. Nations which have strong balance of payments positions may be designated to receive other members' S.D.R.s in exchange for convertible currencies, but they cannot be obliged to accept more than twice the amounts of their own allocations of S.D.R.s. The incentive to accept S.D.R.s from another member lies in the fact that they will be gold guaranteed and carry an interest payment.

Devaluation

When a country is experiencing a serious and persistent balance of payments deficit there will be a strong downward pressure on the value of its currency in the foreign exchange market. The value of its imports (=supply of domestic currency) will exceed the value of its exports (=demand for domestic currency) and the price of the currency, in terms of other currencies, will fall. Under a system of fixed exchange rates, or relatively fixed rates such as the I.M.F. system, the country will be obliged to intervene in the foreign exchange market in order to support the value of its currency – it will have to buy its own currency in order to prevent its value falling below the agreed parity. A persistent deficit, therefore, would soon lead to a serious depletion of the nation's foreign currency reserves. Before such a desperate situation develops such a country must take steps to remedy the cause of the imbalance in its foreign transactions. It may, of course, borrow foreign currency on a short term basis in order to protect its reserves while the corrective measures are taking effect. Apart from the use of tariffs, exchange controls, and quotas, there are two other possibilities.

1. *Reducing the Internal Price Level* (*Deflation*)

Under present-day conditions this method is not likely to commend itself to governments. Prices are extremely inflexible in a downward direction and domestic policies which aim to reduce aggregate demand are much more likely to lead to falling output and falling employment. The decline in output and employment it seems would have to reach intolerable levels before any significant downward movement of prices could be achieved.

2. *Reducing the External Value of the Currency* (*Devaluation*)

Devaluation is the process of changing the fixed parity of a currency by lowering its value in terms of gold. If the parities of other currencies have not been changed, devaluation will reduce the value of a currency in terms of other currencies.

Britain has carried out two such devaluations since the war. In 1949 the pound sterling was devalued from £1 = \$4·03 to £1 = \$2·8. In 1967, Britain again devalued. On that occasion the value of the pound was lowered from £1 = \$2·8 to £1 = \$2·4. The immediate effect of devaluation (assuming no change in the value of other currencies) is to change the relative prices of imports and exports.

Exports become cheaper in terms of foreign currency.

Imports become dearer in terms of home currency

Example:

Before devaluation, £1 = \$2·8

A British car, price £1,000 costs \$2,800 in the U.S.A.

An American machine, price \$10,000, costs £3,571 (approx.) in the U.K.

After devaluation, £1 = \$2·4

A British car, price £1,000, costs \$2,400 in the U.S.A.

An American machine, price \$10,000 costs £4,167 (approx.) in the U.K.

The price effects of devaluation, therefore, should lead to an increase in the volume of exports and a decrease in the volume of imports. But the aim of devaluation is to bring about an improvement in the balance of payments and this is a relationship between income and expenditure. Devaluation alters relative *prices* and will only be beneficial if it changes the *values* of total exports and total imports favourably. The relevant concept here, then, is that of elasticity of demand. Export earnings will increase if the demand for exports is elastic; it is necessary for the volume of exports to increase by a greater percentage than the percentage fall in their foreign currency prices. A rise in import prices will reduce the foreign currency expenditures as long as the volume falls. Since the foreign currency prices of imports have not changed any fall in the volume of imports will reduce foreign currency expenditures.

There are several other problems which influence the effectiveness of devaluation as a remedy for a balance of payments disequilibrium. It can only lead to favourable price movements if major trading rivals do not retaliate by devaluing their own currencies. If other countries follow suit by devaluing their currencies to the same extent, exchange rates will remain unchanged.

The situation with regard to the supply of exports must also be considered. The fall in the foreign prices of exports will increase the quantities demanded, but this increased demand must be met by an increase in supply. If the devaluing country is operating at full employment capacity more goods can only be supplied in the export markets at the expense of the home market. Heavy taxation and monetary measures to reduce demand may have to be used in order to release goods for the expanding export markets. Devaluation may not work unless it is accompanied by some measure of deflation.

One effect of devaluation is to increase the real burden of overseas indebtedness. Since foreign debts are expressed in terms of foreign currency, the repayment of any given loan requires a larger volume of exports in order to earn that given amount of foreign currency.

It is also necessary to bear in mind the income effects of devaluation. If it succeeds in reducing imports substantially, other countries will be suffering a corresponding fall in their exports. This loss of income will reduce their ability to buy foreign goods. The country undertaking devaluation may well suffer some loss of export markets due to this income effect.

Chapter 29

International Economic Cooperation

Two important international bodies, the I.M.F. and G.A.T.T. have been described in the preceding chapters. This chapter deals with some further examples of international integration.

The Sterling Area

In the nineteenth century, the British Empire comprised a large number of relatively underdeveloped territories whose trade was predominantly with Britain and which relied heavily upon Britain for their capital requirements and for the provision of banking, insurance and merchanting services. These close financial and commercial links made it necessary for the colonial banks to maintain working balances and monetary reserves in London. As these countries gradually gained independence, the close economic links remained; Britain is still the major market for many of them. They have continued to maintain substantial balances in London and to link their currencies to sterling. This, then, was the origin of the sterling area, centred on London, which, before 1914, was also very important as the centre of the Gold Standard area.

Sterling, before 1914, was the major currency used in international payments so that many other nations, particularly those which had a substantial trade with Britain, also kept large balances in sterling. With the collapse of the Gold Standard in the 1930s, when many currencies were allowed to go free, these nations chose to link their currencies to sterling and declared a stable exchange rate between their own currencies and sterling. The arrangements were of an informal nature and there was no institutional framework created to operate the system.

At the outbreak of the Second World War, several countries left the sterling area, which, for the first time, was given legal status and a set of rules. The present members of the sterling area are all the Commonwealth countries (except Canada), Eire, Libya, Iceland, Jordan and Kuwait. During the period 1945–58, when most currencies were not convertible, the sterling area provided a large trading area where currencies were convertible and in which a form of multilateral trade could take place.

Today, the sterling area has the following characteristics:

1. Most overseas members hold a major part of their external reserves in sterling, and find the London money market a convenient centre in which to employ reserves and working balances profitably. These reserves, held in sterling, are freely convertible into other currencies.

2. Members use sterling as their main international currency in settling accounts with each other and with other countries. Such foreign currencies as they need, or come by, they purchase, or sell in London. About one third of world trade is conducted on a sterling basis.

3. The currencies of all members are freely convertible into sterling at a fixed rate.

4. The United Kingdom is still a major source of new capital, public and private, for the oversea sterling area countries.

5. There are no restrictions on the movement of sterling from the U.K. to other sterling area countries.

The outlays by the U.K., in overseas theatres of war, from 1939 to 1945, led to a great growth in other countries' holdings of sterling. These balances have remained at a high level since the war. They are liabilities from the United Kingdom's point of view since they are subject to withdrawal, and, since sterling is convertible, they can be withdrawn in the form of foreign currency. These liabilities greatly exceed the U.K.'s reserves of gold and foreign currency.

Table 29. *The United Kingdom – Net external liabilities: 1973* (£ *million*)

Overseas sterling area countries	4,255
Non-Sterling countries	1,542
International organisations (excluding I.M.F.)	271
I.M.F.	1,132
	7,200
Official reserves	2,085

The International Bank for Reconstruction and Development

The I.B.R.D. (known as the World Bank) was established as a result of the Bretton Woods conference. It is the sister institution of the I.M.F. While the purpose of the I.M.F. is to provide short-term assistance to nations in balance of payments difficulties, that of the World Bank is to provide long-term assistance for reconstruction and development purposes.

Member nations were called upon to subscribe to the capital stock of the bank, each being given a quota which was based upon the economic strength of the member. This capital stock is not the major source of the Bank's lending powers. Each member nation is only called upon to pay a small part of the amount which it has agreed to pay. For example, in 1965, the authorised capital of the World Bank was $21,000 million of which members had paid in $2,000 million. The remaining 90 per cent of each subscription constitutes a guarantee fund – the Bank has the right to request members to pay the outstanding amounts of their subscriptions. The Bank obtains most of its funds by borrowing in the world's capital markets. It is able to borrow on very favourable terms because it has first-class security in the form of the guarantees of the member governments. The World Bank tends to set fairly stringent conditions on its lending. A general feeling that somewhat easier terms should be made available to developing countries led to the formation, in 1960, of the International Development Association (I.D.A.) as an affiliate of the I.B.R.D. Loans by the I.D.A. are free of interest, although they carry a small service charge. The repayment period may be as long as 50 years.

Up to 1970, the I.B.R.D. and the I.D.A. had made about 950 loans, totalling some 17 billion dollars. Of these the overwhelming majority have been for specific projects such as schools, irrigation dams, power plants, and roads.

In the earlier years of the Bank's existence, the major part of its lending was to European countries for purposes of reconstruction. Since the early postwar years, World Bank loans have gone increasingly to the developing nations. The Bank's loans are made either to governments or to private corporations, providing the latter can obtain a government guarantee.

The borrowers' applications for loans are carefully examined by World Bank experts who must be satisfied that the project is designed to strengthen the economy of the borrowing country and forms part of a sound economic development plan. One of the most valuable services of the Bank is the advice available to member countries from its teams of experts who are often called upon to make detailed studies of the economic problems facing the developing countries.

The I.B.R.D. has been able to supplement the investment capital available to those borrowers who would have had great difficulty in raising the funds on the basis of their own securities. The projects financed have been in the fields of electric power (e.g. the Volta Dam), transportation, communications, agriculture, forestry and industry.

The Bank will, generally, finance only part of the cost of a project, insisting that the borrowing country should have some financial stake in the proposal.

The European Economic Communities

After the Second World War, there was a strong desire to work for much greater unity in Europe, and to establish political and economic ties which would put an end to nationalist conflicts and give new strength to the shattered continent. In the economic sphere there has been considerable progress along the road to European unity. When in 1948 the U.S.A. inaugurated its massive programme of economic aid for Europe (the Marshall Plan), the European countries formed the Organisation for European Economic Co-operation (O.E.E.C.) to administer the aid in a coordinated manner. O.E.E.C. continued to operate after Marshall Aid had come to an end and much valuable work was done in liberalising European trade. This valuable experience in economic cooperation encouraged further experiments. In practice these communities are being gradually merged and proposals for having a single Treaty for this purpose are now being studied.

In 1961, the O.E.E.C. was replaced by the Organisation for European Cooperation and Development (the O.E.C.D.) which, in addition to most European countries now has the U.S.A., Canada, and Japan as full members.

European Coal and Steel Community (E.C.S.C.)

In 1950 M. Robert Schuman proposed the creation of a Community to integrate the coal and steel resources of Europe. This was taken up and a treaty instituting the European Coal and Steel Community was signed in 1951. E.C.S.C. began its work in 1952. The six nations forming the community were West Germany, France, Italy, Belgium, the Netherlands and Luxembourg. The aims of E.C.S.C. are economic – to promote industrial expansion by creating a common market in coal and steel, i.e. by removing all discrimination and restrictions in the production and distribution of these products both between the member states and internally.

This was an important experiment and its success led to further proposals for closer association between the six countries. A meeting of the foreign ministers of the Six at Messina, in 1955, led to the signing of the Treaties of Rome, in 1957, which brought into being two more communities.

The European Economic Community (E.E.C.)

This community, better known as the Common Market, has, as its main features, the creation of a common market through the elimination of all restrictions on the free movement of goods, capital, and persons between member countries, the harmonisation of their economic policies, and the consolidation of their external tariffs into a single tariff system applying to all imports from outside the community.

The European Atomic Energy Community (*Euratom*)

The aim of this body is to coordinate nuclear research and power projects within the Community.

All these treaties provide for the application for membership from other European countries wishing to join the Community. While the express aims of the treaties are economic, the creators undoubtedly saw these developments as a first step towards some form of political unity.

THE INSTITUTIONS

In the earlier stages, the three separate communities each had its own executive and legislative authorities. This has now been changed and there is a single legislative and a single executive authority for all three communities. The major institutions of the European Communities are as follows:

A Council of Ministers

This is the supreme decision making body which has the power to issue regulations and directives. These orders are legally binding on all member countries. The council is composed of ministers from member governments. For very important decisions it is necessary for them to attain unanimity, but on other issues majority voting is permitted. The votes in the latter case are weighted: France, Germany, and Italy each having four votes, Belgium and the Netherlands two votes each, and Luxembourg one vote.

The Commission

The Commission is the executive body consisting of nine full-time members who are appointed by agreement between the national governments. Each member of the Commission is independent – he is not there to represent the particular interests of his national government. The Commission is committed to European policies. Its role is to draft policies and present them to the Council of Ministers, and to implement the day-to-day running of the Communities. Some 7,000 civil servants are employed by the Commission.

The Court of Justice

The European Communities are subject to strict judicial control. The European Court of Justice sits in the Hague and decides whether there have been breaches of the treaties which established the Communities.

The European Parliament

This Parliament is made up of 142 delegates from the member parliaments. It aims to influence policies and it has power to dismiss the Commission by a vote of censure carried by a two-thirds majority. It cannot, however, appoint a new Commission and it has no authority over the Council of Ministers. It has the right to be consulted and it may question the Commission on policy matters.

There are, in addition, a number of subsidiary organisations:

The Economic and Social Committee must be consulted by the Commission before it can take action on matters concerning trade, industry, the trade unions, the professions and so on.

The European Investment Bank promotes investment in the less developed areas of E.E.C.

The European Development Fund exists to provide aid to the overseas associates of the Six countries. It is managed by the Commission.

The European Social Fund was set up to improve employment opportunities and the mobility of labour (both occupational and geographical).

The European Agriculture Guidance and Guarantee Fund exists to implement the common agricultural policy.

The Treaty of Rome brought into association with the Community the non-European territorities which had special relations with the Six countries. Most of these were the former African colonies of France. These associated territories gain duty-free entry for their exports to the Common Market, but they are allowed to impose certain restrictions on their imports from the E.E.C. Greece and Turkey also have special relationships with the E.E.C.

THE COMMON MARKET – AIMS AND DEVELOPMENT

Broadly the intention is to replace the separate national markets by a huge single market containing some 185 million people; a home market as large as that enjoyed by producers in the U.S.A. and Soviet Russia. The major aims of the Community are as follows:

(a) *Eliminating Barriers to Trade*

The Rome Treaty which took effect on 1 January 1958 provided for the elimination of barriers to trade over a period of twelve years. By July 1968, eighteen n ·nths ahead of schedule, all restrictions on trade in industrial goods, and in the majority of agricultural products had been abolished.

(b) *A Common External Tariff*

The separate external tariffs of member states have been replaced by a single common external tariff which is now considerably lower than the arithmetic mean of the previous separate tariff barriers.

(c) *The Free Movement of Labour, Capital, and Services*

The free movement of labour has already been achieved. No work permits are needed by E.E.C. citizens and all are treated equally in each member country in respect of social security rights, residential qualifications, and trade union rights. The unrestricted movements of services, however, has been held up by the failure to achieve standard recognition of qualifications. The free movement of capital has also been impeded by monetary crises and independent national monetary policies.

(d) A Common Agricultural Policy

This has proved, as was expected, to be one of the most difficult objectives. Agriculture is a much more dominant industry in Europe than it is in the U.K. The traditional high-cost structure of very small farms has been allowed to survive behind high tariff walls. The common agricultural policy aims to establish common price levels within the E.E.C. for each of a wide range of agricultural products. These prices are to be maintained by means of levies on imports, subsidies on exports, and by a system of support buying in the produce markets. Official agencies intervene when the prices fall below some agreed level. Progress has been difficult, but by the end of 1970, 95 per cent of the Community's output was covered by common prices. The cost of supporting agriculture, however, has risen very sharply in recent years. This support is carried out by the Agriculture Guidance and Guarantee Fund and each member must pay to the Fund all its import levies on food together with a progressive amount of its customs duties. From 1975 the Fund will receive all levies and customs duties together with up to 1 per cent of the revenue arising from the value added tax which will, by that time, be harmonised throughout the Community. In 1971 expenditure of the A.G.G.F. is expected to exceed 3,600 million dollars. There are plans to reduce the financial burden by a substantial restructuring of agriculture – taking large areas out of cultivation and increasing the average size of farms.

(e) A Common Transport Policy

The aim of this policy is to eliminate discrimination in rates and harmonise conditions of competition. Some progress has been made on harmonising rates and working conditions on intra-Community road transport.

(f) Common Rules for 'Fair' Competition

Agreements which restrict competition and monopolies are subject to control by the Treaty of Rome which applies principles very similar to those in the British legislation on this matter. The Commission has already imposed heavy fines on firms operating cartels.

(g) Coordinated Economic and Monetary Policies

Although there is a great deal of consultation between members, economic

335

policy making has remained a national prerogative. In February 1971, however, the Council of Ministers announced a plan for full economic union by 1980. This would entail a common currency for the members of the Community and complete harmonisation of budgetary and monetary policies.

THE ECONOMIC ARGUMENTS

1. *Greater Specialisation – Economies of Scale*

Supporters of the idea of a customs union argue that the creation of a greatly expanded 'home' market enables the more efficient producers to expand their scales of production and hence produce at lower cost. The removal of the trade barriers will allow more scope for the application of the principle of comparative advantage. Regional cost differentials will reveal themselves as differences in market prices and this will lead to a much greater degree of regional specialisation.

2. *Greater Competition*

The removal of the barriers to trade between members will lead to an intensification of competition – provided the rules of 'fair' competition are enforced. This will bring about the elimination of the less efficient firms and a more efficient pattern of production.

3. *Increased Exports*

The greater efficiency of the Community producers, brought about by the increases in the sale of production will, it is argued, enable them to compete much more effectively in world markets.

4. *More Investment*

The rising prosperity of the group as a whole will make it possible to provide more funds to help the less developed parts of the Community, and to provide more aid to the developing countries in other parts of the world.

5. *The Dynamic Effect*

It is held by many economists that one of the major advantages of the formation of a common market is the dynamic effect. Economic activity is influenced in an important manner by the expectations of entrepreneurs. The prospects of a much greater potential market and of increased competition will, it is believed, act as a stimulant to investment both for purposes of expansion and for modernisation. These actions, based upon the expectations of growth will, in fact, help to bring about that growth.

But there may well be disadvantages in such regional groupings. The trading bloc may pursue an inward looking policy, concentrating on its own problems while operating behind a protective common tariff. It may, therefore, show little interest in the liberalisation of world trade and in the growth of multilateralism. If the common tariff is protective in respect of certain products, then more efficient producers outside the bloc are being handicapped. Furthermore, the economies of scale argument should not be pressed too far. In many modern industries, national markets in countries such as the U.K., Germany, and France should be large enough to achieve substantial economies of scale. Recent studies show that higher productivity may be due more to managerial skills than to scale of production. The arguments for a huge home market may be somewhat exaggerated if the region as a whole is not a homogeneous group and consumption patterns have strong national characteristics.

E.E.C. – PROGRESS

Since it came into being, the E.E.C. has made substantial progress. Intra-Community trade has grown very rapidly. In 1969 both imports from and exports to member countries accounted for some 50 per cent of total Community imports and exports as compared to about 30 per cent in each category in 1958. By 1971 the absolute trade of most member countries had quadrupled. The common external tariff compares favourably with other industrial countries and by 1972 the average common tariff on imported manufactured goods will be about 7·6 per cent compared with 11·3 per cent in the U.S.A. and 10·6 per cent in the U.K. The most important claims made on behalf of the E.E.C., however, lie in the field of economic growth.

When the growth rates of the Six are compared with that of the U.K. they appear extremely favourable, but when compared with the growth rates of these Six countries in the years before the formation of the E.E.C., or when they are compared with rates in some other industrial countries the performance is in no way exceptional.

Table 30 shows that output per employee in the E.E.C. grew faster in 1958–69 than in 1950–58, but so it did in the rest of Europe. In fact *the increase* was greater in the rest of Europe, and such countries as Denmark, Switzerland, and Sweden have equalled the E.E.C. performance.

Table 30. *Annual rates per cent*

	Output per employee		Gross National Product	
	1950–58	1958–69	1950–58	1958–69
E.E.C.	4·2	5·2	5·6	5·4
Other O.E.C.D. Europe	2·5	3·7	3·2	4·3

Nevertheless growth rates in E.E.C. provide a marked contrast with those achieved by the United Kingdom. In the decade 1960–70, G.N.P.

per head increased on average at an annual rate of $2\frac{1}{2}$ per cent in the U.K. compared with a range in the E.E.C. from 3·7 per cent (Holland) to 4·8 per cent (Italy). This fairly narrow spread of fairly high growth rates is seen by some economists as evidence that the Community is moving towards a common economic policy.

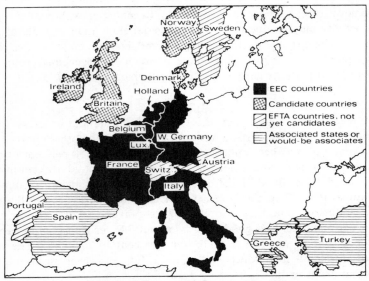

European Economic Community 1971

Figure 62

Source: *Economist*, 16 May 1970.

Britain and Europe: E.E.C. and E.F.T.A.

The formation of the European Communities presented a number of problems to other Western European countries. They had to consider the effect on their trade and upon the possibility of a serious division of interests arising in Europe. On the other hand, many of them hesitated to undertake the decisive step of entering the Communities since it appeared to involve a great sacrifice of independence. These problems were particularly acute for Britain.

Britain was reluctant to accept the degree of integration into European economic and political affairs which membership seemed to imply. Joining the Common Market would mean a considerable loss of independence as far as economic policies were concerned. Britain would not be able to adjust her tariffs independently – this would be a matter for the

Commission; she could not operate entirely independent monetary and fiscal policies, for these would be subject to consultation with member states and the Commission; it would mean a drastic change in her policy for agriculture, but the greatest stumbling block of all would be the special trading relationships with the Commonwealth.

The first two points are fairly clear, but the others require some explanation. Britain, like other European countries, protects its agriculture; the British system is one of guaranteed prices. Most foodstuffs enter Britain

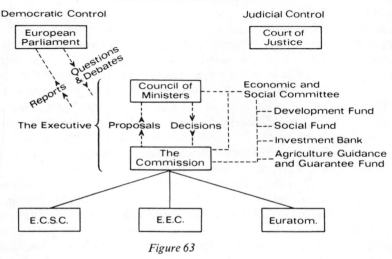

Figure 63

duty free and are sold in the British market at world prices which are generally below the British farmers' costs of production. The farmer is guaranteed a minimum price for his output and he receives the difference between the market price and this guaranteed price in the form of a subsidy from the government. If he sells meat at £5 per cwt, when the guaranteed price is £7 per cwt, he will receive a subsidy of £2 per cwt. The E.E.C. system of protection makes use of tariffs which raise the prices of imported foodstuffs to levels which enable the European farmer to market his products and cover his costs of production. Consumers in the Common Market will pay prices equal to the higher domestic costs of production while the British consumer pays the lower world prices, but has to contribute, in taxation, large sums to meet the costs of the subsidy. A change to

339

the European system would mean higher food prices but lower taxes. There is also the question of Britain's contribution to the Agricultural Guidance and Guarantee Fund. Under present plans this would be very substantial indeed. As a major food importer Britain would collect large levies on these imports and these would be paid over to the Community. In addition, eventually, she would have to pay to the Community's Budget all her customs duties on industrial goods together with the yield of up to 1 per cent on a value added tax. As an efficient agricultural producer, Britain, with less than 3 per cent of her labour force working on the land, will qualify for relatively little assistance from the A.G.G.F.

BRITAIN AND THE COMMONWEALTH

At present, Britain obtains about one-third of her imports from the Commonwealth countries and sends to the Commonwealth a slightly larger proportion of her exports. Under the Commonwealth Preference system most Commonwealth goods enter Britain duty free and many receive preferences because there is an import duty (or a higher duty) on goods from other countries. In return, Britain enjoys preferences (i.e. tariff reductions) in some parts of the Commonwealth. But the liberalisation of world trade, together with the policy of protecting infant industries pursued by the developing countries, has greatly reduced the importance of these preferences to Britain. The British market is, however, a vitally important market to many Commonwealth countries.

Entry into the Common Market would mean the end of Commonwealth preference in its present form, for Britain would have to adopt the common external tariff of the E.E.C. Many Commonwealth products, now entering Britain duty free, would have to surmount a tariff wall, and others, that enter on preferential terms, would lose such preferences. In addition, many Commonwealth products would find keen competition, in the British market, from goods entering Britain from Europe, duty free.

THE EUROPEAN FREE TRADE AREA

These considerations, and others, persuaded Britain to seek alternative arrangements. Before the Treaty of Rome was signed she attempted to form a large European Free Trade Area embracing all the members of O.E.E.C. but this venture was not successful. Later, Britain took part in the negotiations which led to the formation of a smaller, industrial European Free Trade Area with seven members, The United Kingdom, Norway, Sweden, Denmark, Austria, Switzerland, and Portugal. E.F.T.A. was formed in 1959 and began to operate in 1960.

A free trade area is a different concept from that of a common market. It is a much more flexible organisation, there are no supra-national institutions as in the Six. Nations retain a large measure of economic independence and it amounts to little more than an agreement between members states to establish a free market by the abolition of trade restrictions. They remain free to decide their own external tariffs – there is no common external tariff.

E.F.T.A. is an *industrial* free trade area with a population of about 100 million people, but there have been some special agreements to lower barriers on some non-industrial products (e.g. Danish bacon).

The programme of tariff reductions has been deliberately arranged to keep in step with the programme of the E.E.C. Tariff reductions are being harmonised with those of the Common Market in the hope that some link between the two associations might be arranged. As is the case in E.E.C., there has been a significant increase in the amount of trade between members of E.F.T.A.

RECENT DEVELOPMENTS

As the E.E.C. developed, Britain's policy towards it underwent a decisive change and in 1961 she made a formal application for membership. After protracted negotiations the French vetoed the application in 1963. The French view appeared to be that Britain was asking for too many modifications of the Rome Treaty in her attempt to obtain special concessions for some Commonwealth trade.

In 1967 the British government made a second attempt to join the Common Market. The major problems at that time were stated to be, an adequate transition period to allow Britain to adjust to the Common Market agricultural policy, and adequate safeguards for New Zealand dairy products and for West Indian sugar. Ireland, Norway and Denmark submitted applications for entry at the same time. France argued that the British economy was not strong enough to stand up to the immediate strains which entry to the E.E.C. would entail. Since approval of new entrants requires unanimity, Britain's application remained unanswered.

In 1969, however, political developments in Europe led to more favourable attitudes towards enlargement of the Community, and, at the same time, there was a strong recovery in the British balance of payments position. In 1970 negotiations on Britain's application were resumed. Britain has stated that she is prepared to accept the E.E.C. agricultural policy. This would mean a rise in the prices of foodstuffs in Britain and it was probably this fact which led to a swing in public opinion in Britain (in 1969–70) against entry. In the early stages of the negotiations a transitional period of five years was agreed.

Britain formally entered the Common Market on January 1st 1973. Two other countries, Eire and Denmark also joined bringing the membership of the E.E.C. to 9 countries.

Chapter 30

Aid to Underdeveloped Countries·

The Nature of Underdevelopment

The term 'underdeveloped' is rather misleading, in this context, since it can be interpreted as implying a situation where the potential resources of a nation are not fully developed. If this were the meaning, then Australia and Canada must be classed as underdeveloped nations. In fact, the term is used in a relative sense to indicate those countries where the national income per head, and the general standard of living, are much lower than in the advanced countries of North America, Western Europe, Australia and New Zealand.

There is no completely satisfactory measure of the level of economic development, but national income per head is normally taken as the indicator for most official purposes. Although this may be misleading (see Chapter 15), we cannot escape the fact that there are very great differences between the standards of living in the advanced nations and in most others. The national income per head in the U.S.A. is about $3,500, while in India it is about $90.

About two-thirds of the world's peoples live in regions which are classified as seriously underdeveloped and which make up the greater part of the inhabited areas of the world. The underdeveloped world comprises most of Asia, the greater part of Africa, most of South America, Central America, the Middle East and parts of Southern Europe. Table 31 gives some idea of the wide range of economic development.

Table 31. *Per capita Gross National Product. Selected countries – 1965 (U.S. dollars)*

United States	3,520
Sweden	2,270
Western Germany	1,700
United Kingdom	1,620
Greece	660
Spain	640
Chile	520
Mexico	470

Egypt	160
Ceylon	150
Thailand	130
India	90
Pakistan	90
Nigeria	80

Rich Countries and the Poor Countries

The already wide gap between the rich and the poor countries is growing wider. Barbara Ward illustrates this fact as follows: 'To give you only one example, in 1964 the United States *added* to its national income an equivalent of the entire national income of the African continent – some 30,000 million dollars. This shows the sort of built-in accelerating process which growth on top of wealth implies.'[1] If two nations with widely different national incomes grow at the same *percentage rate*, the *absolute difference* between their national incomes will grow ever wider.

In spite of the fact that there are great differences between the developing nations, there are certain generalisations which can be made about them.

1. The great majority of the people is engaged in agriculture; in some as much as 80 per cent of the labour force. Yet productivity, by western standards, is extremely low.

2. Most of the working population is completely lacking in formal education, and in the skills appropriate to modern production methods.

3. The basic structure necessary for economic development, i.e. good roads and railway networks, adequate power and water supplies, etc., is seriously deficient.

4. Many of them are experiencing what has been called 'a population explosion' which is greatly handicapping their efforts to raise output per head.

5. A number of underdeveloped countries are heavily dependent, for their earnings of foreign currency, on the exports of one or two major products. For example:

Sugar accounts for about 76 per cent of the exports of Barbados.
Sugar accounts for about 74 per cent of the exports of Cuba.

Coffee accounts for about 71 per cent of the exports of Colombia.
Cocoa accounts for about 61 per cent of the exports of Ghana.

6. In all of them there is 'a vicious circle of poverty'. Economic growth depends upon a higher level of investment – a higher level of investment depends upon a higher level of savings – a higher level of savings depends

[1] *The Decade of Development—a study in Frustration*, Overseas Development Institute, page 5.

upon a higher standard of living – a higher standard of living depends upon economic growth. Most of these countries cannot break out of this circle unless they obtain most of their capital requirements from the wealthier nations.

Motives for giving Aid

There are three principal motives for giving aid:

Humanitarian Motives
The plight of hundreds of millions of people living in abject poverty must deeply shock all who realise it, and humanitarianism demands that the richer countries should help them.

Political Motives
Both the communist and the non-communist worlds have given some economic aid in the hope of winning the political allegiance of the recipients.

Economic Motives
If the underdeveloped countries succeed in achieving a faster rate of economic growth, they will be able to enter more extensively into world trade and provide growing markets for the output of other countries.

Forms of Aid

The United Nations considers that economic aid consists only of outright grants and long-term loans for non-military purposes, but the chief aid-giving countries take a much broader view and include private capital investment and export credits. In fact, the term 'aid' is being increasingly replaced by 'development assistance'. Economic aid may take several forms.

1. Gifts of Consumer Goods
This form of aid has consisted, mostly, of the free distribution of American stockpiles of foodstuffs, mainly wheat. There are several problems associated with this form of aid. The kind of food stock-piled in the West may not be suitable in the East, and a large release of such commodities may upset world prices and affect the earnings of other producers.

2. Long-term Loans and Grants
These may be earmarked by the donor for some specific project, or they may be 'tied', i.e. they must be spent in the country which is providing the loan. The problem here is that aid in the form of loans gives rise to

interest charges and repayments which impose a burden on the balance of payments of the borrowing country. Many of them have already found such loan charges a heavy liability.

3. *Technical assistance.*

The advanced nations can provide technical experts to advise and assist the developing nations in their efforts to industrialise. In a number of cases the advanced nations have undertaken the building of steelworks or power stations as a direct form of aid. They may also undertake the training of technicians.

4. *Education*

Most of the wealthier countries provide facilities for overseas students to attend universities and colleges and provide them with scholarships. In addition, they may send teachers and instructors overseas.

5. *Specialist Services*

The World Bank, the I.M.F., and the United Nations, as well as individual countries, carry out economic surveys and offer financial advisory services to developing nations.

6. *Trade*

Although it may be possible to increase the productive capacity of the poorer nations, it will only be effective if these nations are able to increase their exports so that they can earn sufficient foreign currency to repay their foreign loans and to raise the level of their imports of capital equipment. It does not make much sense for the developed nations to assist the industrialisation of the poorer countries, and then to exclude the exports of these countries on the grounds that they are the products of low-wage labour. The fall in the world prices of some primary products in recent years meant that some developing countries suffered losses in their earnings of foreign currencies which exceeded the value of their economic aid. The advanced countries will have to adopt more liberal trading policies in respect of the goods exported by developing countries.

Channels of Aid

By far the greater part of economic aid is provided bilaterally on a government-to-government basis. Government aid makes up about 50 per cent of economic assistance, about 40 per cent is in the form of private capital investment (mainly to oil producing areas), and the remaining 10 per cent is provided by international agencies. It is probable that the developing countries would welcome a move to channel a greater share of the aid through international bodies. The acceptance of such aid would not imply any political obligation to a particular country or political grouping, and the recipients would be much readier to allow internal supervision of a development project, if the loan came from a body such as the United Nations. There is a number of such international agencies.

The Colombo Plan is a scheme for the economic development of South and South East Asia operated by the U.S.A., the U.K., Canada, Japan, New Zealand, Australia and sixteen countries in South and South East Asia. The assistance is mainly of a technical nature.

The E.E.C. Development Fund was established by members of the E.E.C to promote social and economic development in the overseas countries with which they have special links (mainly former possessions in Africa).

The Organisation of American States (*O.A.S.*) established, in 1960, a programme of technical cooperation to help the countries of Latin America to solve the problem of shortages of highly trained technicians.

The United Nations has a number of agencies for the purpose of rendering various forms of economic assistance. There is the Special Fund (SUNFED) to finance economic surveys; the Expanded Programme for Technical Assistance to provide the services of experts and to develop training programmes; UNICEF which provides aid in the field of education, and UNRRA which operates a relief and rehabilitation programme.

The World Bank, the I.F.C., and the I.D.A., provide financial assistance for long term development projects. The International Finance Corporation and the International Development Association are affiliates of the World Bank and were established to provide loans, in particular circumstances, on more favourable terms than those granted by the World Bank.

Although aid from the wealthier countries is increasing, the fact that they are growing wealthier has meant that, proportionate to national income, assistance has begun to fall. Nearly all the developed nations give less than 1 per cent of their national income to developing countries.[1]

[1] Barbara Ward, page 5.

Chapter 31

Current Economic Problems

Economists are concerned with 'what is' rather than 'what ought to be'. Economics is the study of the ways in which man goes about his daily business of earning a living and not with how he 'ought to' conduct himself in the matters of producing and consuming wealth. But we all have our ideas on what 'ought to be' and we therefore tend to advocate this policy and condemn that policy.

When we take up a particular position with regard to the ways in which things ought to be done, we are acting as *politicians* rather than as economists. It is the job of the politician to persuade us that this or that particular route is better than the alternatives. The economist can examine the policy proposals and point to the possible economic consequences. In doing this he can help the politician to base his decisions on a wider knowledge of all the implications of his proposed line of action.

In this chapter we shall look at some of the economic policies and problems which are the subject of continuing controversy. We have, of course, already discussed several important aspects of government economic policy. In particular, government policy with regard to employment, monopolies, industrial location, taxation, and the supply of money have been dealt with in some detail. We now turn to a short discussion of some of the broader issues of economic policy.

Economic Planning

The word 'planning' is used in many different senses in current literature. Professor Arthur Lewis[1] indicates six different meanings of the word:

1. Where it is used to refer to the geographical zoning of factories, residential buildings, and open spaces. This is sometimes referred to as Town and Country Planning.

2. It is sometimes used in government statements to describe their planned expenditure in the future. It simply means what the government will spend over the next five years or so if it has the money to spend.

3. It may mean a fully planned economy where each production unit is allocated a quota of resources and is given a production target which it is

[1] *The Principles of Economic Planning*, Allen and Unwin.

called upon to meet. Producers must operate within a central plan, prepared and controlled by a central authority.

4. Planning may mean nothing more than the setting of production targets, by the government, for private and public enterprise in a selected number of key industries.

5. The fifth type is a logical development of the fourth. The government tries to set targets for the economy as a whole and to indicate the necessary allocation of resources. The result is a series of interlocking statistical tables. The British National Plan, published in 1965, was an example of this type of planning.

6. Finally, the word 'planning' is used to describe the means by which governments try to enforce their targets on the private sector of the economy.

We shall consider, briefly, the third type which is usually identified as *planning by direction*, and the last three types which may be described as *planning through the market*.

The alternative to any form of planning is a system of free or unfettered competition with an absolute minimum of State intervention in the production and distribution of wealth – a system known as *laissez faire*. Very few people would argue for complete *laissez faire*, most would accept the case for some degree of government control of economic affairs. The disputes arise on the question of *how much* planning, and whether that planning should be by direction or through the market.

PLANNING BY DIRECTION

Planning by direction, if fully adopted, would mean that all the fundamental economic decisions would be taken by centralised planning committees. These committees would decide how the economic resources of the country should be used. Production targets would be established for each industry and each production unit, and resources would be allocated accordingly. Incomes would be determined by the planning authorities and the distribution of the goods produced would have to be controlled by some system of rationing (i.e. by coupons or by prices). This is an enormous task and would require a vast bureaucratic machine constantly to assess the resources available and the allocation of these resources to the many thousands of different uses.

Complete planning by direction is not possible in any economically developed society, because it cannot be applied to consumption. Although the Government may be allowed to spend part of the national income on behalf of the people (e.g. on education, health and defence), by and large the citizens demand freedom of choice in consumption. There must, therefore, be money and a consumers' market. This makes planning by direction very difficult, for production must be extremely flexible in order to meet the constantly changing pattern of consumer wants, as they are freely expressed in the market place.

Workers generally demand the freedom to choose their own jobs, but centrally planned production targets can only be met effectively by allocating (i.e. directing) labour to where it is required. The direction of labour would be politically unpopular and is likely to be economically inefficient.

Planning by direction is likely to be very inflexible. Once the planners have made the thousands of calculations necessary for the formulation of the economic plan and have issued the necessary permits, licences and directions, it will be extremely difficult to effect any modification. Centralised planning will tend to reduce variety. It is much easier to plan the output of a standard suit of clothes than a wide variety of styles and fashions. For this latter reason, planning by direction is likely to be much more effective in an underdeveloped nation than in an advanced nation.

PLANNING THROUGH THE MARKET

It is possible for economic planning to operate by retaining the market mechanism and using the price system to influence the development of the economy. This would mean retaining a wide freedom of choice in the consumers' market and in the market for labour. It would also provide for a much greater degree of flexibility, for the price system can adjust from day to day. Changes in demand are reflected in price changes which, in turn, will be reflected in production changes. The State operates its plan, not by direction, but by manipulation of the market.

If it wishes firms to make more goods of a particular type and less of another kind, it does not need to use a complicated system of licences and controls, it merely subsidises the production of those goods which it wishes to encourage, and taxes the goods it wishes to discourage. Should the State desire to see more investment and less consumption, then it can give generous tax allowances on investment, or carry out the investment itself, and discourage consumption by means of taxation. The State may use its fiscal and monetary weapons to induce changes in the economy, resorting to price controls and rationing only as short term measures while the supply situation is adjusted. Even so, where resources are very immobile some direct controls may be necessary; for example, the use of building controls in the London area in order to persuade firms to move into the provinces.

THE BRITISH ECONOMIC PLAN

As in most western countries, planning in Britain has been a mixture of the two methods, with the emphasis largely on planning by inducement. Recent British planning has been described as 'indicative' rather than 'imperative'. The idea is that the publication of targets will create a stimulus and an incentive to meet these targets, but the Government is prepared to use its fiscal and monetary powers to help in the realisation of the plan. In addition the Government controls a large public sector (e.g. the nationalised industries) which enables it to exert considerable direct influence on the economy. There is also an element of planning by direction by the use of vetoes (e.g. the Town and Country Planning Acts control the siting of industrial and commercial buildings).

In February 1962 the Government set up the National Economic Development Council consisting of people drawn from industry, the trade unions, and Government, together with some leading economists. Its functions were:

1. To examine the economic performance of the nation and to prepare plans for the future.
2. To consider what are the obstacles to quicker growth, and what can be done to improve efficiency.
3. To seek agreement upon ways of improving economic performance, competitive power, and efficiency.

The first task of the N.E.D.C. (Neddy) was the publication of a programme for growth for the period 1961–6 on the assumption that the economy would grow at an annual rate of 4 per cent. The Council considered how the needs of industry for capital, labour, and raw materials would be affected by this growth rate, and whether the additional imports could be paid for by increased exports. Its report discussed the special policy measures which would be needed in specific areas to back up the growth programme.

The next step was the setting up of economic development councils (E.D.C.s) to cover particular industries. These 'Little Neddies', as they are called, have the same broad structure as the N.E.D.C. Their objectives are to examine the performance, prospects, and plans of particular industries in relation to the planned objective set out by the N.E.D.C. There are now twenty-one of these E.D.C.s.

The third phase of the evolution of the planning process came with the setting up of the Department of Economic Affairs, in 1964, with the object of drawing up and putting into operation a National Plan. The initiation of planning work now lay with the D.E.A., but the N.E.D.C. and the E.D.C.s were intimately linked with this department and the head of the D.E.A. was also chairman of the N.E.D.C. Economic planning councils for the various regions have also been established. (See page 113.)

The National Plan was published in September 1965 and set out, in detail, an analysis of the requirements for a 25 per cent increase in the Gross National Product between 1964 and 1970.

In 1969 the Department of Economic Affairs was disbanded and its functions transferred to the Treasury which now has overall responsibility for the Government's economic strategy.

Early in 1965 the Government established a National Board for Prices and Incomes whose role was to examine and pronounce upon proposed wage and price increases. It also made suggestions for improving productivity and wage negotiating machinery in the industries which were brought to its attention.

An Incomes Policy

It seems appropriate at this point to say something about a problem which is of great concern to the Governments of most Western European countries and to that of Great Britain in particular, namely, the problem of implementing an effective incomes policy.

The fundamental problem is that of bringing to an end a spiral of rising incomes and rising prices. Since the war, incomes in Britain have been rising much more rapidly than productivity. More precisely we can say that demand has persistently outstripped supply with the inevitable result – rising prices. A rising price level, as we saw when discussing inflation, causes serious economic problems, both at home and in relation to our export performance. There appears to be widespread agreement that inflation (persistently rising prices) is undesirable and that some attempt must be made to achieve stable prices. One solution would be to tackle the problem at its source by ensuring that incomes rise at the same rate as productivity. This is the aim of an incomes policy. A further aim of incomes policy is often stated to be the achievement of a greater measure of social justice in the distribution of incomes.

In order to appreciate the developments which give rise to demands for an incomes policy, it will be instructive to refer back to Fig. 43 (p. 182) which illustrates recent trends in productivity, prices, and earnings. It is also necessary to bear in mind the pattern of income distribution. An incomes policy is designed to influence the movements in all incomes, but since wages and salaries (the return to labour) make up about 70 per cent of all factor incomes, there will be a tendency to concentrate on movements in wage rates.

We shall begin by examining the trends of government policy and then proceed to consider some of the fundamental difficulties involved in trying to operate an effective incomes policy.

GOVERNMENT POLICY IN BRITAIN

Since there are three features of this economic problem, movements in prices, movements in incomes and movements in productivity, government policy must be directed towards three ends: (*a*) influencing prices, (*b*) influencing incomes and (*c*) influencing productivity.

With regard to productivity, the Government aims to increase the rate of growth by using its powers of persuasion, by using the instrument of taxation, and by granting financial assistance in order to stimulate investment in those industries which offer the greatest scope for expansion. It can provide incentives for industry to modernise by granting relief from taxation to firms which purchase new industrial equipment. Government grants can be made available to finance research projects which have a direct bearing on productivity. The standards of industrial performance may be raised by an expansion of technical education and by the introduction of schemes designed to improve industrial training. Persuasion and exhortation are the methods by which the Government hopes to eliminate the restrictive practices which are a brake on the development of British industry.

In launching the incomes policy the first practical step took the form of government consultation with unions and employers which resulted in the publication of a Statement of Intent (in December 1964). In this statement, representatives of employers and workers undertook to cooperate with the Government in (1) removing obstacles to efficiency; (2) keeping under review the movement of prices and incomes; (3) examining particular cases in order to ascertain whether proposed increases in prices or incomes were in the national interest.

The second stage was the establishment of machinery to carry out these objectives. It was agreed that the National Economic Development Council should maintain a continuous review of price and income movements and that a National Board for Prices and Incomes should be established to investigate particular cases. This board, established early in 1965, had nine members and worked in two divisions, the Prices Review Division and the Incomes Review Division.

To serve as a guide, on matters of policy, the Government published, in April 1965, a White Paper which set out the criteria by which the Board should judge the cases brought before it. In this document it was indicated that exceptional pay increases (i.e. above the norm) should be confined to circumstances where:

(*a*) changes in working practices made a direct contribution towards increasing productivity, but some part of the gain should accrue to the public in the form of lower prices;

(*b*) the changing of wage differentials was necessary to increase labour mobility;

(*c*) existing wages were considered to be too low to maintain a reasonable standard of living;

(*d*) where the pay of a certain group of workers had fallen seriously out of line with the level of remuneration for similar work elsewhere.

The White Paper also indicated the cases where an increase in prices might be justified. They are:

(a) where productivity could not be increased sufficiently to allow wages and salaries to increase at a rate consistent with the criteria for incomes given above;

(b) where there were unavoidable increases in non-labour costs such as: materials, fuels, services or marketing, which could not be fully absorbed by increases in productivity;

(c) where there were unavoidable increases in capital costs which could not be offset;

(d) where the enterprise could not secure the capital it required to maintain efficiency.

The aim of the prices policy is to maintain stable prices, but this does not mean that all prices should remain unchanged. In an average year, there are something like three million price changes, including both increases and decreases. A stable price level would mean more reductions and fewer increases than in recent years. For practical reasons, the Prices and Incomes Board could only deal with the more important cases – those proposed price increases which would have a significant effect on the cost of living, on industrial costs, or on export costs. References to the Board were made by the Secretary of State for Economic Affairs and it was the duty of the Board to examine, critically, the proposed changes in prices or incomes and then to make recommendations. For example, in the first report, the Board said that the proposed increase of 5 per cent in road haulage rates was not in the interests of the industry or of its customers and should be withdrawn. But the report also contained proposals concerned with ways of increasing productivity in the industry and with changes in the wage-negotiating machinery.

It was hoped that the Board's findings would be voluntarily accepted by the parties concerned, but, in 1966, the voluntary system proved ineffective to deal with the situation. Incomes had been rising much faster than productivity. In the first quarter of 1966, incomes rose by $7\frac{3}{4}$ per cent, whereas output rose by only $1\frac{1}{2}$ per cent.

In July 1966, the government introduced *a standstill* by proposing to hold incomes and prices, at their July levels, until December 1966. This standstill was to be followed by a further period (six months) of severe restraint. Initially, the government appealed for voluntary cooperation, although, at the same time, it introduced legislation which gave it compulsory powers.

After some signs of a breakdown in voluntary cooperation, the government, in October 1966, decided to make use of their compulsory powers; prices and incomes were fixed, at the levels obtaining in July, for a period

353

of six months (July to December). From June 1967 the Government proposed to return to a voluntary incomes policy by allowing its powers to make orders that specified pay and price increases should be vetoed to lapse. It did, however, propose to continue Part II of the 1966 Prices and Incomes Act which required that certain proposed pay and price increases should be notified to the Government which then had the power to delay these increases. These proposals were contained in the 1967 Prices and Incomes Act which gave the Government power to delay pay and price increases for up to seven months subject to a reference to the National Board for Prices and Incomes. The N.B.P.I. was to continue to apply the criteria set out earlier.

For the years 1968 and 1969 the Government announced a ceiling of $3\frac{1}{2}$ per cent per annum for wages and salaries; a similar ceiling was to be applied to company dividends. Although the Government's delaying powers were renewed, and the powers to delay extended to cover a period of twelve months, the policy was ineffective in preventing a sharp escalation in wage settlements in 1969 and 1970. In January 1970 the Government reduced the period for which it could delay a settlement to four months.

The election of a Conservative government in 1970 brought a change of policy. It was announced that an official incomes policy of the kind pursued by the previous Government would not be applied, and in November 1970 it was announced that the National Board for Prices and Incomes would be wound up. In 1971 it was replaced by the Office of Manpower Economics whose brief is to look at: the way employers are dealing with the introduction of equal pay; the relationship between different methods of wage bargaining and the eventual level of earnings; and the general shift to measured day work systems under which workers are paid an agreed rate in return for a specified level of performance.[1]

An incomes policy must cover profit and rent as well as wages and salaries. Profits can be controlled by means of price controls or by means of taxation, or the level of dividends may be subject to statutory regulation. The incomes derived from rents may be limited by a Rent Control Act or by means of taxation. These measures will be discussed in the next section.

PRACTICAL PROBLEMS

We shall deal first with wages and salaries. Broadly speaking there are three major tasks facing those responsible for putting a wage policy into effect.

1. A decision must be reached on the permitted (or recommended) increase in the total wage bill for the period ahead, normally one year.

[1] The quickening pace of inflation in 1972 forced the Government to resort to statutory control of prices and incomes.

2. The second step must be to decide upon the distribution of this total sum among the various groups of wage earners.

3. The third and most difficult problem is to give effect to these decisions by setting up some machinery for enforcement.

The Government is obliged to indicate a 'norm' or recommended ceiling for the general increase in wages during the coming year. In 1965 it was recommended that 3–3½ per cent was the annual increase in money incomes which would be consistent with price stability. It was estimated that productivity, for the next few years, would increase at this annual rate.

Major difficulties begin to arise when the second step is reached. Even if we assume that general agreement is reached on the *average* wage rise, it does not mean that all workers should receive the agreed annual increase in pay. If all workers received the same percentage rise in wages, differentials would be frozen and there would be no incentives for labour to move, either geographically or occupationally. We need labour to move from less essential or declining industries to the expanding industries. Those trades or industries where the rate of recruitment is below requirements must be permitted to grant increases above the average in order to attract workers. This will mean that other workers must accept an increase below the national average, thus raising all kinds of difficulties with regard to the accepted notions of 'fair' wages. The changing differentials are likely to cause feelings of injustice among those whose rise in pay has been below the 'norm'. Quite apart from the needs of the expanding industries, it will be very difficult to assess the appropriate rise in pay for those occupations which have a special case to plead, especially those which are supported by widespread public sympathy (e.g. nurses).

Another problem arises because movements in productivity vary enormously as between industries. Some industries, especially those which are science-based (chemicals) and those which can gain very great technical economies of scale (e.g. the motor industry), are capable of achieving large annual increases in productivity. Workers in these industries will be obliged to accept annual percentage increases in pay which are well below the percentage increases in productivity achieved by their own industries. It has been the experience of other countries (e.g. Holland) which have attempted to limit wage movements to the changes in *national* productivity, that workers have felt that they should benefit from rises in productivity in *their own* industries.

A wages policy must start at some given moment of time, and if it is announced, for example, that future wage rises, in general, should not exceed 3 per cent per annum, there is an assumption that the existing pattern of wage differentials is acceptable. This is not the case. At the time when the wage policy is introduced, there are bound to be some claims 'in the pipeline' and a number of unresolved wage grievances. The groups of workers who are in this position will feel that the queue has been abolished just when they were nearing its head. They will demand special treatment and will plead exemption from the proposed limitations on wage increases. A large number of such 'special cases' will make it very difficult to get the norm or guiding light generally accepted.

Perhaps the most difficult task of all is that of enforcement. In a society such as that of Britain, with its traditional method of wage settlement by freely conducted collective bargaining, and with powerful unions committed to retaining their freedom to negotiate on behalf of their members, it does not seem that any permanent statutory enforcement of wage levels is a practical proposition.

What can be done to control the level of profits? Distributed profits may be limited by (1) legislation which places a ceiling on dividends; (2) a form of price control which fixes prices on a cost-plus basis (during the last war many prices were fixed in this manner, profits being limited to 10 per cent of costs); (3) the use of a variable profits tax which could be adjusted so as to keep distributed profits to an acceptable figure.

The great drawback to all these schemes is that they involve a loss of the incentive to reduce costs. In the case of (2) it could be argued that there is a positive incentive to increase costs. Increased efficiency would not lead to higher profits. The stimulus to embark upon new projects, adopt new methods or to introduce new products, all risky enterprises, would certainly be diminished under a régime of profit limitation. Another problem would be that of distinguishing between industries. Capital is only attracted to the more risky enterprises when there is the prospect of higher than average profits, and it must be borne in mind that export markets are much more competitive and uncertain than the home market. Yet Britain requires her industries to make greater efforts in these markets. In spite of all these difficulties, some limitation on profits is necessary if other income groups are to be persuaded to accept restrictions on their ability to obtain the maximum income possible.

The control of rents in Britain has generally taken the form of statutory rent restriction. The rents of privately owned houses are fixed at the levels in force at the time of legislation. The landlord is only able to raise his rent by permission of some public rent tribunal which must be satisfied that the increased rent is justified by some improvement in the property. There are some serious economic disadvantages to a system of rent control. During periods of inflation such as Britain has experienced since the last war the controlled rent becomes increasingly unrealistic. The landlord's return on his investment becomes progressively less attractive compared with the earnings of capital in other fields. Costs of maintenance and administration rise and landlords tend to neglect their properties as a means of reducing costs and maintaining a reasonable return on their investment. Rent control in the past has generally resulted in a reduction in the supply of privately owned houses to rent. When a house, which has previously been let, becomes vacant, landlords have often sold the house to prospective owner-occupiers, in order to recover their capital in liquid form and invest it in other fields.

There are obviously very serious difficulties involved in the operation of an incomes policy. Perhaps the greatest single economic gain from such an exercise is an indirect one. The publicity and public discussion which accompanies the preparation and introduction of an incomes policy should have important educational and psychological effects. There might be a greater awareness of the national economic problems and a better appreciation of the necessity for restraint. If this were so, then the aims of an incomes policy would stand a much better chance of being realised.

Nationalisation

Nationalisation is the process of bringing an industry into public ownership. It is not essential to planning, because a government has many ways open to it if it wishes to control industry. For example:

1. It may control the prices of the industry's products and/or fix a limit to the profits and dividends.
2. It may take up shares in public companies and place its representatives on the boards of management.
3. A government may exercise a constant supervision of the costs and prices policies of firms in an industry.
4. It is possible for a government to take over the wholesale stage, and, hence, exercise an effective control over prices in that industry.
5. It may lay down statutory specifications for the products of the industry.

Nationalisation is only one of many ways of achieving ends. It has been advocated on a number of grounds. Some advocates regard it as a means of confiscating the property of the rich, but, in Britain, this is not the practice, because the former owners are paid compensation. In more recent years nationalisation has been thought necessary where capitalists have not been putting enough money into an industry. In Britain this has been put forward as one of the justifications for nationalising the railways and the coal industry. Moreover, nationalisation is part of the political programme of those who object to working for private employers who own the means of production. Public ownership, they believe, will enable workers to take a greater share in management. A further suggested ground for nationalisation is where unitary control of the industry would be more efficient than a competitive structure. The economic argument here is that for monopoly (see page 144). Unitary control does not necessarily mean nationalisation, but, where a monopoly is economically desirable it is argued that the monopoly should be subject to public control, and the most complete form of public control is nationalisation.

But, again, nationalisation need not be monopolistic – it may be possible to control an industry by nationalising only part of it. In Britain, there has been support for the complete nationalisation of certain basic industries, including gas, electricity, water, transport and coal, on the grounds that the successful operation of these industries was vital to the efficiency of all other industries, and that they should be run with these wider considerations in mind, rather than with a narrow view to profit. But the degree of interdependence of all major industries in a modern economy makes the selection of certain industries for nationalisation rather arbitrary. It is also argued that only by nationalisation can the necessary integration, with the accruing economies of scale, be speedily achieved.

The extent of nationalisation, in Britain, was greatly increased during the period of the Labour Government 1945–51. As we have already seen (Chapter 9), the form of business organisation chosen to run these enterprises has been the public corporation. The procedure adopted for the nationalisation of an industry has been for the Government to compensate the former owners in fixed interest government securities. The amount of the compensation has usually been based upon the Stock Exchange valuation of the company's shares. The following corporations are now operating or controlling large-scale industries or services:

The Post Office
National Coal Board
British Steel Corporation
Electricity Council and Boards in England and Wales
North of Scotland Hydro-Electric Board
South of Scotland Electricity Board
Gas Council and Area Gas Boards
British Overseas Airways Corporation
British European Airways Corporation
British Airports Authority
British Railways Board
National Freight Corporation
British Bus Company
London Transport Board
British Transport Docks Board
British Waterways Board

The nationalised industries are under a statutory obligation to pay their way. A White Paper published in 1961 declared, 'Surpluses on

Revenue Account should be at least sufficient to cover deficits on Revenue Account *over a five year period.*' Several serious problems arise in judging the performance of nationalised industries.

Most of them have monopoly powers which make it difficult to judge the efficiency of their performance. The fact that the industry makes a profit is not necessarily an indication of efficiency, for the profit may have been achieved by the exercise of monopoly power (although several of them are now meeting severe competition from close substitutes). This leads to the problems of their pricing policies. The prices charged by the nationalised industries are subject to ministerial approval. Some of these industries, particularly the railways and the Coal Board have been operating non-commercial enterprises. The railways have continued to provide many non-profitable services when they thought that to do so was in the public interest, and the National Coal Board has pursued a policy of closing down uneconomic pits at a much slower rate than was commercially desirable because of the serious unemployment problems such a policy would create in the areas heavily dependent on coal mining. These policies have raised average costs and since it is very difficult (and perhaps unfair) to charge different prices, prices have been based on average cost, so that passengers on one line have been subsidising passengers on another line, and some efficient pits have been subsidising less efficient pits.

It is also very difficult to determine what proportion of the scarce resources should be devoted to the nationalised industries. They do not have to compete with other enterprises in the capital market, because they obtain their loans direct from the Exchequer. In recent years, investment in the nationalised industries has been more than double that in private manufacturing industry.

The railways and the coal industry have accumulated very large deficits and it seems that, as yet, no clear policy has been formulated with regard to the basis on which the nationalised industries should be conducted. There is undoubtedly a public service tradition in the operation of these enterprises, but many experts believe that the public service element in their operations should be clearly separated from their other activities, and subsidised by the taxpayer. This policy has now been adopted in respect of the railways which receive a subsidy on the uneconomic lines kept open in the public interest.

Economic Growth

INTERNATIONAL GROWTH RATES

The economic controversies which seem to attract most attention nowadays are those which are concerned with rates of economic growth. We are constantly presented with 'league' tables which show us that in one country the national income has been growing at 7 per cent per annum, while in another the rate has been a mere 2 per cent.

Economic growth is a characteristic of the modern world. Nations have grown in population, in total production and employment, in real national income, and in the standard of living enjoyed by the mass of the people. But the rates of growth have varied enormously. The United States and Western Europe have doubled their output per head since 1939, but it is doubtful if countries such as India and Indonesia have made any real progress in raising income *per head*. Even among the developed nations themselves there are marked differences in rates of economic growth.

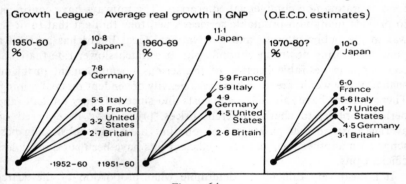

Figure 64
Source: *Economist*, 5 September 1970.

Economic growth is generally taken to mean a growth in real output per head. It is output per head which determines the standard of living, and the worldwide efforts to raise the pace of economic growth reflect the desires of peoples everywhere, in rich and poor countries alike, to raise their levels of material welfare. The British National Plan, published in 1965, set a target for economic growth of about 4 per cent per annum for the period 1964–70. In this particular case, the growth rate refers to total output.

DETERMINANTS OF ECONOMIC GROWTH

We are not saying that it is always a good thing to have a fast rate of economic growth – it might well involve a sacrifice of certain freedoms, of leisure, and of other non-economic aspects of human welfare. We are only concerned with what is meant by economic growth and what determines the rate of growth.

The *rate of investment* is one very important determinant. Increasing the stock of capital relative to labour and land will normally raise productivity in the future. This rate of capital accumulation is dependent upon the level of savings, so that greater output in the future depends upon the extent to which the community is prepared to sacrifice current consumption.

But the *type of investment* is also very important. Large-scale investment in houses, schools, hospitals, coffee bars, and opulent shopping centres will have some effect on productivity by raising the health, educational standards and morale of the people, but these economic effects will be felt only very slowly. Investment in new factories, improved machinery, and modern transport facilities is likely to make a much greater and more immediate impact upon output per head. The *quality of the investment* is also very important. France, Germany and Japan had much of their industry destroyed during the Second World War. Starting from scratch after wartime devastation, they were able to rebuild entire industries with larger production units and modern layouts. This is likely to be much more effective than modernisation by piecemeal replacements.

One of the greatest barriers to economic growth is the immobility of the factors of production, especially the immobility of labour. Rapid growth requires speedy adjustment to changes in demand. In the case of Britain, it is vital that industrial changes keep pace with the changing patterns of demand in world markets. Resources must be moved to those industries which are capable of supplying the growing markets.

Where there is a reluctance to change jobs, to learn new skills, to accept new methods of production, or where there are other barriers to such changes, economic growth will be retarded. A recent survey[1] shows many instances in Britain where new techniques of production have been adopted and where the required amounts of labour have been greatly reduced, but where workers, or management, have insisted on retaining the old 'manning' schedules. This can only mean a considerable under-employment of labour with the consequent sacrifice of output elsewhere.

The quality of the labour force is another critical factor, and faster economic growth requires an efficient system of industrial and commercial training and retraining.

In many industries large increases in productivity can be achieved by increasing the size of the firm or production unit, in order to obtain economies of scale. In the new and larger steel plants, output per worker is several times higher than in the older ones. In the retail trade, sales per employee in the supermarkets are more than 50 per cent higher than in the counter-service shops.

One of the barriers to economic growth may be a lack of enterprise or a shortage of able entrepreneurs. The decisions to undertake production, or to make radical changes in production, or to launch a new product,

[1] *The Sunday Times*, 20 February 1966.

often call for judgments of a high order and require considerable courage. When society accords a low status to business, the best talents are often drawn into other activities such as law, the church, the army or the civil service. A society seeking a rapid rate of economic growth must encourage the entrepreneur and the innovator.

When discussing the underdeveloped nations it was pointed out that poverty seems to be self-perpetuating – there is a vicious circle of poverty. It appears that economic growth is also self-perpetuating. It seems that if an economy could get itself on the development path, the forces of growth might carry it forward indefinitely. The problem is how to get on the path.

The 'Take-off' Theory

W. W. Rostow,[1] a leading American economist, after studying the course of economic development in the developed nations, put forward a theory of *the Take-Off*, suggesting that economic development begins with a rush – it is not a long slow gradual process. Economic growth begins in a relatively short period of radical change which must be preceded by a preliminary period of build up. In the preliminary period it is necessary to establish a basic framework of central government, to have a class of people devoted to economic progress, and to remove the serious barriers to the mobility of capital and labour. There must follow a great increase in the rate of technological change, a large increase in the percentage of output devoted to investment, and a fundamental change in the structure of industrial organisation involving the adoption of large-scale, more specialised methods of production. This process makes heavy demands on the labour force, since it requires a high degree of mobility and the acceptance of the disciplines of the factory system. It requires, too, a supply of able entrepreneurs. Rostow believes that an increase in the rate of savings and investment from something less than 5 per cent of total output to something more than 10 per cent is necessary; if this rate can be achieved a 'break-through' or 'take-off' is possible.

Table 32. *Rostow's dating of various take-offs*

Great Britain	1783–1802
France	1830–1860
Belgium	1833–1860
U.S.A.	1843–1860
Germany	1850–1873
Japan	1878–1900
U.S.S.R.	1890–1914

[1] W. W. Rostow, *The Stages of Economic Growth*.

Reading List

The following sources are intended to give some guidance on material which supplements the subject matter of this book, and on the kind of texts to which the student might proceed from the stage he has now reached.

STANLAKE, G. F. *Objective Tests in Economics*, 2nd edn. Longman, 1971. This is a book of multiple choice questions based largely on the material in Introductory Economics.

Economic Textbooks: General

BENHAM, F. *Economics*, 8th edn. Pitman, 1967.

CAIRNCROSS, A. K. *An Introduction to Economics*, 4th edn. Butterworth, 1966.

HARBURY, G. D. *Descriptive Economics*, 3rd edn. Pitman, 1968.

HARVEY, J. and JOHNSON, M. K. *Modern Economics*, Macmillan, 1969.

LIPSEY, R. G. *An Introduction to Positive Economics*, 3rd edn. Weidenfeld and Nicolson, 1973.

MARSHALL, B. V. *Comprehensive Economics*, Longmans, 1967.

NEVIN, E. T. *A Textbook of Economic Analysis*, 3rd edn. Macmillan, 1967.

SAMUELSON, P. *Economics*, 8th edn. McGraw Hill, 1970.

STONIER, A. W. and HAGUE, D. C. *A Textbook of Economic Theory*, 4th edn. Longman, 1972.

Industry and Trade

ALLEN, G. C. *British Industries and their Organisation*. Longman, 1970.

— *The Structure of Industry in Britain*. Longmans, 1970.

BEACHAM, A. and CUNNINGHAM. *Economics of Industrial Organisation*, 4th edn., 1962.

DUNNING, J. H. and THOMAS, C. J. *British Industry*. Hutchinson (University Library), 1966.

EDWARDS, R. S. and TOWNSEND, H. *Business Enterprise*. Macmillan, 1958.

Business Organisation and Finance

FERRIS, P. *The City*. Penguin, 1965.

GEARY, H. V. R. *The Background of Business*, 3rd edn. O.U.P., 1963.

PACKMAN, R. *A Guide to the Business World*, 2nd edn. Longman, 1971.

PAISH, F. W. *Business Finance*, 4th edn. Pitman, 1968.

363

Competition and Monopoly

ALLEN, G. C. *Monopoly and Restrictive Practices*. Allen and Unwin, 1968.

BROWN, E. H. P. and WISEMAN, J. *A Course in Applied Economics*. Pitman, 1969.

GUENAULT, P. H. and JACKSON, J. M. *The Control of Monopoly in the U.K.* Longmans, 1967.

GALBRAITH, J. K. *American Capitalism*, new edn. Penguin, 1957.

Money and Banking

CROWTHER, G. *An Outline of Money, new ed.* Nelson, 1948.

DACEY, W. MANNING. *The British Banking Mechanism*, 4th edn., Hutchinson, 1967.

DAY, A. C. L. *The Economics of Money*, 2nd edn. O.U.P., 1968.

HANSON, J. L. *Monetary Theory and Practice*, 3rd edn. Macdonald and Evans, 1965.

SAYERS, R. S. *Modern Banking*, 7th edn. O.U.P., 1967.

Employment and Industrial Relations

BEVERIDGE, LORD. *Full Employment in a Free Society*, 2nd edn. Allen and Unwin, 1960.

ROBERTS, B. C., ed. *Industrial Relations*, 2nd edn. Methuen, 1968.

STEWART, M. *Keynes and After*. Penguin, 1967.

WIGHAM, E. L. *Trade Unions*, 2nd edn. O.U.P., 1969.

International Trade and Cooperation

ASHWORTH, W. *A Short History of the International Economy Since 1850*. Longman, 1970.

BENHAM, F. *Economic Aid to Underdeveloped Countries*. O.U.P., 1961.

LIVINGSTONE, J. M. *Britain and the World Economy*. Penguin, 1966.

POWER, J. *Development Economics*. Longman, 1971.

SWANN, D. *Economics of the Common Market*. Penguin, 1970.

TEW, B. *International Monetary Cooperation*, new edn. Hutchinson, 1967.

The British Economy

DONALDSON, P. *A Guide to the British Economy*. Penguin, 1970.

YOUNGSON, A. J. *The British Economy 1920–1957*. Allen and Unwin, 1960.

Economic Planning and Economic Growth

BRECH, R. *Planning for Prosperity*. Darton, Longman and Todd, 1966.

LEWIS, W. A. *The Principles of Economic Planning*, 2nd edn. Allen and Unwin, 1952.

MISHAN, E. J. *The Costs of Economic Growth*. Penguin, 1967.

ROSTOW, W. W. *The Stages of Economic Growth*. C.U.P., 1960.

Booklets/Pamphlets
Key Discussion Booklets (a wide range of titles). Longman.
Hobart Papers. Institute of Economic Affairs.
Reviews published by the Commercial Banks.
The Bank of England Quarterly Bulletin
Central Office of Information; *Broadsheets on Britain* and *Economic Progress Report*

Statistics
The Annual Abstract of Statistics. H.M.S.O.
National Income and Expenditure (Blue Book). H.M.S.O.
The Monthly Digest of Statistics. H.M.S.O.
Britain – An Official Handbook (Annually). H.M.S.O.

Index